Merger Masters

MERGER
MASTERS

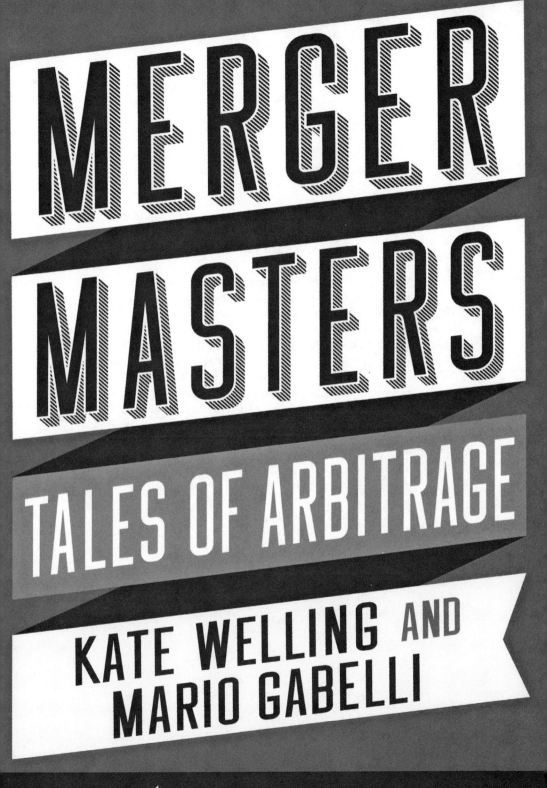

TALES OF ARBITRAGE

KATE WELLING AND MARIO GABELLI

Columbia Business School
Publishing

Columbia University Press
Publishers Since 1893
New York   Chichester, West Sussex
cup.columbia.edu
Copyright © 2018 Kate Welling and Mario Gabelli
All rights reserved

Library of Congress Cataloging-in-Publication Data
Names: Welling, Kate, author. | Gabelli, Mario, author.
Title: Merger masters : tales of arbitrage / Kate Welling and Mario Gabelli.
Description: New York : Columbia University Press, [2018] | Includes index.
Identifiers: LCCN 2018022551 (print) | LCCN 2018025255 (e-book) | ISBN
9780231548915 (e-book) | ISBN 9780231190428 (hardback : alk. paper)
Subjects: LCSH: Arbitrage—Case studies. | Consolidation and merger
of corporations—Case studies. | Investments—Case studies.
Classification: LCC HG4521 (e-book) | LCC HG4521 .W38765 2018 (print) |
DDC 338.8/30922—dc23
LC record available at https://lccn.loc.gov/2018022551

∞

Columbia University Press books are printed on permanent
and durable acid-free paper.
Printed in the United States of America

Cover design: Noah Arlow

Contents

Acknowledgments

KATE WELLING

THE IMPETUS AND inspiration for this book were all Mario J. Gabelli. The concept is Mario's, he convinced me to write it, and he made sure that the not-inconsiderable resources of GAMCO Investors were behind my efforts. For the experience, I'm forever in Mario's debt. The principles of value investing are well known today, in large part because Warren Buffett's monumental success has emblazoned them in the zeitgeist. Think of this volume, as I do, as my old friend Mario's way of highlighting the principles and practices of the other crucial arrow in his investment quiver, merger arbitrage, which has allowed him to translate Wall Street's addiction to deals, deals, and more deals into low-risk, consistent, and non-market-correlated compound returns for clients. The how, once shrouded in mystery, is today both accessible and pretty much infinitely adaptable, as these profiles illustrate. Opportunities are multiplying, even as I write.

This volume would not have been possible, what's more, without the generous cooperation of the arbitrageurs and industrialists profiled. All extraordinary—and extraordinarily different—individuals, they took the time necessary to school me in their own perspectives on deal investing, and I thank them.

I also owe very special thanks to Regina Pitaro, for demystifying risk arbitrage; and to Paolo Vicinelli, Ralph Rocco, Willis Brucker, and the Gabelli merger-arb team for constant and congenial support. Also to Christopher P. Bloomstran, a great friend and better value investor, for constructive commentary on the manuscript.

If I know anything about the craft of financial journalism or the art of writing, it's to the credit of my mentor—columnist and editor—the incomparable Alan Abelson. Any mistakes are my own.

Finally, without the unwavering love and support of my husband of the past forty years, Don Boyle, and our sons, Brian and Tom, I doubt I'd have penned a word.

Abbreviations and Wall Street Terms

10-K	annual corporate financial report filed with SEC
10-Q	quarterly corporate financial report filed with SEC
13D	SEC form that must be filed within 10 days by any person or group acquiring a beneficial interest in more than 5% of a company's securities.
13F	SEC form required quarterly from institutional investment managers with discretion over $100 million or more of regulated securities, listing the names and sizes of holdings
A$	Australian dollars
AUM	assets under management
BA	Bachelor of Arts
Basis point	one hundredth of one percent, used chiefly to describe differences in interest rates
BC	Boston College
Bear hug	an unsolicited and richly priced takeover bid that is potentially so irresistably attractive to the target company's shareholders that a management has little choice but to recommend that its shareholders accept it
Big Board	nickname for the New York Stock Exchange
Bips	Wall Street slang for basis points
BKN AU	ticker symbol of Bradken, an Australian mining equipment supplier
CEO	chief executive officer
CFA	chartered financial analyst
CFO	chief financial officer

CIO	chief investment officer
CLO	collateralized loan obligation. CLOs are derivatives, a form of securitization where payments from multiple middle sized and large business loans are pooled together and passed on to different classes of owners in various tranches.
Convergence trade	A form of arbitrage. Buying one asset forward, for future delivery, and selling a similar asset forward for a higher price, in expectation of profiting from the eventual convergence of their prices.
COO	chief operating officer
DA	district attorney
DIP Loan	debtor in possession financing typically granted during pendency of a bankruptcy case is usually considered senior to all other debt, equity, or other securities of a company. In other words, holders of DIP debt generally go to the front of the line when a bankrupt company's obligations are repaid or it is liquidated.
DIY	do it yourself
DJIA	Dow Jones Industrial Average, or "the DOW," a somewhat dated shorthand for "the market"
DLJ	Donaldson, Lufkin & Jenrette
DOJ	Department of Justice
EBITDA	earnings before tax interest, taxes, depreciation, and amortization
ETE	Energy Transfer Equity's ticker symbol
ETF	exchange traded fund
EU	European Union
FCC	Federal Communications Commission
FDA	Food and Drug Administration
Finco	financial company, a generic term for a corporate financial subsidiary
FTC	Federal Trade Commission. Federal agency with oversight of many corporate transactions
GAAP	generally accepted accounting principles, standardized accounting rules set out by the Financial Accounting Standards Board, invariably more stringent than anything a company reports as "adjusted earnings"

Greenmail	Akin to blackmail, a premium a company pays to buy its own shares back from a potential hostile acquirer.
GM	General Motors
GMAC	General Motors Acceptance Corp.
Highly confident letter	An aggressive financing tool invented by Drexel Burnham in 1983 to permit its corporate raider clients to launch LBO bids before their debt financing was fully in place.
HNG	ticker symbol and nickname for Houston Natural Gas when it was a listed company.
IFB	Ivan F. Boesky's IFB Managing Partnership
IPO	initial public offering
ISS	Institutional Shareholder Services, a proxy advisory firm
JD	Juris Doctor
LBO	leveraged buyout
LTV	Originally the 1960s conglomerate Ling-Temco-Vought, the corporation was the nation's second-largest steelmaker at the time of its 1986 bankruptcy filing.
M&A	mergers and acquisitions
MBA	Master of Business Administration
MO	modus operandi
NYSE	New York Stock Exchange
NYU	New York University
ODP	Office Depot stock ticker
P/E	price/earnings ratio. One fundamental measure of a stock's price relative to corporate profits.
P&G	Procter & Gamble
Pac-Man defense	Like in the video game, this refers to a takeover defense in which the target company attempts to turn the tables on a would-be hostile acquirer by trying to acquire it.
PE	private equity
PhD	Doctor of Philosophy
PM	portfolio manager
Poison pill defense	A shareholder rights plan, a defensive tactic in which a corporate board gives shareholders the right to buy additional shares at a discount if

	a potential acquirer buys a certain number of shares, thereby diluting the potential bidder's stake and increasing the cost of any merger
prop desk	proprietary trading desk at a bank, brokerage firm, etc.
Proxy Statement	A definitive proxy statement must be filed by companies with the SEC and distributed to shareholders prior to soliciting shareholder votes on a merger or some other corporate events. It includes information about the merger, management and board compensation and potential conflicts of interest, among other deal specifics.
QE	quantitative easing
R&D	research and development
REIT	real estate investment trust
S&P 500	Standard & Poor's 500 Index, often "the S&P" as shorthand for "the market"
SEC	Securities and Exchange Commission. Wall Street's federal regulator.
subs	corporate subsidiaries
T-Bill	U.S. Treasury Bills are short-term debt obligation backed by the U.S. government with a maturity of less than one year, sold in denominations of $1,000 up to a maximum purchase of $5 million. Also referred to on Wall Street as "the risk-free rate."
TIG	Tiedemann Investment Group
TWC	Time Warner Cable
UAL	The stock ticker symbol (and long-time Wall Street shorthand) for United Continental Holdings, the parent company of United Airlines and its predecessors. Previously, UAL Inc.was the name of the airline's parent, except for a brief time in 1987, when it was Allegis Corp.
White knight	A company that makes a higher, acceptable offer to buy another company to rescue it from a would-be hostile takeover
White shoe firm	Shorthand, for the most prestigious old-line law and investment banking firms
WMB	Williams Companies' ticker symbol

Merger Masters

INTRODUCTION

Why This Book?

IF THERE'S A better discipline than merger arbitrage to use as the foundation for a career in investing, I haven't found it in my fifty-plus years in the financial industry. It teaches you most of the techniques needed to do deals.

Consider the perpetually self-renewing deal process, the beating heart of Wall Street. Managements looking to do deals are conducting company and industry research. They're getting advisers. They're hiring investment bankers to tell them how to finance deals, how to structure them, how to look at the domestic and global dynamics, how to handle not only the U.S. Federal Trade Commission but the European Union, China, Brazil, and other global regulatory authorities. Legal teams are consulted. Then, assuming a prospective deal can clear those hurdles—and the price seems right—the managements have to look at various currency structures, work the myriad taxation aspects, and oh, by the way, get along well enough with the existing managers of their targets to integrate the operations. Then, if something goes awry—or when the economy periodically goes through a cyclical downturn—restructuring opportunities arise that require many of the same skill sets. Rinse and repeat.

Risk arbitrageurs (commonly known as "arbs") have to be able to assess all of these deal risks. So, if someone wants to get into the investment business—really wants to learn about current mergers and acquisitions (M&A) techniques—the discipline of merger arbitrage is a great starting point. As none other than Warren Buffett put it in his 1988 investor letter, "Give a man a fish and you feed him for a day. Teach him how to arbitrage and you feed him forever."

What is Risk Arbitrage?

So what is arbitrage? The practice can be traced back to antiquity, and probably earlier, to the first time a merchant realized that (usually) small price differentials could exist for the same item in different (often geographically distant) markets and sought to take advantage by buying cheaply in one market and selling dear in the other. Over the millennia, sharp traders engaging in the practice understandably gravitated to describing themselves with a French word, "arbitrageurs," instead of its plain-spoken English equivalent, "scalpers."

In this country, especially since what historians refer to as the "second wave" of Wall Street mediated mergers began creating vertically-integrated industries in the aftermath of the First World War, the term has often been compounded as "risk arbitrage" or "merger arbitrage." The terms are most often used by Street denizens to describe seeking profits by trading securities involved in announced corporate events—mergers, recapitalizations, asset sales, reorganizations, self-tenders, liquidations, and the like—in such a way as to limit the trader's risk, should the expected event fail to happen. Because merger outcomes are not correlated to stock market movements, and an arb hedges his or her positions to eliminate market risk, arbitrage is, in modern parlance, a market-neutral strategy.

What's Ben Graham Got to Do with It?

Although I knew that I wanted to get into the investment business prior to entering Columbia University's Graduate School of Business,

I didn't know how or in what capacity. Then I took a course called Security Analysis, taught by Roger Murray. Professor Murray was the successor at Columbia to value investing gurus Benjamin Graham and David Dodd. It is Ben Graham, of course, whom Warren Buffett credits with most of his success as an investor. Buffett concedes that he was a reasonably successful investor even before he took Security Analysis, but he adds that learning how to take advantage of what Ben Graham called Mr. Market's sometimes violent mood swings is what created his unparalleled success. Those emotional market excesses create opportunities for patient investors to buy stocks with a margin of safety (at depressed prices comfortably below intrinsic values) and to profitably sell them when temporary manic enthusiasms drive prices well above those values. Careful securities analysis and asset valuation expertise show the way. I was hooked.

Today, I often find myself introduced to viewers of financial TV as an authority on deal investing; the founder of GAMCO Investors Inc., a $40-plus billion publicly-owned asset-management and mutual-fund corporation, whose success has made my proprietary Private Market Value (PMV) with a Catalyst™ methodology an analytical standard. GAMCO's separately-managed client accounts have compounded at around 15.5 percent annually for forty years, albeit with four or five down years breaking the compounding chain over that stretch.

What's less widely appreciated is that I founded my first arbitrage hedge fund back in 1985—a year before launching our first mutual fund. Called, simply, the Gabelli Arbitrage Fund, it was funded with just a tad over $9 million—and GAMCO now oversees investments approaching $5 billion in arb strategies. The original Gabelli Arbitrage Fund, renamed the Gabelli Associates Fund has grown to over $230 million and is part of over $1.4 billion managed in our arbitrage hedge fund strategy. Operating without leverage since we absorbed the brutal lessons of 1987, GAF has compounded its initial capital at an annual growth rate of 7.6 percent over the thirty-three years of its existence.

What also is often overlooked is that my PMV with a Catalyst™ methodology is actually based on and is an extension of Ben Graham's classic value investing strategy—with an overlay of deal dynamics, risk analysis, and sensitivity to the time value of money, which is derived from my appreciation of the compounding magic of the consistent, non-market correlated returns that the risk-arbitrage discipline

GABELLI ARBITRAGE FUND

A private arbitrage partnership organized under the laws of the State of New York.

$9,175,000

The undersigned arranged the private placement of these securities

———————

GABELLI & COMPANY, INC.

January 31, 1985

GAF Tombstone. Courtesy of GAMCO.

generates. Thus, while our original arb hedge fund's long-term compound annual return is less, obviously, than the 10 percent real plus inflation that we target in numerous long-only equity strategies, it's also lower risk. In fact, a conservatively implemented merger-arb strategy like ours actually is a low-risk way to earn an even better absolute return than in a low-cost money fund. On a long-term basis, we hope to earn the risk-arb premium, which historically is about 400 to 500 basis points above the T-Bill rate.

Pretty much from the arbitrage fund's onset, we have sent letters to our limited partners that detail individual arb transactions we are invested in—why we bought it, the hurdle rates, what the risks and rates of return were, the investment rationale. I've always felt that we should be transparent, operating in a fishbowl. Clients should know how we do things. So we communicate about the deals in the fund's pipeline. Our monthly letters always give the investors at least one detailed example of a deal that we think illustrates a very clear path to success. (A sampling of recent deal examples is distilled in Appendix II, at the back of this volume.) Even as early as 1985, there were already a couple of SEC rules mandating us to make some disclosures—13F, requiring a quarterly report of holdings by institutions with at least $100 million in AUM; and 13D, which meant we as a firm had to file any time we owned 5 percent of something—so we weren't giving away a lot of the secret sauce in our client letters. Besides, we agreed with Buffett that educating investors about arbitrage is the appropriate thing to do.

Lifting the Veil

That effort culminated—until now—in the 1999 publication by Gabelli University Press of *Deals . . . Deals . . . And More Deals* by Regina M. Pitaro with Paolo Vicinelli. A concise yet example-rich volume, *Deals* has gone through three printings in English and translations into languages ranging from Chinese and Japanese to Italian. This authoritative volume deftly and completely lifts the veil of mystery that—as recently as the turn of *this* century—still shrouded the mechanics of merger and acquisition arbitrage on Wall Street.

In it, Pitaro (whom I'm lucky to also call my wife), a managing director at GAMCO, draws on her master's degree in anthropology, her MBA at Columbia, and her research at Lehman Brothers to make brilliant use of an ancient fable—versions of which exist in a number of cultures—to vividly illustrate the true mathematical miracle of compounding. In doing so, she unmasks it as the source of risk arbitrage's "black magic." The tale involves a peasant who does a good deed and then bankrupts his ruler in a month's time by modestly requesting as his reward but a single grain of rice—the amount of which was to be doubled daily. With that daily compounding, the single rice grain quickly amounts to more than a billion rice grains a day. As *Deals* put it, "In no style of investment is the magic of compounding more evident than in risk arbitrage, making it an essential component in an investor's portfolio." Indeed, I can't emphasize enough that if you don't break the chain of success in generating absolute returns and compounding the interest on those returns, you can make a lot of money in merger arb over an extended period—even starting with what looks like small grains of rice.

Deals drew heavily on the collective wisdom and collaborative efforts of our entire risk-arbitrage group and made liberal use of our proprietary research on hundreds of deals. Our intention was to build on the foundation of Guy Wyser-Pratte's groundbreaking NYU thesis, *Risk Arbitrage*. Written in 1969, it was the first publication to reveal the arbitrageurs' "black magic" to professionals outside of what was then a tight-knit fraternity of risk-arb practitioners. Ivan Boesky's 1985 book, *Merger Mania*, had briefly helped popularize the discipline among ordinary investors by bombastically promising to reveal "Wall Street's best kept money-making secret" as its subtitle put it. But it was thoroughly discredited when it was discovered that Boesky omitted his own dark secret—insider trading.

Pitaro took an entirely different tack, clearly and dispassionately guiding readers, step-by-step, through a "pilot's checklist" of the tasks required to professionally research and analyze some of the biggest deals of the late twentieth century—or any era [Updated in Appendix I]. What's more, that eminently readable treatise lays bare for investors of all stripes the Gabelli Arbitrage team's proven strategies for success in merger and acquisition arbitrage—elucidating just what's in the secret sauce: how you can make low-risk money in announced deals; exactly what spreads are; and explaining the steps required to create consistent, uncorrelated, absolute returns in risk arbitrage.

It's Not Complicated

That's the background. Why I wanted to publish this new book is not complicated, either. I wanted to capture the essence of those individuals who have been successful at risk arbitrage over the years—allow them to teach the craft by talking about some of the elements of the art and science that they daily go through—or went through—while they were trying to figure out what deals were going to break, how they were going to make money, how they lost money on occasion, what they do if a deal does break, and so on. Then I also wanted to help illuminate the other side of the equation—to spotlight some of the extraordinary corporate managers whose companies were at times allied with, and at other times were targeted by, risk arbitrageurs or activist investors. I wanted to explore how they handled the arbitrage community while deals were in process; how they would respond to the myriad questions posed by risk arbs; how they would play defense and offense; how they sometimes used arbs to further corporate goals but at other times tried to avoid being abused by arbs whose short-term incentives were in conflict, perhaps, with the executives' longer-term corporate goals.

Then the next question is why have Kate Welling, the editor and publisher of an independent investment journal, *Welling on Wall St.*, write this book, as opposed to doing this one, too, in house? The answer reaches back into what, for many plying the Street today, is ancient history. Kate and I met sometime in the late 1970s, not long after I started my firm. I had already met her boss, Alan Abelson, and had started sending him a series of reports that I had been doing on underappreciated asset plays, numbers one through ten, trying to drum up interest in my new firm's research. So, around New Year's, 1979, I sent a research report on Chris-Craft to Alan, along with a note along these lines:

> Alan, enclosed is my most recent asset play #7. It's Chris-Craft. I hope you publish it. First, it's a great value play. Second, my clients are long. Third, and perhaps really #1, I understand you pay "contributors" $50 if you publish it, and I could use the money.

Remember, in the late 1970s, you could buy a taxicab medallion for $35,000—and a seat on the New York Stock Exchange for around the same price.

I was in luck. Abelson, then the managing editor of *Barron's*, published a feature based on my Chris-Craft piece and followed up with an invitation to be interviewed over lunch in the magazine's rather grungy old lower Manhattan offices at 22 Cortlandt Street. Lo and behold, there were five or six *Barron's* editors and writers, including Kate Welling, Larry Armour, and Shirley Lazo, as well as Abelson, sitting at the table, peppering me with questions as I was putting pepper on my salad. Kate Welling edited and published that interview in March 1979 and, somehow, my ideas worked. Then Abelson stuck me on the annual *Barron's* Roundtable, beginning in January 1980, and Kate and I started interfacing frequently.

I found that Kate understood the markets, grasped the dynamics instantly, and knew what stocks are up to. She simply wasn't the typical Wall Street reporter. She was up-to-date and she did the research. She was at the time—still really is—very knowledgeable about the world of the markets, and that was good. Then, after she partnered with Weeden & Co. to launch *Welling@Weeden* in 1999, we kept in touch because she was in Greenwich where I have an office and we would often go to breakfast or lunch. She went off entirely on her own in 2012 and started publishing from eastern Long Island, but I became a charter subscriber and a staunch supporter of *Welling on Wall St.* So when I started thinking about this book—to prepare people for what I see as the next round of significant M&A dynamics in the market— I wanted to recruit a brilliant writer who knows markets. I know she thinks that's debatable. But when I said, "Hey Kate, do you want to write a book about risk arbs?" She said, "Whoa. Interesting."

What's in this Book

Actually, Kate insists her recollection is a mite different. But I am nothing if not persistent. Also, generous. So I prevailed, happily ensuring that the literature of merger arbitrage now includes stories, reflections, and insights about the strategic, tactical, and, especially, human aspects of a part of the investment business too long shrouded in needless mystery. The eighteen über-successful arbitrageurs profiled here are fascinating, many-faceted characters. No two are alike— the infinite variations and complexities of the deal business attract all sorts. What's more, the ways they implement the risk-arb discipline range all across the spectrum from low-risk, conservative, announced-deal investing to aggressive activism. But all would agree with York Capital Management's Jamie Dinan when he says, later in these pages (chapter 14), "If you love investing and you love human psychology, risk arbitrage is an amazing business."

Likewise extraordinary are the trio of corporate executives whose profiles comprise the special section which is this volume's final chapters. Their thought-provoking interviews add "the other side's" perspective on deal-making and risk arbitrage to the narrative. They also raise some profound questions about the current state of the capital markets and the evolving role of financial capitalism in modern society. All of which is exceedingly timely, as a monumental fifth wave of booming merger and acquisition activity—counting the wave driven by the swashbuckling conglomerateurs of the 1960s that I followed as a neophyte analyst as the first—is now beginning to wash over the global markets. Over the next decade, the stock markets will likely generate, in my judgment, total returns of 6, 7, 8 percent a year, and interest rates will probably float up moderately. In that environment, risk arbitrage will generate good *nominal*, as well as absolute, returns.

Meanwhile, I also believe we're going to witness a surge in merger activity propelled by financial engineering dynamics. With the corporate tax changes in the United States, companies will know what they can do, they'll understand how much leverage they can use, and private equity will figure out ways to finance the deals—they always do. Plus, you'll get both the private equity entities and the strategic buyers back in the market in a big way in the next couple years in a merger and acquisition wave that will be more global this time around. In sum, there could scarcely be a better time to focus investor attention on the arb world. Warren Buffett's sage observation about giving individual investors the knowledge and tools needed to become an arbitrageur has seldom been timelier.

Corporations inherently want to grow and the big ones now have rich currencies—their shares—to use in mergers. You're already starting to see some of these deals in various sectors, and you're just going to see the deal making accelerate. Sure, we hear people asking, "Is this deal activity good for the company that's the subject of a takeover? Is it good for its employees?" That's a different issue, especially when corporate constituencies beyond their shareholders are taken into consideration. However, a takeover target's existing shareholders get cash

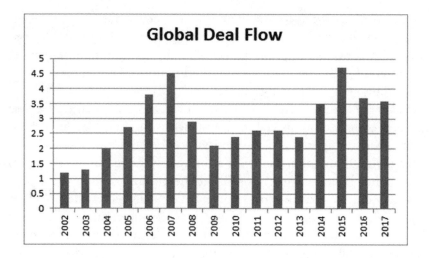

Merger Activity Chart. Courtesy of GAMCO. Data from Thomson Reuters.

and/or the takeover currency—and that currency, they can arb out, sell. So the existing shareholders of the target do well in a takeover. The upshot is that money is fungible. Wherever investors think they can make better returns, relative to other alternatives, money flows into those tactics and strategies.

Mistakes Will Happen

Nevertheless, there's no getting around it: each deal must be evaluated on its own merits. AOL's top-of-the-internet bubble takeover of Time Warner in 2000 was a classic case of a merger that might not have worked out for the existing shareholders of the target, due to AOL's rich valuation. As I recall, that particular announcement came out on a Monday in January while we were doing the *Barron's* Roundtable and I was long Time Warner, technically the target, though it was the larger company. I said, "Hey, this is not for me." But as Time Warner shares traded higher on news of the deal, that gave us an opportunity to unwind our really significant position in its shares. I used our fundamental research to become a seller of Time Warner.

Subsequently, we reestablished a position in Time Warner's depressed shares. Then it changed managements and Jeff Bewkes started the long restructuring process—started unwinding Time Inc., unwinding Time Warner Cable, unwinding AOL and trying to marry up with a potential buyer, who was Randall Stephenson at AT&T. The reality is, we're in a world with 7.5 billion people today. Sixty years ago, there were only 2.5 billion people on the planet. Today, many of these people carry around smartphones. And they have apps on those devices on which they can watch podcasts, watch short stories, video clips. Television has become very mobile. Why shouldn't content and transmission marry? The notion of storytelling for these new "walk-around viewers" has to be completely different. You can't do thirty or sixty minutes of *Walking Dead*. You've got to try to tell a story in ten minutes. The world's a-changing.

More typical of the risk-arb deals pursued by the Gabelli merger-arb team, which has been led by GAMCO managing partner Ralph Rocco for nearly a quarter of a century, are situations in which they can piggyback on GAMCO's deep research into undervalued assets to gain an edge in assessing the likely ultimate value of transactions. The 1999 takeover of Hudson General, detailed at length in *Deals*, was a great example. In short, because Gabelli Asset Management had deemed Hudson General an asset play, trading at a steep discount to its private market value, long before any bid was announced, the firm had built up a 49.5 percent position in the stock in client equity accounts. When a group of Hudson General's senior executives offered $100 million, or $57.25 a share, for the company in November 1998—a bid amounting to only a 5 percent premium to the company's pre-offer trading level—the Gabelli arb team instantly recognized it for the lowball bid it was. They also realized that buying more shares, in risk-arb accounts, even at the $56.375 price they'd risen to on news of the offer, provided an unusually attractive risk/reward opportunity. Downside was limited to the pre-deal price of $54.625, only about $1.50 lower than where it was trading. Potential upside was substantial.

In fact, after analyzing the three major assets on Hudson General's balance sheet, Gabelli's analysts had concluded it was worth about $75 a share. So the arb unit built a position and waited for a bidding war to commence. It quickly did in February 1999. Hudson General ultimately attracted four suitors and a winning bid of $76 a share from German airline Lufthansa—a 35 percent premium over the purchase price the Gabelli arb team had put up just three months earlier. That outcome was a perfect illustration of why I've long considered management-led leveraged buyouts to potentially be the most egregious form of insider trading. If a management participates in a buyout group, you know they have hidden jewels.

Experience Before Theory

Although I couldn't read a formal theory of risk arbitrage until Guy Wyser-Pratte's groundbreaking MBA thesis started circulating around Wall Street in the early 1970s, I remember being exposed to the practical aspects of deal investing shortly after landing my first brokerage firm job. I was working as an analyst for Loeb, Rhoades straight out of the Columbia Graduate School of Business, in 1967. Michael Steinhardt had just left to create Steinhardt, Fine, Berkowitz & Company, one of the best-performing early hedge funds, and I inherited his research coverage. Let's just say the files were lean.

But that meant I picked up coverage of Steinhardt's industries—consumer durables like autos, producer durables like farm equipment, and also conglomerates. Companies like Gulf & Western, ITT, and Textron, where the key was to watch how they were doing transactions. Only about a year later, the merger of MCA into Westinghouse was announced—on a Sunday, July 28, 1968—and John Loeb, the senior partner, asked me to look at the deal. That's when I started working closely with Loeb, Rhoades's arb department. We stayed in touch even after I migrated over to William D. Witter in the early 1970s. All of the arbitrageurs of the day, guys like Carl Ichan, would call and ask me about deals. Even Ivan Boesky.

Letting Individual Investors In

The appeal of risk arb as a strategy markedly broadened after May Day, 1975, the SEC-mandated end of the era of fixed brokerage commissions. Until then, the arbs' frequent reliance on narrow spreads for profitability made risk-arb strategies economic only for exchange members who didn't pay commissions. Post-May Day, the rapidly declining commission structure allowed individuals—or small firms like mine—to participate in the spreads, which then proceeded to grow quite fat on a nominal basis by the end of the decade as nominal interest rates soared. So when I started Gabelli & Co. in 1977, I used part of my firm's capital to do arbitrage deals as a way to earn consistent, low-volatility, non-market-correlated returns tied to deal specifics. This was done in part because we had a research background edge, and in part because I understood how conglomerates worked. Luckily, it worked out quite well, preserving capital and even acting as a hedge against rising rates—because the arb premium of 4–5 percent above the risk-free rate is a constant. That is, arb spreads almost always trade 4–5 percent wider than short-term rates. So as short-term interest rates rise, and the 4–5 percent arb premium to those rates stays constant, nominal arbitrage returns rise alongside rates.

Understanding how conglomerates worked in the 1960s allowed you to understand how smaller, aggressive companies—the ones run by the conglomerateurs—could be buying much larger companies. How they handled the currency—high-priced equities—that they used in terms of the trade, how they dealt with the regulatory environment—which may, or may not, have been as encompassing then as it is now. But the conglomerate era basically ended in 1969 when Chemical Bank successfully spurned Saul Steinberg's raid. Then there was some accounting pushback, some new regulations that changed the market's dynamics in the early 1970s. Still, the deals and the market dynamics of the conglomerate era provided a baseline for what we're doing in risk arbitrage.

Clearly, the deal market has morphed over the succeeding decades. There was the 1980s boom in debt-financed hostile mergers. It was the age of greenmail and LBOs; T. Boone Pickens; highly leveraged oil, banking, pharma and airline mergers; high-yield or "junk" bonds; and Drexel Burnham "highly confident letters." A bonanza for deal investors while it lasted, the market's exuberance was tamped down at decade's end by insider trading prosecutions unveiled just as the failure of a management buyout of UAL Corp. at the market's 1989 peak ushered in a bear market. But plentiful arbitrage opportunities reemerged in a wave of horizontal industry consolidation in the 1990s, culminating in the internet bubble. After the dot-coms popped, the early 2000s saw a recession and increasing numbers of distressed corporations being restructured, with and without resort to the bankruptcy courts. And ever-resourceful arbitrageurs found ways to profit amid the upheaval. More recently, in the environment of exceedingly low interest rates that has characterized post-financial crisis economies, so-called event-driven strategies have dominated deal making.

Through it all, the risk-arb team at GAMCO has stayed singularly focused on generating consistent low-risk returns in deals. It has also remained ever vigilant to take advantage of those rare instances when arbs, for whatever reason, are forced to liquidate everything. Amid a crisis like the crash of October of 1987, or 1998's Long-Term Capital Management panic, or in the great financial crisis in 2008, when over-extended arbs are all forced to sell at once, spreads blow out to offer 50 percent, 60 percent, even 100 percent returns—that's a great time to have some liquidity to use to buy those spreads.

Analytical Advantage

While lawyers always think they have an edge in everything—and I concede a certain amount of inevitable bias because my training is as an analyst—there's little doubt in my mind that analysts have an edge in risk-arbitrage situations. In the most fraught of market moments, an analyst following an industry or a company, with accumulated and compounded knowledge, can put a valuation on a stock—understand how a private equity firm or a corporate rival thinks about the business, how they could buy it today, and how they'd plan to get out of it in five or ten years. Analysts also have strategic insights. They naturally look at eliminating certain cost structures, squeezing out synergies. Every industry has different flavors and the analysts are on top of those flavors of the decade: they are prepared for things like spinoffs and takeovers of spinoffs, liquidations—the list goes on and on. That's why we combine research with arbitrage. There is one risk-arb strategy that the GAMCO arb team never touches, however. We don't buy the debt of a company in bankruptcy; try to get control of the assets for pennies on the dollar. We recognize that is a very different niche, one that's very lawyer-intensive—a different facet of this diamond that we call merger arbitrage.

Instead, the arb group at Gabelli likes to follow certain individuals and organizations. It's valuable to us to know which companies tend to do spinoffs—in part, for a favorable tax structure; in part, because they figure out that somebody would buy the asset on a stand-alone basis—and that the deal would be more tax-efficient as well as get a higher valuation if it were spun out. We follow guys like Ed Breen who took over Tyco after the Dennis Koslowski fiasco and did a fabulous job of splitting it up and selling off the parts. Now Breen is at DuPont, working to make the same magic. We track that kind of individual because he's done it. He understands the virtues of doing spinoffs. Then we also look at the companies he's spun off because we know, at some point, somebody is going to buy them.

John Malone is another great example of an individual we follow. Not just because he accumulates companies but also because he tries to understand—even before he starts buying—who the logical eventual buyers for that asset might be. Malone sold his first cable television foray to AT&T way back when it was a different AT&T. Then, just a year and a half ago, he sold DirecTV to Randall Stephenson, who runs the "new" AT&T. Now Malone has a cable company that intrigues me, called Liberty Latin America. It has cable operators all across Latin America and at some point they're going to consolidate.

Clearly, opportunities to profit from deals continue to have me jumping out of bed in the morning, even after five decades in the business. There's always something worthwhile, even in the very interesting world we inhabit today. Of course, there are worries, too—always. As some of the arbs in this book mention, they have to be careful in structuring their portfolios. They have to worry if everyone is doing a certain style of deal; whether they want to finance positions with high-yield debt; if they—or everyone else—have too much leverage. They worry about what the Europeans are doing or about tax inversion deals. And now they are worried about deals associated with China. If the guy running that country wants to run it for another five or ten years, is he stopping capital outflows just for the moment? Or is he doing things that will stop deals? Will the United States, in turn, retaliate with tariffs? Nonetheless, as I look today at the Risk Arbitrage Decision Tree that we published as an appendix in *Deals*, really, the only changes since 1999 are a few details about the regulatory issues. [An updated version appears as Appendix I in this volume.]

So amid all the uncertainty of these interesting times, how can you earn returns that are non-market-correlated and do it on a global basis? Unlike in the 1960s or the 1970s or the early 1980s, when very few foreign companies were buying American assets, this is now a global marketplace. You'll get a lot of cross-European deals, you'll get Asian companies buying global assets. Those challenges are to be relished.

The good news for me—as Warren Buffett says about himself—and it applies to others, too, is that you don't have to have good hand-to-eye coordination to be a good investor if you have the benefit of accumulated and compounded knowledge.

On the other hand, you've got to get out of your comfort zone as an investor. Get into the digital revolution that's taking place and do other new things. You've got to transition. We just had our forty-first annual auto parts conference and its theme was that there will be driverless cars, there will be no car owners, and maybe you won't even have to have roads. Maybe you'll have cars that levitate quickly and fly the way drones do. It's one reason we have to find ways to revive the IPO market in this country. Initial public offerings are good for the system. That's how you get capital to flow into new ideas. But I digress.

I like it that Bob Dylan, who wrote "The Times They Are a-Changin'," got a Nobel Prize in Literature. You can say the same thing about Wall Street, about politics, about global relations—but change breeds opportunities. So my thanks to Kate, for helping investors prepare for the next round of significant dynamics in the marketplace and in merger arb.

—Mario J. Gabelli
Founder, Chairman, CEO, and CIO
GAMCO Investors
March 2018

PART ONE

The Arbs' Perspectives

CHAPTER ONE

Guy Wyser-Pratte

Catching the guys at Houston Natural Gas red-handed—that's what really motivated me. Every time I'd catch some skullduggery going on, on the part of a corporate board, at the expense of shareholders, I really was energized to go after them . . .

I'm not a passive person, and just sitting anywhere, passively sweating out individual risk-arb deals—I couldn't deal with it any longer. So in the 1990s, I started to go after managements in the United States that were not doing right by their shareholders.

THE OFFICES OF Wyser-Pratte & Co. are nestled in the gilded countryside on the northeastern edge of Westchester County, New York. A visitor must traverse miles of hilly and winding two-lane roads through fields dotted with artfully repurposed barns and imposing estates to arrive at Guard Hill Road. There, an insistent series of speed bumps slows progress until the path narrows to not much more than a tree-lined country lane. Potholes in this path, now genteelly worn down almost to the dirt, take over the task of impeding passage. Finally, a mailbox marks the narrow, uphill gravel driveway that crosses precariously over a gully and practically grazes a quaint cottage before revealing the red barn turned office tucked into the hillside. Its entrance is around the far side, up a steep stepping-stone path, past the tennis court. From the inside, a floor-to-ceiling wall of glass provides an expansive view of rolling pastures—as well as plenty of warning should anyone approach.

Guy Wyser-Pratte, it's quickly clear, has forgotten not a whit of his long-ago Marine Corps training in logistical advantage. Tall, ramrod straight, and broad-shouldered even in his mid-1970s, he springs from behind his document-piled desk to greet a guest. Then he proudly shows off mementoes of his long career, which line the walls and fill multiple volumes of scrapbooks that meticulously record nearly five decades of the "Rambo *der Kapitalmärkte*'s" deals, deals, and more deals. But the quiet hum of voices punctuated by ringing phones arising from the four-person trading desk on one side of the open office—accompanied by the electronic pings of quote screens and news feeds—belie the pastoral setting, announcing in unmistakable terms that Guy Wyser-Pratte and his eponymous firm, with roughly $250 million in assets under management, are still actively engaged in the Wall Street art of risk arbitrage.

For Wyser-Pratte, it's the family business. His Hungarian-born father, Eugene, founded Wyser-Pratte & Co. in Paris in 1929. "He had been working for an Austrian bank (owned by a family friend) as their Paris representative. They were doing arbitrage the old-fashioned way"—buying assets in cheaper markets and selling where they commanded a premium. "He made a good living. He and my Austrian-born mother enjoyed café society in Paris in the days of Gertrude Stein, F. Scott Fitzgerald, and that whole crowd." Then, of course, came the Second World War. Guy was born as France fell to the Nazis, on June 21, 1940, in Vichy, France, and emigrated with his family to the United States in early 1946. "I was always told that my father had worked until the day war broke out, and after that, I don't quite know what he was up to. I suspect something with the underground. He wouldn't talk about it." When the family sailed from Le Havre, it was on a troop ship, the USS *Hood*, crammed with GIs coming home from Europe.

"What a Great Country!"

After passing through Ellis Island, Wyser-Pratte remembers walking up First Avenue with his parents. "Everybody was smiling and celebrating. I said, 'What a great country. Everybody's having such a good time.' But my father shrugged, 'It's St. Patrick's Day.'" Adds Wyser-Pratte, "Everyone was frolicking in and out of all of the bars. I thought it was pretty amusing. I wasn't quite six." The youngster was also a mite slow to appreciate the implications of the family's journey. "I didn't expect that we'd stay in the States. We wound up living in the St. Moritz Hotel for three months. One day my father comes into Rumplemeyer's—where I always was at lunchtime—and says, 'I bought a house.' I thought, 'That's the end of my friends and my toys.' But I never turned back."

The elder Wyser-Pratte reestablished his arbitrage business on Wall Street, and in due course, Guy, his two older brothers, and his parents became U.S. citizens. It was only as an adult, says Guy, that he learned his father had "some pretty bitter stories about France, though he would go back all the time on business." "He was a crusty guy, to say the least," allows the son. After attending the University of Rochester on a Naval ROTC scholarship, the younger Wyser-Pratte was the only member of his class commissioned into the Marine Corps. The "fun-loving frat boy" quickly found himself in Okinawa, in February 1963, as a platoon commander with the Third Reconnaissance Battalion, Third Marine Division. He twice volunteered for service in Vietnam but never made it there, leaving active duty as a captain in June 1966. The crossed officers' swords, multiple photos, and a vintage recruiting poster declaring, "If you want to fight, join the Marines" on his office walls leave little doubt that Wyser-Pratte relished his military service.

But Wyser-Pratte père made sure the young officer didn't forget the family business. "My father insisted on having the *Wall Street Journal*

sent to me, even in the field. And I'd steal away to read my *Journal*."
When he got out of the marines and explained that he wanted to get
an MBA on the GI Bill, recalls Wyser-Pratte, his old-school father
replied, "Good, you do that at night and you come work for me in
the daytime." Guy Wyser-Pratte dutifully complied and soon found his
first assignment thoroughly enjoyable. "My father had all these business contacts in Europe, and he wanted me to get familiar with them.
The minute I got discharged, he said, 'Get your suitcase and go.' What
a time! Really rough duty. He had me staying with all the family connections." But his "basic training" was cut regrettably short, Wyser-
Pratte ruefully recalls. "I was in Paris enjoying the life of a young blade,
when my father sent a note, saying, 'Come home, we're merging.'
I sent back word, 'I'm not coming home.' He got on the phone and
said, 'Then I'm cutting off your support.' I said, 'I'll be right there.' "

The merger between Wyser-Pratte Co. and Bache & Co. took place
in July 1967, giving the risk-arbitrage operation access to a much
larger capital base and the brokerage firm a highly profitable trading
desk that provided the majority of its profits in many subsequent years.
"Harold Bache was running the place back then and was happy to
have me as a second to my father." The younger Wyser-Pratte quickly
fell into a work/school routine. He reminisces: "It was great. The
office was at 50 Broadway, just around the corner from where New
York University's Graduate School of Business Administration held
classes on Church Street. I'd go right after work and have, as professors, practitioners right off the Street. Then, as my master's thesis, in
June 1969, I wrote *Risk Arbitrage*."

Guy Wyser-Pratte's highly technical thesis, which explained not
only the theory but also the ins and outs of the practice of securities arbitrage, set off shockwaves on Wall Street, where the workings
of arbitrageurs always had been shrouded in secrecy. Poorly Xeroxed
copies of the thesis were passed hand-to-hand until May 1971, when
a reedited version was published in NYU's Bulletin of the Institute
of Finance. Westchester Capital's Roy Behren speaks for many in the
trade when he reports that his first inquiries into the business were
met with, "You've got to read Guy Wyser-Pratte's book." Behren did
as instructed, tracking a copy down "in some office at NYU Press" and
devouring it. It wasn't until 1982 that *Risk Arbitrage*, already a cult
classic, was published in actual book form by the Salomon Brothers
Center for the Study of Financial Institutions at the NYU Graduate

School of Business Administration. More recently, in 2009, Wyser-Pratte updated the volume for inclusion in the Wiley Investment Classics series.

Lifting the Veil

Why did Wyser-Pratte lift the veil on his father's business—and Wall Street's entire arbitrage community? In part, it was simple, he explains. "Nobody had ever written about it before—and I had the best teacher in the world, in my father. He was the best example I could have had. I took the book right from what he was teaching me. He was a mathematical genius. While I had gotten good grades in college in physics and math, I didn't *see the numbers* the way he did. He could *see* spreads where no one else could see them, and he taught me how."

But the younger Wyser-Pratte was also on a mission of sorts. "I'd come out of the marines a captain, a proud dude, okay? I thought I was going to meet the captains of industry on Wall Street. But after meeting some of the arbs competing with my father, I was totally unimpressed. The lack of character and backbone was stunning to me. I couldn't deal with the backstabbing. It's not the way I had been trained or raised." In fact, recalls Wyser-Pratte, "After six months on the job, I was ready to go back to the Marine Corps. But my father urged me, 'Stick it out for a while longer, and you'll see.'" Now, with better than a half century of arbitrage behind him, and his own son, Jamie, working in his firm, it's clear that Wyser-Pratte found a way to thrive in a business whose culture he'd at first found alien and inhospitable, in part by helping it evolve with his book's disinfecting dose of sunlight. "I had gotten a little bit fed up with all the secrecy and arcane practices of these guys with shadowy European backgrounds. I was a marine officer, and I didn't have anything shadowy about me."

Pressed to elaborate, Wyser-Pratte adds, "I have to be a little bit careful what I say here—but I was not part of the arbitrage syndicate on the floor of the New York Stock Exchange. These guys used to swap inside information, with Bunny Lasker and veteran traders like him leading the syndicate." Bernard J. "Bunny" Lasker started on Wall Street as a runner in 1927, became a member of the NYSE in 1939, and by 1968 was senior partner in Lasker, Stone & Stern. He served as chairman of the Big Board from 1969 to 1971—and was never charged, much less convicted, of insider trading. Lasker's name color-fully surfaced, however, in the investigation of the insider-trading scan-dal that helped bring the super-heated takeover boom of the 1980s to a screeching halt. As chronicled in James B. Stewart's Pulitzer Prize–winning nonfiction book, *Den of Thieves*, the convictions of Robert Freeman, the risk-arbitrage head at Goldman Sachs, and Martin Siegel, an investment banker at Kidder Peabody, were based in part on a wire-tap that recorded Siegel responding, "Your Bunny has a good nose," to a question from Freeman about a deal Lasker allegedly told him was in trouble. Wyser-Pratte continues, "What that gang did was, if Goldman was doing a deal that L. F. Rothschild wasn't in, Rothschild could trade it and Goldman would give them the information. And vice versa. I didn't want to be part of that. Besides, I had my own floor broker, a guy who was very smart, very clever, very quick on his feet on the floor—back in the day when hustle there meant something. He pulled things off for me. I could figure out deals as well as other guys, and I didn't want the problems inside information could lead to."

A Charming Guy

Fast-forward four years. It is 1971 and the senior Wyser-Pratte wants to retire. The challenge was convincing John Leslie, then Bache's chairman, that the brash thirty-one-year-old could run the arb desk. Indeed, says Wyser-Pratte, it was only through the intervention of Clark Clifford, a former defense secretary, Washington lawyer, and long-time counselor to presidents going back to Harry Truman, that he got to succeed his father. Clifford phoned the Bache chairman, Wyser-Pratte recalls, and said, "John, I know this young man. He knows his stuff. You have to give him a chance." Clifford had become a Wyser-Pratte client after returning to his law firm from the Pentagon in early 1969 and discovering that Wyser-Pratte was a client of the firm's antitrust practice. "Mr. Clifford called me up one day and said, 'I understand you've written a thesis. Come down here.' So I went down to his office in D.C.—what a charming guy."

It was the beginning of a long and close relationship that endured until Clifford's death, at age ninety-one, in 1998. Wyser-Pratte contin-ues, "A week later, he sent me a check in the mail for like a half-million dollars, and said, 'Invest it.'" Clifford had incurred big capital losses selling his defense stocks in 1968, when Lyndon B. Johnson asked him to run the Pentagon, explains Wyser-Pratte. "So we, in doing arb deals for him, made up his losses—and used up all his tax loss carryforwards—so he didn't pay a cent of taxes. He was thrilled." Small wonder, then, that Clifford put in a good word for the young man with Bache. "From that time on," boasts Wyser-Pratte, "risk arb was the most profitable operation Bache ever had. Every year, Leslie—and then Harry Jacobs, who took over from him—would come to me near the end of the year and ask, 'How much are you going to make this year?' Because they would pay the entire firm's bonuses out of the arbitrage desk's profits. I had eight employees and the rest of the firm had 12,000. But we made money hand over fist for a long time." Indeed, beginning in the early 1970s, annual stories about Wyser-Pratte earning more than anyone else at Bache became a staple of tabloid financial pages. (As one of the first publicly traded brokerage firms, Bache had to report compensation to its shareholders, much to the chagrin of Wall Street's intensely private old guard.)

Deal making, and the arbs who facilitated the transactions, proliferated and splashed into the headlines with increasing frequency throughout the 1970s. Novel, aggressive, and flexible deal structures like hostile bids, two-tiered offers, and white knights, as well as the players' outsized paydays, entered the public consciousness. The boom in deals arose partly because the long and grinding bear market that cratered the "Nifty-Fifty" and ended the go-go years of the 1960s drove the shares of many companies down to bargain levels, ones that made it cheaper for companies to buy assets on Wall Street than to invest to build them. It was also in part because, in the decade's frequent bear markets, takeovers of one sort or another often provided the only game in town for beleaguered bulls—who stampeded from rumor stock to rumor stock.

Merger Mania

In the increasingly fevered deal atmosphere and trailed by a growing band of inquisitive financial journalists that the deals attracted, arbs also began to find it increasingly difficult to operate under the radar as the 1970s progressed. Especially after an aggressive newcomer and shameless self-promoter named Ivan Boesky came onto the scene at mid-decade. Trained as a lawyer, accountant, and securities analyst,

Boesky used his wife's family money to set himself up as a risk arbitrageur. To attract limited partners, Boesky shredded the arb community's unwritten rule, which prohibited publicity seeking. He courted journalists and penned a mass-market book, *Merger Mania*, touting arbitrage as "Wall Street's Best Kept Money-Making Secret," earning for himself the unending enmity of many rivals and a nickname, "Piggy," albeit it one only uttered behind his back.

In October 1977, old-line arbs were aghast to pick up the new issue of *Fortune* and find, beginning on page 266, a four-page spread featuring a large color photo of the arriviste arb grinning from phone-pressed ear to phone-pressed ear under the headline, "A Killing in Babcock & Wilcox." The story by Eleanor Johnson Tracy focused on a bidding war between United Technologies and J. Ray McDermott & Co. for the prize of the old-line boiler maker. It breathlessly recounted how four "fearless young arbitrageurs made $30 million while the year's biggest corporate takeover battle was underway." It dubbed them "the Four Horsemen; the acknowledged leaders of the younger generation of arbitrageurs"—though it carefully specified that the four "do not work as a group." Boesky boasted in the article that he had been a winner in 90 percent of the deals he'd invested in since opening his firm a scant two years earlier. The writer, snowed, breathlessly reported Boesky's impressive qualifications to excel in risk arb—by virtue of education, experience, ambition—and because he was said to need only four hours of sleep nightly. According to *Fortune*, Boesky had boldly taken a large stake in Babcock at $40, on news of the first bid, seeing it as "a good buy" there.

The magazine spilled comparatively little ink on its other "Horsemen." Goldman Sachs's Bob Rubin briefly acknowledged being successful, "on balance," over his eleven years on the arb desk to that point, but he also cannily admitted to "on occasion" losing more than

---

The Four Horsemen of Arbitrage

Ivan Boesky
Guy Wyser-Pratte
Richard Rosenthal
Robert Rubin

Fortune's four horsemen of arbitrage, October 1977.

$1 million in a single arbitrage deal. Dick Rosenthal, a partner and executive committee member at Salomon Brothers was evidently even more circumspect. *Fortune* carried nary a quote from him, merely a few scraps of biographical info. Then there was Guy Wyser-Pratte. Along with his basic résumé data and a mention of his treatise, the *Fortune* reporter rehashed the latest tabloid reports of Wyser-Pratte's eye-watering compensation package and then reported that the Bache arb head took a "working vacation" to Martha's Vineyard and Booth Bay Harbor, Maine, while the deal hung in the balance, leaving his partners in New York stewing over the capital he'd put at risk. According to *Fortune*, "Wyser-Pratte stopped buying for Bache three weeks before September 3 [when the tender expired], and, in the end, succeeded in clearing $15 a share. He ended up with the largest position (probably some $15 million) Bache had ever taken in arbitrage." Rubin, according to the magazine, had settled for a good bit narrower spread, but took considerably less deal risk, buying 100,000 shares of Babcock, at 59¾, just four days before the tender expired. (McDermott had committed to paying $65 a share for the stock a few months' hence.)

A Glossy Image's Downside

The glossy *Fortune* piece amped up a land rush into the risk-arb world, with investment capital—and would-be portfolio jocks—pouring into the space, eager to share in the seemingly easy profits. What followed, entirely predictably, was a narrowing of arbitrage spreads and a decline in the profitability of the business, even as the deal flow continued pumping along. As Wyser-Pratte himself had explained in his treatise (*Risk Arbitrage*, Wiley 2009), "The arb's return on investment is a direct function of the demand for that particular spread. With five or six arbs willing to trade a deal for no less than a 25 percent annualized return, the arrival of a new player who is willing to accept 20 percent compresses the profit available to the others. The new player will bid up the target's price while selling down the acquirer's price, leaving those who require a higher return outside or 'away' from the market."

The "Four Horseman" article was scarcely Wyser-Pratte's only close encounter with Boesky. In Wall Street's still relatively small, albeit growing, arb community, some sort of relationship was all but inevitable, and the two became occasional tennis partners. It was a *Wall Street Journal* reporter, says Wyser-Pratte, who may have inadvertently kept him from being dragged through the mud in Boesky's insider trading prosecution:

> I was lucky. Boesky insisted on having a private wire into my office because I had written the book. We would even socialize occasionally. His wife, Seema, and I got along very well. But one day, Priscilla Meyer, who worked for the *Journal*, came down to my Bache office. We were talking deals and she baited me a little bit—and I was a little naïve. She said, "You know, Piggy says,"—referring to Ivan—and I replied, "Yeah, Piggy, that is the way he would view this." Then I said, "Now, you're not going to quote me on this." I thought she promised, "Absolutely." But the next day, in the *Journal*, I read, "Guy says Piggy . . ." I tried to apologize. I picked up the private wire, he slammed it down; he pulled it out. This was in 1986. I called on an outside line, and he said, "You're an expletive deleted!" and hung up. The next thing I know, he's wearing wires and trying to give the government enough evidence on others' insider trading to mitigate his own penalties.

It's perhaps no accident that one of the more arresting curios in Wyser-Pratte's office hangs above the office privy: A framed yellowed copy of the front page of the *New York Post*, dated November 15, 1989. Dominated by a large photo of a shifty-eyed derelict with flowing white hair and a wild beard, the tabloid's headline screams, "Look what jail's done to . . . Ivan Boesky!" The editors thoughtfully included a small two-year-old headshot of "the dapper Wall Street mogul," just in case any of their readers had forgotten Boesky's Wall Street mien.

As Wyser-Pratte entered his second decade running Bache's arb desk, a market flooded with new money cooled his enthusiasm for shrinking traditional arb spreads. Indeed, he admits, he became "kind of bored with doing just risk arbitrage. I was not a passive person, and to be sitting there, just passively sweating out individual arb deals—I couldn't deal with that." When he started in the business, Wyser-Pratte points out, "risk arbs wouldn't go into a deal if there wasn't an unlevered 35 percent–40 percent return" on offer. "You sweated even those deals, because the Justice Department could come in at the last minute and drive everybody nuts. I just hated being subject to someone else's whims, so I started to look for ways to push the values myself." Thus, the more dumb money flowed into the risk-arb space amid the merger mania of the 1980s, the more diligently Wyser-Pratte focused on creating an activist business.

Standing Up to Corporates

Wyser-Pratte had gotten his first taste of activism way back in 1974, in an encounter with Denver-based Great Western United. Wyser-Pratte's risk-arb operation had picked up a large chunk of cumulative preferred shares in a Great Western subsidiary, Great Western Sugar. The sub was materially in arrears on dividends, so Wyser-Pratte began digging into the parent, discovering it was "making money hand over fist. So I wrote a letter, demanding the preferred dividends that they owed us. They refused. So I sued in federal district court in Delaware. A week later, I got a check in the mail for the entire amount of the preferred arrearages. I said, 'Aha. If you stand up to these corporates, you see what happens.' That just launched me into the activist side of the business."

Traditional risk arbitrageurs, he explains, use their capacity for risk-bearing and expertise in corporate valuation to take positions in corporate transactions that appear sufficiently rewarding—thereby providing liquidity that helps ensure efficient outcomes. Activist arbs use those same skills and resources to take the process one step further. They recognize situations where inept corporate managements have created "value gaps" and where they can employ their capital to catalyze change.

Manifestly proud of his military service and a staunch believer in democratic capitalism, Wyser-Pratte easily took up cudgels for shareholders' rights. When he found an undervalued company being managed in the interests not of its shareholders but managers and insiders, he acquired equity stakes and pressured management to improve returns to shareholders. Hostile takeovers, mergers, spinoffs, share buy-backs—Wyser-Pratte quickly became known for using any weapon at hand to achieve his goals.

Not all of his early forays into activism were as quickly or as satisfactorily concluded as his quick win against Great Western. His very public jousting with the chairman of Gerber Products at its 1977 annual meeting came to naught. The baby food company's board simply refused to consider a takeover bid from Anderson Clayton

& Co.—despite the bid's substantial premium to Gerber's trading price. But Wyser-Pratte's protest at the meeting grabbed national headlines. So did the lawsuit Wyser-Pratte subsequently filed, even though a judge in Gerber's hometown foiled its prosecution. The wide publicity on Gerber, Wyser-Pratte says, encouraged other activists to begin challenging corporate management—and him to continue, with relish—though his litigious, activist style of risk arbitrage not infrequently proved awkward, to say the least, for Bache's brass. Especially because Wyser-Pratte sat on the board of Bache, and—later—Prudential Bache, "It actually used to drive them nuts when I would do it."

Wyser-Pratte cites American Express's 1979 unsolicited offer for the publishing house McGraw-Hill—at the time one of the richest takeover bids ever, at some $830 million—as a case in point. The credit card company's opening salvo was essentially twice the publisher's trading price. But the publisher's board simply said no. Rather than sue, Wyser-Pratte put together a "shareholder protective committee" and sought to demonstrate that the majority of holders favored selling. The tactic was famously disparaged as a "children's campaign" by Martin Lipton, a renowned M&A attorney who represented McGraw-Hill and whose threat of litigation, recalls Wyser-Pratte, scared other members of his group "into folding like a tent." The collapse of his committee did not stop Wyser-Pratte, though, from taking to the floor at McGraw-Hill's annual meeting to ream the publisher's chairman for "arrogant disregard" of shareholders. The former marine evolved an approach to activist arbitrage resembling a military campaign. Not every charge succeeded on its own, but taken together, his unrelenting attacks helped plant the idea—among shareholders, professional investors, lawyers, and the financial media—that the interests of shareholders could not simply be swept under the rug.

Getting Under Pru-Bache's Skin

Wyser-Pratte recalls with some relish that he "really" got under the skin of Pru-Bache's board when he sued Houston Natural Gas (HNG) in 1984. Coastal States' founder Oscar Wyatt had made a merger proposal to HNG that February, which the utility fended off by paying "greenmail" to its suitor (buying back its shares in HNG at a fat premium). "Every arb got bagged, me included," Wyser-Pratte recalls. "Just about as that was happening, a Lazard Frères investment banker sent me a letter demonstrating that a Lazard client, Transco Corp., was willing to offer a higher price for HNG than Coastal had—but HNG's chairman wouldn't even allow the letter into his boardroom." That letter, plus Wyser-Pratte's visceral distaste for the greenmailing tactic HNG had used to protect its management, was more than the arbitrageur could abide. He sued in federal district court in Houston.

The lawsuit proved the undoing of Houston Natural's chairman, M. D. Matthews, Wyser-Pratte chuckles, nearly thirty-five years after the fact. "I'll never forget it." In the discovery process, "We caught them writing standstill agreements with anyone and everyone—except Transco—who might potentially bid for Houston Natural Gas, out of a makeshift office in the basement of First Boston's head-quarters. But the utility's board had never approved any standstills. When it came out, they fired Matthews. The rest, unfortunately, is history. Houston Natural Gas became a part of InterNorth, which evolved into you-know-who, eventually—the bad guys, Enron."

Just after Matthews was fired, Wyser-Pratte continues, "Pru-Bache chairman George Ball—the little tyrant—comes down to my office and says, 'I want you to settle this thing with Houston—*now*.' It turned out it they had the other buyer—InterNorth—for HNG. But first the lawsuit had to be settled. So I settled. Nonetheless, catching the guys at Houston Natural Gas red-handed—that's what really motivated me. Every time I'd catch some skullduggery going on, on the part of a corporate board, at the expense of shareholders, I really was energized to go after them."

By that point, Wyser-Pratte was clearly less than enchanted with Pru-Bache's management. But busily minting coin in arbitrage amid the decade's leveraged-buyout-fueled merger mania, he now says with chagrin that he didn't notice the nefarious activity of immense propor-tions going on elsewhere in Bache all through the 1980s. Fraudulent deals packaged and promoted by Pru-Bache's tax-shelter department corrupted thousands of its retail brokers, who swindled clients out of life savings. The losses aggregated in the billions and enmeshed Pru-Bache executives in a pattern of "backstabbing, lying, embez-zling, cover-ups" as Kurt Eichenwald put it on the cover of his exposé, *Serpent on the Rock* (HarperCollins 1995). By 1990, chinks started appearing in the legal obstacles Pru-Bache and its corporate parent had been throwing up to prevent aggrieved clients from suing. State securities regulators from coast to coast were either filing charges or pursuing investigations. Even the somnolent watchdogs at the SEC and the Justice Department were becoming aroused. By August, Ball, the Pru-Bache chairman, already on a vanishingly short leash with Prudential's top brass, didn't dare balk when he was ordered to slash the capital available to Wyser-Pratte's risk-arb department—even though, recounts Wyser-Pratte, Ball had told consultants earlier that same year that risk arb was key to the firm's profits and a core asset.

His available capital abruptly slashed to only $25 million, Wyser-Pratte was forced to dump multiple positions and his P&L commenced bleeding. By mid-December, Ball was looking at an annual loss of $250 million at Pru-Bache (and no prospect, that year, of a bailout from the capital-starved risk-arb desk). He sent out a memo announcing a drastic restructuring. Most notably, Pru-Bache's risk-arbitrage department was shuttered and its director, Wyser-Pratte, a twenty-year Bache veteran, was instantly locked out of his office. "They wanted to instill the impression that I was responsible for their losses, that the arb desk lost all that money," says Wyser-Pratte. "It's not true. They made me sell out the positions. The world would find that out—but only gradually, *afterwards*. The real sources of all their losses were the fraud-infested partnerships they'd sold—what a can of worms."

Indeed, it took four more years, but in late 1994, federal prosecutors in Manhattan finally filed a criminal complaint against the company, charging that its sale of energy-income partnerships had been laced with fraud throughout the 1980s. It was accompanied by a deferred prosecution agreement, effectively putting the firm on probation for three years. It ultimately admitted after more than three years of denials that it had broken the law, and it agreed to top up the penalties it paid to more than $700 million. The SEC and various states and private attorneys eventually won additional judgments, but Eichenwald's book documents that Pru-Bache and its corporate parent, Prudential Insurance, were remarkably successful overall in abusing the legal system to shield themselves from ever paying a price commensurate with the damage their fraud inflicted on clients.

For Wyser-Pratte, his abrupt expulsion from Pru-Bache "was tough for a while. They tried to prevent me from setting up my own risk-arbitrage operation. They wouldn't give me any of my records— tried to stop me from getting the data I needed to reestablish my track record. It was really bad news on their part. But I managed to re-create everything. Luckily, some of my guys still worked there, and they were walking out of the office every night with knapsacks full of records, so that we could re-create our performance." Eventually, says Wyser-Pratte, he could put together a couple-inch-thick book documenting his record. And the SEC decreed, "It's good enough for us."

Freer to Do Activist Things

Meanwhile, a former Bache investment banking colleague with broad experience in Europe volunteered to raise capital for Wyser-Pratte. "He went out and raised money for our Euro Partners Arbitrage Fund. It did very well, mostly doing risk-arb deals. Once I got out on my own, I resurrected Wyser-Pratte & Co. on February 1, 1991." With his own name on the door, Wyser-Pratte "felt a lot freer to do activist things. From 1991 through today, I have done over a hundred activist arbitrage deals. They're far more interesting to me than the straight risk-arb deals that I was doing earlier in my career. I'm not a passive person, and just sitting anywhere, passively sweating out individual risk-arb deals—I couldn't deal with it any longer. So I started to go after managements in the United States that were not doing right by their shareholders." Never shy about judiciously bringing his activist exploits to the attention of the media, Wyser-Pratte's activities eventually piqued the curiosity of some friends in Europe. Companies overseas, he had observed, seemed to be at least a decade, if not two, behind their peers in the United States in terms of democratizing corporate governance.

These days, claims Wyser-Pratte, he finds more risk-arb situations pregnant with profits waiting to be exploited in Europe than in the United States. He positively delights in aggravating the "ancien régime" by taking aim at sprawling, underperforming conglomerates being run "to cosset close relatives and to outwit the Centre des Impôts," France's IRS. In Germany, he has frequently been quoted arguing that making a profit is not a "sin." All over the Continent, he has battled staunch resistance from entrenched insiders. He has been harassed by police and securities and customs officials, barred from social gatherings, and subjected to creative name-calling. "*Le* Rambo *du capitalisme*," "*Der* Rambo *des Kapitalmärkte*," "the John Wayne of finance," and "Schwarzkopf" (an homage of sorts to the Gulf War hero) are among the more printable of his sobriquets.

Theatrics aside, Wyser-Pratte's investment modus operandi always starts with identifying undervalued securities and analyzing what problems in management, strategy, asset mix, corporate governance, shareholder conflicts, or any of a host of global or local forces are weighing on the stock. Wyser-Pratte then uses peer-group analysis and related financial statistics to estimate what the company might be worth without those burdens—and calculates his activist-arbitrage "spread" as the distance between that estimate and the company's current market price (as opposed to the difference between a takeover premium and the actual market price in more traditional risk arbitrage, centered on announced transactions). This "value gap" represents the potential return that might be gained for shareholders by agitating for the desired changes.

His all-time best activist-arbitrage deal—so far—boasts Wyser-Pratte, required seemingly endless patience. It grew out of a relationship established in 2000, when Wyser-Pratte took his activist investor act into Germany. "I went after Rheinmetall, the big defense contractor. It was controlled by the Röchling family, and the company needed some international investor to enter their market and draw attention to it, which I did. The stock was languishing at €8 when I bought it, and I sold it a year later at €18. The German press called it 'the financial transaction of the decade' in their home market."

Nothing to sniff at, to be sure, but the relationship Wyser-Pratte struck up over the course of that year with Rheinmetall's supervisory chairman, Werner Engelhardt, paid even greater dividends. The two stayed in touch and in 2003, says Wyser-Pratte, Engelhardt, by then retired, came to dinner in New York and said, "I have another one for you. I used to work for a company called IWKA, on the French border. I know the chairman. He's too rich; he doesn't need the money, so he's not working very hard. The company's jewel is the robotics division. You should sell everything else.'"

At the time, IWKA, a manufacturer and provider of engineering services, mostly for automotive markets, was trading between €11 and €12 a share, "but Werner told me it was worth three times what it was selling for," recalls Wyser-Pratte. He quickly amassed a 5 percent holding and announced he was looking forward to working with IWKA management to maximize its value. Over the next several months, he recalls, "I met with the company and we wined and dined." Then, just before its annual meeting, IWKA said it was selling three businesses, but not an underperforming packaging division Wyser-Pratte had been urging them to jettison. He threatened a proxy fight if IWKA didn't dump the unit within a year. IWKA responded by hiring Goldman Sachs. Wyser-Pratte, in turn, hired an old friend, Sebastian Freitag, whose Freitag & Co. is a leading corporate-finance advisory in Germany. Freitag, reports Wyser-Pratte, simply "outfoxed the Goldman guys." IWGA's CEO announced his resignation on the morning of its 2005 annual meeting, "and that was the start of all the billiard balls rolling in one after the other. The chairman resigned, the rest of the board resigned." Wyser-Pratte increased his stake in the company as it continued selling off noncore operations. By late 2007, IWGA announced its first dividend since 2005, giving Wyser-Pratte a chance to close out his campaign with an annualized rate of return of 24.51 percent.

KUKA Won and Lost

That was not, however, the end of Wyser-Pratte's involvement in IWGA—or KUKA, as it soon renamed itself, reflecting the prowess of its KUKA-brand robotics production equipment business. Despite the name change, Wyser-Pratte and Freitag weren't satisfied with the pace of the company's attempts to sell robots beyond the auto sector. Another new management was recruited and Freitag "found another investment group to come in and take a 25 percent position." Wyser-Pratte reestablished a 10 percent stake in February 2009, and the two investor groups took control of the board that September.

From then, says Wyser-Pratte, "to make a long story short, the stock soared from €11 to €85, on strong earnings gains, wider margins, and several strategic acquisitions." In March 2015, Wyser-Pratte liquidated his position. It was with immense satisfaction that Wyser-Pratte reflected, at that time, "KUKA is now the premier robotics manufacturer in Europe. One of the top three robotics companies in the world. It provides the robotics that all of the German automobile manufacturers use. But now they also do robotics for many other industries. Yet if we hadn't forced the old management to sell off its other divisions, the company would have gone bankrupt. They used the cash they raised to restructure, so KUKA became a huge success."

There is, however, a coda to the KUKA story, one that leaves Wyser-Pratte expressing mixed emotions. Shortly after he closed his position and stepped down from KUKA's board, Midea Group, of China, took a 10 percent stake. Says Wyser-Pratte, "I could see the writing on the wall. If KUKA were an American company, I would have tried to stop them cold. I am an immigrant here and I am a real believer, a patriot. I just didn't want to see the Chinese grab the technology."

The erstwhile marine swung into action, calling and writing KUKA's CEO, warning of Midea's motives. "They need the robots in China. They have the lowest penetration per capita of any nation in the civilized world!" He was outflanked though, when Midea quickly announced a preemptive €115 a share buyout. Today, despite his qualms about KUKA's buyer, Wyser-Pratte, the pragmatic capitalist, can't help himself. "From €11 to €115! What a journey!"

What strikes a listener as Wyser-Pratte reminisces about deals—and friends—won and lost over his storied career aren't so much the gilded names liberally dropped, but his insights into the motivations and vulnerabilities of the astonishing range of characters he has encountered on Wall Street, in Washington, and in companies and markets around the world—and his audacious willingness to use those insights. Also, his recurring emphasis on duty, honor, and fair dealing as a vocal advocate of applying the "Marine Corps way," meaning the principles of maneuver warfare (as described in *The Marine Corps Way: Using Maneuver Warfare to Lead a Winning Organization* by Jason A. Stantamaria, Fincent Martino and Eric K. Clemons, McGraw-Hill, 2005) to running his own business—as well as to virtually any other business. Combining those principles with the solid understanding of deal-spread analysis so fortuitously bequeathed to him by his father, Wyser-Pratte has parlayed the use of bold surprise attacks to confuse and confound his adversaries—along with the targeting of vulnerabilities to overwhelm opponents' defenses—into a winning strategy for activist arbitrage investing around the globe.

CHAPTER TWO

Jeffrey Tarr

I used to look at myself as being in a kind of drug business—not like I was peddling marijuana, but in terms of needing to do research constantly. I experimented in 5 percent of the portfolio. I did all kinds of crazy things, created all kinds of securities. We didn't know if we could arbitrage them. But I'd try it, and if it didn't work, I called it "garbitrage." If it did work, I called it "arbitrage." It was always changing.

JEFF TARR OPENS the door just as the elevator doors slide sideways, revealing his art-filled apartment's private entrance at the San Remo on Manhattan's Upper West Side. Clad in comfortable khakis and a golf shirt, the family shih tzu yapping around his ankles, the white-haired Tarr's first impression is more prosperous retiree than Wall Street master of the universe. That's perhaps unsurprising considering it has been more than twenty years since Tarr shuttered Risk Arbitrage Partners, his extraordinarily successful risk-arbitrage firm—the first to successfully marry the power of computing to arb strategies. Then again, the discreet and unpretentious Tarr was never one to swagger or to tout privately-held Risk Arbitrage Partners' eye-popping returns, which averaged 30 percent a year, *every year*, from the partnership's founding on January 16, 1981 through 1995. So there were no head-lines when Tarr turned fifty and—telling his wife that he harbored no ambition to be "the richest guy in the graveyard"—simply closed Risk Arbitrage Partners to embark on a series of globetrotting adventures with friends. (Tarr's Junction Partners—JCT are his initials—which served as the managing partner of Risk Arbitrage Partners, survives as his personal business vehicle.)

Even at two decades' remove, Tarr would still clearly prefer to avoid calling unneeded attention to his achievements in risk arb, deflect-ing a visitor's attention instead either to his canine companion or to the multiple professorships and scholarships he has endowed at his alma mater, Harvard, and at Yale, for which he ran money. Those topics exhausted, Tarr digs back further, reminiscing about Operation Match, the world's first computerized dating service, which he and a buddy cooked up, essentially on a lark, while still Harvard undergrads. That business, Tarr has no qualms about touting, then or now.

Risk arb is another matter. Still a secretive, if lucrative, back-office business conducted largely by a few trading desks at brokerage firms when Tarr arrived on Wall Street in 1968, it wasn't much changed by 1981 when he formed Risk Arbitrage Partners. The hedge fund had practical as well as tactical reasons to take pains to be discreet. Especially in its early years, before the Tax Reform Act 1986 sharply curtailed the availability of tax shelters, a hefty chunk of its alpha owed to Tarr applying his mathematical wizardry to the tax code—using loopholes that created tax losses and that permitted the fund to avoid or indefinitely delay realizing gains, allowing its profits to compound virtually untaxed.

Lucky Guy

Today, the passage of time and a subdural hematoma suffered in a biking accident have dimmed in Tarr's mind the details of the deals on which Risk Arbitrage Partners built that sterling record. But he has no trouble at all recalling the fun he had constructing it. Jeff Tarr, as he is the first to admit, is one of those lucky guys blessed with a combination of brains and the ability to recognize when he was in the right place at the right time—along with the calculating wile and gambling instincts required to take advantage of favorable odds.

Tarr's luck started early. A small-town kid with big-time math skills, Tarr took top honors in his home state of Maine in an actuarial contest while still in high school. This lead to scholarship offers from Harvard and Yale. Warned off Yale by a student who confided, "New Haven's the armpit of the universe," Tarr headed for Cambridge. Besides, he adds, "Harvard offered me more money."

He majored in math, Tarr says, "because you always play from your strengths," and snared an internship in New York City after his freshman year at the National Bureau of Casualty Underwriters. The job itself was a snore. "It was only much later that I discovered that actuaries are accountants with personality," Tarr jokes. Nonetheless, Tarr made a discovery that summer that changed his life. "I got used to using these big 'IBM machines'—that's what they were called in those days—not 'computers.'" The math major was immediately taken with their numbers-crunching prowess.

Back on campus in the spring of his junior year, Tarr and classmate Vaughn Morrill were pursuing the age-old quest of college guys everywhere: trying to find dates. One day, while commiserating with some similarly "geeky" friends, inspiration struck the duo. Their then-novel idea: Use a computer to match single men with compatible women seeking dates. If it worked, maybe even they'd get lucky. "Using a computer for dating match-ups wasn't on anyone's radar," explains Tarr. "Computers were used only for industrial purposes. We were the first. Operation Match, we called it."

The budding entrepreneurs figured they'd spend ten hours a week on the project, but it quickly consumed more than twelve hours a day. "I was very oral, very creative. So I wrote the very short questionnaire. The other guy was very anal and put everything where it should be.

The questionnaire was printed on an envelope that was self-folding for mailing, and people who wanted matches put $3 in." Responses about topics like musical preferences, literary influences, and a self-reported "sexual experience ranking" were transferred to punch cards and fed into an IBM 1401, which generated "compatibility matches"—but only during the wee hours of Sunday mornings because that was when it was cheapest to rent computer time.

To get things rolling, Tarr and friends pitched Operation Match to student newspapers on nearby campuses. The *Boston Globe* soon picked up the story. "They came over to see me one morning when I happened to be late for class," Tarr reminisces. "I had to shave. So while shaving, I made up stuff to tell them. Like that our research showed that different sorts of women liked different aftershaves. 'There are Old Spice women and English Leather women.' It wasn't really a lie; I was just a college kid having fun. But they printed it on the cover of the Sunday edition, under the headline, 'You can fall in love with this business.'"

It was a February 1966 *Look* magazine cover story, "The Great God Computer," by Gene Shalit, that sent Operation Match into orbit, however, with the article decreeing, "punch bowls are out, punch cards are in." Tarr was invited to flog the dating service to Johnny Carson on the *Tonight Show* as well as in appearances on *To Tell the Truth* and *I've Got a Secret*. The business went wild. "I went to no classes my senior year," Tarr says. "My tutor—I was an honor student—worked for me. I would have dropped out of college, but I couldn't—or didn't dare to—because of the Vietnam War."

Over the next year, more than 100,000 completed questionnaires poured into Operation Match from students coast to coast. At least a hundred nuptials were celebrated. After graduating from Harvard, Tarr took the whole operation down to New York City where, theoretically at least, he was to attend graduate school. "I tested well, so I got in everywhere. I went to Columbia Business School and, in theory, to Columbia Law and to Fordham Law. But I didn't really go; I just registered. When I showed up for finals for the first semester, I found that they thought I had dropped out and that classroom participation was half the grade. So my grades weren't so great. But I didn't care because I was getting a lot out of my job with Operation Match."

It didn't take long, however, for competitive dating services to appear and Tarr and pals were well aware, he says, that they were riding a fad. So less than three years in, they sold their brainchild "for not very much money."

Discovering Risk Arbitrage

Around that time, a New York acquaintance suggested Tarr might like working in risk arbitrage. "I thought he meant arbitrating disputes between two people," remembers Tarr. The acquaintance set him straight, adding, "My brother works at Goldman Sachs, why don't you go for an interview?" Tarr did and was offered a job working with Robert Rubin, who, only five years Tarr's senior, was already turning heads on Goldman's arbitrage desk.

But Tarr had another idea. "I always had wanted to work for the government; John F. Kennedy was my hero. 'Ask not what your country can do for you . . . ,'" Tarr explains. "So I took a job offer in D.C. from McKensey & Co. They took only one out of 100 applicants. They put me through eight rounds of interviews. I remember the eighth. I was sent down to Philadelphia to see a psychiatrist and he rubber hosed me. When I left I was so sweaty, I was rubbing my hands on my pants. But they hired me. I thought it was the greatest job in the world; thought I'd work on big projects. But I was only in Washington for two months before I realized it was the most corrupt city in history."

Returning to New York City, Tarr says he was on his way to see Goldman about the arb job he'd so rashly turned down when he ran into another acquaintance—"this guy I hardly knew"—while walking to the subway. After he explained that D.C. hadn't worked out, says Tarr, the fellow urged, "Well, come have lunch with my boss. He would love you."

"So I go lunch," Tarr says. "His boss was Sam Hunter at Smith Barney. He says to me, 'Well, if you check out, you can run the whole arb department.' I was only twenty-three. I didn't have any money. They offered me the opportunity to make eight times what Goldman had offered." Naturally, Tarr accepted the Smith Barney offer and began a crash course in risk arbitrage and the ways of Wall Street.

As Tarr tells it, at the end of his first year at Smith Barney he was owed a bonus but was told, "We can't pay you; it's too much money." When Tarr objected, he was put off with a promise, "Don't worry, I'll make it up to you next year." When the same scene unfolded again the following year, Tarr announced his intention to quit and collected, over a weekend, "in essence, five offers." Only when Tarr marched in that Monday to formally resign, he remembers, did Smith Barney offer to pay him what he was owed.

"I said, 'no.' Then I bounced around a bit. First, to Neuberger Berman, until they merged with a firm that had a veteran arbitrage operation, and I didn't want to work for anyone. Then Oppenheimer offered me a job and I went there. That time, when they offered me an incentive deal, I got it in writing." It proved a good move. "One year Oppenheimer lost money and wanted me not to take my bonus," Tarr recalls. "I said, 'Look, if I lost money and you made money, would you pay me?' They just smiled." So Tarr kept his bonus. Nonetheless, Tarr remembers fondly the many lessons he learned while working alongside Willy Weinstein, a legendary Oppenheimer trader, and Jack Nash, the firm's cofounder. For one, why they wanted his arb desk to operate independently. "They thought risk arbitrage was a good hedge for their market exposure because it is not market-related. In theory, that's true because you take the risk of the deal as distinct from the risk of the market. Except in a crash, when everything goes down, as we all know."

But classic risk arb on announced deals wasn't the half of what Tarr did at Oppenheimer. With his mathematical turn of mind and ever-increasing amounts of computing power, he found almost endless arbitrage opportunities. "The way I thought of risk arbitrage," Tarr continues, "there was a product for all seasons. In the summer, it would be hot tender offers; in the winter, it would be bankruptcies. Among the latter, I remember we had a major position in Penn Central. What sticks in my mind is that every night for two weeks, I was spending two hours reading the documents. It was so complicated. But I finally figured it out. Not that I had any idea what it was worth. What I saw was that there were common shares and bonds that were equal in terms of rights—emerging from the settlement—trading at different prices. So I arbitraged those. Penn Central was major. Even when the settlement got very clear, there was still a good spread, and the uncertainty was gone."

Analytical Edge

The thing was, Tarr explains,

> when I went to Wall Street, few others used computers. But I did. In all these deals, I would figure out different ways to hedge. Mostly, they were back-of-the-envelope kinds of transactions. So tenders,

exchange offers—I didn't even know the word *algorithm*. But I'd have everything—maybe 100 deals that we were in some stage of doing—on the computer. We would have them all handicapped—a very seat-of-the-pants process. Then we'd run the computer once a day. It was not like today, with all the computers running nonstop. The following morning, we would do a quick review and we'd see these things—maybe in two of the deals the spreads would either close or open up—and we'd think about whatever would precipitate out. It was a good way to watch; to find opportunities. We didn't restrict ourselves to equities, we did listed warrants, options. When I started, we used over-the-counter options dealers.

Then the 1974 creation of the Chicago Board Options Exchange opened new opportunities. Savvy arbs took advantage of arcane exchange rules that permitted them to delay assigning options trades to investment accounts until the winners were evident, while losers could be chalked off as business expenses. Tax arbitrage opportunities blossomed right and left.

Tarr recalls, "Often, what I did were box spreads. I bought and sold puts and calls on hot stocks—hedged them so that I would break even. What would happen is that we'd create ordinary losses in a market-making account and short-term capital gains in an investment account. But every thirty days, there'd be one or another option that would be way up and I'd put it in the investment account with a very favorable basis. In the early days, before the Reagan tax changes, by having certain mixes of ordinary losses and short-term and long-term capital gains, you could actually make money from the government. It was silly. But that's how I converted short-term ordinary income into capital." Tarr continues, "There were any number of loopholes that we used quite regularly—it was all quite legal, at the time. Since I also ran tax arbitrage for Oppenheimer, I got to model all of these just glorious transactions."

By the end of 1980, Tarr wanted his own business and Oppenheimer was amenable as long as they could retain a piece of his genius. Risk Arbitrage Partners came into existence as a joint venture, capitalized at $20 million by Tarr and a few friends, including Oppenheimer. That $20 million grew to $500 million over the next fourteen years, and the hedge fund never took in any new money. Tarr's 25 percent stake made him the largest investor and he retained firm control.

Loopholes and Other Rules

In the partnership's early years, Tarr recalls, "I made it a project—I wanted to see if I could *not* pay any taxes. Our tax counsel was a really well-respected guy named Dick Valentine, the head of the tax department at Seward & Kissel, and I remember him saying he'd never found anyone like me. I could always figure out these things that I thought were wrong in the tax code—but as long as the loopholes were legal, we'd use them. It was fun to figure out. But we didn't talk about them because if we did everyone would have been doing them—or the government would have fixed the loopholes." Which, of course, Congress at least partially did in 1986 by passing Reagan's tax overhaul. While that legislation was being hammered out, Tarr relates, he got a phone call from a key Congressional staffer, "who had heard I was doing crazy things with loopholes. I remember saying to him, 'You must have the wrong guy. There's no one here but us chickens.' And he says, 'Look, we're going to do it anyway. Can I come in and see you?' So he came and we talked a long time about the loopholes. I told them they shouldn't be. But as long as it was legal, we were using loopholes.'"

Tarr says one partner in Risk Arbitrage Partners, whom he got to know fairly well, "a learned gentleman from Chicago named Milton Friedman, convinced me there should be no rules." (Friedman, of course, later won the Nobel Prize in Economics for *A Monetary History of the United States* and demonstrated his own disdain for the rules of fair play when he did not share the prize with his coauthor, economist Anna J. Schwartz.) But, adds Tarr, "There *are* rules in Wall Street and you have to follow them." So at the hedge fund, and at Oppenheimer before it, "We made most of our money doing mathematical arbitrage, whether of stocks, other securities, or tax rules. We didn't talk to people. I didn't even *try* to talk to people."

Tarr was aware, to be sure, that other arbitrageurs sometimes played differently. "Actually, I remember when one guy wanted to be my friend. He called me up six different times and gave me inside information on deals. I just listened, more out of curiosity than anything. Then I decided that he was so promotional that I should bet the opposite of what he was saying. I didn't bet win, place, show. I bet to show—I was just having fun, going to the track—but all six times, I won." Not long afterwards, Tarr recalls, he brought those tips up while chatting with a lawyer. "He said to me, 'You were betting using inside information.' He was right. I could have gone to jail."

Tarr identifies his wrong-way informant as Martin A. Siegel, the Kidder Peabody investment banker who eventually did land in jail along with Ivan Boesky, Michael Milken, and Bob Rubin's successor as Goldman's arb desk chief, Robert Freeman, as a result of the insider trading scandals of the late 1980s. "Marty was notorious in the business. I didn't really *want* to be his friend. I wanted *to get along*, but I didn't want to—you know."

Relying on Numbers, Not People

In similar vein, Tarr insists that it was essentially his Yankee skepticism of Wall Street mores that kept him from getting entangled, amid the 1980s leveraged-buyout (LBO) boom, in Milken's Drexel financing daisy chains. While Risk Arbitrage Partners never took in additional equity capital, Tarr "used Morgan Stanley to raise some debt financing for us, because there was a lot to do and there were some tax advantages." While that loan was in the works, Tarr adds, "Mike called me up and offered me more money, at lower cost, no questions asked. I said, 'No.' I knew he was pushing the envelope and didn't want to get involved."

"That was the best decision I ever made," Tarr declares. "I didn't trust him. I knew him pretty well. Now, after prison and prostate cancer, I think he's totally different; working very hard to do some good things for humanity. But then, he had all these guys. We used to have a name for them: It was a play on 3M's stock symbol—'the Triple-Ms, Milken's Mental Midgets.' They would do anything Milken wanted, and they would help each other. They're still around. It was all very questionable."

Tarr continues, "But a lot of guys back then thought *that* was how you did risk-arb research. Goldman Sachs was the big one—the king. Gus Levy [Goldman's seminal trader and senior partner from 1969 until his death in 1973] was *the king*. They used to tell stories about how when Gus was on all these boards, he'd find inside information and his wife would buy the stocks."

"Or remember Felix Royhatyn?" asks Tarr. "Years later he was credited with saving New York City from bankruptcy. But when he was representing the ITT guy—Harold Geneen—in all the 1960s deals that went into building his conglomerate—they [Lazard Frères, Royhatyn's investment bank] had offices in Switzerland and they would buy the stock over there, and it would be legal."

Mathematical relationships, Tarr clearly believed, were a much firmer foundation for his business than the human sort. He reaches back to 1970 for a story illustrating some of the ambiguity on the

Valle's steakhouse. Wikimedia Commons.

slippery slope to insider trading. Tarr was still getting his feet wet in arbitrage when the Campbell Soup Co. made an offer to buy a stock called Valle's Steak House. "Valle's main location was in Portland, Maine, about thirty miles from where I grew up. So I called up Valle's, got a guy on the phone and said, 'We used to go there for holidays, we loved it, it was *the* big place we'd go,'—and that was the truth. Then I went on, 'Hopefully everything's going well.' He said, 'Oh, yeah, going well.' Then I said, 'Well, hopefully the deal will go through.' The guy said, 'Well, I'm not going to be involved. I'm going on a vacation for three weeks and then I'm coming back,'—and he told me the day. I wrote down the date and on that Monday, before 9 A.M., I called, 'Hi, this is your friend from Maine. I just wanted to check on how the deal is coming.' He said, 'I can't talk to you.' I sold my stock when the market opened. At 11 A.M., the deal was called off. Did I rely on inside information?"

Tarr continues, "Most people trading on inside information *lose* money, but the government only goes after those that make money. I also think that if you really look at 'inside information'—depending to some extent on how you define it—everything is in the stock." So Risk Arbitrage Partners, says Tarr, "ran like an insurance company. Strictly by the numbers." And his numerical focus helped keep the fund's expenses lower than many of its rivals. "I remember when a number of arbitrage firms started hiring lawyers. Pretty soon I figured out that they had hired so many lawyers that the deals were fairly well-handicapped—which was already reflected in the prices of the stocks. So I didn't hire any lawyers."

Patience and Humor

Another way Tarr managed Risk Arbitrage Partners' exposures was with calculated patience. A deal would be announced, but Tarr would sit tight on the sidelines waiting for any and all controversies to be cleared up, for good or for bad. "Everyone else would work on it for months, but I didn't. When all the dust settled, I either bet on it or didn't bet on it. We could go either way; we could go long or short."

He adds, "You've got to be lucky in arbitrage. It isn't all luck, but it's most of it. Being mathematically-driven helped a lot. I'm not saying it required any brains but just having experience with a computer was a big edge when I started in the business—and it helped that the markets weren't as efficient as they are today. In fact, in the 1960s, when I started, there was an MIT professor who believed that the markets were so efficient there was no need to do research. He was right. He was just fifty years too early! Back then, though, a lot of people liked doing arbitrage because it felt like going to the track. If they knew Secretariat was running, they had to bet on him. We had a much better system to handicap the race though—and the introduction of all sorts of options meant we could arbitrage puts and calls on all sorts of stuff."

His experience taught him, says Tarr, "that if you were deaf, dumb, and blind, you could make 1 percent a month in the market—just by swimming with the current. Then, if you brought some—I guess they call it 'alpha' today—to it, you could make more. So we averaged 3 percent a month."

In October 1987, Tarr admits, "I did have 'inside information.' The week before the crash I couldn't sleep. My insides were in tumult. So I sold out 75 percent of our portfolio. Everyone thought I had gone crazy. Then the market crashed. Well, for that calendar year we were still up 12 percent. And on our fiscal year basis, we made 57 percent in the 12 months that included the crash. But I only made that because my 'insides' wouldn't let me sleep. It was an unusual situation. But the moral of the story is that unusual things happen. That's why you have to diversify."

In the immediate aftermath of the crash, Tarr continues, he had no idea what would happen next. "I was on the board of the Lincoln Center Theater and they had an opening scheduled for that very night, of the play, *Anything Goes*. I called the guy who was running the theater and said, 'It was such a hard day, I don't think I'm going to be able to make it.' Then I added, 'But I have something you ought to do, for today only.' He said, 'What's that?' I said, 'Change the play's name from *Anything Goes* to *Everything Went*.' "

Tarr pauses for a beat, then adds, "I've always had a sick sense of humor. He didn't laugh."

CHAPTER THREE

Martin Gruss

"The business has changed so much," laments Martin D. Gruss. "I remember in the early 1970s, there'd be a bid for a company at $25 a share. Most risk arbs would get together and give their orders to one broker—and the stock would open at $23. Everybody made a very nice living off of that. Nowadays, if there's a bid at $25, the stock opens at $27. There's no spread. People have wised up to the hope of a competitive deal." Yet, observes the veteran arbitrageur, "Merger arb is still alive and kicking. It's not booming—the players are different and the capabilities are different. But arbs are still underwriting the risk in corporate deals in exchange for a rate of return—still providing

a valuable service to shareholders who may not want to take the risk
of a deal successfully closing. And many still provide uncorrelated
long-term market-beating returns, as well as capital preservation,
for investors."

———————————

MARTIN GRUSS'S ART-FILLED family office is perched on a high
floor in Phillips Point, an exclusive complex on West Palm Beach's
South Flagler Drive. The workspace overlooks the gilded islet and the
Atlantic Ocean. These days, Gruss is a pillar of Palm Beach society, an
avid collector of vintage sports cars, which he drives in road rallies, and
he pays closer attention to fluctuations in the price of gold than he
does to M&A news. ("Everybody should own a little bit of gold. It's
owning disaster insurance.")

In his younger days, Gruss, now seventy-four, skillfully piloted privately-held Gruss & Co. through much of the turbulent 1970s, the
leveraged-buyout fueled 1980s, the mega-deals of the 1990s, and into
this century. Gruss began transitioning his firm to a new generation
of partners, restructuring it as a hedge fund in 2000. As Gruss Capital
Management, the Manhattan-based firm continues to manage money
in alternative strategies but now for outside investors as well as for
Gruss family members.

Gruss, who didn't fully retire until 2009, comments, "We had a pretty
good run from 2000 to 2009. The S&P 500 index fell 15 percent,
while Gruss Arb was up 78 percent. We substantially outperformed the
S&P, although our returns were much, much lower than in preceding
decades due to the extremely low interest rates. Not to mention that a
lot of guys were carried out on their backs in 2007–2008. We've never
really gotten caught out severely." In fact, he avers, there's scarcely a
better illustration of the power of risk arb's uncorrelated returns and its
protection of capital in a bear market than Gruss's performance in the
difficult markets of that decade. "And, if you look at longer periods of
time," notes Gruss, "our arb partnership enjoyed a much higher rate of
return than the S&P."

Says John Paulson, who got his start in risk arbitrage in Gruss's
shop, "Marty has a very impressive track record. He compounded over
twenty years at about 20 percent." Indeed, it was Gruss's example that

fired the younger man's ambition to build his own firm. "Marty came into Gruss & Co.'s office one morning and made many, many millions in one deal," Paulson recalls.

No Sure Thing

Yet, to hear Martin Gruss tell it, his success in risk arbitrage was anything but foreordained. During the 1960s, Gruss & Co., the New York City-based risk-arbitrage firm that Gruss's father, Joseph, built after fleeing the Nazis in 1939, ranked as one of Wall Street's top-ten investment banks, based on capital—and it was all Joe Gruss's capital. By the early 1970s, the senior Gruss, who had started investing in oil and gas deals in the 1950s, essentially as a tax-shelter, had become increasingly captivated by "his very nice little oil business," according to his son. "He was very happy if he could recover a dollar for every dollar he invested—because that invested dollar only cost him 90 cents, considering the high marginal tax rates. Then, in 1973, the Arab oil embargo hit and the price of oil soared to $30 a barrel from $3. Suddenly my dad found that he had a very nice, pretty big oil company. He became quite happy to focus on Gruss Petroleum."

Joe Gruss also diverted most of his capital into the booming oil patch. By the time Martin entered the arb arena in 1974, Gruss & Co.'s arb presence was "very small," he recalls. "My father basically had retired" from risk arb and the company's Broad Street office housed "just my father and a couple of accountants." The son stepped in with trepidation. Joe Gruss is revered to this day in philanthropic circles for his support of Jewish education but his relationship with his only son was fraught. His old-world father, born in 1903 in what is now part of Ukraine, recounts Gruss, was "mercurial, and could be very difficult to work with."

He concedes, "My father was forty when I was born and he was a bit anxious for me to learn his business." But as a young man, the son was not particularly career-focused. He played polo, "which didn't sit especially well with his old man," recalls a business associate of the elder Gruss. The upshot was that Marty Gruss didn't join Gruss & Co. until in his early thirties, after college, law school, and three years in corporate finance at Kuhn, Loeb & Co.

Something New and Unfriendly

"I started very small. Within a few months, International Nickel made a $28-a-share hostile bid for a battery company called ESB Inc. It was the first-ever *unfriendly* tender offer made by a blue-chip company—*and* it had the backing of Morgan Stanley, a leading corporate underwriting firm. Until then, backing hostile deals was just *not* something that the white-shoe firms had been willing to do." They weren't done by old line companies, either—only by arriviste conglomerators.

But this bid, clearly, was something new, says Gruss, "So I bought ESB—which had been trading at 19½, before the bid—on the open, which was around 25. A couple of days later, it was trading at 27—and my father thought I was smart, for a change. Like I said, Dad could be difficult. If the trade had gone the other way, I'm not sure where I'd be today." The younger Gruss's quick trade got even better as ESB hired Goldman Sachs and they, in turn, brought in industrialist Harry Gray's United Aircraft (soon to become United Technologies through mergers of its own) as a white knight. The rivals bid the price of ESB up to $41 a share before Inco walked away with the "prize." Those quote marks denote that—not seven years later—Inco quit the battery business after posting hundreds of millions in losses from its failed attempt to exploit what it had thought was a monopoly in nickel with extensive research in nickel battery technology. Only a classic case study for finance textbooks survives from the misadventure.

That cast absolutely no shadow, however, over the immediate and resounding success of Martin Gruss's first big risk-arb trade. He was hooked. In short order, he and his father recapitalized Gruss & Co. "I had a little capital that my father had built up for me in a trust fund, so I contributed $250,000—which was a lot of money for me in those days—he contributed $1.75 million, and off we went."

"It was a great time to start in risk arbitrage," Gruss recalls fondly. "We had double-digit risk-free rates. We would make two or three times that. We thought we were geniuses. But all we were doing was making two or three times the risk-free rate." What's more, a whole new range of behavior was gaining acceptance in corporate finance. "White-shoe companies were making hostile bids and acting as white knights—greenmail and 'highly confident letters' were soon to enter the picture. It was a new era." Gruss continues, "Deals were happening left, right, and center. Lots of arbitrage opportunities. We—my long-time partner, Richard Novick and I—were fortunate to be able to take advantage of them—and success feeds on success. We were lucky, too, to have very talented people come through the office. John Paulson and John Bader, to mention just a couple."

It was, however, a young man's game, and the elder Gruss "one day showed up in the office," his son remembers, "and announced, 'I want out. My heart can't take this.' That's just how he was." By that time, Gruss estimates, his father's capital in arb had grown to about $20 million. "I came back the next day and proposed that we pay him out over five years. He said, 'That's fine.' So we, in effect, did a leveraged buyout of his interest."

Particularly in the first decade he ran Gruss & Co.—before arbitrageur Ivan Boesky's arrest for insider trading—the younger Gruss recalls, "rumors were rife and you could see stocks starting to bubble and trade higher. There were technical patterns that you would look for to confirm rumors. I mean, everybody *knew* the rumors. Not everybody *played* the rumors, but the rumors were no secrets. A lot of leaks were coming out of investment banks and law firms and the guys at the printers' offices the night before."

A Disciplined Focus

What Gruss, "in the day," emphasized more than sheer brainpower was discipline, he says; avoiding a preponderance of the busted deals and making sure the potential rewards in deals it participated in far outweighed the downside risk. His foremost discipline, Gruss recalls, was "a focus on finding a free call. If you were risking a really small sum of money but there was a chance for the bid to be increased, we liked to load up." There were times, Gruss acknowledges, "when we were super-leveraged. But we were also always very risk-averse. There were times we would not like where it looked like the market was going and so we'd get out. Which is important, because all boats—yachts

The Gruss & Co. logo. Used with permission from Martin Gruss.

and rowboats—go down together in a severe market decline. And if you're highly leveraged, you'll be carried out." Gruss credits this risk-aversion with protecting his firm in 1987, 2000, and 2007–2008. In each, Gruss had deleveraged, bought puts, and scaled back its long positions to very manageable proportions before the crisis hit—and then was able to take advantage of the panic selling to establish newly attractive positions.

From Arb to Activist

Gruss also occasionally "actually became an acquirer or potential acquirer." This happened most prominently in a deal which resulted in Anderson Clayton Corp., an amalgam of cotton mills, salad dressings, and Gaines dog food, being acquired in 1986 by Quaker Oats after an often rancorous six-month takeover battle shaped by Gruss & Co. "The Clayton family—headed by four elderly daughters of one of the founders—owned 33 percent of the stock but had only recently gotten control of it, from a trust," Gruss recounts. "One day, we read that the family wanted to cash out. The company proposed an elaborate restructuring—basically, paying the sisters $45 a share to keep management intact. A quick, back-of-the-envelope analysis said the price was egregiously low."

He continues, "So we started building a position. Then I talked it over with Bob Steinberg, a friend who was running the arb department at Bear Stearns. He started taking a position, too. A couple of days later, I called a friend who had a hedge fund, we talked it over, and he started taking a position, too. A few days after that, I asked another friend, 'Do you know anybody who'd like to own a pet food company?' He said, 'Why don't you call so-and-so in Chicago? He might be able to help.' So I did, and told *him* about Anderson Clayton. Within a couple of hours, he calls back, saying, 'Quaker Oats would love to buy the pet food division.' That was the start."

After several months of negotiations—and armed with financing from Quaker Oats—Gruss and Bear Stearns quietly made a $54-a-share tender offer for Anderson Clayton. Gruss and Bear Stearns banker Michael Tarnopol flew to the target's Houston headquarters to convey the bid while Quaker Oats kept to the wings. "Quaker had put up a great deal of the money in return for a security convertible into

100 percent of the pet food company," explains Gruss. If the tender succeeded, Quaker would get Gaines for about $238 million, while Gruss and Bear Stearns would profit by selling the rest.

"Let's Put on a Show"

Gruss and Tarnopol's reception in Houston was icy. Anderson Clayton brass stonewalled them. So the arbs publicly announced their $54 bid just days before a shareholder vote Anderson Clayton had called on its recapitalization plan. The financial press had a field day. The *New York Times* quoted Gruss telling a Bear Stearns executive, "You can sing, I can dance and someone else can provide the music. Let's put on a show" ("Quaker Stars in a Wall Street Soap," Fred R. Beakley, October 26, 1986).

Public skirmishes flared all summer. Anderson Clayton first raised its own bid for the Clayton block to $56. Gruss and Bear then made a public hostile tender, also at $56, and sued in Delaware Chancery Court, which quickly sided with the arbs. The court issued injunctions halting the restructuring and self-tender, citing the company's desultory attempts to find higher bidders.

But Anderson Clayton also had begun courting a white knight, Ralston Purina, whose number 1 position in the pet food market might have proved vulnerable if Quaker captured Gaines. In mid-September, Ralston's chairman, William Stiritz, shrewdly unveiled a plan to have his board vote on a $62-a-share takeover of Anderson Clayton. With $62 in prospect, the deal was getting a mite rich for the arbs' blood. They told Quaker they'd stay in the bidding only if it upped its financing commitment. Suddenly, Gaines was a tad rich for Quaker's taste, too. But allowing Ralston to capture a dominant share of the dog food market was at least as distasteful.

Bear and Gruss did their best to advance the notion that Quaker's best shot was to go after Anderson Clayton on its own, selling off the parts it didn't want to drive its cost for Gaines below $250 million. At that juncture, the two arb firms had considerable paper profits on their block of 7 percent-plus of Anderson Clayton's shares—and also stood to split a $7 million banking fee from Quaker if the deal closed. They obligingly withdrew their tender so Quaker could buy Anderson Clayton shares on the open market, which it did with gusto. Quaker quickly swept up 23 percent of the shares at $64, mostly from arbs, Bear Stearns among them. But Gruss held out.

His memory is now hazy on the details, but contemporary reports had investment bankers speculating that Gruss was miffed at Quaker for ignoring advice to negotiate for the elderly sisters' 33 percent block *before* hoovering up the Street's shares. Bleakley's *Times* piece cited above, for one, quoted Gruss saying, "I did not think it was particularly intelligent for any Anderson Clayton shareholder to sell when the bidding process was just beginning." He proved correct. Anderson Clayton shares spiked to $64, and white knight Ralston raised its ante. Stiritz *first* arranged to buy the family's stake at $64, *and then* went into the open market and swept up 14 percent of Anderson Clayton at $70—a block that included Gruss's more than 300,000 shares.

Out of Victory . . .

It looked like Ralston had won, having corralled more than 51 percent of Anderson Clayton's shares. But the sisters insisted on a board vote to finalize their sale, and it was scheduled for the next night— opening the door for yet another bid for the family block. Investment bankers told both Ralston and Quaker to make their best bids. Stiritz quickly responded that Ralston was holding firm at $64 a share. Quaker wasn't in that loop, however. It held a marathon, all-night teleconference that ended with its brass signing a merger agreement at dawn for $66 a share, or $812 million—effectively bidding against themselves to raise the deal's price that final $2 a share.

The whole long, drawn-out battle, Gruss reminisces, was "very interesting. It's very exciting when you see the tombstone ad crediting your firm in a public takeover. Suddenly, you can even get a good table in a New York City restaurant." Yet that was Gruss & Co.'s last foray into public activism. "Personally, Anderson Clayton took a lot out of me. I found doing public deals much more time-consuming than trading in private. The publicity was unrelenting and the research kept evolving. I became 100 percent preoccupied. Paid no attention to my family—and I just didn't like where I was going as a person. You have to love being out there and want fiercely to succeed. If you don't, your reputation and future prospects become tarnished. I decided to go back to plain vanilla risk arbitrage. It was profitable *enough*." Acknowledging that work/life balance wasn't the norm on the Street then and isn't now, Gruss adds, "I just enjoyed watching my children grow up; thought it important as a father to be around. As the Duke of Wellington said, 'Do the business of the day in the day.' I'd leave the office by five—and *usually* be able to check my brain until the next day."

Even thirty years later, however, Gruss still reflects proudly on his Anderson Clayton deal. "I'm not sure any merger arbitrageur, *ever before*, had gone all the way to making a tender offer to bring out value." In the end, Quaker did win the pet food unit it coveted. It also was able to sell most of the rest of Anderson Clayton the next year to Kraft. But it realized only $235 million on that deal, considerably short of what it had expected. Was Gaines worth it? Quaker Oats phased out of its disappointing pet food business in the very next decade.

To this day, Gruss says, he still vividly remembers "going to bed thinking that this or that deal was a certainty, only to wake up the next morning and read that it had been called off." The lesson was unmistakable. "There's no such thing as a 'sure thing' and deals can break for a whole host of reasons—which really can't be foreseen. What's more, my experiences also taught me that the insiders very often don't know how it will turn out. Deals get done by human beings, and humans can be fickle. Attitudes can turn on a dime. So much so that maybe a degree in psychology would be good preparation for merger arbitrage."

CHAPTER FOUR

Paul Singer

There's a set of mind that is an absolute requirement. If you're not a person whose starting point is "what am I missing?" rather than "how frickin' great am I?" you are missing something essential to survival. "What am I missing?" is like oxygen. If you're asking, "How great am I?" you're the *Night of the Living Dead*.

TAKE IT AS a given, based on that quote, that you're not going to encounter Paul Singer tooting his own horn—though he is reputed to rock the piano, strictly among friends. To be sure, Singer, the founder, president, and co-CEO at Elliott Management Corporation, the $34 billion hedge fund he founded with $1.3 million of family and friends' money in 1977, doesn't have to boast. His fearsome reputation precedes him.

Widely perceived as tough, aggressive, scary-smart, and fiercely unyielding, Singer, seventy-three, is often described in print as a combative Wall Street investor and activist who has faced down nations, from Argentina and Peru to the Republic of Congo, to be paid his due on Elliott Management's investments on defaulted sovereigns—once even having the Argentine navy's tall ship impounded to press his claims. Nor do either a target's size or its reputation seem to daunt Elliott Management. In the spring of 2017, Elliott went public with demands that Australia's BHP, the world's largest mining company, spin off its U.S. oil assets. The Australians grudgingly complied, announcing they would seek to exit their U.S. shale ventures. Late that summer, Singer thwarted Warren Buffett's Berkshire Hathaway's planned takeover of a long-troubled Texas utility, Oncor Electric Delivery Co., by demanding his bid be sweetened by at least $300 million. Singer's fund had picked up a slug of Oncor's junior debt in bankruptcy and that sizeable increase in the bid would have put it in the money. When the famously value-conscious Berkshire Hathaway chairman refused to budge, San Diego-based Sempra Energy swooped in with a bid of $9.45 billion for 100 percent of Oncor's parent, Energy Future Holdings Corp, which amounted to $450 million more than Buffett's offer. (Energy Future, the erstwhile TXU Corp., was subjected to a spectacularly ill-timed leveraged buyout—at $45 billion, the largest ever—in 2007 and finally emerged from its long-running bankruptcy when the Sempra deal was completed in March 2018.)

Singer's Elliott Management is also credited as the activist fund responsible for driving EMC Corp. into the arms of Dell in 2016, creating the largest tech merger in history. It has likewise played the activist role in a long line of liquidity events in technology companies, including Mentor Graphics, LifeLock, Polycom, Compuware, Informatica, Novell, Riverbed, and Qlik Technologies, among others. In the tech sector, says Singer, Elliott has frequently "found itself knocking on an open door." Managements were relieved, in other words, in one way or another, to find Singer's fund coming up with solutions to issues that may have seemed intractable from the inside. Elliott Management's activism has likewise reshaped industries outside of the tech sector. Its sudden appearance as a large and dissatisfied shareholder in Cabela's, in 2015, for instance, ended up driving the outdoor outfitter's merger with rival Bass Pro Shops a year later.

A Prescient Warning

Shortly before the financial crisis, in early 2007, Singer warned the G-7 finance ministers—to no avail—about the critical vulnerability of major banks. During the Obama administration's bailout of Detroit, it was Singer's last-minute intervention in tense negotiations with the U.S. Treasury's auto task force that permitted crucial General Motors supplier Delphi Automotive to emerge from bankruptcy and allowed GM to reopen plants. More recently, after the Brexit vote hammered the value of the pound, Elliott Management was one of several large shareholders that succeeded in convincing Anheuser-Busch to increase its original cash bid for SABMiller to compensate shareholders for the decline in the British currency.

Then there is South Korea, where Elliott Management has arguably had more impact in the past few years on the nation's government and its powerful chaebol business interests than any other investor within or outside of Korea. Elliott Management's 2015 attempt to prevent Samsung C&T Corp., in which it had taken a large share position, from merging with another Samsung affiliate, Cheil Industries, for $8 billion—a value the activist argued was woefully inadequate—ostensibly failed. The Korean National Pension Service, a key shareholder, acted against its own financial self-interest by rejecting Elliott Management's suits and voting against Elliott's proxy, throwing the ugly battle—shadowed by blatant appeals to xenophobia and anti-Semitism—to Samsung's management. The conglomerate then quickly restructured to cement its control by the founding Lee family while dodging a potentially massive and looming inheritance tax hit. (Lee Kun-hee, officially Samsung's chairman, hasn't been seen in public since a 2014 heart attack reportedly left him severely debilitated.)

Yet, two years later, South Korea has a new president, Moon Jae-in. His predecessor, Park Geun-hye, was impeached in December 2016 and ousted in March 2017. Then, in April 2018, she was sentenced to 28 years in prison on bribery and related charges. Her bestie, Choi Soon-sil, who had already been sentenced to three years in prison on charges of abusing her influence, in February 2018 got a 20-year term for extortion, bribery and other criminal offenses. Perhaps even more astonishing, in late August 2017, a South Korean court found

Samsung Group heir and the conglomerate's de facto leader, Vice Chairman Jay Y. Lee, guilty of bribery, embezzlement, and perjury in the corruption scandal that brought down Park, and sentenced the billionaire corporate scion to a five-year jail term. Then again, Lee's lawyers filed an immediate appeal and Lee was released—to the dismay of anti-corruption activists—after less than a year in jail and his sentence was suspended in February 2018. Among the allegations: Then-President Park, after three meetings with the younger Lee in the summer of 2015, asked for $38 million in "payments" to foundations and businesses run by Choi—outlays which grew out of the same corrupt relationship that involved government support for the Samsung C&T and Cheil merger. This corrupt relationship, according to prosecutors, explained the South Korea National Pension Service's vote of its large block of shares in favor of the merger, though the pension service lost at least $123 million on the deal. They also alleged it bolstered the value of the Lee family's convoluted holdings in Samsung Group by $758 million or more.

Forcing the Activist's Hand

"Samsung C&T didn't start out as an activist position at all," notes Singer. Elliott established its stake based on "what, at the time, was knowledge that the Street also had about the Lee family's situation— about the family's stated and assumed need to restructure," Singer explains. "Also, on lots of conversations with the company in which we got the clear impression that they were thinking about it the same way the Street was thinking about it. But then they came out with a terrible, unfair restructuring proposal."

"When they did that," Singer continues, "we had a big position, and so had a big mark-to-market loss against us and had to decide what to do. That's why we launched into activist mode to oppose the merger and ran into this nationalism ginned up by the company's leadership. The people who were being hurt by Samsung were criticizing *us* for being foreigners. It felt like the shareholders were saying to management, 'I know this is going to harm me economically, but I'm voting for this merger because it's the patriotic thing to do and I'm trusting that you'll find some way to make it up to us.' Yet it was a slam dunk, in terms of rationality, to vote with us—to vote against the deal."

Instead, Singer goes on, "all of a sudden, the company sold—to an ally—a block of treasury shares that Samsung couldn't vote, and the National Pension Service voted Samsung's way, not ours." The merger sailed through with nearly 70 percent of the vote and Elliott then unloaded the majority of its position.

But fast-forwarding a year and a half, Singer pointed out, the former chair of the National Pension Service had already been convicted of corruption and charges lodged against the former South Korean president, her close advisor, and Samsung scion Jay Y. Lee. "We believe the evidence at these trials and in public statements has been overwhelming that there was a corrupt relationship between the Korean government and Samsung, and that advisors from the Blue House had meetings with the National Pension Service [NPS], which controlled the swing vote. We believe the intent was to make sure we, the foreigners, lost." Finally, adds Singer, upper management at the NPS took voting authority out of the normal channels "to cast the deciding vote against us."

Singer, an erudite, silver-haired bantam of a man whose stylish, closely-cropped beard and owlish wire-rimmed glasses lend him a professorial air, reflects, "There are so many ironies in this situation. What we were doing, sure, was trying to protect our position. But protecting our positions sometimes—including in this situation—has the effect also of moving a defective system or corporate culture in a positive direction. South Korea's corporate elites can't do things like this and attract global capital on a sustaining basis. Investors figure this stuff out. These are important data points. We're defending ourselves."

No Losses, No Excuses

Singer is crystal clear on the principle that has guided his career. "I don't want to lose money, ever, with no excuses. My goal with investors is a combination of underpromising and overdelivering whenever I can. And I try not to be benchmarked. We just try to make a moderate return—as high as possible—given that our goal is not to lose money." Elliott's performance over its forty-year history offers abundant evidence that he's rarely failed to sail over that bar. News reports cite his fund's track record of consistent returns (around 13.5 percent annually, on average), including only two down years (1998 and 2008) out of more than forty.

Singer's firm, Elliott Management (Elliott is his middle name), now employs more than four hundred people in five cities: Manhattan, London, Hong Kong, Tokyo, and Menlo Park. But when founded in 1977, it was decidedly a party of one. Raised in Teaneck, New Jersey, one of three children of a Manhattan pharmacist and a homemaker, Singer grew up thinking he'd become "a courtroom lawyer, someone like Perry Mason." Pursuing that goal, he picked up a BS in psychology in 1966 from the University of Rochester, and then a JD in 1969 from Harvard.

Finance didn't even enter his thoughts, Singer says, until after he was admitted to Harvard Law and his proud and excited father told him, "You have to learn how to invest." He was coming of age, of course, in the eye of Wall Street's go-go years. Singer continues, "So he and I started trading stocks together. I was so 'clever' that I was shorting and buying on margin and trading at the same time I was reading about investing. I was the kind of person who went to the library and took out all the books on investing. I read everything written on cycles in the late 1960s. Then I started reading *Barron's*. It became my bible and my rabbi was Alan Abelson. 'A battle of wits between unarmed opponents,' is an Abelson line I use a lot." Yet all of Singer's reading wasn't getting him very far. "Basically, my dad and I found every conceivable way to lose money, on the long side, the short side. It was pathetic. But what that engendered was a deep desire to figure it out."

The Reluctant Attorney

Although Singer practiced law for a few years after earning his degree, first in Newark and then in New York City in the real estate division of Donaldson Luftkin & Jenrette, it was only because he "needed a job," says Singer. "It's probably an exaggeration to say I hated every minute [working as a lawyer] but I don't think it's too much of an exaggeration. I just wasn't into it. It was actually very stressful, working for somebody, all the deadlines—and I don't think I was very good at it." At the same time, Singer relates, not even the end of the 1960s bull market cooled his enthusiasm for markets. "I was really interested in trading. When I think back now to the beginnings of what I do, what I remember is that I started writing an investment letter around then, which I distributed for free to my friends and acquaintances. It was called the *Hamilton Investment Letter*." The noted donor to Republican causes adds, "I've found a couple of copies, and it reflects basically the same arch-conservative, hard-money, pro-gold views I still have."

The core lesson Singer took from his market experiences in the 1960s and 1970s, he says, "was to try as much as possible to control my own destiny. If I had to broad brush it, I'd say there's one thing I'm never going to get out of my head: I don't know enough—and neither does any guru" about the direction of the markets. Singer continues, "By the way, if there's any one person who put me into business, it was Marty Zweig. He was Alan Abelson's pal and always getting quoted in *Barron's* in those days. I was looking for insight and Marty had five or so perfect market calls. Of course, I was reading every issue and soaking everything up. I never spoke to the guy, but I also subscribed to the *Zweig Forecast*, his investment letter."

His Guru Stumbles

Singer continues, "So I started orienting my trading with Marty's calls. There was only one problem. There we were in the fall of '73, and for truly the last time in my life I was bullish on the stock market. I was long, I was leveraged, and, of course, Marty missed the imposition of the Arab oil embargo. But then he also missed the 25 percent-ish crack that happened immediately thereafter." To make matters worse, Singer goes on,

> Marty went bearish close to the bottom, and then the market rallied into January, February, and March. Marty got bullish in January 1974 and then never changed his mind. But starting in April, that market began coming down hard. In that July, August, and September, it was a cascade. There wasn't a single, dramatic crash day, but that summer I believe there were never more than three days when the market wasn't going down. I was so depressed at that point that I called up *Barron's* and offered them my entire collection—every single issue of the magazine for ten years. When they didn't make a decision after several calls, I threw every single issue down the incinerator. I was losing so much money. Two weeks later,

the woman at *Barron's* calls me up and offers me $200 for my collection. It's a true story. It was horrible. The market didn't start to bottom until the first week of October. Actually, it double bottomed. After that, Marty changed his signals and stopped publishing his complete record. But the reason I say he put me in business is because that was it for me. I realized that no one got that one right, and that's what is typical in the market.

By 1976, says Singer, he was still working as a lawyer, but was also "running little family and friend partnerships on the side, having survived—barely—the '74 market collapse." The experience, he adds, had only made him "more determined to figure out how to trade and *not* lose money." Then came two fortuitous events. "Somebody introduced me to convertible hedging—there were reasonable interest rates back then. And the guys running the DLJ subsidiary I worked in got fired, and they shut the place down. I went to my wife—we had two little kids—and said, 'I really want to do this investment, trading stuff.' She asked, 'Can we pay the bills?' We lived in an apartment and owned an old car—there was no lifestyle—so I said, 'Yeah.' I pooled the accounts and formed Elliott in February of 1977."

The Important Stuff Is Personal

Asked to reflect on what has contributed the most to his investment success in the years since, Singer says, "I actually think the technical skills are secondary. The important stuff is creativity and a little intelligence. You have to be good at numbers and have the ability to analyze. The legal background was good—really important. As a lawyer, you're supposed to be able to read complicated documents, analyze complicated situations, learn about new things your client is doing, figure it out, and drill down to the essence. As an investor, you need tenacity, resilience. Everybody makes mistakes—sometimes big—and you have to have resilience to come back, survive, make decisions amid ambiguity."

What's more, insists Singer, "You have to have character. You have to be trustworthy. If you're trading with the Street, you have to be straight. You often hear complaints about Wall Street. 'Oh, Wall Street is terrible; its people are terrible.' But I haven't encountered another business or profession with higher ethics than I've seen in the Street over my forty-year career." Another required attribute, says Singer, is "physical stamina—it's not exactly the same as resilience, but it's close. I mean, you have to keep doing it—and you have to have flexibility and subtlety to be able to work at it through different phases of your life." The key, he continues, "for anyone in the business for a long time, no matter what he or she starts with—and most start with nothing—is to be able to apply the same rigor and effort when you're *not* poor. Then, when you're *really* not poor, you can't let up, *ever*."

Evolution to Distressed

The other critical variable behind his success, Singer explains, has been "risk management. It is something that needs to be central to every investor's and every money manager's consciousness. It's so odd how most people don't bother looking at history and asking, 'Has anyone ever consistently gauged turning points, timed markets?' Sure, people can get it right once, twice. But then they're dead the third time or the fourth time. I mean dead. I mean, buried." Singer then points to the crash of 1987—which his erstwhile guru, Marty Zweig, ironically enough, predicted on Lou Rukeyser's TV show—to prove his point. "The strategy that had worked for us for ten years at that point was convertible bond arbitrage. Long the bond, short the stock—generate a big positive cash flow, a couple of bucks trading profit, and you're done. Not too much leverage—I'm not a big fan of leverage. It did the job, meaning that it produced consistent, modest returns, making money more or less all of the time. Then the crash of '87 comes as a big surprise." But, Singer emphasizes, "I survived the crash by being hedged." And his commitment to his goal, not to lose money, was reinforced once more.

A specialized form of arbitrage, convertible bond hedging was a quiet but lucrative backwater in the investment world when Singer started plying the trade in the mid-1970s. "The ownership of convertibles used to be 20 percent arbs and 80 percent institutions," he recalls. "Then it shifted, and over a period of ten or fifteen years became the opposite. It became dominated by arbs, very competitive and very quantitative. People started using computers, the arbs were monetizing volatility, and pricing became completely ridiculous. Plus, there were two or three convertible hedging crashes in the last twenty years. So the business became very uninteresting to me."

Luckily for Elliott's clients, however, another business had begun to catch Singer's eye—even during the heyday of convertible hedging—in the 1980s. It is called distressed investing—buying the securities, usually bonds, of distressed companies at bargain prices and holding on to profit via repricings, redemptions, or conversions into equity in a restructured entity. "I'm a curious guy, good at math," he explains, "also a tell-me-a-story kind of guy. So I got involved in distressed investing early. There was Western Union's liquidity crisis in '84, I believe. I know that LTV's Chapter 11 [at that time, the largest in history, with $4 billion in liabilities] was in the summer of '86. [LTV Corp. was the second-largest steelmaker in the United States.] Then Public Service New Hampshire's bankruptcy in '88 was another opportunity, and there were others—El Paso Gas & Electric a year or two later." In fact, Singer allows, "I don't want to rank our businesses, but one of our strengths is distressed situations. The only problem is that it comes and goes. So it's parenthetically interesting that there have been some intriguing distressed positions—Caesar's restructuring, the entire energy sector—in recent years, despite the nine-year bull market. It's actually weird to have this juxtaposition of a bull market with a real collapse in the securities of energy companies." Don't think Singer is complaining, however.

He observes, "It's not an accident that when Mike Milken's high-yield business created this pool of preprogrammed distressed stuff—this asset class, the Macy's and the Federated, the Southmark—that it was arbs who mostly were the first to populate the world that Milken had helped create. Sure, there was a Marty Whitman, a curmudgeon who had been a lawyer for distressed clients, who became a distressed value investor [M.J. Whitman & Co. and Third Avenue Managment]. But more typical were the guys at Angelo, Gordon & Co. and me—I mean, we were arbs—and it was an easy migration from arbitrage into distressed."

Delphi Automotive: The Big Workout

One of the most well-known (infamous) distressed deals Singer and Elliott have successfully navigated was the exceedingly fraught reorganization of Delphi Automotive out of bankruptcy at the tail end of the financial crisis. Looking back, says Singer, "The number of forces and factors that converged for a process and result with Delphi Automotive made it particularly interesting." He continues, "If you remember, when President Obama came into office in January '09, the auto industry was on the brink. We got involved with Chrysler, with Chrysler Financial Co., with GMAC and General Motors, with a variety of securities. We had Chrysler Finco bank debt—among others. There were a lot of things happening back then, but the first major thing that happened in the reorganization world was that the government basically worked out a deal for Chrysler that gave its unions a recovery much, much greater than their pari passu recovery."

Singer goes on:

> They stuffed it to the creditors. The president's team actually threatened to call out the creditors *personally* if they didn't sign up for that deal. As in, "You sign up for this deal by 6:00 p.m. tonight or the president is going to name you tomorrow during his press conference." That was the threat made to the holders of Chrysler Finco bank debt. So we, the "combative" Elliott, immediately folded. We folded because the bid/ask spread actually wasn't far away from the president's price. We thought that the administration's behavior was wrong on so many levels—but we also thought that, at the end of the day, the judge might approve it.
>
> I'm telling you that just to set up the environment we were operating in back then. Because the next thing that happened—just a few weeks later, as I recall—was the General Motors bailout. It was also a completely ridiculous, contentious, and unfair process. The unions win, the bond holders lose; creditors' committees screaming, yelling, battling, surrendering. All that is context. I think we managed to make some money. We were left with some bonds but resigned from the creditors' committees because we just weren't in the mood to go through all that nonsense again.

What set Delphi somewhat apart from the rest of the beleaguered auto industry during the meltdown, points out Singer, was that "it had been sinking for years." Quite publicly. In fact, the former GM parts subsidiary had had to disclose "accounting irregularities" in 2004 and filed for Chapter 11 protection from its creditors the very next year, even though automotive industry sales were still chugging along. "There followed two or three attempts to do restructurings," recalls

Singer, "and the latest attempt had been David Tepper's—Appaloosa Management's—agreement to put in a large amount of money." [Appaloosa committed $2.55 billion in equity to a $3.4 billion deal with Cerberus Capital Management to bail out Delphi, in a plan announced in 2006, but not accepted by the U.S. Bankruptcy Court until August 2007—after major revisions.] "Then Tepper backed out in April 2008," Singer goes on, "because there had been a melt of value, obviously, in all of these businesses—but Delphi really had a big head start in the melt."

Appaloosa's exit sent both GM and its former subsidiary scrambling for reorganization financing to keep critical auto plants running. "In late April or May of '09," recalls Singer, "there was such lender exhaustion—hatred, whatever—that there was an opportunity. It was like they needed muscle. They needed a fresh, vigorous force to enter the negotiations. So we looked at it. There were three tranches of the DIP loan—and the third and largest tranche was only going to be repaid about 20 cents on the dollar in the proposed reorganization. The debtor-in-possession loan—busted! It was such a mess. In terms of the company's business, as I recall, Delphi had a bunch of foreign facilities, some of which were highly profitable."

No Compelling Interest

Singer continues, "What was problematic was that the government guys were going to sell the foreign plants to their pals. So, when we decided to step into Delphi, it was with knowledge that almost all of our peers had looked at Delphi and said, 'Cars, government, unions—no way!'" Nonetheless, Singer adds, what Elliott realized was "the government had no compelling interest in that financing arrangement at all. They certainly had a compelling interest in the U.S. plants and in keeping General Motors alive, but there was no necessity for them to sell the foreign stuff to Platinum Equity. I mean, it was unbelievable."

Platinum, a Beverly Hills-based private equity firm, had spent three years trying to structure a $3.6 billion reorganization deal for Delphi, with almost all of the funding coming from GM or the federal government—and only $250 million in cash plus an additional $250 million credit line coming from Platinum investors—who nonetheless would have ended up in control of Delphi's extensive foreign operations. Platinum's "sweetheart" reorganization plan also provided for very little in terms of debt repayment for Delphi's creditors and, when filed with the bankruptcy court, understandably made the parts maker's creditors go ballistic.

The creditors found the reinforcement they were looking for in Elliott Management. Reminisces Singer, "So we march into court—because the government was still making 'my way or the highway' noises—but we knew that they didn't have a compelling interest in Platinum's plan for Delphi. I mean, they did have compelling interests in the General Motors and Chrysler bailouts. Even so, they should have done them in a different way. What they did [to those creditors] was tough and people remember it to this day."

A Happy Ending

At any rate, Singer continues, "We march into bankruptcy court and say that we—the actual creditors of Delphi—would in effect take over the company." The lenders would make a "credit bid"—use the debt they were owed to, as it were, pay for the takeover. "Elliott could do that because by that time we owned a number of different tranches of the deal," Singer adds. "So we convinced the judge to let us, the creditors, make our proposal. He made this amazing remark to the effect of that 'if those guys in suits could buy this, why can't these other guys in suits buy this?'" Under the creditors' plan, GM would still take back four factories and Delphi's steering business, the financier explains, "but part of our proposal was ponying up cash for the U.S. plants to give General Motors and the government sort of a dowry. And the judge let us creditors propose to buy the foreign subs. In all, it was more cash and better terms than Platinum Equity was going to put up—and we also agreed to backstop a rights offering."

Singer's satisfaction is manifest as he adds, "When the smoke had cleared just a couple of months later, we owned a lot of stock and we loved the company that remained." Delphi stock has risen nearly 105-fold since the investment was made, resulting in astronomical compound annual returns since the 2009 investment of more than 75 percent per year, over nearly a full decade. He goes on, "I'm telling that story because we approached the opportunity creatively, and the whole thing was fast. It wasn't one of those five-year bankruptcies, at least in terms of our involvement. We conceptualized it accurately when those around us did not. In terms of the amount of money, the elegance of the approach, the lessons learned, that was a great result."

Mergers with Hair

Although distressed investing is clearly Singer's first love, the cyclicality of distressed opportunities and his own restless curiosity led him to dabble in the booming merger business as early as the 1980s. Singer remarks, "We've been trading mergers, in one way or another, for thirty-five years. I became interested not as a continuous player but in the occasional merger deal and came to feel—especially because of my experience in the LTV workout—that creating value, making something happen, was both a driver of value and a risk mitigator. In other words, a way to try to control my own destiny." Indeed, he points out, "Elliott has never engaged in a pure risk-arb business, like the old Bear Stearns merger-arb desk. We've always been highly selective. I'm not a fan of investing in vanilla, low-risk mergers. In that game, you get nine right and then you give it all back with the tenth. The merger business we tend to do is stuff that's complicated; has hair on it. We want something that we can get involved in, where we can make something happen, where we can make some money at the edges."

Singer now frequently refers to Elliott's activism as "situational investing—things with returns that are either uncorrelated to the market or involve a great deal of complexity." He explains that while Elliott "has found it essential to be always hedged, we've also found it productive to be consistently applying our full set of tools—analytical talent, media strategists, proxy advisors—to the task of creating value through equity activism." Instead of passively waiting for deals to come to him, Singer is always looking to make things go his way—as he did in Oncor Electric. Situational activism, the savvy Elliott Management founder elaborates, requires applying his firm's full range of skills and knowledge: "There are a lot of linkages between merger arb, distressed, activist distressed, activist arbitrage, activist equity. Similar skill sets are required in each of these areas."

As an arcane example, Singer points to deals involving what are known as "domination agreements" in European takeovers, especially in Germany. In essence, a type of squeeze out, these agreements come into play when would-be acquirers need to control a certain number of shares to force a company's hand. In Germany, the magic number of shares is 75 percent of the outstanding. Once there, an acquirer can make a target's management do its bidding and can immediately consolidate income statements. "They are complex situations," allows Singer, "but offer the opportunity to make money pretty consistently. Still, you've got to keep at it. You've got to be willing to stand your ground: in effect, talking to the target company and trying to make something happen." Elliott has accomplished that in numerous instances. In one, Elliott acquired a 15 percent stake in German machine tool company DMG Mori Aktiengesellschaft, which it then soon sold, quite profitably, to an acquirer, Japan's DMG Mori Co. Ltd., which needed the shares to solidify its control of what had been its German joint venture. "We get involved in deals that have different characteristics, where we can trade effort for risk or complexity for risk—and that's why our pattern of returns is so different than others'," notes Singer.

"Global investing that has an active component is very, very tricky," emphasizes Singer. "But look, it's part of our expertise. We're supposed to be able to invest in complicated places, figure things out; figure out the accounting, the legal issues, the enforceability, the culture. Obviously, mostly we do. But when you get it wrong, as we did in the Samsung C&T fight, it can be costly." There's a coda, however, to Elliott's wrenching 2015 loss to the Lee dynasty in the battle over Samsung's restructuring. "We learned a lot about the Samsung Group," says Singer, with studied understatement. "There's no such thing as moral victory in this business. We're trying to make money, *always*. But that did ultimately prove to be a credibility-enhancing loss."

Singer explains, "We took a new position in Samsung Electronics in October 2016—and this time, it was ultra-polite. We made some proposals that basically were just stating—nicely—from the outside, things we thought they should or could easily decide to do." While Samsung still refused to restructure along the lines Elliott suggested, and the South Korean conglomerate's own legal difficulties affected that and other governance issues, it did pay its first-ever quarterly dividend—and said it would cancel billions of dollars' worth of treasury shares to bolster its balance sheet. Since then, boasts Singer, "Samsung Electronics' stock has gone crazy on the upside—despite Jay Y. Lee being arrested, tried, and convicted. There's no way anyone could get bored with this business."

Nor is the billionaire investor going to be hemmed in by borders of another sort. With the recent opening of Elliott's newest office in Menlo Park, Singer is moving to formalize the firm's private equity activities—essentially so that he can seize profit opportunities when and how he sees them. "You run an activist campaign and maybe the company gets put up for sale. A couple of times, despite the fact that we teed up everything for the private equity world, we got shut out when we wanted to participate in the buyout. What are we, chopped liver? Well, we *were* chopped liver—but we're not going to be anymore," Singer avers.

CHAPTER FIVE

Michael Price

"If someone is paying $400 million for a cement plant, you can back out from that number, how many dollars they're paying for a ton of cement capacity. Then, if there are comparable cement plants, you can plug that number into your valuations of what those other cement plants are worth." In that way, notes Price, even risk-arbitrage deals that he does not invest in directly still provide significant value in the form of a chance "to fine-tune, to sharpen our pencils on corporate valuations."

BILLIONAIRE INVESTOR MICHAEL Price has a famously keen eye for value, whether in underappreciated stocks, activist situations or in "vulture" assets undergoing reorganization. That faculty, employed in increasing size and with characteristically relentless and unflinching drive during deal-happy stretches of the 1980s and 1990s, propelled Price's once under-the-radar Heine Securities Corp. and its Mutual Shares series of funds to more than $17 billion in assets under management by the time he sold the fund management company to Franklin Resources in 1996. That transaction, in which Price personally pocketed some $670 million for the funds company—only eight years after acquiring it for little more than $4 million (under the terms of the estate of his mentor and partner, legendary value investor Max Heine)—only burnished his reputation as a canny surfacer of value.

Not that his reputation needed spiffing up. Just the prior year, Price's blunt and no-nonsense activism had, in a brief six months' time, driven patrician Chase Manhattan into the arms of Chemical Bank (which quickly adopted the far tonier Chase moniker). The merger created the then-largest bank in the United States—and millions in profits for Mutual Shares' investors. What's considerably less well appreciated is the central role that risk arbitrage—what Price calls the "invisible hand" of Wall Street—has played in the money manager's storied career. Indeed, the discipline continues to crucially figure in Price's asset allocation decisions, portfolio construction, and, especially, valuation process.

Chat with Price in his unassuming research-stacked office at MFP Investors, his family's Manhattan-based limited partnership, and risk arb soon becomes a recurring meme—it is a critical link, as Price views it, in the proper functioning of the markets and economy. There is an overarching and virtuous financial cycle in which, as Price puts it, "a cheap stock becomes an M&A deal, becomes a bankruptcy, becomes a cheap stock, becomes M&A, becomes a bankruptcy"—risk arbitrage is the essential grease that keeps it all turning—and as value investors, "we want to participate in that whole cycle."

Not by riding the shares of over-leveraged companies into bankruptcy, Price quickly clarifies, but by staying on the profitable side of the capital cycle. The valuation savvy and discipline accumulated through his career-long fascination with risk arbitrage is invaluable in figuring out where to be, when, and at what price. "Suppose oil and gas stocks are cheap, so we buy them. Then, the commodity's price rises. The shares rise and the companies start to borrow to drill and do mergers and to explore. That virtuous circle goes on for three or four years until too much supply and competition enter the market, pressuring the whole group—and the companies start doing spinoffs, asset sales, and bankruptcies to try to stay ahead of their creditors."

Ideally, says Price, he will have ridden the entire cycle, selling the formerly cheap stocks as they inflated; getting out of the way as the run-up turned to excess and as equity multiples soared into the stratosphere. He then stands aside in short-term liquidity—which includes risk-arb deals as well as cash—watching. Waiting. Eventually, opportunity reappears, perhaps as bonds that the troubled companies issued to finance their late-cycle flings tank and become Price's next tickets to value creation. Picked up for 30 to 50 cents on the dollar, and sometimes held through what, he concedes, can be a long and torturous bankruptcy process, what Price banks on is the bonds eventually becoming not only money good but getting laced with equity sweeteners. And that then those options will again be transformed via the endless cycle of capitalism into cheap stocks pregnant with anticipated run-ups.

"It's like the *Lion King*'s 'Circle of Life,'" Price offers, with just the slightest suggestion of a twinkle softening the piercing intensity of his dark eyes. It's an apt analogy, coming from a man who set his sights on a career as an investor at a tender age. "I knew the names of every bone in the body when I was in fifth grade. My cousins were doctors and I was going to be a doctor," Price reminisces. "Then I bought a stock and it tripled—and that was that."

To Wall Street, Via Oklahoma

Luck? Perhaps. It was surely lucky for the budding investor that one of his father's golf buddies was a fellow named Stanley Schiff who ran the Drexel Burnham arbitrage department. For Price wasn't headed to Wharton, his father's alma mater, or any of the other Ivies from which Wall Street typically recruits. "I didn't have the grades to get into Wharton," Price matter-of-factly recalls. He'd paid more attention to playing lacrosse and football for his suburban Long Island high school than to his grades. "But I grew up a Sooner football fan," so it wasn't much of a stretch that he ended up in Norman, Oklahoma, studying business at the University of Oklahoma. "Not exactly the center of value investing or risk arb," Price dryly remarks, although the class of 1973 alum has done his part to change that. In 1997 Price donated $18 million—at the time the largest single donation ever to a public university—to the Sooner business school, which was renamed the Michael F. Price College of Business.

But that's getting ahead of the story. One day, barely out of high school, Price wrangled an invitation to visit Stanley Schiff's office at Drexel. There was nothing showy about it but Price was quickly mesmerized. Schiff and his small team "were classic risk arbs—long the target, short the buyer—only investing in announced deals with signed contracts." But, oh, the outsized returns they generated on only very short-term exposures to stocks. His father's Seventh Avenue business paled in comparison.

Price began to spend as much time as he could hanging around Drexel's risk-arb unit trying to learn everything he could about the Street's still-secretive arb business. By 1971, Price, still an undergrad, had gotten his hands on Guy Wyser-Pratte's pioneering 1969 New York University MBA thesis, *Risk Arbitrage*, and found himself perfectly prepared for a stock-picking competition one of his professors was running back in Oklahoma. "It wasn't real money, just a paper portfolio," Price explains, "but having spent more time in Drexel's risk-arb department that prior summer, I was aware of certain situations. So I put 100 percent of my paper portfolio in a company that I knew there was a high likelihood of getting taken over by Greyhound. Sure enough, that semester it got taken over. My whole portfolio doubled because I'd literally bet everything on that one stock." None of his classmates, as Price remembers it, made any paper profits in the exercise.

Obsessed with Arbitrage

"From then on, I started reading every article I could find about mergers," Price adds. Realizing that what operators of other businesses were willing to pay for a target was perhaps the best indicator of value he could find, Price "studied every announced deal." And within a year of picking up his diploma in 1973—through another stroke of good fortune—Price found himself in another small Wall Street office interviewing with Max Heine. Already an icon by the early 1970s to New York's then-tiny circle of value investors, Heine had founded

Mutual Shares Corp. in 1949 and, recalls Price, "My father's stock broker, who was Max's partner, told me, 'You are interested in mergers, so go meet Max.'"

What then transpired is perhaps the greatest Wall Street job interview story ever: "Max walks into the room and says, 'So what do you like?'" Price reminisces. "Well, I'd just spent days reading about and analyzing the Manufacturers Hanover takeover of a company called Ritter Financial. It had just been announced and the stocks were trading at a certain spread. I knew every fact about the deal. I knew the timing, about the buyer and the seller. Everything. I told Max the story. He gets up and buys 20,000 shares—during my first job interview! That was it. Off to the races. . . . I learned the value business from Max and bankruptcy investing from his partner, Hans Jacobson." The lucrative but little-known practice of investing in the busted—but richly asset-backed—bonds of bankrupt railroads was Jacobson's specialty. Price proved a quick study. Hired as a $200-a-week research assistant in 1974, by 1982 he was Max Heine's full partner in managing Mutual Shares' swelling portfolios.

Bumps in the Road

This is not to say that Price's career has been all smooth sailing. Like all investors of his generation, Price early on was bloodied in an encounter with a ferocious bear market. Heine Fishbein, the brokerage firm associated with Mutual Shares, essentially went broke in the depths of the late 1970s bear market. Price's job was spared only because he followed Heine and the money management business into another small broker dealer, which became Herzog Heine. It was a quick and harsh introduction into the downside of Wall Street's "eat what you kill" culture. But the painful reorganization also indirectly led to Price's chance first encounter with another now-famed value investor and risk-arbitrage practitioner, Mario Gabelli.

The two don't remember the story in precisely the same way, Price chuckles. But here is Price's version: As Heine Fishbein's trading business foundered, Heine and Price were forced to vacate Heine Fishbein's space in One State Street Plaza, a stark and imposing 1960s glass and steel tower on the edge of the harbor. Heine had to move the fund's operations, including his young research assistant, Price, into the new firm's considerably more modest digs at 170 Broadway, a well-worn Wall Street fixture of a building.

"We were even selling our desks. So who comes in one afternoon looking to buy a desk on the cheap? Mario Gabelli. Mario had just left Loeb Rhoades to start Gabelli & Co. and what better place for a value investor to buy a desk than from a failing brokerage firm?" Gabelli's bargain-hunting clearly left an impression. But something else Price remembers has really stuck with him. "While he's looking at desks, what does Mario do? He takes a research report that I had just written for Max right off my desk! I remember this like yesterday. Mario insists he didn't steal anything; he just 'borrowed it.' But that report laid out this complex of mining companies listed on the New York Stock Exchange and on the Amex that were all controlled—through a maze of interlocking corporate structures—by a fellow named Lewis Harder who was the chairman and president of International Mining Corp.

"They controlled Molycorp, Fresnillo Mining, Rosario Resources, Kawecki Berylco, and some others. I had laid out all of the relationships and all of the numbers in that report for Max, and we were starting to buy every one of those mostly obscure stocks because they were all cheap. Anyway, that is how I met Mario. Just a few years ago, he actually found that old report in his files and sent it back to me!"

Ask Price about the best arb trade he ever made and he's likely to reach even further back for the research that actually led him to International Mining. The tale shows Price doggedly pulling at obscure threads of information until they fell into a pattern revealing unimagined value. It revolves around an old-line Chicago company named Fansteel that made specialty components for the aerospace industry and other users of exotic metals. While its telling has Price using research tools that seem almost unimaginably quaint today— the New York City Yellow Pages and *Webster's Dictionary*—its impetus and lessons for investors are timeless.

Watch the Smart Guys

He came across the opportunity, says Price, because he'd made it a habit to keep an eye on what top investors and business leaders were doing. "Watch what the smart guys do" is one of his mantras. "Today, that might be a Jeff Immelt or Seth Klarman; Warren Buffett or Charlie Munger," Price offers. But back then, "One of the *machers* was an old-school industrialist named Thomas Mellon Evans; his company was Crane Co., a maker of plumbing supplies. So I'm sitting at my desk one day and across the news ticker comes a story that Thomas Mellon Evans has bought 8 percent of Fansteel, a maker of refractory metals."

Price was still just a kid, twenty-four or so, but that tidbit sparked his curiosity. "Why would this smart guy, a bona fide industrialist, buy shares in a little company making refractory metals? And what the heck are refractory metals?" Price was especially intrigued because some base metals, which had been depressed for as long as he could remember, had just recently started showing signs of life. "So I literally picked up the dictionary—the internet didn't exist—to look up the definition of 'refractory metals.'" He learned that they have certain useful properties: "the ability to withstand high temperatures, high tensile strength, that sort of thing and that there were five or six different kinds." Then he looked at Fansteel's financial statement "and saw its balance sheet was okay and that it produced four of the refractory metals. If I remember right: niobium, tantalum, tungsten, and molybdenum."

Price continues, "I had never heard of them outside of the context of the old periodic table of elements, so I tried to figure out what they were used for. I don't know why, but I grabbed the New York City Yellow Pages, looked up tantalum, and found a company called the Tantalum Corp. of America. I'm not making this up. I picked up the phone, called the number, and some guy answers. I introduce myself, say that I work at a little mutual fund, and that I'm working on tantalum because Thomas Mellon Evans just bought 8 percent of Fansteel."

Price pauses at that point for effect, then adds, "I hear silence at the other end of the line. Then the guy utters, his voice rising, 'He did?'" Price immediately assured the Tantalum Corp. man that his information was good and in the same breath asked, "Why would he?" The answer came back: "Well, obviously, because Fansteel has all these warehouses in Baltimore full of tantalum and its price just jumped from $20 a pound to $200 a pound." With that, Price hung up the phone and started buying Fansteel "that instant, at $9 a share; it was subsequently taken over at $25. 'Hello,' as my sister would say. 'Let your fingers do the walking.' Here I had a smart guy buying a company that has warehouses full of what was called Thai slag, which has tantalum in it."

These days, says Price, his family office, MFP Investors, "just tries to be smart investors—principals." Price likens it to "barbless fly fishing, because if you take your fly and clip off the barbs, it's much harder to catch a trout or bonefish—meaning, we're investing without the cushion of big management and performance fees." Nonetheless, his portfolio looks much like it did "twenty, thirty, even forty years ago: A hodgepodge of value names, some special situations—including risk arbitrage. A smattering of cash. And now we are starting to get a few liquidations—bankruptcies in the oil and gas and metals and mining spaces."

The hodgepodge is deliberate, Price explains, with around 30 percent of the portfolio usually allocated to positions in risk arb and liquidations, which act as diversifiers and hedges against untoward movements in the more market-sensitive value equities that dominate his portfolio. Although the downside in value stocks during market selloffs tends to be buffered because "they are trading so far below intrinsic value that they can't get too hurt," Price observes, they are nonetheless prone to following Mr. Market's lead in both his manic and depressive episodes.

To moderate that market sensitivity, Price has long invested in risk-arbitrage stocks that tend to move with the idiosyncratic progress of individual merger and arb deals, rather than with the market. When interest rates were more normal than they've been in the post financial crisis era of zero interest rates, he wistfully recalls, spreads on arb deals tended to be above the cost of funds and, as the time to merger shrank, the spread would come in, leaving the arbs on the receiving end of fat profits. For people who "did it the old-fashioned way," arbitraging only announced deals and, carefully using only moderate amounts of leverage, risk arb provided very good rates of return, he recalls. "And we would always also sit with cash and positions in liquidations and bankruptcies, so a third of the portfolio is effectively insulated from market gyrations."

As much as Price prizes the insulating qualities—hedging properties—of his risk-arb and liquidation positions, their primary attraction for him, it is clear as he talks deals, is that the analytical processes and techniques he hones in them give him a valuation edge. "They make us smarter on what corporate values are," as he puts it. "When a merger is announced, its terms will go to a multiple of earnings, a multiple of book, a multiple of cash flow." That tells you, in other words, "what business people are buying and for what price.

If someone is paying $400 million for a cement plant, you can back out from that number, how many dollars they're paying for a ton of cement capacity. Then, if there are comparable cement plants, you can plug that number into your valuations of what those other cement plants are worth. In that way, notes Price, even risk-arbitrage deals that he does not invest in directly still provide significant value in the form of a chance "to fine tune, to sharpen our pencils on corporate valuations."

Risk-Arb Lessons

Reflecting on lessons learned doing risk arb, Price says, "You have to be quantitative. You have to develop a really good Rolodex or contact list of people who can help you understand different industries—the antitrust aspects of proposed deals, the financial aspects. You have to be able to talk to bond desks and bank lenders as well as to antitrust lawyers."

Hard-won experience is also crucial to success in risk arb, argues Price, however daunting that may be to neophytes. "Only with experience do you learn how to figure out which deals should go through, which deals make sense, how to psych out why a deal is happening or what's driving the personalities. That's why you don't start in the risk-arb business, you start working for someone in the business."

Four or five young analysts work for Price at MFP at any given time, analyzing deals. "I give them a little rope, like Max gave me. But in the risk-arb business some deals are much higher risk than others. And you have got to understand where the risk comes from. Today it could be financing; there's effectively no second-lien market. It could be antitrust; under Obama there was really high antitrust risk. Look at Staples and Office Depot. They'd been working on that deal for a year when the government said, 'No, you can't do it.'"

Price continues, "Or look at the proposed merger of Halliburton and Baker Hughes. They had agreed to sell $7 billion of assets but still couldn't get feedback from the regulators—and ultimately couldn't overcome objections from the Justice Department and governments abroad—despite more than a year of trying."

Price and his analysts at MFP spent a month after the Halliburton-Baker Hughes deal was announced, he says, "just figuring out who would buy what and whether they could get it done—how those buyers could finance the asset sales that were clearly needed to win approvals." Yet when the government didn't give the companies or the markets any feedback on their plan to sell assets, the arbs couldn't have much confidence in their analysis. "So you then tend to take only a very small position until you get more confidence. You don't take a big position at the beginning. Position sizing in arbitrage really matters because that's what determines your success. You've got to be right, but if you have tiny positions in the deals that happen and a big position in one that doesn't, you're done. You're toast."

Psyching Out the Players

Always cognizant of the myriad risks in risk arb, Price approaches the business as a challenging, multi-dimensional puzzle. "You think about why a businessman is doing something and, in the best cases, antici-pate what they might be doing. Where is the CEO going with this company? What's his motivation?" He continues, "My first and most important thought process when a new deal emerges is why is there a deal? Why does this deal make sense? Mergers are not just company A buying company B. It's people, it's integration, it's business strat-egy, and strategic plans and synergies. In other words, it's 'Why is this deal happening and does that make sense?' You have to know the cast of characters. We don't talk to them. I don't like to make those calls. Don't like to ask people questions like that. But I think about it."

Price says he tells his young analysts: "Put on your thinking caps as if you're in the board room. Think about what they're talking about for this business. They make widgets and there are currency problems and there is a raw materials bottleneck. How is that board going to react to those circumstances in the next three years if you're a direc-tor? Or, if you're the CEO, what are you going to say to your board? If you're an independent director, how are you going to press the CEO?" It's not until he can put himself in their places and think about what they are thinking, Price insists, that a merger-arb analyst can envision what a company caught up in M&A might do.

"Sometimes, they give you clues in quarterly earnings calls, in the president's letters in their annuals, or in other presentations they make, and sometimes they don't give you any clues. But you can psych out what these people should be thinking about. Besides that, you have to know if they're likely to use stock or cash in mergers. If they use their stock, they're telling you they think their shares are fully priced. If they won't use their shares, they're saying they like their stock." Price's next question then goes to figuring out how much confidence he is going to place in what a management is saying. "Do they own a lot of stock?" Price is emphatic on this score, in fact: "That's crucial. The proxy statement is just as important in the analytical process as the 10-Q and the 10-K. How do they pay themselves?"

Nothing Frivolous

That is not to say, however, that Price treats risk arb like anything as frivolous as a game. "The risk-arb business is an essential part of Wall Street. It has to exist. I think it's gotten a better image lately, certainly versus the Boesky days, which were horrible. People understand today, when there are huge mergers, that arbitrageurs provide liquidity for people who don't want to wait for those mergers to close or don't want to take the risk that they don't close. So the mechanism of Wall Street is fine. And the spreads reflect current interest rates and the risks of a deal, as they always have, so that hasn't changed. The risk-arbitrage business just plays a very important role in providing liquidity to the markets. The classic risk-arb business was levered at the broker-dealer level where they could borrow the shares in a stock-swap merger very cheaply or they could use the firm's capital and lever their positions, getting pretty good returns with the leverage."

Price adds, "Then we went through a period when it became very popular for hedge funds to get into the risk-arb business and that flood of money, for a while, tended to narrow spreads as the new arbs competed to establish positions. Happily, that sort of thing tends to be self-limiting, as the drying up of profitability pushes out less skilled or less lucky arbs. Risk arb can be a tough business for hedge funds because they aren't layering into it the negative cost of doing business that a brokerage firm enjoyed with its own capital. Instead, they're sticking clients with fees of 2 percent and 20 percent. It's a whole different equation."

To make risk-arb returns work with a 2 and 20 fee load, Price continues, "you've got to run more risk and/or more leverage. That's just not the same economics or the same risk/reward as in the classic arb business where a member firm used its own capital to lever up the positions judiciously and had no stock loan costs, no margins costs. Of course, then you had Boesky, who I think charged 3 and 50 in his last year or two in the business before being indicted. He could get away with that because he was cheating and seemed to be creating excess returns—like someone else we know about today, who 'Madoff' with above-market fees because he was cheating."

And regardless of who is doing it, warns Price, risk arbitrage is not immune to market-wide landslides, like the crashes of 1987, 2000–2002, and 2008. "No matter how much I spoke earlier about arb stocks tending not to move with the market—moving instead with the idiosyncratic progress of deal—in fact, arb stocks get pounded in extreme market situations. And that's true whether it's your basic cyclical crash, as '87 proved to be, or crashes that are actual harbingers of recessions and economic crises, like more recent examples. Indeed, when you have a big market disruption, arb stocks often get killed even worse than the averages. That's because the arbs are often long in both fewer positions and larger positions than other investors, so when they've got to lighten up because they're overleveraged or have redemptions, their concentrated selling tends to wreak havoc."

Yet the crisis Price remembers as especially painful for fellow arbitrageurs wasn't any of those, but the Black Friday mini-crash on October 13, 1989:

> Nick Brady was the secretary of the Treasury in the first year of Bush forty-one's presidency, and Coniston Partners, who were dear friends of mine, were running a big proxy fight against United Airlines's parent, UAL Corp. We had been going through the LBO craze, in which Drexel Burnham Lambert and other firms did lots of financings using junk bonds to allow highly leveraged deals to get done. All of which lead to United Airlines. Coniston was pushing United Airlines' parent to do some sort of a deal. The pilots wanted to buy the airline in an LBO and speculation had driven the stock quite high. Then, basically the Treasury Department, under Nick Brady, came out on Friday the thirteenth and said, 'No more LBOs.' The whole group of arb stocks—those with announced deals—took gas. More significantly, all the speculative arb deals that were only anticipated, not announced, crashed. Time Warner—actually still

Time Inc. back then—was one of them. The whole market was just ugly. Nasty.

Opportunities Amid Pain

But Price notes there are other times when arb deals crack and actually create opportunities for alert investors "if you can stand in there and buy when the speculative or over-leveraged arb positions get blown out. For instance, we wound up buying a stock amid the market's sharp downside correction in January 2016. There was an announced deal, with a $10 acquisition price, and the buyer was a well-financed private equity firm. In fact, we thought there was 100 percent financing in place, including equity participation from some of the owners of the publicly-listed company that was being rolled into a private-equity deal. Yet that listed stock quickly slid from like $9.60 to $9. The deal was to close in only two months. So that was a 10 percent arb spread to be earned over two months or a 60 percent annualized return. We thought about it and talked about it and then tripled our position. That's why we come in every day."

According to Price, the key is "having the judgment to act. Any young MBA can do the math. But you need judgment, experience to know when to get involved. Even then, no one is right all the time, so part of risk arb—and all investing—is managing losses, and that goes first to position sizing. You don't want to be caught holding a big position when a deal falls apart. You've got to have small positions. But something else Max taught me was that sometimes, when deals break, you buy more." When? "When selling by the arbs causes a stock to sell below its basic trading value until their positions are sold out— because then it should bounce back up. At Mutual Shares, where we always kept a cash reserve, we sometimes would opportunistically take advantage of that."

Acting opportunistically is another key for Price:

We could take advantage of worries—there were times when there were announced deals, after a contract was signed but before the shareholder vote or before whatever final approval was needed came through, and there would be a scare for one reason or another about the deal. The scare could be an antitrust issue, the scare could be a disappointing earnings quarter, it could maybe be that an asset sale had to happen and it was not happening—lots of things. I remember a number of times being able to buy positions from really smart sellers because we had good sources and a good understanding of the people in deals. We knew the deals would happen or that they would change the terms to make sure the deals happened.

I remember standing at the desk at Mutual Shares and buying a lot of stock from Goldman and Salomon when they were selling out of a particular position. Max looked at me and said, "Are you sure you ought to be doing that?" And I said, "I'm sure." Because I just knew that this board and this CEO were going to figure a way to get the deal done. Maybe on slightly different terms, but that deal would close. Goldman and Salomon just didn't know the players the way I knew them. It wasn't that I talked to them. There weren't conversations. It was that I had an understanding of the psyche of the key person. I knew that he wanted to get this company sold because the buyer was ideal, because they could shelter the earnings with a tax loss, and because it was a fantastic opportunity. Now, you still need to have reasonable risk parameters, but that deal was going to close in a few days. So you had reasonable risk parameters. And you bought 60,000 shares, not 600,000. But I remember that distinctly. When it's right, you have to act—like we did on that $10 deal.

When merger proxies are filed with the SEC, Price notes, "there's actually a paragraph called 'Reasons for the Merger.'" But that comes out only several months after the announcement. "You've got to anticipate what the reasons are. You have to—on the day it's announced—say, 'Oh, this makes sense' or 'This doesn't.' A deal should be a big opportunity for the buyer or a big opportunity for the seller. Or, maybe it's caused by sketchy factors. You've got to be aware of funny money, of funny paper. Not just of debt but of someone's stock being overvalued."

As an example, Price points to Bill Ackman's Platform Specialty Products Corp. "He put it together and then used its stock to do roll-ups with a lot of leverage. The stock went from $10 to $28 to $5. You have to be careful. Valeant is another great example. I'm always leery of tax-driven deals as opposed to deals driven by real business reasons." When it comes down to analyzing prospective deals, says Price, "I like to take the taxes out of the equation: I don't like to pay for tax-loss carryforwards and I don't like to use tax arbitrage as a reason for merger.

That is just trying to pump earnings and I'm leery of that. Another red flag is a lot of debt financing. Another is sketchy earnings. You look through the products, you look through the people."

Always, the goal is the same. Picking up dollars for pennies. It's the investment environment that changes, making it a challenge to find those pregnant pennies. Price notes, "Zero interest rates forced big changes in the business, people added leverage, and there were a lot of deals. Then we went through a period for several years when buyers' stocks would take off and guys could play both sides of a deal. Maybe they would get short the buyer or maybe they'd get long the buyer and the target and everything would lift while the deal closed. Now that's stopped. The stocks of buyers have stopped going up on the prospects for synergies or expanding P/Es. The market's changed."

The endless cycling and recycling of investments in Wall Street is just fine, from Price's practiced perspective. "Wall Street serves an essential purpose in financing innovation and growth, developing new resources; also by financing mergers and trading the securities involved in business combinations and restructurings. It's not a bad thing. It is what permits the economy to evolve so that capital flows to growing areas and needy areas. If an Elon Musk wants to build electric cars, solar plants, and rockets to wherever—Mars—we're going to finance him. Now, maybe Elon Musk is blowing up, maybe he's going to blow up in the future. But money is available to the Elon Musks of the world because investors know there will be other investors for that paper. And if a particular deal doesn't work out, they know other investors will be there to buy the paper when it's in default—and that they'll swap it into control of that busted solar plant or whatever, for 10 cents on the dollar after the bankruptcy," Price says.

"So you know, it's fine. You've just got to make sure you're in the right part of the cycle and in the right securities."

Odds are, Mike Price will be fine. Tesla, anyone?

CHAPTER SIX

Peter Schoenfeld

Every once in a while—at least once a year—something really irks us, where the gap between what we think can be created and what is being created is so great that it's worth the effort. We see that gap as potential profit if there is a clear road map to get to where we want to be. So, unlike some other risk-arbitrage houses, we add an activist element when our moral compass and our financial compass are both pointing in the same direction.

TALL, DARK-HAIRED, and ramrod straight, with only the slightest sprinkle of gray at the temples hinting at his seniority, Peter Schoenfeld is a commanding presence, whether he's stepping into a conference room or onto a half-court, where the "deal junkie" still regularly plays competitive basketball to let off the steam generated in the event-driven investment arena. But the erudite and soft-spoken Schoenfeld, the founder, CEO, Chairman, CIO, and portfolio manager of hedge fund P. Schoenfeld Asset Management (PSAM) eschews the bluster and headlines often courted by activist investors. Indeed, he'd rather downplay the whole activist vibe. "I'd say 80 to 90 percent of what we do in merger arb is plain vanilla research—doing deep dives to understand what's driving the deal, what the performers look like; trying to build a merger model; trying to understand shareholders' wishes; antitrust and other regulatory issues; and all the other key considerations."

It's not, concedes Schoenfeld, that the $3 billion-plus PSAM can't be "pretty tough when we have to be. But we prefer to be quiet about it." Though he also admits, "To us, activism is the more exciting part of the business." He's simply found it often more effective to speak softly than to brandish a big stick. Merger-arb event-driven investing, the frequently professorial Schoenfeld explains, can be run "in a very dull fashion, which is perfectly fine for many investors. Even when they see inappropriate behavior, many portfolio managers just say, 'Let's ignore it. We know management's not doing what they ought to be doing but why should we take on that risk?' They may even be right in the long run. And at least 50 percent of the time they're right in the short run." Thus, Schoenfeld says that PSAM, too, "often will just avoid a deal because it's very time-consuming to go down the activist road."

But, Schoenfeld goes on, slipping into his steely-eyed executive persona, "every once in a while—at least once a year—something really irks us, where the gap between what we think can be created and what's being created is so great that it's worth the effort. We see that gap as a potential profit if there's a clear road map to get to where we want to be. So, unlike some other risk-arbitrage houses, we add an activist element when our moral compass and our financial compass are both pointing in the same direction. Very often in these situations we prefer to get a seat at the table—as we do in credit restructurings—to get our views heard. Having had a certain amount of success at times in the past when we have surfaced as activists, we tend to get that seat at the table."

Reputational Cred

In a sense, Schoenfeld acknowledges, it's all about perceptions. "If, in the past, you've shown yourself to be willing to go beyond writing a letter, then they're going to be advised to pay more attention to you. They don't doubt that we could gain support if we wanted to take our objections to the deal public. There are certainly funds that are bigger than us that have a lot more influence. But I'd say within our small world, we're one of the few that tend to stand up aggressively." Schoenfeld quickly qualifies, "It takes a lot for us to get to that point and we have to feel highly confident that we're going to succeed before we do it. But as I look back, there have been quite a few situations where we've mixed it up with companies in M&A deals quite successfully. In fact, I can't think of a case where we've surfaced hard and lost. Not that we haven't lost money. We've lost plenty in deals. But where we've been proactive and out there aggressively our batting average is perfect as far as I can recall."

A native New Yorker, Schoenfeld grew up in Washington Heights, at the far northwest tip of Manhattan, and in 1966 earned his BA in economics at New York University in the Bronx. Then he headed down to lower Manhattan and in 1968 earned his MBA at NYU's Stern School of Business. He stayed there, pursuing post-graduate studies in economic concentration, from 1969 to 1973 until he discovered risk arb. "I was doing research and went to a couple of arb desks to get data on current deals before it was available elsewhere and realized, 'these guys aren't exactly rocket scientists and they're making a lot of money. What am I doing working on my PhD?'"

Schoenfeld quickly backtracks. "Actually, they were very smart and very clever. I was talking to Salomon Brothers, L.F. Rothschild, Goldman Sachs, Bear Stearns, all the traditional trading houses. They were a likeable bunch of guys, very high-intensity and extremely knowledgeable." Schoenfeld soon talked himself into a job on the arbitrage desk at White Weld and then moved, in 1978, to Schroder Wertheim & Co. There, he started out managing proprietary trading and expanded into overseeing arbitrage and convertible securities, then created an asset management vehicle for outside capital. From 1986 to 1989, Schoenfeld served as a managing director at Schroder and as its vice chairman from 1989 to 1996 when he left to start PSAM.

Founded to focus on global investing in event-driven transactions, PSAM uses fundamental research to analyze corporate events that may alter the control, capital, or strategy of an organization in the belief that such events frequently create mispricing of securities relative to their inherent or ultimate realizable value. "There's a tendency," says Schoenfeld, "to look at risk arbitrage as a pretty perfunctory business but, depending on how you approach it, it can take on a lot of different dimensions. We do speak out a little bit more than others, I guess."

What's the Value?

Schoenfeld continues, "If there is a common theme running through everything we do—whether it's a credit situation, or M&A, or even special situations—it's trying to determine value gaps and what type of catalyst is going to compress it. So, for instance, if a company is trying to spin out assets, you have to ask yourself, 'Why?' They have probably been approached by a suitor recently. Under U.S. tax laws—which are totally outdated in this respect—you can't sell a subsidiary without taking a tax hit at the corporate level. Everywhere else in the world, you can sell with minimal tax friction. Here, you need to go through this intermediate step of spinning it off and letting it mature in the market a bit before it can get acquired without triggering taxes. The complexity of our strategy is intellectually challenging on a day-to-day basis. But it's fun to be around people who are forced to think in a similar fashion. You can share ideas and every once in a while you get to do something proactive that can help change the landscape on a particular deal."

Schoenfeld's global focus at PSAM provides broad diversification and opportunity sets that "serve our investors well. The merger portion of what we do is cyclical and can be limited but also varies around the globe. During a slowdown in the United States, perhaps you find opportunities in Europe or Australia, the Pacific Rim, or even Asia." Schoenfeld adds, "If you're immersed in game theory as well as in financial theories, then investing globally is fun because the takeover codes are different. Antitrust laws are becoming more uniform in the way they're interpreted, and becoming more Anglo-Saxon-like around the globe, which also is encouraging in certain respects. Of course, political crosswinds come into play from time to time."

Egos and Excitement

A lot of risk-arb investors, Schoenfeld observes, come out of investment banking after being frustrated by clients "inadequately executing
their great ideas" or simply because they are tired of slaving away to
bring someone else's vision into reality. By contrast, he says, "being in
the market, and looking at the deals that have been announced, the
ones that might be occurring because of stakebuilding and things of
that nature is exciting. Assessing the risks includes recognizing that
there are some huge egos at play in this arena on the corporate, legal,
and on the banking sides. Sometimes bankers are quite instrumental
strategically in getting their clients to move; yet on other deals, they're
merely executing block trades." So it's crucial, he says, "to assess who
is pulling the strings and to understand what assumptions they are
operating under and to assess whether they are realistic or not. Any
major disappointments along the way before closing the deal mean
there may have to be reevaluations of the terms and of the willingness
of the board to proceed."

Despite superficial changes in the merger-arb business over his career,
says Schoenfeld—through instantaneous distribution of information,
changing governance rules, and shifts in capital committed—the fundamentals of the analysis are the same. "Reading and understanding
the contracts underpinning a deal is still extremely important. They
are the result, typically, of a lot of hard work on the part of the companies and their lawyers and reflect the negotiating strengths of the
various parties. There are subtleties to be read in those documents.
The whole business, at least on the senior level, is very much an art
form and it pays to be able to draw upon history. The nuances of the
regulatory environment, the contracts, the defenses available in the
case of a hostile deal, the tactics, can all be telling and instructive in
calculating probabilities and risk-adjusted return."

Risks and Returns

PSAM makes a distinction between M&A and special situations in
its portfolio, says Schoenfeld. The latter are "softer catalyst situations where companies are making capital allocation changes, maybe

spinning off certain businesses, undergoing proxy fights, or may be responding to dramatic changes elsewhere in their industry. Obviously, those are much less defined than M&A transactions with a formal bid outstanding or a contract among the parties. But we can demand a much higher rate of return for the higher-risk situations. On the credit side, we may be doing very hard bankruptcy analysis and think we're eventually going to be paid off in full. Or perhaps we'll get equitized in some way."

Adds Schoenfeld, "In any takeover situation, we generally look across the entire capital structure. We're not just looking at the equity. We're trying to see whether there may be a more interesting part of the capital structure to play where the risk/rewards are better aligned than they might be in a pure equity transaction. Many bonds, for instance, have change of control provisions; many have potential for upgrade or downgrade as a result of the transaction. Critically, for PSAM clients, the firm often can lever its research in one strategy to continue investing in a situation as opportunities mutate through the economic cycle from a distressed situation into a 'special situation' and occasionally into a takeover target."

As final edits were being made on this volume, Schoenfeld added, "Entering 2018, we see huge pent-up demand for U.S. M&A that was postponed awaiting the passage of the Trump administration's recent tax legislation. With clarity restored and substantial benefits embodied in the new law for the corporate community, we expect significant positive energy in U.S. board rooms for both M&A and large capital expenditures."

M&A in Distressed Investing

Schoenfeld observes, "M&A even creeps into distressed investing." He points to the 2009 bankruptcy of Smurfit-Stone—a $7.4 billion casualty of the great financial crisis—as one of the instances in which PSAM brought its M&A expertise to bear on a distressed investment. "We'd taken a look at the speed at which they were trying to exit bankruptcy and felt they really had not done a proper job. Management hadn't done the heavy lifting; had not closed the number of plants and mills that it should have. At that point, we publicly stated that Smurfit-Stone should be sold because its management just didn't have sufficient depth to revive it. They were slashing debt by swapping it for equity and restriking their options and doing all the things managements tend to like to do so they'd get a second bite at the apple."

PSAM then went public, arguing at a Bloomberg conference that Smurfit's management had done such a sloppy job that its revival was doubtful. Peter Faulkner, head of PSAM's credit team, objected to the enterprise value Smurfit's advisors put on the company and protested that the proposed plan unfairly favored certain creditors. At the same time, the hedge fund added an equity stake in Smurfit, picked up for pennies a share, and "contacted a number of strategic investors and a few private equity firms to encourage them to bid for Smurfit while it was in bankruptcy to offer a superior alternative," says Schoenfeld. In the end, prospective merger partners elected to wait to see Smurfit's post-bankruptcy capital structure. "But within three months," adds Schoenfeld, "there were bids in the market for the company. We held onto our bonds, we became equitized, and hedged by shorting out a basket of similar packaging companies. The M&A transaction occurred in a relatively short time and it all worked out quite well."

French media company Vivendi also has taken heat from PSAM. Schoenfeld explains that prior to waging its 2015 proxy battle, PSAM "had owned Vivendi stock for two-plus years on a basic sum-of the-parts valuation as a special situation. We looked at the telecom assets, at the music assets, at their shareholdings in game companies, and we just saw an extreme discount. There had been management upheaval going back to Jean-Marie Messier's tenure at the turn of the century. Plus, they were running into credit issues because they had a lot of minority stakes that they couldn't consolidate into cash flow. The stock traded very badly."

During that time, Schoenfeld also discovered that French industrialist Vincent Bollore had designs on Vivendi. "He ultimately was able to take control of Vivendi with a relatively small stake (in the mid-teens), taking advantage of this unusual structure France has where a holder of the stock, after a couple of years, gets double voting rights. It's a perfect example of how you need to understand the rules in different countries." But as Vivendi's 2015 annual meeting approached, says Schoenfeld, he saw that Bollore had built up "an extraordinary cash pool" by selling some Vivendi investments and, based on the Frenchman's track record, Schoenfeld says he "had a feeling Bollore was going to try to use Vivendi as a glorified hedge fund or private equity fund." Then, claims Schoenfeld, Bollore announced a dividend policy "so extremely minimal, we were offended, and wrote him a couple of letters but he stonewalled us." This time, Schoenfeld adds, French law favored PSAM: announced corporate dividends have to be ratified by all shareholders at an annual meeting. PSAM's teams widely published a white paper, spearheaded by portfolio manager Rich Bilotti, detailing Vivendi's strengths. PSAM also filed a proxy proposing an additional $5 billion dividend to shareholders over staggered quarters. "He fought us and the board fought us on it for a while and I'm not sure if we would have won the vote. But at the eleventh hour, Bollore called and worked out a settlement including enhanced dividends plus some buybacks. He distributed a huge amount and we have become frenemies," concludes Schoenfeld dryly.

Taking Up Cudgels

In the United States, Schoenfeld credits "heavy lifting" by institutional investors with taming the worst excesses of the M&A markets of yore. The poison pills, the restrictive state takeover statutes, and the rest have diminished influence today, he contends, because "85 percent of the companies in the S&P 500 have now destaggered their boards," under pressure from corporate governance-minded institutional investors. "With the entire board up for a vote each year, you're vulnerable. If somebody is serious about doing something, they can replace the entire board. So anybody with a strong argument and a strong bid in the market has a lot of influence today."

Adds Schoenfeld, "the best and most high-profile activist deal we've done was MetroPCS's 2013 takeover by Deutsche Telekom"—basically, its merger with T-Mobile USA, which the German company already owned. "The parties had a merger proposal in place," explains Schoenfeld, when PSAM got involved "on the strength of analysis by Rich Bilotti," who runs its special situation group and was a top-ranked telecom and media analyst at Morgan Stanley for a decade before joining the hedge fund. Says Schoenfeld, "We had a strong view that the MetroPCS board was giving away control. The board chairman was quite ill; there were three private equity directors who wanted to free up their money for their next-generation fund. From our perspective, they had negotiated a terrible deal with Deutsche Telekom. We also had the benefits of the insight of Peter Faulkner's credit team who saw significant upside via an adjustment to the capital structure."

PSAM took a holistic approach when they wrote to the board, suggesting adjustments to both the transaction itself and the capital structure. "Not only was the contribution analysis wrong but the debt structure was extremely onerous in an industry that has to buy spectrum and build out systems—too much debt." When rebuffed, PSAM went public with a proxy fight to block the deal, arguing Deutsche Telekom could improve the terms either by reducing the debt or adjusting its contribution analysis—or both—because MetroPCS's spectrum value alone was in excess of the offer price. Also, because Deutsche Telekom needed to take its T-Mobile USA unit public by acquiring MetroPCS instead of retaining full control.

Recalls Schoenfeld, "They fought hard but we received the support of both [institutional proxy advisory firms] ISS and Glass Lewis, which is very hard to do. It's even harder to get arbs to say, 'No, we're not going to take the deal on the table. We're going to risk doing nothing and remain independent.' But we did. That may have been one of our finest moments. We were doing full webcasts with the public, with institutional holders, and we ultimately defeated them." Deutsche Telekom then "negotiated along the lines of our original letter and adjusted the capital structure," adds Schoenfeld, "reducing the combined company's debt by $3.8 billion and lowering the interest rate. Both stocks did extremely well, post-closing."

Biomet's Scourge

Schoenfeld has also gotten irked enough to take an activist role in several healthcare deals involving private equity groups. "We got in the way when we didn't think a company had been properly shopped or had accounting or management issues," shrugs Schoenfeld. In Biomet, he found plenty of the latter in 2006. That year, the then-U.S. attorney for New Jersey, Chris Christie, forced four makers of artificial joints, including Biomet, to pay a combined $311 million to settle kickback charges. A few months later, a last-minute discovery of options backdating improprieties scuttled Biomet's planned merger with its U.K.-based rival Smith & Nephew. After that setback, the artificial joint company hastily agreed to fall into the arms of a private equity consortium.

"We blocked that deal," recalls Schoenfeld, "and convinced them to reopen the process. It was a large PE consortium, with KKR,

Blackstone, Goldman Sachs Capital Partners, and TPG, so we made a lot of enemies. But they did everything we asked: raised their bid and went to a tender offer as opposed to a merger, because a merger would have required a 75 percent vote. For some reason—and to this day, I don't know why—Smith & Nephew, which had had a better bid, didn't resurface. So we got a price bump but not the competitive bidding we'd hoped for. Ultimately of course, the PE group sold Biomet to another of its rivals, so now it's Zimmer Biomet."

In other cases, observes Schoenfeld, "the market isn't really appreciating how potent a merger is—that the company is going to get significantly rerated as a result. In those, we may choose to convert the M&A and stay with the combined company rather than quickly closing out the arbitrage." The 2013 merger of U.S. Airways and American Airlines was an example. "American was totally mispriced after the combination, relative to the peer group, so we stayed with it. We actually created as much of the equity as we could and hedged out our exposure with a basket of other airlines. Then we just waited for the multiples to make sense. I mean, once we've done all the hard work to understand the merger, the valuation, and everything else, why settle? Although plenty of times, pure merger arbitrage yields a great rate of return."

Every mega-merger, Schoenfeld cautions, is not an opportunity. "You wonder how some deals even got out of the board room. Like a Baker Hughes/Halliburton. How did they ever think, in 2014, they were going to get that merger through the Obama administration's antitrust review without pre-lining up someone to buy certain operations? The seller, Baker Hughes, clearly understood that there was a big risk—the $3.5 billion breakup fee in the contract told you that. It was a significant chunk of money when the deal was signed—and even more significant when it was terminated because the whole oil service industry had collapsed." Still, Schoenfeld mused presciently in May 2016, the strategic impetus for that broken deal made sense. "We do think there was a buyer for those assets: GE. But the value of oil patch assets diminished so significantly while that deal was pending—and GE itself was under a bit of activist pressure, from Trian and others, that it wasn't going to happen then. Still, GE's weakest link is its oil service business. They have never reached scale there, so they are the logical buyer, and I bet they're going to buy Baker Hughes within a year-and-a-half."

In the end, it took only five months, until late that October, for GE to make its move, adding yet another notch in Schoenfeld's belt.

CHAPTER SEVEN

John Paulson

It does take—I call it a sixth sense. You can guess and be right once or twice, but to be right almost all the time, to generate smooth returns, it does take a sixth sense. You've got to be 100 percent focused because there are a lot of deals, and the way you get or find things is by 100 percent focus and constant digging, finding information, and understanding the relevance of that information—because when you look back, there are always clues. You want to find those clues before the event happens.

PAULSON & CO.'S eponymous founder, John Paulson, wasn't referring in the quote above to his legendary series of big bets against the housing bubble—"The Greatest Trade Ever," as author Greg Zuckerman collectively dubbed them in the title to his 2009 book by the same name, subtitled: "The Behind-the-Scenes Story of How John Paulson Defied Wall Street and Made Financial History." Those audacious trades made his hedge fund over $15 billion (and Paulson alone more than $4 billion) in the first year of the financial crisis. They also catapulted the slightly-built, buttoned-down hedge fund manager from Queens squarely into the investment pantheon alongside the likes of Warren Buffett, John Templeton and George Soros.

The soft-spoken Paulson uttered the remarks above, instead, as he allowed himself to kick back just a little, sliding partway out of his expensive loafers, in the hedge fund's conference room high above Rockefeller Center—a rather ordinary space, but for its fine art and sculpture—as he began to expound on the strategy that lured him to Wall Street and that continues to be a central focus of three of his funds—risk arbitrage.

His fascination was sparked, Paulson relates, by one of his NYU professors, who "loved risk arbitrage" and brought top partners from Wall Street into his classroom. In the late 1970s, the professor's favorite guest was Robert Rubin, then the head of Goldman Sachs's arb desk—at the time, its most profitable junior partner.

The young Paulson became fixated on risk arbitrage. "There was such an aura around it. The risk-arb groups were small, usually five to ten people, but could produce, say, a $200 million annual profit without working long hours. In investment banking, you might have a hundred people trying to earn fees and working all hours just to maybe make a similar profit. That's how Ace Greenberg, who ran risk arbitrage, became chairman of Bear Stearns. He produced more profits than anyone. That's how it worked."

Obstacles Hurdled

But the entrance hurdles were daunting. "I was told, 'if you want to go into risk arbitrage, you've got to get experience in mergers and acquisitions. Then, if you do well, *they'll pick you* to go into risk arbitrage.'" He applied forthwith but was told, "You can't join

M&A until you have an MBA—and we basically hire from Harvard."
Undeterred, Paulson got admitted and graduated in the top 5 percent
of his Harvard Business School class. But that was in 1980, when the
best and the brightest were heading anywhere but to the fading, bear
market–battered canyons of Wall Street. Paulson accepted a research
gig at Boston Consulting Group but soon was scouting opportunities
in finance. When a job opened up with renowned investors Leon Levy
and Jack Nash at Odyssey Partners, Paulson jumped to the Street—
soon parlaying that job into an M&A post at Bear Stearns. Paulson
rapidly made partner but wouldn't be diverted from his goal. He had
cultivated relationships with arbs at Bear Stearns and elsewhere—networking that ultimately led to a partnership offer from the risk-arb
powerhouse Gruss & Co. Paulson leapt at the opportunity.

"Gruss had no clients, they only managed their own money,"
Paulson recalls. Gruss's founder, Joseph Gruss, had essentially retired
and his son Martin had taken the reins by the time Paulson joined.
"Marty had a very impressive track record." [Gruss compounded over
twenty years in double digits.] "The business at the time was less
crowded, so the spreads were bigger. When there were competitive
bids, they would make a fortune."

The younger Gruss made a lasting impression on Paulson in October
1988 when Philip Morris made a hostile bid for Kraft at $90 a share,
a fat premium to the food company's prebid price of $65.125 a share.
"Marty was very sharp. He bought a big slug of shares right off the
bat." Gruss was betting the cash-rich tobacco company would pre-
vail, despite Kraft's initial resistance. Sure enough, Kraft settled, within
two weeks, for $106 a share. That left Gruss with an enviably quick
multimillion-dollar profit. "I paid my dues in M&A, which was fine,
but I wanted to invest. The money you can make in arbitrage—when
you have money—is so much greater. You can make so much more as
a principal than you can as an agent."

Going His Way

Paulson worked as a partner at Gruss for four years. When he felt
he understood the business well enough, he left and started Paulson
Partners in 1994, "to do risk arbitrage—mostly mergers—and the flip-
side of mergers, which is bankruptcy reorganizations." The practices

are countercyclical, explains Paulson. "You really need both skills to keep busy all the time." When he started, Paulson recalls, "I probably had one hundred times more capital from outside people than I had myself." Nor was he by any means the only young Wall Street buck hanging out a shingle as hedge funds boomed. They were all taking advantage, notes Paulson, of a huge increase in the supply of Wall Street's capital available to risk-arb hedge funds. Before, almost all risk-arb capital was partnership capital. "Now, you could go out with your hedge fund and raise many multiples of your equity from outside investors. The path was no longer: analyst, portfolio manager, partner at Goldman or Bear. If you had the skills, you'd raise a huge pile of cash—and go do the same things for yourself."

Ultimately, the flood of rivals with fresh capital into risk arbitrage started weighing on arbs' profitability. "Not everyone was skilled as an arbitrageur. It's a unique business," observes Paulson. "A lot of people just started doing spreads, diversifying across every deal. Well, you *can* do that, but you're *not* adding value. You don't know which spreads are good; you can't weight the good ones, and avoid the bad ones, and you end up in deals that break. You also get some competitive bidders but overall you start to produce average returns—the whole return profile in the industry came down—gradually starting to approach the general level of interest rates."

Today, says Paulson, "a 400-to-600 basis point premium to the risk-free rate is a reasonable expectation for unlevered, long-term average returns in risk arbitrage." It's possible, he adds, "to add value above that—through research, by weighting, by managing the portfolio—if you can eliminate deals that break, weight the portfolio to competitive bidding situations, and optimize spreads, you can add 200 to 400 basis points to returns."

Leverage isn't a tool Paulson recommends in arb deals. "If you use some, you can boost returns," Paulson allows, "while volatility and drawdowns are low. The problem with leverage as a tool is that in the wrong hands it leads to disastrous results. Some arbs doing very diversified portfolios will lever as much as 6:1. But while some of the early arbs did it, there's no way you can handle 6:1 today; you eventually blow up. Boesky was a very levered player. He blew up. You can't *always* get it right. If you have leverage when you slip, it takes you down."

Staples/Office Depot

Paulson makes no claims of infallibility, pointing to the Staples/ Office Depot merger saga over 2015 and 2016 as a prime example of the pitfalls of arbitrage. When the deal was first announced, he recalls thinking, "Gee whiz, that's a stretch. This isn't going to get done." He adds, "The two had tried to merge once before, way back in 1997, and it was a big busted deal. The FTC blocked it." Paulson had read the FTC's 2013 decision permitting Office Depot and OfficeMax to merge, "*and part of the reason they approved it was that Staples was a competitor.* It seemed to us that the FTC wouldn't approve this latest deal."

Though Wall Street was bullish on the proposed tie-up, Paulson & Co. stayed away. But when the FTC blocked the deal, Paulson recalls, "all the arbs came out and the spread blew out to $4.50—which was where it would be if the deal broke." Tempted, Paulson read more about the FTC's position. He felt the agency was overly empowered by the Obama administration, but he knew the key issue in antitrust is market definition. "They don't want overconcentration." As he dug, Paulson saw, "the FTC was so antibusiness that they kept willy-nilly defining the market so narrowly—like Amazon's not a competitor, Walmart's not a competitor." They ignored mid-sized businesses, retail customers. "They defined the relevant market as only the one hundred largest corporations—as if *they* could *only* buy from Staples and Office Depot!"

Paulson grows heated, abandoning his usual decorum. "I read the pleadings and I said, 'That is ridiculous!' We put on the spread at $4.50, albeit only a small position. The FTC is supposed to look after consumers. Why were they looking after the one hundred largest corporations in America?" The more he studied the legal filings, the more incensed Paulson became. "They also cherry-picked the products. Paper and pencils didn't count, just toner cartridges. It was a gerrymandered definition of a market for a narrow group of products to prove the deal was anticompetitive. We thought the FTC had a weak case. With Office Depot trading as if the deal had broken, it didn't have much downside. We thought it was at least fifty-fifty we could win. We spoke to the companies, and they were very angry and bullish."

In court, Paulson says, "It looked like the judge was siding with Office Depot, questioning the FTC's market definition. Amazon testified that it was growing its business-to-business platform, adding, 'We're huge, we can drop ship to anyone, in any quantity.'" What's more, Paulson notes, "The judge reprimanded the FTC for doing some not-appropriate things to try to jig the case; he seemed angry at the FTC all through the hearings." As they awaited the decision, says Paulson ruefully, "it still seemed very possible he'd allow the deal to proceed, driving the spread to zero." But the judge sided with the FTC, proving to Paulson once again that courts can be capricious—but also reaffirming his wisdom in not heavily weighting the position.

Pfizer/Allergan

He wasn't as lucky, Paulson admits, in the proposed "inversion" merger between Pfizer and Allergan, which the Treasury Department had killed just days before he was interviewed for this volume. "We got caught with our hands in our pants—it was our largest position." The way he'd looked at that deal, Paulson says, the Treasury had already issued new regulations, in November 2015, to discourage inversions—and had bluntly added, "Congress has to act if it wants to block these deals." Since the Pfizer/Allergan plan "ticked all the boxes" in the Treasury's rules, "and we knew Congress wasn't going to act anytime soon," says Paulson, "we thought there was a 90 percent probability the merger would close. I met with Ian Read, who runs Pfizer, I met with Brent Saunders, the CEO of Allergan. We went through all the issues. We understood the law. We understood the regulations. We understood how they structured the deal.It wasn't even an inversion; technically it was a merger of equals."

What they didn't anticipate, says a still-fuming Paulson, was the Treasury's "unprecedented, very draconian, heavy-handed, and punitive action. They way overstepped their bounds but because of how the legal system works there's really nothing to be done." It's very likely, Paulson opines, that the new regulations would not stand up if challenged in court. "But you'd have to complete the merger to have standing to sue and endure years of uncertainty during the litigation.

Neither company is going to do that. Treasury was hell-bent on preventing Pfizer from leaving U.S. jurisdiction for tax purposes—and accomplished that."

Fortunately, while some deals break, others work out better than expected. Business judgment proved crucial for Paulson in late 2015 when he played a "preannouncement" arb situation in another specialty drug stock, Salix Pharmaceuticals. He had passed on buying the stock early that year when it was being bruited about as a potential merger partner for Allergan. It had quickly soared to 170, from 130, before sliding down to 140 as merger hopes faded. But then, in November, Salix unexpectedly announced that it, inexplicably, had been stuffing wholesale channels to inflate sales. Immediately, the stock price was cut in half. "It was quite unfortunate," remarks Paulson. "Their script volume was actually pretty good. They just wanted even more." That's where Paulson's keen business judgment came in. He knew Salix's sales to actual end users were growing well. It would take time to work through the excess inventory, but the management responsible, Paulson felt certain, was getting the boot. He speculated, "This was an acquisition target before. It's probably worth as much now. Anyone who buys it will be basing the price on prospective sales, not on temporarily depressed ones. And this board will be desperate to sell. Someone will come in."

It took Paulson the morning, he says, to figure it out. "We started buying the stock that afternoon. By the end of the day, the stock had bounced back to $90 from $70 and we just kept buying until the end of December when we held 10 million shares, or 9.9 percent of the company, at an average cost of $105 a share. Then we waited. We didn't have to wait long. In February, Valeant offered $158, then Endo bid $170, and Valeant came back with $173. The deal closed March 31.We made $68 a share on 10 million shares, or $680 million. We got the timing and the amount perfectly. We were the largest shareholders." "Activism"—taking a position in a stock and then agitating for its management to enhance shareholder value—is another strategy increasingly embraced by arbs. Paulson sometimes gets active but generally in a collaborative way with management. "We generally don't like adversarial situations," he stresses. In the 2008 takeover of specialty chemical maker Rohm & Haas by Dow Chemical, Paulson's helpful activism rescued Dow from almost certain bankruptcy.

The Dow Dance

In June 2008, Dow Chemical had broken up a pending sale of Rohm & Haas to German chemicals behemoth BASF with a higher bid. To give up BASF and go with Dow, "Rohm & Haas wanted an ironclad merger agreement and was represented by Wachtell, Lipton, arguably the best law firm on mergers," Paulson recounts. "So Dow signed a *very tight* merger agreement—no financing out, no material adverse change out—and agreed to pay all cash. That was fine with Dow, as they coveted Rohm & Haas. The spread initially traded at a 12 percent return. We said, 'We'll just put on a couple percentage points and watch this deal.'"

Then Lehman failed, the economy and stock market collapsed, and along with them the cyclical chemicals stocks. Dow, which had been planning to finance the Rolm & Haas deal, in part, with proceeds from a sale of a joint venture to Kuwait for $8 billion, saw the kingdom pull out of that deal. "Dow had no recourse," Paulson adds. "The spread on its $80 offer for Rohm & Haas blew out to $30—a 60 percent gross spread. Dow's own shares, around $55 when the deal was inked, plunged to a low of $6 and its management took to TV saying they couldn't close the deal."

Dow had commitments for financing, intended as a backup for the Kuwaiti funds, Paulson observes, but "there was no way the banks wanted to fund them" in the midst of the financial crisis. Still, Dow had paid a commitment fee so the banks couldn't just leave, says Paulson. "We read the credit agreement. It was tight." The banks had only one out—if Dow failed to maintain an investment-grade credit rating.

Meanwhile, the merger agreement gave Dow no wiggle room. Explains Paulson, "it didn't matter whether the banks gave them money or not. There was no financing out. They still had to buy Rohm & Haas or be liable. Wachtell was giving no ground, refusing to negotiate. Dow claimed they'd sue to get out of the deal. But we read the agreement—not just me, I had Harvard lawyers that specialize in M&A on my staff—and *we* decided Dow could sue all they wanted but would likely lose and be forced to perform. So we thought the merger would survive Dow's lawsuit and we took an enormous position in Rohm & Haas."

A Collective, "Oh, Shit"

Things got dicier amid the spiraling financial crisis when Dow's credit rating was dropped to triple B-minus. Paulson recalls, "if they were downgraded just one more tick, they'd no longer be investment grade, the bank financing would go away, and Dow might have to file for bankruptcy protection." The reaction at Paulson & Co. was a collective, "Oh, shit." They'd been relying on their analysis of Dow's *legal* position but not on their financial capacity. "Suddenly we realized Dow might not be able to fulfill its commitment *financially*, regardless of the legal outcomes."

Paulson swung into action. "I contacted the CEO of Dow, Andy Liveris, and said, 'Perhaps we could provide you with equity to allow you to meet your commitment.' His investment banker, Bob Greenhill, the Chairman of Greenhill & Co. and former head of M&A at Morgan Stanley was quickly on the phone, asking, 'Are you serious? Why don't you come meet with Andy?' I met with them, and they were a great management team with a solid strategic plan. They just got caught in a financial bind in the midst of the financial crisis. It turns out that the banks had told Dow to raise $1.5 billion in fresh equity to reduce their financing commitment—or they would lose their investment-grade rating."

There were literally no equity providers at that time, Paulson recounts. "Plus, with the company's shares down almost 90 percent, even if they could find buyers, a sale of common equity would be highly dilutive to Dow." Paulson goes on, "we concocted this 'deferred dividend preferred' that hadn't been used since Drexel days. Basically, it doesn't pay a cash dividend, just pays dividends in additional preferred shares." Since it had no cash requirement, Moody's agreed to count it as equity, Paulson adds. He reckoned "it would likely be money good" even if Dow failed, because it was senior to the common. The chemicals giant had $8 billion in preferred previously outstanding, $3.5 billion of which was held by Warren Buffett. Paulson insisted his new paper "had to be *pari passu* with Buffett's preferred, so if Dow went under, we wouldn't be junior to Buffett." Once Buffett signed off, Paulson presented the deal to the Rohm & Haas family shareholders. "We said, 'Look, if Dow doesn't raise this $1.5 billion they could go bankrupt and we may get nothing. So split the funding of this restructuring with me—to allow the merger.'

We both agreed. Then Rohm & Haas hesitated. The family could only take $500 million of the $750.I ended up buying $250 million of their commitment for a $50 million discount or $200 million; taking on $1 billion of preferred in total.I was dealing in *a lot* of cash."

Says Paulson, "We funded it overnight. Dow kept their investment-grade rating and the banks funded the takeover. Importantly for us they closed the merger in ten days. We made $600 million on that $30 a share spread; we had 20 million shares, maybe more. When we funded Dow, Rohm & Haas ran up to 74 from 50. A week later the deal closed and we got 82. That was the big game," Paulson concludes with evident relish.

He was still holding $1 billion of Dow's preferred, which Moody's had insisted they make non-callable for two years. Paulson didn't want to further encumber Dow with a 12 percent preferred, so he allowed Dow to pre-pay early without penalty if they could refinance. The takeover closed in February of 2009, the market bottomed early the next month, and stocks took off. By April, the investment grade bond market opened up and Goldman did a refinancing for Dow to allow the chemicals giant to pay off the expensive preferred. Dow common quickly recovered. "Within two months, we got paid back the $1 billion, made an extra $50 million on the Rohm & Hass piece we took down, plus fees and the 12 percent dividend—*and got out of the deal*." says Paulson. "We saved that deal. *Very* quickly. No one else could have done that."

CHAPTER EIGHT

Paul Gould

Risk arbitrage is a great discipline to learn. It helps with understanding the investment world. The strategy takes into account a lot of different aspects of the investment business and is a good skill set to acquire. But it's not a business for all seasons.

AS ALLEN & Co. managing director Paul Gould explains, winding down the firm's risk-arb business at the end of 2015 was "a matter of allocation of resources and focusing even more on client relationships."

Gould, a tall, dominating presence with the broad-shoulders of the athlete, started the very private boutique merchant bank's small but potent risk-arbitrage arm in 1975 and ran it, quite profitably, for over forty years. Gould has also long been deeply involved in Allen & Co.'s high-powered merger and acquisition advisory practice and serves on the board of a couple of John Malone's media companies. He observes, "we don't do all things for all people, and the move was more of a reflection of the firm's direction than it was on risk arbitrage—though spreads had narrowed quite a bit."

An emeritus trustee of Cornell University, which he attended before graduating from Farleigh Dickinson University, Gould went to work on Wall Street in 1969 and soon gravitated into trading convertible bonds. "In 1971 to '72, convertibles were a pretty active market. There were a lot of real estate investment trusts doing unit offerings, with a bond, equity, and a warrant—and the warrant very often was exercisable with the bond. So if the bond sold at a discount, which very often they did, you could use discounted dollars to exercise the warrant—and therefore buy the stock cheaper." The young trader soon discovered, "you could fool around with all those variables." He was entranced. By 1972, Gould—by then toiling at Allen & Co.—had discovered another under-the-radar investment discipline involving intriguing variables, risk arbitrage. "We ended up taking a couple of small positions. I got great backing here, and we just started doing risk arb."

Maturity Matters

In the intervening forty-plus years, Gould reflects, "risk arbitrage has gone from being a very immature business to what was an overly mature business, seven or eight years ago. In the 1970s, nobody had any idea what the business was about. The flamboyant way Ivan Boesky seemed to do things intrigued people, but—other than that—there was very little known about it. There certainly wasn't a research product being put out. It was almost impossible to even get public filings. They came up to New York a day late. Sometimes if you *really* wanted to see something, you got somebody to hang around a courthouse or the SEC and you waited until the filing could be read to you."

The rigors of the trade weren't without their compensating balances, however, Gould recalls with evident relish. "I'm sure you've heard about

'Friday night specials.' In those days, you could complete an unfriendly cash tender offer in seven days. Somebody would drop an offer on somebody's desk on a Friday night," and the whole thing would be over by the end of the next week. The annualized rates of returns were eye-popping. "But it went from that to, in 2005, I remember walking by this conference room one day and one of the guys working for us was in here with two different firms pitching their arb research. I knew then it was probably the top of the market. If there's one theme that survives in risk arb, it's that having a contrarian bent pays."

It was thirty years earlier, in the teeth of the 1975 bear market, as it happened, that Allen & Co.'s fledgling risk-arb fund picked up a key institutional account. Gould reminisces, "the Yankees were playing the Red Sox in the playoffs while we were up in Boston—we were the first outside managers Harvard ever hired—and its investment arm had never even shorted a security before. That shows how immature the business was at that point. It took us about six months just to work out a mechanism for them to short stocks." But shortly thereafter, Gould adds, "Cambridge Associates invited us to an endowment meeting in Charleston, South Carolina. I went down and pitched our arb fund and ended up with the World Bank, Case Western, Johns Hopkins—about ten different accounts, in all. We grew that to about a billion dollars by the late 1980s."

You've Got a Friend

Not bad for a team of just four professionals, as Gould recounts, that initially looked to sell its risk-arbitrage services to institutions as a way to cement client relationships. "We went out and got those endowments," says Gould, because "Allen & Co. was bidding for the Irvine Ranch, out in Orange County, California, against Mobil Corp.'s real estate arm. We had almost no institutional friendships at that point to call on to come in as investors. That's why I ended up forming those relationships with Harvard and the others. Now, obviously, we have a ton of relationships—many because of the Sun Valley conference we run, which blows our minds."

To be sure, the frenetic takeover boom of the 1980s hit a wall at the decade's end, as Boesky went to prison on insider trading charges and the prolific originator of "highly confident letters" and junk-bond-fueled corporate daisy chains, Drexel's Michael Milken, likewise headed for jail. The proliferation of "poison pills" also dampened merger activities, Gould remembers, while the 1990 recession relegated arb desks to sifting through "boring bank deals in which we couldn't do better than the prevailing interest rate."

It wasn't Allen & Co.'s cup of tea. Explains Gould, "a good portion of our billion dollars under management had always been our own money, and the premise always was, 'whatever we're going to do with your money, we're going to do with our own money—so if we don't want to invest it, we'll let you know.'" Which was what Allen & Co. did. "In 1990 we sent a letter suggesting clients take their risk-arb money back. The opportunities weren't there. We managed to get the fund down to about $120 million. But most of our accounts stayed with us as much smaller investors. We just ran the business in a very mild way for four or five years, until the risk-arb business got better." Allen's clients ultimately were well-served. "Luckily, up until 2005 or 2006, we never had a losing year," reports Gould. "Maybe you could say we didn't take enough risk—if you don't take risk, you're not going to lose anything—but some years we had 25 percent to 30 percent returns."

Crisis Management

Gould credits their critical and contrary thinking habits with keeping his risk-arb team in the black in the market crises of both 1987 and 2007–2009. "In 1987 we hardly got hurt at all when the whole M&A business was coming down with Boesky and Milken. Some 70 percent or 80 percent of the deals at that point actively depended on Drexel financing—that was just way too much correlation for us. We were quite risk-averse and very conscious of avoiding concentrating our positions in industries or sectors or with a specific investment banker. So we only had one or two Milken deals—ones we thought were the better deals—and they ended up closing—though obviously I had no idea anyone was getting indicted."

Gould shares an anecdote, however, that speaks to the cloud of suspicion and fear that descended on Wall Street in 1987, as news spread that Boesky was cooperating with the government. "It turned out that Boesky had me out for drinks while he was wired. A friend—I can't mention his name—actually had been offered cash by Boesky the week before. It was a scary time. People were being indicted and you didn't know if somebody was going to say something about you that may not have been true."

Unsurprisingly, Gould remembers being immediately suspicious when Boesky "insisted on meeting me." Allen & Co. "had very little to do with the guy for a number of reasons, including the fact that we very definitely thought there was something going on," adds Gould. Nonetheless, he met with Boesky. "I'll never forget—it was at the Harvard Club. He walked in and right away, I started talking about our sons and wrestling—his kid and mine actually wrestled against each other—that's all I would talk about. About halfway through the drinks, Boesky stood up and walked out. That was it. A few months later, the whole story hit the wires."

Common Sense Investing

The core of a good risk-arb strategy has always been "and remains, even today, despite all the computers, just common sense about where the risks are," says Gould, "and how they correlate and don't correlate—things that machines can't necessarily tell you. The analysis of deal dynamics and of people's motivations." On that score, Gould admits, working in Allen & Co., with its deep relationships with corporate movers and shakers, was an advantage. The firm's corporate advisory expertise, Gould reflects, meant that he "could always have substantive conversations about a business and what was going on and why people were doing things."

At the same time, Gould stresses, "The last thing you ever wanted to hear" from a corporate advisory colleague or any banker, "was that, say, someone is going to raise their bid $3 tomorrow. Inside information just got you in trouble. We wouldn't do it. We felt strongly that Boesky—I hate to use this word, but it fits—screwed the industry mightily for about ten years by driving spreads out of whack; cost other arbs considerable money." Boesky's machinations were manifestly obvious to other arbs, Gould adds, and inspired copycat trading. "Something would trade up and it wasn't justified. Obviously, Boesky had information you didn't have. So either you never bought the security or you ended up holding it as it started trading down because the deal was in trouble. Or you bought more because you thought he knew more than you—and it ended up not occurring." It was also clear to the savvy eye, Gould adds, "that Boesky was tipped off by someone at Kidder. It was Martin Siegel who was caught, but I had suspicions about others, too."

As the markets headed into the 2007–2008 crisis, Gould says, Allen & Co.'s contrarian bent and well-honed investment banking toolset helped it again avoid major pitfalls. "The risk-arb market got increasingly scary beginning around 2005 when many private equity firms started coming in and buying companies for no discernible strategic reasons." Realizing "there were no real synergies as motivators for completing the transactions" if the market or economy stumbled, Gould steered clear of all but strategic deals.

Leverage? No, Thanks

Allen & Co. also deviated from common arb business strategy when it came to using leverage. It never used the stuff. Explains Gould, "the idea was not to be forced. If you thought you were a pretty good judge of risk/reward, you didn't want to be forced to sell if the market sold off. The standing joke is that you know it's the bottom of the market only when your boss walks in and tells you to sell everything."

Gould is no fan either of risk-arb hedge funds pursuing activist investing. "Of course, 'hedge fund' can mean anything and everything," he allows, but a lot of what activists are doing "is not a lot different from what Milken was doing in the 1980s. Let's face it, Milken (or a member of Drexel's junk-bond-financing circle) bought big positions and forced companies to increase shareholder value in the short run. Sometimes, unfortunately, this was just by cutting expenses and slashing R&D."

He goes on, "In today's world sometimes that doesn't work— because they've already done that, in many cases. But also because today's businesses—especially in technology—have to invest a lot in R&D to survive. You can't milk technology like an old-line business. If you try, you're just not going to be competitive." Gould adds, "It's too bad, but the world in general has become too short-term oriented. The worst offenders are probably the funds of funds. Their job is to move assets around, so I'm not blaming them. If they make investments and then sit there, they're not justifying their own fee on top of a fee."

The good news, says Gould, is that some companies are developing mechanisms to fend off activists' short-term demands. "A way to get around them is to have companies that are closely controlled, so you don't worry about it. Ferrari did this in their IPO. They issued a class of securities to the Elkann-Agnelli family, which agreed not to sell them for a time in exchange for super-voting rights. With economic ownership of 20 percent or so, they control the vote."

Contrary to the Core

More broadly, "There will always be opportunities for contrarians" in the markets, comments Gould. In a tough current environment for classic risk arb, he sees better prospects in selective arb activity. Investors, Gould suggests, should find an arb fund that "isn't strictly M&A focused—one that also has a distressed debt component, because the strategies tend to move in different cycles." Gould stresses that 40 percent of his arb book was in distressed going into 2007–2008, and adds that related strategies shouldn't be overlooked, "spinoffs, options trading—whatever. Some of the best opportunities, even amid the crisis, were not buying equity, but buying debt."

CHAPTER NINE

George Kellner

Part of the attraction of risk arbitrage has always been that it's open-ended, a little free-ranging, and you can make a lot of money. Don't think for a second that it was not a factor. I could see that you could get really good and make a lot of money. It was apparent what some of the partners in some of the funds were making—and that appealed to me. You're not going to get that in a corporate structure. But it takes a certain willingness to take risk. If someone is looking for stability and safety, risk arbitrage has never been the right business.

"I COULD HAVE been the bow tie king, that *was* an option," says George Kellner, with just enough bemused and self-confident disdain in his voice to telegraph that it was *not* one he ever seriously considered. Although the niche fashion business was his immigrant family's economic life raft and bridge to the American dream in the 1950s and 1960s, recounts Kellner, it wasn't lost on him that his father had always "loathed the schlocky rag trade." So Kellner, whose parents fled Hungary in 1947 with their three-year-old "and the stereotypical $30 sewn into the back of a belt," used the educational opportunities afforded him by his parents' bow-tie-making success to chart a decidedly different course—through Columbia Law School, a white-shoe law firm, and a stint as a corporate-counsel-turned-securities-analyst at an early mutual fund company—into the top ranks of the specialized corner of Wall Street called risk arbitrage.

One of Wall Street's pioneers as an independent risk arbitrageur, in February 1981 Kellner joined forces with Phil DiLeo (whose previous gig had been trading for Ivan Boesky) to form merger-arb shop Kellner DiLeo & Co., just as merger activity—and before too long the entire stock market—started to percolate like mad. Contemporary press clips breathlessly pegged the size of the young partnership's arb portfolio at $1 billion (probably including leverage) before it ran into the market buzz saw otherwise known as the crash of 1987. Demurs Kellner at this remove, "I was not overly ambitious, so I never raised a ton of money. At the peak, I think we had $600 or $700 million in capital and that was it." What is indisputable is that Kellner's firm, rebranded Kellner Capital, successfully navigated not only that long-ago crash but also the numerous other corrections, retreats, and crashes that have buffeted the business since. Today, Kellner Capital manages around a quarter of a billion dollars in a hedge fund and in a variety of alternative investment strategies for institutional and family office investors, as well as in a family of alternative mutual funds. But that's getting ahead of the story.

"Like most immigrants, my parents came here not because they wanted to but because they *had* to," recalls their only child, "but they made a go of it." Kellner adds, "They were educated and had been people of means. My father was a PhD economist who left a senior position at the National Bank of Hungary but he had no practical skills. He spoke four languages, none of them English." Luckily, though, his mother knew how to sew. "My father was unsuccessfully selling light bulbs door-to-door when she got a job in a bow tie factory. She ended up as the forelady—literally in about four months—and six months later said to my father, 'Hey, I now know how to make ties and you're an ex-banker. We should get into this business.' By the time they retired in 1967 or 1968, they had the largest bow tie factory in America."

They brought his grandmother over from Hungary, relates Kellner, "and she basically raised me until my parents—because they didn't know any better—sent me off to military school. That's one of the few things Donald Trump and I have in common." Unlike the president's, Kellner's own tenure in a military school was exceedingly brief. "Military academies back then were really kind of reform schools, and I had a teacher who quietly told my parents they should send me elsewhere. So I went off to a boarding school." From that point on, Kellner observes, "Bow ties put me in very rarefied company." Nonetheless, he had no inclination to take over the family business. Instead, Kellner went from Trinity College to law school and practiced law for a couple of years. Until, Kellner recalls, he recognized that his "forty-four-year-old boss was working hours almost as long as me. We were working until midnight and eating sandwiches at the printer's together while the investment bankers and their clients were leaving at 6:00 p.m. and eating at the Four Seasons. I thought I'd rather eat at the Four Seasons eventually."

Discovering Risk Arbitrage

Kellner found his way out in the early 1970s, through his college roommate's wife. She was a daughter of Edward Merkel, the CEO of the Madison Fund Inc., a large closed-end fund. "I started as house counsel," remembers Kellner, but before long earned his CFA, shifted into securities analysis and, ultimately, portfolio management. He stayed about five years. "Then Ed retired. I would have liked to run the firm but nobody asked," shrugs Kellner. Besides, he had already become intrigued with risk arbitrage. "I had run into Bob Rubin and others at Goldman Sachs—Bob was already running their arbitrage desk. Gus Levy had retired. In any event, I noted what he was doing and thought it was pretty interesting. We talked a little bit about it. One of my frustrations as an analyst, and even as a portfolio guy, was that you could do a lot of work on a stock and be absolutely right on the fundamentals—but dead wrong on the price. So many factors go into the pricing of securities, there's a real disconnect between the fundamental analytical process and the outcome. Whereas, in merger arbitrage—at least as we practice it—if you follow the dots and you do the work, the outcome is pretty predictable and I like that." As a consequence, Kellner continues, "I kept my eye out for how to get into the game."

This time, it was a school connection of his young son's that led to Kellner's break. "He was going to the Allen-Stevenson School and one of the guys who also had a son in the class was Carl Tiedemann, who at that point was running Donaldson, Lufkin & Jenrette. One day, we were both at some class event and I could feel Tiedemann looking at me. Carl was a very large guy—and I'm a small guy—so he really had me wondering, 'what's going on?' But it turned out that he was starting an arb department at DLJ. Long story short, I went to work at DLJ in 1976–77—basically launched their merger-arbitrage business. They may have had one, or toyed with the idea when they first formed the firm, but it hadn't worked out for whatever reason. So I restarted it and worked happily there until 1981 when I got the itch, for a variety of reasons, to take a shot at going out on my own. So I did, with Phil DiLeo. He was my co-founder and head trader and we stayed together for close to fifteen years until he retired."

Early Days

Originally, recalls Kellner, "We were a pure partnership. I didn't know what a hedge fund was. Our structure was not dissimilar to the other independent partnerships that were entering the risk-arb business back then, people like Guy Wyser-Pratte and Mario Gabelli. While Boesky attracted most of the publicity, the real difference was that we were naturally honest while he wasn't." But at any rate, their timing could scarcely have been better, Kellner reminisces. "Merger arbitrage, certainly in the 1970s and 1980s, was an extraordinarily profitable business—one with very high rates of return and not a crowded space. It was just the brokerage firms doing it, along with a few independent practitioners like myself." And the good times rolled, Kellner adds, "probably until the early 1990s," when new entrants flooded into the business.

More recently, Kellner sighs, "The rates of return from risk arb have been very pedestrian relative to those good old days because a component of its returns is interest rates. With interest rates at zero, if you make 4 percent or 5 percent, that's pretty damn good—which is what we've done and all we can do—based on how we manage our risk, until rates go up." The only exceptions, he adds, "are in a few bespoke and highly-levered accounts willing to accept a lot more risk." Kellner's response has been to diversify. "In 1990 we got into convertible arbitrage. Then in the late 1990s and early 2000s we diversified further, into event-related strategies, both domestic and offshore. But I never added short-only funds and never went back into a Madison Fund–like long-only investment business. Primarily, I think, because of my experience there. I just didn't have a lot of confidence in the predictability of the outcome from fundamental stock picking. I always wanted something that I could look at and analyze that would have a catalyst associated with it—some trigger."

Taxing Rules

Too be sure, Kellner adds, his firm was scarcely immune to the vicissitudes that periodically plague the markets. He remembers the crash of 1987 with a shudder. "I almost got blown up in 1987 because we were members of the New York Stock Exchange for tax reasons. You may remember that back then you could transform short-term capital gains into long-term ones by being a member of the Exchange. So we had great returns *and* we were tax-efficient. But to be really tax-efficient, as I said, you had to be a member of the NYSE. That enabled you to short stocks without putting up any margin to carry positions."

The downside of that considerable benefit was that Exchange members were subject to all of the NYSE's rules. Kellner recalls, "when October of 1987 came around—and the proverbial fan got hit—I got a phone call from the Exchange saying, 'You're in violation of the capital rules. You've got to sell.' They basically forced me to liquidate about 90 percent of my portfolio *in a week*, which was extremely painful. Some of my peers who were *not* Exchange members just held on to their positions through the crash—and ended the year up, actually. The only good news in all of this for my firm, though, was that we had been up about 140 percent on the year when October happened, so I had some buffer. But we took about a 100 percent hit. We were down pretty substantially. In fact, 1987 ended up being one of the only three years the firm has been down in its thirty-five-year history."

Stuff Happens

Kellner continues, "But being taken to the edge of the abyss and forced to look down, it taught me something very important—and here's the point of this story: Up until then, I had thought, 'Maybe somebody else sits down on the potty, but I don't. I do it differently.' It was a very valuable lesson. Also humiliating and frightening. I learned that you're not as smart as you think you are—and bad things can happen totally unexpectedly." From today's vantage point, Kellner credits his harrowing 1987 experience, in a sense, for his firm's longevity, despite the succession of "some pretty ugly periods"—1990, 1994, 2000–2001, 2007–2008—that followed, because it prompted him to implement a number of very strong risk-control and risk-management procedures. "The game plan is *not* to be the Babe Ruth of the business. The game plan is to be the Stan Musial of the business. In other words, I want to have a .300 batting average whenever possible, but I don't need to hit sixty-one home runs, or whatever Roger Maris hit, to break the Babe's record. Consistently hitting singles and doubles is just fine. And that has been our MO from 1987 forward. We almost never employ leverage greater than 1.3–1.4 in our hedge fund—even less in the mutual fund."

While Kellner cops to "probably running portfolios that are a little more concentrated than a lot of arbs' might be," he's also quick to point out, "our concentration is thirty to fifty positions, not fifty to a hundred. And fifty is going to be the top side of positions you'll find in our portfolios—unless everything is so wonderful that you just have to keep eating cake until you're sick of chocolate."

Disciplined Risk Analysis

To Kellner, the huge advantage the risk-arbitrage business has over fundamental stock picking arises from its discipline of risk analysis and predictability. "In any investment business, if you make a mistake, you try to figure out, 'How come?' But when I first started to think that way, back when I was a securities analyst and portfolio manager, I couldn't really figure it out. Maybe my timing was lousy or there was

Babe Ruth. In investing, he would be the home run king—swinging for the fences with riskier investments; this works excellently in baseball but not so well in arbitrage. Wikimedia Commons.

Stan Musial. In investing, his good batting average translates to consistency, which is key in arbitrage. Wikimedia Commons.

some exogenous event in Timbuktu that was totally unpredictable." By comparison he says, "in the merger-arbitrage business, most of the risk is antitrust. And you can do some 20/20 hindsight work and see where you went wrong—so you can hope, *that mistake*, you won't make again, or that at least you'll make it in a lesser degree."

Kellner cites, for example, recent controversial merger proposals that involved tax inversions. "We were well aware of inversions—we were in Shire Plc., to begin with, in 2014 [it was in negotiations with AbbVie Inc. for an 'inversion deal' which ultimately foundered on Obama administration efforts to deter foreign mergers driven by tax advantages]. And we were also in Allergan (before the Treasury in April 2016 scuppered Pfizer's deal to buy it and move their combined headquarters to Ireland.) So now you might ask, 'George, you've been talking about how much you've learned. How come you were so stupid as to be in Allergan after having that Shire experience?' The answer is that, first of all, we're in a business where we take risk. Prospective *risk-adjusted returns* are what we look at."

Then too, Kellner continues, "When assessing deals, the most important factor for us—whether they're inversions or not—is whether there is strategic merit to the combination. Is there a strategic reason why these people are getting together? Or is it just a financial deal or a tax deal or some other motivation, which is not as strong or not as good? Shire is the perfect example of a situation that looked like they had a strategic reason—and those optics were reinforced the week before the deal broke when the chairman of AbbVie publicly reiterated that they loved Shire, were really committed for strategic reasons. He was ringing the bell, trying to drum up enthusiasm among Shire employees. That's when we took a full position; he sucked us in—and a lot of others, too. Then, a week later, the whole thing fell apart. In the Allergan situation, we were well aware that Treasury could come back and do *something*. But, like most people, we had no idea how *draconian* their action would be. We also, maybe foolishly, thought that the Treasury secretary would comply with the law."

"Them's the Facts"

His ire unmistakable, Kellner continues, "If Pfizer actually went to court—this is my opinion and it's shared by people who make a specialty of this sort of law—they would have a very high probability of getting these regs thrown out or overturned. But they're not going to spend the time and money to do it. I admit, I didn't think Treasury would come out and do something as right on the edge as they did—now, [former Treasury Secretary Jacob] Lew is never going to admit that—but 'them's the facts,' as they say. Did we learn something from it? Yes. We learned that—at least the Obama administration was willing to take things to the edge. That lesson cost us something. But it didn't cost us more than our risk parameters allow. We basically limit our positions to 2 percent of the portfolio, which is what we had. So our basic metric is that in the worst case we can anticipate, we're not going to lose more than 2 percent of our capital. Over the many years, that's worked pretty well for us. In fact, that's what happened in both Shire and Allergan."

There is no broad agreement in the risk-arb community about how to handle investments in broken deals, and Kellner is in the "it depends" camp. "Sometimes we sell right away, sometimes we don't, depending on the circumstances. With Shire, we traded out of the position over some time because right when a deal breaks is very often the worst possible time to sell. A lot of the institutional types will sell immediately, as a matter of discipline, as we well know. We tend to let them do what they're going to do. Then, since we have a fairly good idea, we think, where these stocks *ought* to trade on their fundamentals, once the dust settles we will tend to leg out of the positions.

"But if, for whatever the reason, they're trading at a price that's attractive to us at the time a deal breaks—or there are so many other opportunities that it's foolish to hang on to the position—then it's better to take your licking and move into something else that will help you to make up the differential. Again, there's no hard and fast rule. A lot of people tell you, 'When the deal breaks, we sell out immediately.' That's a discipline—just not the discipline we follow. We try to be a little more *artistic* than that."

Being Different

Acknowledges Kellner, "I suspect that most people who are in this business are a little bit—different. What I mean is they're mostly outliers. If I had wanted to be a conventional guy, I would have joined Goldman—well, I don't know if they would have hired me—but

I would have gone with some sort of white-shoe investment banking firm—done things on a more conventional basis. Arbitrage was not a conventional business. It was not even a highly regarded business, back in the 1970s and 1980s—but it was fascinating. Two things that appealed to me strongly were that, one, it was a business in which it looked like I could use my background and interests much more effectively and, two, there wasn't a lot of structure to it. You weren't locked into some hierarchy where you'd have to fight to stay alive for a long time to have a chance to succeed. Today, for example, a lot of young people are going into entrepreneurial businesses on the West Coast for many of the same reasons. They'd rather work in entrepreneurial unicorns than work at Goldman for 150 hours a week. Part of the attraction of risk arbitrage has always been that it's open-ended, a little free-ranging, and you can make a lot of money. Don't think for a second that it was not a factor. I could see that you could get really good and make a lot of money. It was apparent what some of the partners in some of the funds were making—and that appealed to me. You're not going to get that in a corporate structure."

Kellner goes on, "But it takes a certain willingness to take risk. If someone is looking for stability and safety, risk arbitrage has never been the right business. There was a guy back in the late 1970s and 1980s who, in my opinion, was one of the smarter people ever to work in arbitrage. He worked for a name-brand firm, but in the early '80s, when people like me were making 50 percent-plus, compounded annually, he was making maybe 20 percent or 30 percent—underperforming everybody. The reason—in some ways—was that he was smarter than the rest of us. When he looked at a situation, he saw every possible permutation and it paralyzed him. He could not prioritize what was important. He made a mountain out of every molehill and ended up being too risk-averse, too conservative, at a time when aggression paid. That was the beauty of the 1980s and even portions of the 1990s. If you were wrong—and all of us were, on occasion—you got punished for a week and a half. Then another deal came along and you could make it up. One of the major differences in the business today is that if you're wrong, it takes much longer to make up your losses. That's why risk management has become so much more important."

A good arb, says Kellner, quickly sorts what's important from what's not and processes that information consistently and accurately. "It requires someone intellectually flexible who is able to say, 'Boy, can

I be wrong.' In this business, you can't be dogmatic and intellectually stiff. A Donald Trump would be a horrible arb because he's always right and always a genius. This business is humiliating and humbling because you are frequently wrong. You have to be driven by facts, not ego. You also have to have enough common sense not to push the edge of the envelope." In other words, he says, hubris and bravado have no place in arbitrage. "Probably the best thing you can do, if a deal looks a little spooky, is not do it. The fail rate in announced deals is pretty low—90 percent or 95 percent of announced deals close. But the downside of the business is that when you're wrong, it's *very* painful. So you can't be too wrong, too frequently—which makes avoiding busted deals really the name of the game. Figuring out what that risk is and the probability of that risk—which is not a science, it's a little bit of an art—is the key."

CHAPTER TEN

Roy Behren and
Michael Shannon

What we both find interesting about merger arbitrage is that there's such variety. One day you're working on a merger of laser companies and another day it's a merger of airlines or biotech companies or oil and gas companies. So we're always reading about interesting companies. Then, too, no deal ever proceeds the same way; there are different timelines. Now, with the internationalization of the capital markets, we're investing in deals where the target may be in the U.S. and the

acquirer may be overseas, or vice versa. Or both companies may be
overseas. It constantly keeps us engaged.

—ROY BEHREN

Our deals are most often in industries that are dynamic. Because if there
are mergers, what's happening? There's a grab for assets. The targets are
obviously valuable to somebody, for some reason. The fun thing about
it is finding out why and who's next?

—MICHAEL SHANNON

Or sometimes we have companies consolidating out of weakness. The
oil sector, for instance, can't support all the existing companies with the
price of oil at multi-decade lows.

—ROY BEHREN

So the nice thing about risk arbitrage is that we can play both sides of
the economic cycle.

—MICHAEL SHANNON

ROY BEHREN AND Mike Shannon complete each other's thoughts
with the unselfconscious ease of guys who have worked together
practically every business day for twenty-two years—and then spent
untold after-hours on the links. All that time, focused fairly singularly
on growing a business from roughly $60 million when they joined
to more than $6 billion currently. The magic their chemistry has
produced owes to a highly disciplined risk-arbitrage strategy used to
generate consistent positive returns as well as to preserve capital for
clients—facilitated by the low correlation of the deals they invest in
with the stock market.

They've also been fortunate. Their track record was importantly
bolstered by close-to-flat performance in the "crucible" of the 2008
financial crisis. While Westchester Capital Management's mutual
funds—which offered daily liquidity throughout the crisis—saw inevitable outflows amid the panic, as investors raised cash wherever they
could put their hands on it, those flows turned prodigiously positive
in its aftermath. Westchester Capital stood out prominently among
the myriad fund purveyors for making good on downside protection

promises to clients in its "liquid alternative" mutual fund—the now-$5.6 billion Merger Fund—as well as to clients who had invested in its event-driven WCM Alternatives mutual fund and related structures, which now boasts some $720 million in assets under management.

Though they grew up just miles apart on the south shore of Long Island, Behren and Shannon—now comanaging members and coportfolio managers for the mutual fund company, Westchester Capital Management, LLC, and affiliates, and for Westchester Capital Partners, LLC, its allied hedge fund advisor—didn't meet until 1996. And then it was more or less by chance.

Shannon's Wall Street career almost ended before it began, in the fall of 1987. The Boston College senior was living the good life with his college buddies, waiting for the start date of his Salomon Brothers training program, when the market crashed. "I come home from a bar at like two o'clock in the morning, and my roommate says, "An hour ago, a Salomon guy called. The message was, 'Call me whenever you get in. I'll be here.' The market had crashed three or four days before, so I thought, 'Oh, shit. This is my job.'" He was right. Shannon was one of fifty trainees the bond house jettisoned.

Shannon scrambled, got lucky, "and ended up getting a job in JPMorgan's training program." He remembers enjoying bouncing as a trainee among the investment bank's many departments. Once "pigeonholed," however, as first an oil and gas analyst and later a banking analyst, Shannon chafed at narrow investment banking mandates. Finally, eight years after his BC graduation, Shannon discovered merger arbitrage when asked to fill in on Morgan's risk-arb desk. The business, Shannon remembers thinking, was "kind of cool." It got even cooler when he learned that risk arb was at least as lucrative as M&A, but didn't regularly consume weekends. Shannon briefly returned to his M&A post but devoted himself from then on to exploring risk arbitrage.

Barron's Pointed the Way

"Soon, I came across your *Barron's* article on Fred and Bonnie," Shannon recalls. That would be Westchester Capital Management founder Frederick W. Green and his long-time partner, Bonnie L. Smith. Enthralled by the deals he saw percolating in 1980, Green left Goldman Sachs, where he had been a senior portfolio strategist and a member of the investment policy committee, and started Westchester Capital expressly to pursue risk-arbitrage strategies. Smith joined in 1986, becoming Green's indispensable partner in risk-arbitrage research and portfolio management, serving as vice president of Westchester Capital and as partner in Green & Smith Investment, their hedge fund affiliate.

Shannon's timing in reading the 1993 Barron's cover interview with the duo that I penned was fortuitous. The article—focused on Green and Smith's groundbreaking 1989 launch of the first risk-arbitrage mutual fund, creatively dubbed the Merger Fund, as well as on its impressive subsequent performance—had sparked a significant growth spurt at Westchester Capital. As Shannon recalls, "I'm like, 'Look at this! There aren't many people there and now they're managing maybe $100 million.'" He wasted little time in seeking a job interview. Behren, who had been hired by Westchester Capital only months earlier, answered the phone. As Shannon recalls the conversation, "Roy said, 'Why don't you come up? We'll have fun.'" To be sure, formal interviews with Green and Smith followed but Shannon soon found himself enthusiastically working alongside Behren, as he does to this day.

It clearly didn't take Green and Smith long to recognize that by teaming Shannon with Behren, they in effect backed themselves with a young risk-arb dream team—combining Shannon's experience as an M&A banker with Behren's considerable expertise in corporate and securities law. Behren had picked up a BS in economics at the Wharton School, a JD at the University of Miami, and a master's in corporate law at NYU—all before spending seven years working in the SEC's enforcement division. But the ambitious young lawyer grew increasingly restless when assigned to collecting supposedly long-settled Drexel-era judgments for the agency. Friends who had made a beeline for Wall Street straight out of college boasted at weekly poker games about bids and asks, block trades, and soft dollars. "It just sounded so exciting," Behren reminisces. "Finally, after I'd been complaining for a couple of years, one of the guys challenged me to take a week off from the SEC and sit with him at his trading desk. He said, 'I'll teach you what it's like on an arb desk. You'll see if it's something you want—at the very least, you'll be able to talk intelligently in an interview."

Behren grabbed the opportunity and hasn't looked back. "While I was visiting that desk, one of the analysts, who was friendly with Bonnie, mentioned that her firm was hiring." Behren quickly set up an interview at Westchester Capital and made his pitch: "I'm fairly quantitative; I have a decent legal background, it seems there's a lot of litigation that goes on with merger arbitrage; and I'm a quick learner. I have no risk-arb experience, obviously, but I've read a lot." Green responded, "Don't worry. Whatever you need to know, I'll teach you," recalls Behren.

Picking Up Quant Tricks

Behren and Shannon have worked together ever since, except for about a year in 2004–2005, when Shannon took "an offer he couldn't refuse" from quant shop D. E. Shaw & Co. Working as Shaw's senior vice president in charge of mergers and special situations, Shannon reflects now, "was a very good learning experience. They were very smart guys and very nice, but it was a different culture, very quantitative."

Interjects Behren, "Mike's detour to Shaw proved very helpful." When Shannon came back, he explains, "We implemented a quantitative overlay to our portfolio to help analyze whether an investment is attractive on a risk-adjusted basis—whether the reward [the spread paid for the target company] compensates you for the risk you're taking. So if, for example, a company is being acquired for $20 in cash and it has traded up to $19 from $10 since the announcement, it has (at least) $9 of downside if it's terminated and a dollar to make if the deal is completed. One way to look at that is that the market is pricing in a 90 percent likelihood that the deal's going to be successfully completed."

Behren continues, "Why risk $9 for the chance to make $1? That's where our overlay comes in, calculating the market-implied odds that the deal will be completed. If our forecasted odds are 95 percent, then the stock may be an attractive buy. Additionally, our model compares the anticipated profit of each deal to the potential downside in a way that calculates the return per unit of risk, or standard deviation. If we invest in a diversified portfolio of mispriced investments like that, we can optimize the risk-adjusted returns of the portfolio. The quantitative overlay also helps us compare deals with different characteristics—we may be looking at a drug deal with a three-month tender timeframe and comparing it to a public utilities deal that may take two years to close, and to a hotel deal that has nine months to close. They all may have different upsides and downsides—the quantitative methodology helps us decide which deals to put our money in."

"It's not," Shannon quickly chimes in, "that we have a black box. What we do have is almost like a modified Sharpe ratio or Sortino ratio, applied to assessing relative deal risks, instead of to portfolio risks in a fund. Right now [June 2016], for instance, we're tracking two hundred deals around the world, all with different upsides and downsides and probabilities of success. This tool helps us concentrate our time and effort on the deals that offer the best returns for given levels of risk. Using our quantitative overlay is one thing that probably sets us apart from other arbs."

Generational Transition

Shannon's 2006 return to Westchester Capital marked the beginning of its generational transition. Bonnie Smith soon moved out of portfolio management to concentrate full-time on running the investment companies as chief operating officer. Fred Green, meanwhile, worked out a plan to transfer control of the firm to the two younger portfolio managers over the course of the following four years. "Then Fred moved out to Arizona," remarks Behren, to focus on his already-in-progress second career—as an award-winning producer of films including PBS's *Guns & Mothers* and *A Prairie Home Companion*. "It was a very smooth transition," Behren observes, "the investors already knew Mike and me; we actually gained assets as the handoff played out."

Since taking the reins, Behren and Shannon have made sure to follow the lessons Green inculcated in them. Especially staying on the conservative side of the risk-arbitrage spectrum. Westchester doesn't speculate on prospective targets or on rumors. It doesn't buy speculative stakes in companies in consolidating industries. It invests only after a public announcement of a merger proposal, a hostile approach, or a company putting itself on the block. "If a company announces it has retained bankers, we may consider it," concedes Behren, "but the important thing for us is to squeeze out any directional exposure. Our goal in managing the merger-arbitrage portfolio is to create a market-neutral vehicle to provide absolute returns for our investors."

He goes on, "in a stock-for-stock deal, this means, first, that you hedge out the directional exposure by selling short the shares of the acquiring company that you're going to get. In a cash deal, you don't need to do that because you're going to get the same value as consideration regardless of whether the acquirer's stock goes up or down in price. In an international deal, we'll also hedge out the currency exposure. The second step? Carefully reading the merger agreement for every deal we invest in—it spells out the rights and obligations of the parties. We also review the antitrust implications of the deal; the Hart-Scott-Rodino application if government approval is required. We have specialized outside counsel for all of that. In drug deals, we use FDA counsel. There's been a lot of activity in the communications sector, so we have FCC counsel, too. For public utilities deals, we retain the appropriate state public utilities commission counsel. Then, since we invest internationally, we have EU counsel, Australian Competition Commission counsel, even Ministry of Competition counsel in China."

"Something else very unusual, if not entirely unique, about our research," breaks in Shannon, "is that we actually go visit companies. They're like, 'Why are you here? Why aren't you just asking questions on the conference call?' But risk arbitrage is like the insurance business. We're taking on the risk that the deal won't close. If you're writing a life insurance policy on someone, wouldn't you want to take a look, make sure they're healthy?" Though he's quick to disclaim using anything with a whiff of inside information, Shannon says visits to companies occasionally produce insight or add depth and subtext to Westchester Capital's understanding of how committed the parties are to a transaction. "If there's a glitch between the announcement and the closing, we want to know, how committed is the buyer? Typically, companies are responsive to our calls because our size means we tend to be a top-ten holder of their stock by that point—and we're friendly because we want the deal to close."

Avoiding Nasty Surprises

Behren swiftly amplifies, "There are a lot of larger multistrategy firms and a lot of larger global macro firms. A ton of companies manage more capital than us. But there aren't many that have as much dedicated merger-arb assets as we do—probably fewer than you could count on one hand. Most are in the $50-to-$150 million range." Adds Shannon, "Everything is done with the goal of determining the ultimate likelihood of the deal closing successfully. To state the obvious, we want to avoid deals that are going to break, sending the target stock into a steep dive. Another stumbling block we run into from time to time is the emergence of cultural issues between the companies. They always get pooh-poohed at first, 'We get along great!' But then the agreement slowly starts to break down." The proposed merger of advertising giants Publicis Groupe and Omnicom Group is exhibit A. Unveiled with great fanfare in July 2013, it was called off the following May after headline-making clashes of culture, tax issues, legal questions and disagreements over who would run what—all of which emerged piecemeal. Says Shannon, "We were skeptical about the strategic rationale from the onset and figured that at some point they'd realize, 'You have Coke and we have Pepsi.' Neither could afford to lose such a big client. We just didn't think it would work. The risk/reward profile in risk arb is always asymmetric, and the wide spread between the post-announcement market price and deal price in that case rightfully reflected the low odds of the deal succeeding."

But most announced deals, Behren notes, have a fairly high likelihood of being completed. "They've retained lawyers, hired bankers and accountants, done all the work—and they tend to be strategic in nature." Which usually leads to fairly tight spreads. So Behren and Shannon hunt for inefficiently priced transactions—ones "that reflect a lower likelihood of successful completion than we believe is correct. If a deal is trading at, for example, a 75 percent market implied likelihood of success, but we figure the deal has a 90 percent to 95 percent chance of closing, it's an attractive opportunity for us."

Shannon clarifies, "We look at the value and risk of each trade against the interest rate environment. With rates as low as they are, it would be a bummer to have a 100-basis-point loss on a deal. So, knowing where the downside is on trades, we manage our position sizes accordingly. We keep a close watch on value at risk."

But the most critical part of their process, stresses Behren, is the deep, fundamental, qualitative research that Westchester Capital is known for. They talk to customers, clients, and, as noted, the companies themselves to figure out the strategic rationale for a deal—if there is one. "You can see LBO deals where the buyer may be very well-financed," warns Behren. "But if there's no strategic rationale, it doesn't take much—a bad quarter, say—to make the buyer considerably less motivated to close the deal. Whereas, in a strategic deal, with fantastic product overlap and a good bit of sales force overlap, there are tons of synergies to be realized—and the strategic acquirer is likely to take a much longer-term view of the deal than a private equity buyer."

Shannon again jumps in with a qualifier. "But if the strategic rationale is too strong, our next thought is that the deal might be vulnerable on antitrust grounds. Other times, the companies may seem enthusiastic and there are no antitrust issues—but look as we might, we can't figure out why they're doing the deal. It makes no sense." The ultimate reason Westchester Capital is religious about doing its fundamental and quantitative research, sums up Behren, "is to come to our own conclusion about the deal's likelihood of success."

A Fund for All Seasons

He adds, "We're up to 400,000 or so investors in the mutual fund because we've stuck to our knitting. We don't promise people we're going to be up 30 percent. We're about preserving capital while providing attractive risk-adjusted returns in almost any market environment—with the emphasis on risk-adjusted." Amplifies Shannon, "Our investment rationale is to provide a diversification tool with a stable rate of return in all market environments—and to preserve capital in market drawdowns. So, yes, we will 'underperform' in a bull market, but during a bear market people will be glad to be invested with us."

Behren agrees, "Exactly. As Fred used to say, 'Equity-like returns with bond-like risk.' So despite our notional returns going down, along with interest rates, to record low levels, the strategy and our vehicle remain attractive because we can generate a pick-up over whatever prevailing interest rates are. The value proposition for a vehicle like ours is that something with an equivalent standard deviation, which historically would be a short- to medium-term bond fund, will give you all of fifty basis points or so today."

Now Shannon breaks in, "Don't forget, the Merger Fund has had only two down years in its existence. Since Roy and I took over, we've had one down year. It was frustrating for a while, before the financial crisis, to be out talking to potential clients and be told there was another guy with returns just as stable but who did 200 to 300 basis points a year better than us with less standard deviation. It didn't seem possible. I remember being very bummed out walking out of an investor meeting after hearing that. How could we possibly raise money against performance like that? Of course, about three years later it came out that the investor had funneled all that money to Madoff, and he'd been cooking the books. I still can't believe it."

While Behren and Shannon continue to embrace Green and Smith's conservative arbitrage principles, they nonetheless are flexible in adapting them to the ever-fluid investment environment. Westchester Capital's investment in Time Warner Cable shares during that company's long-running takeover battle is a prime example. In capsule summary, Charter Communications, backed by billionaire John C. Malone, was widely rumored as early as the first half of 2013 to have designs on TWC. But Charter's initial publicly announced offer for the cable operator didn't emerge until January 2014 and—at $37.8 billion, or $132.50 a share—it got an immediate thumbs-down from TWC. Its chief executive called the bid a "nonstarter," adding that TWC had already told Charter it would take a bid of at least $47.5 billion, or $160 a share, to win its affections amid mounting interest in consolidating the cable industry. Unfazed, Charter responded by nominating a full slate of directors to TWC's board and began executing other pressure maneuvers. But the very next month, Comcast stepped in and seemingly outflanked Charter with a bid that practically matched TWC's asking price—more than $45 billion. With that, Westchester Capital, along with many other risk-arb groups, quickly amassed positions in TWC shares—even though the Comcast-TWC deal faced numerous public relations and regulatory hurdles. Including, significantly, the continuing proxy battle in which Charter was noisily urging TWC shareholders to scotch the Comcast deal.

"It's very rare," explains Shannon, "that we will play in a deal we think has just a 75 percent chance of happening. We're usually in the 85, 90, 95 percent confidence range. But we didn't see a lot of downside in the TWC trade. We thought, 'If this deal doesn't happen, we know Charter is there. They keep saying they want to buy it, every day.' It was almost like they were telling the regulators, 'Block it. We're here. We're a better buyer, so why let Comcast get it?'" Then again, Shannon adds, Westchester Capital also knew "that Comcast had as many friends in D.C. as anybody," so there "was a chance Comcast would get this deal through and we'd make money."

The jockeying for position, public hearings, and closed-door sessions continued for over a year. Finally, in April of 2015, faced with strong signals that both the Justice Department and the FCC were about to block its merger, Comcast withdrew its bid. Charter then added to the melodrama and high anxiety in investment circles by waiting about month as smaller deals percolated through the cable space before making arbs' dreams come true with an offer worth $55 billion for TWC—a merger, when completed, that created a significantly stronger competitor to Comcast. Hedging, says Shannon, kept Westchester Capital from losing money on its TWC stake in the Comcast fiasco. And its thorough analysis—and patience—were finally rewarded when Charter won all the necessarily regulatory approvals and closed its TWC acquisition.

Expect the Unexpected

The most painful deal for risk arbs that Shannon and Behren recall involved the failed 1998 merger of two telecommunications equipment suppliers, Ciena Corp. and Tellabs Inc.—an event also inextricably linked in their memories to that fall's subsequent failure of hedge fund Long-Term Capital Management, which spawned a financial crisis that brought the global financial system to its knees. Says Shannon, "The Ciena-Tellabs story itself is extraordinary because the deal seemed like such a good fit and came so close to closing. Tellabs was literally in the midst of its annual meeting, about to bang the gavel down on the shareholder vote approving the merger, when someone came up and whispered in its CEO's ear. Ciena had just lost its most important client relationship—with AT&T—which had been expected to chip in one-third of its revenue. Just like that, the deal was off. It was unbelievable. It stunk for us and all the arbs who lost a lot of money, as Ciena shares immediately collapsed. At least we were pretty diversified, with seventy or so positions, so it was only 2 percent or 3 percent of our portfolio."

But the story didn't end there, Shannon adds. "Unbeknownst to us, a large arbitrage hedge fund competitor [Long Term Capital] at that point had a book of ten equity risk-arb positions, all levered ten to fifteen times, and one of them happened to be Ciena/Tellabs." It didn't take long for signs of distressed selling to start showing up in the market for arb stocks. "The ensuing financial crisis made life especially miserable for virtually all arbs," says Shannon—and ordinary investors, as well. "The troubled firm's equity arbitrage book was blowing out in the fall of 1998, at the same time the Russian debt crisis was starting to play havoc with convergence trades. As the hedge fund started dumping its equity arb positions, all of our risk-arb spreads blew out by huge amounts." While that created opportunities to establish new positions at fat spreads, most investors were caught by surprise. Shannon shakes his head. "We could guess who was doing the selling and why it was happening. But we were getting our butts kicked, along with everyone else."

Genius, Lacking in Common Sense

That a highly-leveraged risk portfolio would blow up shouldn't have come as a surprise, adds Shannon, "if you knew the history of arbitrage." He explains, "I remember the risk-arb prop desk at JPMorgan being opened and closed every three or four years. It was this stable, low-rate-of-return-type strategy—until there'd be a broken deal and the head of trading would shut it down. The problem was, they weren't doing the numbers on the risk and—because the bank had a 5 percent capital ratio—they'd be levered twenty-to-one on that arb book." The 1998 crisis was likewise made worse, notes Shannon, because the hedge fund at the center of the crisis decided they could "lever the crap out" of a few concentrated positions since their strategy had a low standard deviation. "What was missing was common sense. If you only sell ten life insurance policies and one guy dies, it wipes out all the premium. You can't do it, you have to be more diversified."

Behren interjects, "Inevitably, there will be broken deals. There may be a fraud at a company, there may be a natural disaster—anything can happen. We've found that despite our best efforts, probably 2 percent of the deals we invest in won't be successfully completed. We deal with that by limiting our position sizes and properly diversifying. What's more, we hold to a general philosophy that making valuation bets on companies is not our business. So, if a deal breaks, we work our way out of related positions—ideally, methodically and carefully." He explains, "When a deal is first terminated, the stock tends to overshoot to the downside. Some investors have mandates that force them to sell immediately. We've often found it valuable to work our way out of positions slowly. We hedge it out first and then exit, sometimes selling call options to realize a little extra value as we do."

Behren stresses, "We're not a trading shop. We tend to hold positions unless there is a significant change in the probability of the deal closing. We don't trade around positions, trying to scalp nickels and dimes. Nor will we play what we call 'last mile trades,' which involve taking positions in deals that are almost certain to happen—ones with four or five days to closing that you can maybe make a nickel in. To us, the asymmetric optics of buying a position to make a nickel, when—God forbid—something could go wrong and you'd lose $8, just can't be explained to a public investor base." The Lockheed Martin/Northrop Grumman deal that fell apart in early 1998 was a case in point, Shannon recalls. "The deal seemingly had gotten DOJ approval and was about a day away from closing when the Pentagon blocked it—that sticks in your head. It goes to show that there's risk in even 'sure things.'"

The Value of Experience

"What we like to tell people," adds Behren, "is that we have been through many market cycles and merger-arb cycles and have learned how to manage through downturns in both. You have to be able to select attractive deals that don't expose you to too much incremental risk, especially during a slow patch in M&A—when you can't have eighty deals in your portfolio—when you can find barely fifty deals you like. Because we don't have an obligation to be 100 percent invested, we won't invest in deals that don't make sense for us. We'd rather be in cash than in a deal that's not attractive on a risk-adjusted basis." Still, notes Shannon, "2002–2003, when the brakes were slammed on M&A activity by a cavalcade of high-profile corporate frauds—Tyco and Enron, Worldcom, and Adelphia Communications—was the only time we raised cash in the portfolio to 30 percent. At that point, we also soft closed the Merger Fund."

Despite current fashion, Behren and Shannon are both emphatic that neither passive indexing nor ETF vehicles are suitable in the merger-arb space. Says Shannon, "I don't know how you do a non-actively managed arb fund. I don't see how you can market cap-weight the positions." Says Behren, "They can't replicate the research-intensive process of our actively managed portfolio. If you're investing in a random selection of deals, you'll end up in some with obvious antitrust problems. An algorithm is not going to know if a deal's financing is committed, or how to evaluate contingencies in the merger agreement." Behren continues, his voice rising, "You have to weight a risk-arbitrage portfolio by the deals you like the most or by the ones with the best risk-adjusted profiles. Statistics say around 91 percent of publicly-announced deals are successfully completed. So a monkey throwing darts is going to be right nine out of ten times—and so will a risk-arb ETF. But that one other time out of the ten, they are going to lose *a lot* relative to what they've invested—and overall, they won't be profitable."

In fact, insists Behren, "the way to tell whether a risk-arb portfolio manager has improved upon the market's return or added alpha is if he has a better track record of picking successful deals than a random selection of merger-arbitrage transactions. Our track record says 98 percent of the deals we invest in are completed because of our research-intensive process. Because we risk-adjust everything, because we have platoons of lawyers advising us, etc., we add alpha. That's why an actively managed fund is better than an index fund in merger arbitrage—unless you're bad at merger arb and have a worse track record than the monkeys with darts."

CHAPTER ELEVEN

Karen Finerman

I remember reading this front-page article in the *Los Angeles Times Magazine* about "Ivan Bow-eh-ski"—that was how I thought you pronounced his name because I'd never heard anyone speak it. This was before the whole insider trading thing—and I thought, "Wow, that sounds really cool. Ivan Boesky makes all this money and it seems exciting and that's what I want to do."

EVEN AT FIFTEEN, Karen Finerman clearly was not your stereotypical Beverly Hills schoolgirl. Something of a tennis prodigy,
she had been allowed to take middle school physical education in
the boys' class. But it is her discovery of that glossy Boesky puff
piece, and with it, the high-stakes world of Wall Street risk arbitrage,
that Finerman remembers as the seminal event in her young life.
As she wrote in her 2013 book, *Finerman's Rules: Secrets I'd Only
Tell My Daughters About Business and Life* (Business Plus/Hachette).
"I wanted to be in the action, and I wanted to be the one making lots
of money. I loved the image of creating my own destiny and being in
control of my world. This wasn't some fantasy future in the way lots
of girls announce that they want to be a fashion designer or a singer.
I had found my calling. This was going to happen. I was destined for
Wall Street."

Remarkably, she got there, step-by-step, beginning by insisting to
her parents that she'd apply for admission *only* to the University of
Pennsylvania's Wharton School. She'd been told it was the fastest track
to the Street—and she ultimately succeeded far beyond even her wildest
teenage dreams. Today, Finerman, invariably smartly-dressed—even in
jeans—is a viewer favorite on CNBC's nightly *Fast Money* program.
An attractive, blue-eyed blonde nicknamed the "the chairwoman," she
stands out on the program because of her gender, but even more for
her perspective as a fundamental value-oriented investor—the perfect
articulate foil for the roster of testosterone-fueled short-term traders
filling out the regular panel.

Finerman has no shortage of the Street cred she needs to command the respect of her fellow panelists, and she effortlessly matches
or sets the pace of their market repartee. While still in her late twen-
ties, in 1992, Finerman joined with lifelong friend Jeffrey Schwarz to
found Metropolitan Capital Advisors LP, a Manhattan-based hedge
fund advisor that the pair not once, but twice built up to roughly a
half-billion dollars under management. They rebounded from a near-
death business experience in 1998 and then, at the end of 2015, she
and Schwarz decided that the glory days of the hedge fund business
were over. He retired. Finerman kept one of their earliest investors, a
large foundation, and is running the fund with that investor and her
family's money.

One of five children of a prominent Beverly Hills orthopedic sur-
geon and a homemaker, Finerman credits her mother with sparking in

Karen Finerman on the set of CNBC's Fast Money. Wikimedia Commons.

all of her children a relentless drive to succeed. A favorite line is that she was "raised a Calvinist" because her mother preached incessantly to her three daughters "that she dressed us exclusively in Calvin Klein fashions so that we'd be driven to figure out how to continue affording them once we'd graduated from college and were on our own." Indeed, Finerman remembers her mother always pushing her children to strive for more, whether in academics, sports, or life. Finerman also recalls recognizing at a tender age that the parent who made all the money held all the power in their household—and in her parents' relationship. It was that insight, she says, that bolstered her resolve to become financially independent by following what she saw of Ivan Boesky's path to riches in Wall Street.

Fresh out of Wharton, Finerman used a family connection to land her first job in finance. Jeffrey Schwarz and Finerman's older sister, Wendy (the Hollywood producer of *Forrest Gump* and a raft of other hits), had become close friends while students at Wharton. Karen Finerman had met Schwarz while she was still in high school, when the two families vacationed near each other in Boca Raton, Florida. "As a sixteen-year-old tomboy, I would play football on the beach with Jeffrey and ask him about his work as a risk arbitrageur. He was the only real-life one I knew."

It was Finerman's good fortune that Schwarz had quickly turned heads as a rising star at Kellner DiLeo amid the super-heated takeover boom of the 1980s. By 1987, just as she was coming out of Wharton, the Belzberg Brothers, billionaire Canadian-developers-turned-corporate-raiders, staked Schwarz to $30 million to run a new risk-arb hedge fund for them. It was a sizeable sum for a hedge fund startup in those days, but the Belzbergs were well known for their aggressive shareholder activism. Just the prior Christmas week, they'd stunned not a few Wall Street bankers with a brazen attempt to break up GTE Corp. The telecom company's indignant chairman complained that Samuel Belzberg's letter, proposing that GTE sell two Canadian units to the family and spin off its Sprint mobile unit had been delivered to his office on December 23—the day *after* the news appeared in the *New York Times*. His formal response was withering: "We do not believe that it is generally in the best interest of GTE shareholders for this corporation to treat its businesses like commodities that are always for sale"—a flat rejection backed up by overwhelming shareholder votes in favor of a variety of takeover defenses at a special meeting quickly held on Christmas Eve.

Working Like Crazy

Schwarz hired Finerman into his nascent fund, she knew, not for whatever financial acumen she'd picked up in her favorite Wharton class, "Options and Speculative Markets." But "because he needed someone to dive in and work like crazy to get the fund up and running." Finerman gladly complied, soaking up all she could about the ins and outs of risk arbitrage along the way. As she reflects now, she was lucky to find in Schwarz "a long-time partner who really wanted to see women succeed. He taught me the ropes."

Finerman quickly started working as a trader, as well as gofer, executing Schwarz's arbitrage trades. Within eighteen months, Finerman had figured out that she wanted to switch to the research side of the business—analyzing deals, their inherent risks, and the probabilities of their completion—because she saw research adding far more value to the firm's business than trading. It had dawned on her that she would have to be able to figure out what companies are worth—and why—to succeed as an arbitrageur.

Characteristically, Finerman wasted little time stewing over that insight or feeling hemmed in by her job description. She went to Schwarz, told him she wanted to switch into research, and boldly asked him *not* to make a planned new hire in research—to use her instead. Then, to demonstrate that she could shoulder research responsibilities, within a few weeks Finerman made an emphatic stock recommendation—"pounding the table" to buy iconic retailer Federated Department Stores. It had just received a $47-a-share takeover bid from Canadian developer Robert Campeau's Allied Stores. She didn't yet have the analytic skills to model the deal, Finerman admits. But her gut instinct (she now declares following it a tenet of her investing philosophy) was that "trophy properties *always* get sold, in *any* market. It doesn't matter what the state of the world is or the financial markets. When a unique financial asset is for sale, egos take over. Someone will *always* step up to buy it and pay either a full price or a ridiculous price. It will be sold." Which is precisely what happened with Federated, the owner of fashionista redoubts the likes of Jordan Marsh, Burdines, Marshall Field's, and Bloomingdale's. A bidding war ensued and Campeau ended up paying an extraordinary $6.6 billion, or $73.50 a share, to keep Macy's from buying Federated—in a deal so overleveraged that he was forced to seek bankruptcy protection within a year. But not before, to be sure, the Belzbergs' risk-arb fund pocketed millions in profits on the deal, Finerman relates.

Not all of Finerman's early positions worked out as well. She recounts in gruesome detail in her book her discovery—during the market-cratering 1989 collapse of UAL's proposed LBO—of the downside of taking asymmetric risks. Especially when, as in that case, the asymmetric risk is amplified using options. The proposed $7.65 billion LBO of the airline by a labor-management group was the capstone of the decade's subprime debt-fueled merger mania—and news that the buyout group's financing fell through hit the stock market squarely in the solar plexus on Friday, Oct. 13, 1989. The DJIA skidded nearly 7 percent—much of it in the last hour of trading—resurrecting for many traders the ghosts of the 1987 market crash.

Says Finerman bluntly, "I totally blew it." She explains that a bidding war had driven UAL shares from the mid $150s that August to roughly $280 in October, where they stalled as shareholders waited for final financing and regulatory issues to be hashed out. Metropolitan stood to make $20 a share on its arb spread, or about $400,000, if the $300-a-share deal closed. "Where I went wrong was that there was a 1-by-2 put spread available, which looked very cheap. I figured there was maybe a 15 percent chance that the stock could drop to $260 a share if there was a snag in closing the deal. I calculated that by purchasing the option spread for $2.625 a share, we would make $20 a share if the deal were delayed. If the deal went through on time, we'd be out what the spread cost us, but we'd still make $20 in the stock." The only thing she didn't consider was the possibility of the deal falling apart entirely. "That 'brilliant' option trade I had devised ended up being to pay $2.65 *to put it on, to later pay $80 to take it off*, which was a disaster of gigantic proportions. I had overlooked the fact that a 1-by-2 put spread could move almost infinitely against us, until UAL hit zero—which it came awfully close to doing."

That sobering episode did not forever sour Finerman on employing options strategies to hedge arbitrage positions. "I remember talking with a well-known arb—I think it was during the NCR and AT&T merger negotiations in 1991. He said something like, 'Why would you buy puts on NCR if you think the deal will go through?' I replied, 'Well, if the puts change the risk/reward from risking 11 to make 3, to risking 3 to make 2, why wouldn't you do it? The deal risk stays the same, but your odds are much more favorable." Finerman concedes, "But that was when the options markets were still pretty new, and options are much more efficiently priced now. In today's options markets, I'm sad to say, I often find that options are appropriately priced. Using them does still allow you to know exactly what you have at risk. It's just that when options were inefficient, they were such a better way to add alpha."

Faking It

It did, however, hasten the rude interruption of what had been Finerman's stratospheric early career trajectory. Economic woes mounted after the mini-crash, as other overly-leveraged takeover artists were forced to join Campeau in filing for bankruptcy—ushering in 1990's steep recession. The Belzbergs weren't forced into bankruptcy, but they did lose control of one of their holdings, a West Coast thrift, in the ensuing savings and loan (S&L) crisis—and closed down Schwarz's risk-arb fund. Finerman was out of a job. Determined to talk her way into another buy-side research perch, despite her short track record in arbitrage, Finerman set about faking her way into as many interviews as she could wrangle. Finally, at Donaldson, Lufkin & Jenrette she met the firm's new head of risk arbitrage, Chris Flynn, who had just been hired away from industry legend Guy Wyser-Pratte's firm. Finerman had loved reading Wyser-Pratte's nuts and bolts treatise, *Risk Arbitrage*, and prepped for her interview by studying every pending deal in the market. She won the job—and a new mentor, who "spoon-fed" her the art of arb research, as *he* wanted it done—"to her supreme good fortune."

The 1990–1992 recession, along with the collapse of the subprime debt boom, was not exactly conducive to fostering lots of the corporate takeovers that risk arbitrageurs thrive on, however. So while Finerman sharpened her research skills at DLJ, she was also watching arb desk after arb desk being disbanded. By the middle of 1992, Finerman says, it had become apparent to her that risk-arb's glory days wouldn't be returning for some time, if ever. But she also saw some other Wall Street specialties—like restructuring the corporate remains of the prior decade's M&A excesses—starting to pick up. She began searching for a fresh opportunity to use her newly acquired skills in valuing companies to generate profits for clients—and herself.

Fortune smiled again. Her old boss and friend, Jeffrey Schwarz, came to Finerman with what even she characterizes as a "pretty outlandish" idea. He wanted to start a new hedge fund and offered to make her a junior partner, she says, because she had done quite a bit of work on the beaten-down banks he wanted to focus on. Their shares battered by the S&L crisis, the good ones (without too many problem loans) at that juncture were classic value opportunities—and Finerman knew how to find the truffles. Presented with that opportunity, avers Finerman, it wasn't hard to leave her job at a brand-name firm for the risk and uncertainty of a hedge fund startup—despite a gigantic pay cut. "I had no mortgage, no kids, no debt, and no other prospects."

Besides, she had been priming herself since high school for just such a calculated bet—one, Finerman quickly concedes, that worked out far, far better than she ever imagined, as Metropolitan Capital grew and prospered. It was also a bet she says she never regretted—even in 1998 when they suffered that "near-death experience" brought on by Russia's debt default. In retrospect, admits Finerman, Metropolitan

Capital's progress up until that point had been so relentless that its partners' hubris had grown with its asset base. But their AUM was swollen with foreign and other hot money with no patience for sticking around when its small-cap value stocks were battered unmercifully in the market retreat. Nor did their hedges work. It was an overwhelmingly miserable experience. But, says Finerman, "I had no better teacher than 1998."

Survival Lessons

Surveying the wreckage—and lessons learned—Schwarz and Finerman rejected throwing in the towel. Some clients, including a very large institution, stuck with them—and it ultimately took the pair just six months to make back the losses of those clients in 1999's much friendlier investment climate. Even though, unable to find value in the era's bubbly internet stocks, the pair bucked fashion and avoided them. As a result, it wasn't until the internet bubble popped in late 2000 that they could again really demonstrate their value investing mettle. Metropolitan Capital returned better than 26 percent in 2000, while the S&P dropped more than 9 percent. Clients and prospective clients took notice. It was another four years before the firm bested its pre-1998 peak in asset size, but Schwarz and Finerman achieved Wall Street redemption and more.

Yet this time, they kept their hubris under control, as reflected in their 2015 decision to wind down Metropolitan Capital, citing a paucity of value opportunities. Explains Finerman, "spreads are tight, there are a lot of hedge funds crowding the market, and it's been very difficult for several years. Especially in the zero-interest-rate environment, the 2 and 20 thing hasn't been working because the absolute return numbers are so low. Even if a spread is two times or three times Treasuries, it's still not enough to compensate for the risks. Stuff happens." Finerman points to the Treasury's April 2016 surprise decision to put the kibosh on pending tax inversion merger deals as illustrative of recent risks. The rule change scuttled a proposed $150 billion combination of Pfizer and Dublin-based Allergan, leaving many risk arbs nursing gaping losses. The move "wasn't even completely out of left field," notes Finerman. "It had been floated. It was no secret that the government didn't like inversions. But everybody thought, 'the government is pissed, but what are they going to do about it? What *can* they really do about it?' Well, they found out."

When a deal breaks suddenly, Finerman says she's learned from hard experience that the best thing for her to do is sell. "I'm out. I'm just out." She continues, "You can revisit the position, even that same day or shortly thereafter. But sell first. There's an objectivity that is lost when you're long and hoping something good is going to somehow happen. Hoping is a terrible strategy. I try to be very disciplined about it—as in, 'I'm here for an event. It didn't happen. We're out.' That is a pretty firm rule for me, and it's painful, but how many times do you see that your first sale was your best sale? My biggest losses always started out as smaller losses."

Her years in arbitrage, says Finerman, taught her a fine appreciation "for the art of the deal" as well as the importance of thinking about risk, assessing risk, and trying to value the unknown. "One of my biggest mistakes in United Airlines was not assigning any probability to the deal breaking, which was absurdly stupid." Hostile deals, Finerman continues, always held special fascination for her. Not just because of the potential for competing bids driving up prices but because she liked analyzing how they might evolve. "They made me think about the notion of 'what's going to happen after that?' Not just what would happen next—looking at the situation as a three-dimensional puzzle instead of a game of checkers. Just the discipline of asking yourself, 'if that happens, then what?' can make you look smart, like you see several steps ahead."

Another attraction of hostile deals for her, Finerman admits, is that she's "always intrigued by egos and by how what a company says—and what it means—can vary. There can be subtleties of language employed in a rejection of a bear hug, say, that can make all of the difference." In analyzing proposed deals, Finerman stresses, she focuses on their strategic rationales, if any. "Even in 2007–2009, when all the spreads blew out, virtually all the strategic deals ultimately closed and people made a lot of money." Also "really important," she says, "are the quality of the assets and the quality of the buyer. And the terms of the merger agreement." Deals with regulatory hurdles, Finerman adds, "I just don't like. And I hate a merger agreement with a market escape clause—I hate it." She continues, "I also care who the lawyers and bankers are. I care if it's the A-team, because the A-teams get deals to the finish line. That's why, when you get to smaller deals, the spreads should be wider because the risks are greater. You're not dealing with the A-team and smaller businesses are inherently more risky. Then, if you get any leverage involved, they are riskier still."

Probing Motivations

Deal dynamics, to Finerman, "are endlessly fascinating. Why do they do these deals? What makes a company attractive?" Very often, she says, "what makes a target attractive is just growth-for-growth's sake." But those deals can prove more tenuous than strategic deals, especially if the going gets rough. She reflects, "I used to be so dismissive of companies that would reject bids, saying, 'We have a plan to do it on our own.' But a lot of times they *were* much better off on their own, over the long term. A 20 percent bump in the price of stock—wow, that's great if you're an arb—and get that over about two months. That's fantastic. But those companies were looking out *years*. Eventually, it made me wonder, 'What did they see?'"

Finerman cites Iowa-based Casey's General Stores as a case in point. "It's a Midwestern chain of gas stations and mini-marts. Back in 2010, they got a bid from a Canadian rival, Alimentation Couche-Tard, that started around $41. It went to $43, then to $45. The stock had been trading around $33 before the bid. But Casey's kept insisting, 'No, no, no, no!' And their shareholders backed them up. So fast-forward a few years. The stock has gone as high as $134. Boy, are its shareholders much better off than they would have been in a Casey's/Couche-Tard deal. That was a big revelation."

Asked why she thinks very few women can be found running arb portfolios or hedge funds—and why there are only somewhat more, here and there, on trading desks—Finerman exclaims, "It's counterintuitive, right? You think of trading as so much more brutish or testosteroney, and of research as more cerebral and refined, yet you *do* find more women in trading—though not a lot." She continues, "I'm still surprised that there aren't more women in the hedge fund business. I asked around about it back while I was writing my book. One of the things I heard, which really rang true, came from a male friend and I put it in my book. I asked him why he had no women analysts on his team. He said, 'Here's the thing. When a guy comes in to pitch me an idea, he pounds the table about how much money I can make. When a woman comes in, she tells me about all the things that could go wrong. I've got this limited pool of capital. I'm a sucker for the upside every time. What do I need the women for if I'm not going to listen to them?'"

"He was very candid," observes Finerman, "and I appreciated it. Then it occurred to me, 'Women *do* tend to present that way.'" Finerman believes it's a risk-minimization tactic, used not just to minimize the risk in the position but their risk in promoting it. To give them an out. "They can say, 'All right. If I told him everything that could go wrong and he bought it anyway, that's on him.' But to advance, *you need it to be on you*. Too many women are not comfortable accepting that responsibility. They prefer consensus decision-making and they don't like being seen as decisive or bullying or aggressive." That said, Finerman continues, "I think there is some meritocracy to this business, in the sense that if you're positively affecting the bottom line, you'll get rewarded—getting to the point where you can experience that is the trick."

Finerman concedes that's she's always found losing other people's money "a tremendous burden. Even if they're tremendously wealthy, it's still a burden." But, she continues, "it's something you just have to live with in this business. Arbitrage taught me that you have to make *lots* of decisions. Some are going to turn out your way, some not. So it's really about being comfortable with your process for making decisions. If it's a case of, 'look, I made a decision at the time, it was reasonable. But it didn't work out.' That, I can live with. And sometimes, it goes the other way. You make a poor decision and get lucky. That happens—less frequently—but it *does* happen." Finerman doesn't rely on luck, however. She's discovered that "luck" favors the well-prepared.

CHAPTER TWELVE

John Bader

What I came to learn is that you can generate alpha not just by selecting the right instruments or allocating to strategies at the right times but also by evolving—which was a very dirty word in the late 1980s, 1990s. Everyone talked about "style drift" and how you shouldn't do it. But I feel if you don't evolve, you die. Joe Gruss, who came to this country in 1939, opened a travel agency, and ultimately turned his nest egg into hundreds of millions, always used to say, "The way you get really rich in this country is you live a really long time and don't lose money—keep it compounding." Almost any year I've been in the business, I'm sure other people have produced much better returns than we have but we've managed to survive by avoiding losing significant amounts of money in any given year, by focusing on the right strategies at the right times and by evolving our strategy mix.

––––––––––––

WHEN JOHN BADER says "we" he is referring to Halcyon Capital Management LP, the global investment solutions provider founded by legendary investor Alan B. Slifka in 1981. Now Halcyon counts around $10 billion in institutional assets under management—in hedge funds, in managed accounts, in CLOs, in bank loans, in opportunistic credit strategies, and in bespoke structures, including litigation investing—all dictated by the idiosyncratic as well as collective needs and preferences of its clients. The Madison Avenue-based firm, with offices in London and Luxembourg, is today owned by its twelve active partners, who average sixteen years with Halcyon. It is run by Bader, fifty-five, who serves as chairman and chief executive, prefers kiteboarding to golf, and has made evolving "to stay ahead of the curve" a central tenet of Halcyon's business plan.

"When I got into the merger-arbitrage business—and certainly people were there before me—there weren't more than maybe twenty proprietary trading desks and boutiques around Wall Street that were doing it. It was a relatively uncrowded business," Bader recalls. "Likewise, when I got into the corporate distressed business, it was the same ten or fifteen bankers and lawyers who were doing everything, and off the top of my head I knew all of the big distressed investors' office numbers, weekend numbers, spouse's names. Then suddenly, in both cases, there were legions of nameless investors doing these things. The question clearly was, how do you stay ahead of the curve?" He continues, "I realized that you want to be doing things that other people *aren't* doing to stay ahead—and that there was big money to be made while the market was inefficient. That's why I moved into the stressed/distressed asset-backed business before many people were engaged in that strategy. So what we've done right is not be wedded to any strategy. We try to focus on the right strategies at the right times and to bring in the best people to help us and to educate us about evolving new strategies."

Bader joined Halcyon as a portfolio manager in 1990 after three years in risk-arbitrage research with Gruss & Co. and a brief baptism-by-fire introduction to Wall Street and merger arb as the junior-most analyst toiling in Ivan Boesky's IFB Managing Partnership in 1985 and 1986—until it was shut down by federal prosecutors in the insider trading case that ultimately undermined the Drexel-led, LBO-fueled merger mania of the 1980s. Though he had entered Harvard in the class of 1984 expecting to go on to law school, Bader became fascinated with mergers and acquisitions during an eighteen-month break from his undergraduate studies. He worked as an intern at a Toronto software company, Bader explains, and spent a lot of time reading about then-rampant takeover battles in the *Wall Street Journal*. His interest grew apace with the "surprising amounts of money" he made placing options bets on the mergers he was reading about. Bader returned to Harvard and picked up his BA in history with the class of 1985, but he had by then abandoned dreams of practicing law and made a beeline for Wall Street upon graduation.

Though the young investor quickly snagged an offer to work for Morgan Stanley, he told his father, "I really want to work for a merger-arbitrage boutique." Bader's father, an academic physician in private practice in New York City, "didn't really know much about business," he recalls. But as Bader tried to explain what he knew about merger arbitrage and who did it, he happened to mention the names of a few arb shops, including Boesky's. "My father responded, 'Oh, Ivan's a patient of mine. I'm sure he'd be happy to meet you.'"

So it was that Bader got his coveted interview—only to hear that Boesky didn't hire analysts without graduate degrees. Nonetheless, Boesky did give his doctor's kid a summer job. "I managed to push back my start date at Morgan Stanley, and that's how I got to work with Ivan Boesky," Bader recalls. "It was very peculiar. Had I ever worked for any other firm, some of the secrecy at Boesky's would have seemed very weird. But I hadn't. At the time, I was a bit miffed that I was not invited to the morning meetings and didn't get to see position sheets, so I really did not know exactly what we were investing in." Bader, who brought to Boesky's firm considerable computer skills (still a rarity on Wall Street at that juncture) spent his days doing an increasing amount of financial modeling for other analysts but still wasn't allowed to accompany them into the morning meeting. In retrospect, Bader speculates, Boesky may have been protecting him.

"I don't know, maybe Ivan already knew he was under investigation at that point."

Regardless, Bader's modeling was sufficiently appreciated for his summer gig to morph into a job offer in the fall of 1985. Says Bader, "I got a chance to learn a lot about the business, got to look at a lot of situations, and was fascinated—even if I never saw a copy of the portfolio, so I didn't know what we owned. Look, there were an awful lot of people doing very hard, honest work at IFB. I remember, for instance, doing analysis to help the director of research on a memo suggesting we get rid of a big Nabisco position." The request surprised Bader, since he "didn't have access to the position sheet. But that memo basically asked, 'Why are we holding this? The fundamentals are bad.'" Bader shakes his head and smiles just a bit sardonically, "Of course, Nabisco got taken over not long after that. I guess Ivan had information that we didn't have."

Riverboat Gambling vs. Principles

His next boss, Bader quickly makes clear, was the polar opposite of the abrasive and publicity-seeking Boesky. "I learned much, much more working for Marty Gruss, who is a really first-class investor. I was very fortunate to go next to Gruss & Co., where I could learn the business in a much more substantive way. Where Boesky liked to be massively leveraged, to bet the ranch—he was a grand riverboat gambler—Marty was, in my view, a much better risk manager, though he was not shy about taking big positions." Bader continues, "Marty operated according to a set of basic principles—a lot of which he learned from his father [Joe Gruss], who shared the office with us in those days. What Marty liked most of all was what he called a free bet. If two people wanted the same asset badly enough to start bidding, like in an auction at Sotheby's or Christie's, he thought that was a great way to make money. Marty actually hated classic merger arb, where the risk/reward is often very asymmetric, and you either make a little or lose a whole lot. He much preferred deals where he could position himself to have a free bet. Another Gruss principle was to seek quality merchandise. Joe Gruss liked to say that he wanted to shop for stocks on Fifth Avenue, not in the South Bronx. Marty listened—he'd always prefer an opportunity to make less of a profit on a real quality asset over the chance to make a larger percentage on a third-rate property."

There were still more lessons Bader learned at Gruss. "Marty was a big believer in what he called, 'not kissing all the girls.'" Bader continues to reminisce, "Marty felt—because we weren't running other people's money, just his—he could live with some volatility, to a degree that, say, a pension fund probably couldn't. He had learned a famous Andrew Carnegie aphorism from his father, 'Put all your eggs in one basket and then watch that basket very carefully.'"

Lessons Stuck

The lessons stuck with Bader as he transitioned into running institutional funds. "I'm a big believer to this day in not being an index, in being selective, and buying quality names," Bader avers. "Of course, I would not put all the eggs in one basket for an institutional account— unless that was the mandate." He also took to heart the attractiveness of strategies uncorrelated to the market, with the important corollary learned during the crash of 1987 that almost every long position *is* correlated, if the downturn is bad enough." He continues, "There are also things I learned on my own at both Boesky and Gruss that aren't so much principles that I was taught as experiences that I liked. I found, for instance, that I really liked finding a compelling investment where I was trading against most of the Street—*and they didn't understand why.*" The first time it happened, Bader recalls, he was still at Boesky's firm.

Bader was tasked with looking into options positioning in one of the two-tier LBO tender offers proliferating at the time. "All these Chicago options brokers put on forward conversions, believing they were engaging in a riskless trade. But that wasn't true in the context of a *two-tier* tender offer. Someone pointed out to me, 'Look, John Mulheren has been buying massive amounts of these outer-month puts. Why?' Well, I certainly wasn't smart or knowledgeable enough to have invented that trade. But I was smart enough—when someone pointed out what Mulheren was doing—to figure it out. The put-call parity theorem does not work in the context of a two-tier tender offer. Those backend puts were *cheap*—and had the potential to go to the moon. So we did that trade and made a lot of money on it. Other people eventually figured it out, but early on that market was very inefficient. That's how I came to realize that if you were ahead of the curve there was big money to be made."

That insight was reinforced in the aftermath of the crash of 1987, Bader says, "in one of the favorite things I ever did." United Airlines, then operating under a misbegotten and mercifully short-lived alias, Allegis, was under pressure from activist Coniston Partners to maximize shareholder value. It had decided shortly before the crash to sell its Hilton, Hertz, and Westin units, and to make an extraordinary distribution of $2 billion to shareholders.

"When the market crashed in 1987, I realized I had a bit of a personal tax problem," Bader recounts. "Marty had always encouraged me to invest along with my Gruss trades. It wasn't a conflict because we never had outside money and it was actually a very valuable lesson. He would always say, 'you're willing to buy it, but are you willing to put your money where your mouth is?' Anyway, I wasn't trading particularly aggressively at the time—the firm was actually up very nicely in 1987. But, personally, I was down a little bit—not a lot—pre-crash. The insight I had was that extraordinary distributions are deemed to be dividend income to the extent of earnings and profits, and a nontaxable distribution on the residual. I realized I might wind up with a big dividend and a capital loss, but those don't offset for tax purposes—and I had no gains to use the loss to shelter."

Problem Solved

Bader goes on, "Then I realized that if I had that problem, Coniston Partners might have a much bigger problem. They owned 11 percent-plus of the stock. I called a fellow at Coniston. He didn't confirm anything but I definitely got the feeling, as I highlighted the problem, that there was concern on the other end of the phone. I thought, 'Wow.'" Then, adds Bader, "I pointed out that Allegis could solve Coniston's (and my) problem if they got that $2 billion to shareholders via a tender offer instead of as an extraordinary dividend. So Gruss put on a big position in what might become backend puts. When Coniston got Allegis to convert the distribution to a tender offer, we profited handsomely." Opportunities like that, Bader concedes, are typically few and far between. But their potential for outsized rewards "has led me to try to do that over and over again—in merger arbitrage, in bankruptcy workouts, and now, even in litigation finance."

Bader left Gruss, which managed only Marty Gruss's money, in early 1990, he explains, in part because he realized he was unlikely to become a partner of "someone else's bank account." But Bader says he also recognized—after the failure of United Airlines's planned LBO plunged the market into the "mini-crash" of October 1989—that he "wasn't sanguine about the prospects of the merger business for the next few years. We were heading into a credit crunch and, I thought, 'boy, the distressed business is going to be where it's at.'"

Besides, Bader reflects now, "I had made several *very good* trades at the end of 1989. We had puts against our entire UAL position, at my recommendation, before the deal blew up. Then there were a couple of arbitrage deals—leveraged buyouts—that I had recommended short-ing instead of playing the spreads: Philips Industries and Birmingham Steel. I had recently met with bankers relating to a potential prin-cipal transaction in connection with another steel company and was extremely mindful of the industry's weak earnings trend. Philips was another management buyout of a company with a poor earnings trend. I felt the risk/reward in both cases was something like one up and fifteen down heading into a recession." Both shorts worked spectacu-larly. The proposed $367 million, $30 a share LBO of Birmingham Steel by Harbert Corp. fell apart in January 1990, for lack of financing, and the stock quickly plunged into the mid-teens. The proposed LBO of Philips Industries, originally priced at $25.50 a share, and then cut to $24 a share, or $672 million, likewise foundered on financing and its shares slid rapidly into the mid-teens.

Time to Part Company

As the credit crunch took hold, Bader got increasingly excited about getting into distressed debt investing. John Paulson, who was also working for Marty Gruss at the time, likewise had been trying to inter-est Gruss in distressed debt. "Though we had bought a position in Texaco's equity and converts, Marty initially did not seem interested in the distressed debt business. But then he hired a good guy, Yakil Pollack, who admittedly, unlike me, had experience at it. While I liked Yakil and knew that he knew much more about distressed investing at the time, I thought for the first time that I should leave Gruss when he was hired. I was convinced that distressed debt would be hot and arbitrage would be dead for the foreseeable future. But I have enormous affection for Marty; he had a tremendously positive influence on me as an investor. And I understood perfectly why he would want someone with distressed expertise. But it was time to go."

When Halcyon beckoned, Bader jumped, starting as a portfolio manager for its multi-strategy funds, including distressed investing. And he quickly built expertise in bankruptcy law that even his rivals describe as "encyclopedic" and "unmatched." It wasn't that he didn't have plenty of company in looking to salvage value from the era's plentiful bankruptcies, Bader quickly notes, "but the reality is that 90 percent of the distressed debt investors out there in the early 1990s were simply trying to make intelligent, value-oriented equity-type investments. That's a valid way to make money, and we certainly did that. But I was much more interested in doing things that looked like arbitrage in the distressed world." Seasoned liquidations, for example. "While liquidations can be fraught with valuation risk, I liked *seasoned* liquidations—ones where the assets had largely been sold, so you didn't have to worry much about the valuation. The numerator was largely cash. You simply needed to determine the valid claims and make a timing estimate."

"We're Experts at Valuing Cash!"

The example Bader cites is Montgomery Ward. "You knew it was a troubled retailer with a credit card company—and the trade claims were trading at 10 cents. When we looked at it, I had no idea what it was worth, and I am less than convinced that anyone else had a better idea. But when GE Credit came along and paid $650 million in cash for the assets, I knew exactly what the value of the numerator was because it was in cash. I like to joke with our investors, 'We're experts at valuing cash!' "

He continues, "The questions then were what was the denominator? And how fast were you going to get paid? A funny thing about a lot of bankruptcies is that the original unliquidated claim amount is oftentimes ludicrous. When we got into Montgomery Ward, the unliquidated claims had already come down to about $5 billion from something like $45 billion—something crazy. There are usually an enormous number of spurious and/or duplicative claims in bankruptcies. The claims resolution process eliminates them. Montgomery Ward had a disclosure statement that said they expected—after five years of court-supervised claims resolution—to get their unliquidated claims number down closer to $2 billion. In other words, the distressed investors were going to get something between $650 million divided by $5 billion and $650 million divided by $2 billion—and the only question was how long it would take. Meanwhile, the stock market could go up or down, but you didn't have to worry about the value of the assets. That really resonated with me," Bader avers.

It got even more tantalizing, Bader admits, when he realized "how few people would focus on a situation like this. There was a data room for the bankruptcy litigation in Chicago. We sent someone there to work on this; he was there for days, but he never saw anybody else in the data room. It was a pretty interesting result for us—especially after we got an insurance company to tender for the claims. But even without that, seasoned liquidations can be very interesting opportunities. They are often very complicated and people don't want to do the claims analysis. But not infrequently, if you actually do the blocking and tackling, it's very straightforward."

Focus on Form

One thing that sets Halcyon apart from other distressed investors, says Bader, is that many tend to think almost exclusively about value. "But we're just as focused on the form of the workout as we are on the value. Old debt in a restructuring or in a reorganization is exchanged into some combination of cash, debt, equity, and then whatever funky other pieces of paper they might give out. Well, we love the cases where we are buying claims that are going to turn into cash. Even if there is less upside, that feels a lot more like merger arbitrage. We also like things that are going to turn into the debt of a less-leveraged restructured company. That is a bit harder to value and subject to a little more volatility, so we don't like those as much as straight cash deals. We also like getting equity that can be hedged, making it more like an arbitrage situation. While we occasionally buy old debt to create straight equity, we are very mindful of how much more volatile the outcome can be."

There's that word again, "arbitrage." Indeed, despite the broad and ever-evolving spread of Halcyon's strategies, talk with its top executive for just a little while and it's clear he brings a successful arb's quick and canny calculating mindset to every investment situation—as well as a finely honed appreciation of the vagaries of human nature. The first question Bader asks about any transaction, he says, is "not the obvious, what's the spread? Or what's the rate of return? It is why?" He elaborates, "What's the motivation? Why are they doing this? Second question: What's the valuation? Does it make any sense? Is it cheap? Is it expensive? I'd much rather invest in a deal—even if nobody comes in and tops the bid—if it's on the low side of fair value because (a) there are that many more chances that something good will happen and (b) there's that much less downside."

But that's only the beginning of risk-arb research, Bader-style. Another crucial element is what he calls "constituency analysis." Asking, "Who wants to do what to whom? How are they being paid? How are they incentivized? Who are other constituencies who might block the deal? What votes are in play? Who are the voters? It's all about probing motivations, which are often neither pure nor simple," Bader observes. "Take a deal like Alza and Abbott Labs, which blew up back in 1999. A lot of people lost a lot of money. I remember talking to a friend before the deal fell apart and he kept telling me how wonderful the contract was. But I said to him, 'It's the world's worst-kept secret that these people hate each other.' They were supposed to be getting married and they really hated each other. So we happily avoided that deal—and those losses. But my point is that it was because we care about—we pay attention to—constituency analysis."

Not that they don't make mistakes, Bader quickly acknowledges, citing Halcyon's worst loss in recent memory. It was on the 2014 inversion deal in which U.K.-based Shire Pharmaceuticals was to be bought by AbbVie, based in North Chicago—and change the combined company's legal address to the U.K. AbbVie called off the plan about a month after the Treasury Department issued new rules "designed specifically to destroy the financial benefits of inversion transactions." Bader explains, "It had been very clear to us that AbbVie's CEO really wanted to do the deal—he was making it very clear to everybody, both in writing and in conversations. But in doing our constituency analysis we neglected one thing that we should always want to at least think about: Does the CEO have his board behind him? In this case

---

▮▬▮ Merger Arbitrage Spreads Have Widened

═══

- For most of the last two years, friendly, non-controversial merger arbitrage spreads were providing gross rates of return of around 3-5% annualized

- On October 16, Abbvie walked away from a $50bn deal to acquire Shire

- Arbitrage spreads on all merger transactions widened dramatically in the wake of this event

  - Fear ⇒ Capital fleeing from strategy

  - Large transactions ⇒ Wide spreads

11

Halcyon marketing slide after 2015 break of the Shire/Abbvie deal resulting in wider spreads. Courtesy of John Bader.

it became obvious too late, unfortunately, that the CEO did *not* have his board's support. We probably lost more than we should have in that transaction [though within our risk limits]—and so did a lot of others. Because the level of desire for the deal he was expressing was pretty extraordinary, we erroneously jumped to the conclusion that his board was in sync. If there's a lesson to be drawn from the experience, it is to avoid politicized deals, which seem to have a tendency not to work out well."

Pressed for another investing principle, Bader offers, "One of the big lessons is that every good investment strategy gets commoditized sooner or later. Strategies get crowded out because people come barreling in and force the question, how do you find the next thing?" Bader almost immediately amends that lesson, "That said, old friends *do* come back. All of the sudden, here we are in March of 2016 and it's possible to put together a highly-diversified merger-arbitrage portfolio—with definitive agreements—and make good returns with good risk/reward ratios. That hasn't been the case in quite some time. But my point is, it's not going to be the case *all* the time."

Barely pausing for emphasis, Bader shrugs, "It comes back to creating alpha by understanding cycles. You have to understand when it's there and when it's not. At the end of the day, I believe there are more ways than people may realize to create alpha: there is the traditional method of individual instrument selection, then there is allocation to the right strategies at the right times, there is strategy evolution, and one can also generate alpha through sourcing and documentation."

Whatever the cycle, it's a good bet that John Bader is using alpha tools that will stay ahead of it.

CHAPTER THIRTEEN

Clint Carlson

One, have passion for the business. You've got to really love it—and to love what you do is the greatest blessing you can have. Two, you've got to be extremely intellectually curious to find out everything you can about all sorts of businesses—that really helps in risk arb—but you also need to be imaginative in identifying risks. You always have to be thinking, "What could go wrong?" Finally, you need a high degree of skepticism—bordering on cynicism. You can't take anything at face value.

"HOW DO YOU explain to clients that your investment strategy is to buy a stock—*after* it's up 40 percent—to make the last 1 percent?"

That pointed query, says Clint Carlson, was directed at him from "another arb who had been in the business since the 1960s," and was meant as a joke. But it crystalized for Carlson the source of the investment opportunity in risk arbitrage. "It's only there because all the guys that owned the stock before—when it was up 20 percent, 30 percent, 40 percent—decided, 'the career risk to me of sticking around for a deal to close is way too high,' so they sold it"—*below* the price on offer, creating a risk-arbitrage spread just waiting to be exploited.

Juicy spreads arise for myriad reasons, Carlson acknowledges. "One time we had one of the big investment banks come in and say, 'This is our whole position. We'll sell it to you, and you'll make 40 cents a share overnight. We don't want to take the risk.' So we did the trade. It was like, Wow, this is pretty cool. What they were worried about had to do with the concept of fraudulent conveyance—that if they were the owner when the LBO closed and were paid cash, then they might have been at risk. If the company subsequently filed for protection under Chapter 11, its creditors might have dragged them into a fraudulent conveyance suit alleging, 'You took the money and left the company insolvent.' Some of the large investment banks at that juncture simply had a policy against running that risk." Carlson Capital, with no such policy, happily exploited the spread.

Indeed, consistently and profitably exploiting arbitrage spreads is part of what fifty-nine-year-old Clint Duane Carlson does through his Dallas-based hedge fund, Carlson Capital, with nearly $9 billion under management. When he's not in his Dallas, New York, Greenwich, Palm Beach, or London offices you're likely to encounter Carlson on some of Aspen's more vertiginous slopes, which explains the name of Double Black Diamond, Carlson's lead multistrategy fund. Founded with just $17.5 million in 1993, Double Black now invests in a changing mix of seven strategies, depending on where Carlson spies the best market opportunities at the moment.

Risk arbitrage, however, is one of the three core strategies on which Carlson founded his empire. "I'd love to say that I did a lot of quantitative work and came up with three strategies that run uncorrelated with one another and have a high Sharpe ratio, but as a matter of fact, when I started the fund, I was doing the three things I knew how to do: risk arb, convertible arb, and 'relative value arbitrage'—essentially, a pairs trading strategy that I developed after looking at hundreds of smaller bank deals and really coming to understand how banks are valued." It was an opportunity Carlson espied as banking went through a wrenching consolidation in the late 1980s and early 1990s. "You could go long one bank and short another and create a really unique risk/reward profile through that trade."

It wasn't long, Carlson recalls, before he expanded his pairs trading strategy into stocks related to Dallas's consuming passion, the energy patch. Then, "in 2002, we added a credit arbitrage strategy—mainly focused on distressed credit." He has continued to gradually add strategies over the years. The correlations between Carlson's seven strategies vary, he explains, but the idea is that "they tend not to be highly correlated most of the time. Sometimes, everything is correlated—but that's not anything you'll get away from." It all goes back to Carlson's philosophy that "all investment businesses are cyclical. If you commit to one narrowly-focused business, there are times when—in either absolute or relative terms—it is not attractive. As an investor, you don't want to do just the best thing that's available in a narrow subset, you want to have the flexibility to move to other places."

Who Dun It?

The only strategy Carlson and his 175-member team have found it necessary to drop from the hedge fund's toolkit in the subsequent twenty-four years is convertible arbitrage. "Back in the late-2000s, it became a very commoditized business and there just wasn't the opportunity." It's not that Carlson doesn't still dabble in convertible arb, as the occasional opportunity arises, he says, "But it's buried in another strategy. You want to maintain the capability—if guys are really smart they can analyze a convertible security—but there is no longer a broad opportunity where you can run $2 billion in convertible arbitrage."

"Technology killed it. For years, we would have a programmer on our desk, constantly refining the convertibles model. Then Bloomberg put a convertibles model on its ubiquitous terminals. When our model, which we thought was very good, came up with pretty much the exact same answers that Bloomberg was coming up with, there really wasn't much to do." The realization hit that "it was going to be hard to make money in the increasingly crowded convertible arb space." At the same time, Carlson saw that the few convertible arbs who were making money at that point were doing so "because they were systematically over-hedging or under-hedging—which wasn't an arbitrage business." Carlson goes on, "This subset of companies that issues convertible bonds—why that's the pond you ought to be fishing in for longs and shorts—I don't know. There are some managers who have been good at it, but it's no place for an arbitrage business *now*. I'm not inclined to say never. But as of now, we haven't missed much over the years by stepping back."

While it's not unusual to hear "old-timers" in risk arbitrage, voice something approaching despair over the challenge of profitably running a risk-arb portfolio in an era of near-zero short-term interest rates, Carlson isn't among them. "Sure, when short rates get back up to 7 percent, 8 percent, you're going to nominally earn very good money—but that's because the risk-arb return should be two times the risk-free rate, unlevered. That's more or less where it is now and where it has been over the long-term. You're getting paid for the risk at that level.

"The amount of leverage Carlson Capital employs has changed over the years, but most recently has run anywhere from 1.8 times to 2 times, figured as long market value divided by capital. That's probably a prudent risk/reward on a diversified portfolio of deals. Now, if you're running a very concentrated portfolio, you need to bring the leverage down. But the wrong strategy is, 'My arb spreads are tight so now I'm going to lever up.' No, you lever up when arb spreads are wide and the opportunity is really good."

How much capital Carlson dedicates to risk arb and to his other strategies varies according to his changing assessments of their relative opportunities. "There have been times when risk arb was our biggest exposure within our multistrategy fund, and at others, it has probably comprised only somewhere between 10 percent and 12 percent. Today [spring 2016] it's 30 percent. That's just because opportunities are really good." That capital was spread across thirty to forty arb deals in Carlson's global risk-arb book at that point, and "twenty were material," in Carlson's description, while "a lot of the others are not that big because of liquidity constraints more than anything." Carlson adds, "I've never figured out which is a leading and which is a lagging indicator, but merger activity tends to peak when markets peak. So how long we have a good market, that's how long the risk-arb cycle will be. Then, the number of new deals will decline. The opportunity set will stay good beyond the peak, but we won't get the refresh. That's when we maybe move on into the distressed debt cycle or something else that's arbitrage-like."

Attracted to Risk Arbitrage

Meanwhile, Carlson observes, "You can't really expect, in this interest rate environment, that you're going to get a 12 percent annualized return on a deal with no identifiable problems—which is a better description than saying a 'safe deal' because there's no such thing as a safe deal." That's why it's called risk arbitrage—a discipline and strategy, Carlson freely admits, he knew nothing about back in 1985, when a friend tipped him to an opening for a risk-arbitrage analyst in Houston. Hooked on the markets since buying his first stock at age twelve, Carlson had picked up a BA and an MBA from Rice University along with a law degree from the University of Houston—but never practiced law after passing the bar. "I was just fascinated with the concept of investing," he explains. Fresh out of law school, he took job in finance at Texas Commerce Bank and then spent a couple of years managing growth stock accounts at Houston's American Capital Asset Management. But Carlson was restless. He was also curious, so his friend's mention of a risk-arb opportunity quickly led him Ivan Boesky's just-published *Merger Mania* (Holt, Rinehart and Winston, 1985), a self-aggrandizing paean to what its book jacket described as "a fraternity of audacious professionals who bet millions of dollars on the outcome of corporate takeovers."

Boesky's book was one of the few places to go for information about the strategy, remembers Carlson, "and I thought, 'This sounds really cool.' Of course, now we know there were large parts of Boesky's risk-arb operation [specifically, trading on inside information] that he left out of the book." Regardless, what Carlson could quickly glean about the practice of risk arbitrage appealed to his fundamental investing mindset, and he realized that his training as an attorney could give him an edge in understanding the legal issues surrounding corporate combinations. "I could speak the language and understood how the process worked—both enormously helpful."

Indeed, to this day, Carlson swears that law school is a better training ground for investment work than an MBA "because of the way they teach you to think. It's about weighing both sides of an issue and developing arguments on both sides. It's about not necessarily going in a direct line to a conclusion, which I think is great training for the investment business. That's not to say that you don't need to know the time value of money and how derivatives work and how to do an earnings model. But all that is secondary to being taught how to think—which law school does so much better."

Does this Make Sense?

The risk-arb job opening turned out to be as comanager of a risk-arb fund within financier Charles Hurwitz's Maxxam Group. "Charles controlled a number of different entities and risk arbitrage at that time was a way to deploy excess capital—we didn't have any outside investors." Carlson found a mentor at Maxxam, portfolio manager Ron Huebsch, who inculcated in the young arb a relentless focus on finding the investment thesis in every deal—and on continuously tracking how things are going relative to that thesis. "Ron said, 'Look, there's one key element that's going to make or break your investment—whether in a risk-arb deal or in a particular stock selection—and you've got to focus on getting that one big thing right.' That's why, to this day, my first question is, 'Does this deal make sense? Should both parties be wanting to do this?' "

As rewarding as Carlson found working with Huebsch, he also recalls that "a big part of our capital, when I worked for Hurwitz, came from his savings and loans, and I figured out after looking at our monthly budget and income statements that every month our real estate write-offs were exactly equal to the arbitrage profits—I thought that might be a problem down the road." Thus, Carlson was primed to move on in 1988, when he "got a call from the Bass brothers up in Fort Worth. Richard Rainwater had just left. Tommy [Thomas M.] Taylor had taken over their investment operations and they were looking for someone to run risk arbitrage. I said, 'Well, that sounds pretty good to me.' "

It was also good for the Bass brothers to have Carlson heading up arbitrage or "non-directional strategies" for them. Combining his predilection for deep fundamental research with the arbitrageurs' probabilistic discipline focused on deal spreads—constantly gauging the upside relative to the downside in the era's steady flow M&A deals—Carlson minted substantial profits for the Bass brothers and their partners. Up until 1993, that is, when Carlson decided—as had several other of Texas's young guns by that point—"These Bass guys are making a bunch of money doing this hedge fund stuff. Let's start one. I can do the same."

Reflects Carlson, "The funny thing about business in general—but especially entrepreneurial ventures—is that they are irrational. If you looked at the probability of success, you'd realize that you shouldn't do it. So you have to have that naiveté, that belief in your own abilities, or you wouldn't do it." Carlson rounded up $17.5 million from initial investors and "thought I had a great start. It's a funny story. I sat down and made my A-list of potential investors, my B-list, and my C-list, figuring that's where I'd raise my capital. But the A-list didn't come through at all, the B-list was decent, the C-list was actually very good. But they all gave me leads on more investors—and it was actually the leads I got by making those calls that came through better than any of the potential investors I knew before starting to raise money. So the secret of money raising is really persistence. Sure, you need a good product—and I thought I had one. But it's about making the calls and making the connections and following up and doing the right things."

For Carlson, in risk arb, the paramount questions are fundamental. "I always try to figure out: What is the industrial logic for this deal? Why are they doing it? Is it accretive, dilutive? I do a lot of valuation work and try to understand the businesses—because if I didn't understand them, I wouldn't know what risks could stand in the way of the completion of the deals." Despite—or perhaps because of—his legal training, Carlson is acutely conscious that risk arb is "always more than, 'Okay, here are the terms, I read the merger agreement, I talked to my regulatory lawyers, and this is what I have'."

For instance, says Carlson, "we always spend a lot more time trying to figure out what the downside could be than we do on the upside—and continuously update the downside calculation over time to track how the values are changing." The lessons he learned in a fundamental shop early in his career, Carlson stresses, remain critical. "Scarily enough, most M&A deals are *not* good ideas, but they happen anyway. A lot of it gets buried, so you never really know. But I don't think there's a ton of value creation in M&A. While there are some very disciplined buyers and they do create a lot of value, most of it is just about getting bigger—or just about ego. Sometimes, ego drives the whole process."

None of which is to say that Carlson sees M&A going away any time soon. "Look, organic growth is really hard to come by, so companies have to find some other way to grow. Financing is very cheap and the only thing that we were missing until the last couple of years was the confidence of management and boards to take that risk. Once they got confidence all hell broke loose." M&A activity surged to record levels in number of deals and deal value in 2015, slowed only barely perceptibly in 2016 and 2017, and has started 2018 at a blistering pace, with the value of announced deals globally surging to more than one trillion dollars before the end of the first quarter, a record, according to Dealogic.

A Question of Desire

When it comes down to it, says Carlson, the core of his risk-arb philosophy is that, "If it's a good deal and both parties want to do it, they will usually find a way to get it done. If there are hiccups along the way, they'll get fixed. But if somebody—the buyer or the seller—decides, 'I don't want to do this anymore,' then you're really at risk. They are looking for the first opportunity to get out of the deal." In practice, Carlson explains, he takes a big picture, long view of arb situations. "Once I've decided this deal is going to get done for this reason, I don't worry so much about the little things that happen along the way." That doesn't mean he's not prepared to change his position if the facts change—but by staying focused on his investment thesis, Carlson tries to avoid being shaken out of positions prematurely. "Trading around arbitrage deals is not a profitable strategy. You pay more in commissions and you're not right as often as you need to be."

He continues, "It's a very simple concept: What is the thesis of the trade? The thesis is: I think the deal's going to close. So I'm going to go long the target, short the acquirer—and if it closes, I make my money." The exception, Carlson adds, is a cash deal, where's there's nothing to do on the acquirer side. "But there, the thesis is still that the deal is going to close. It's a nice, neat thesis." He quickly adds, "I guess the other thing I like about the risk-arb business is that you never really need to worry about selling. I mean, the deal closes and the position just goes away," leaving the profits. "Ask a risk arb, 'What's your sell discipline?' and he can shrug, 'The deal closes!'"

Yet discipline, stresses Carlson, is critical to the practice of risk arbitrage, warning that succumbing to the temptation to "get a little long" in an arb stock that looks undervalued can be deadly to an arbitrageur. "If you do that, small adverse movements in the market will just totally wipe out your spread. If you want a long portfolio, choose your stocks a different way than by looking at arbitrage deals."

That's not to say, Carlson acknowledges, that he doesn't sometimes buy a stock hit by selling after an arb deal breaks "if it's highly accretive and the stock is under pressure because the arbs are dumping it." But those purchases are based on an entirely different investment thesis and are not mixed into his arb book.

"One of the things we emphasize is doing ongoing work on what we think the fundamental downside is in every risk-arb deal. We make a judgment on where fundamental value is." That ongoing fundamental analysis, Carlson emphasizes, is crucial. "Knowing where intrinsic value is means you can take advantage of the technical selling pressure from arbs unwinding—it can create a great opportunity. But you have to have done the work first." Most often, however, when risk-arb deals break, Carlson advises, it's better to just get out and move on: "I'd say, 75 percent of the time, the stocks go immediately to fair value. The hardest thing to do is to say, 'I was wrong here,' and take that loss. But you have to do it from time to time."

Uncorrelated Returns

Risk arbitrage as an investment strategy is very much like fixed income in that it is uncorrelated with the stock market—and that is its value proposition, avers Carlson. "Yes, when there's stress on the deal market, spreads blow out—but the same thing happens to corporate bonds amid a financial crisis. In fact, all correlations go to one, given enough stress. The value proposition for risk arb remains that it's normally uncorrelated. The other way to look at it is, in some sense, as an insurance business. Somebody has to take the risk that the deal doesn't close.

I'm underwriting the deal closing, therefore I'm taking that risk from the long-only guy who owned the stock but who said, 'I don't want to take that risk.' So the arb spread is my underwriting premium. If I have good underwriting standards and if I do it often enough, I will make money over the longer term—but that doesn't mean a house doesn't burn down every now and then." It's up to a risk arb to decide, stresses Carlson, when the spread is attractive enough to write the business and when it isn't.

While sizing up the probability of a given deal being completed is a key part of the analysis behind Carlson's risk-arb positions, he is adamant that his is "not a probabilistic business. For us, it's about fundamentals. I have read the academic papers. I understand that there's research out there that shows if you just buy every deal, you'll earn 90 percent of the return in the strategy. But we don't think that works as well as a fundamental strategy." It's a conclusion Carlson bases not merely on his fundamental bias but on empirical evidence. "We actually developed an index-based risk-arb model in 2003/2004 and we were running it for a while. But it never outperformed our fundamental risk-arb strategy. It was highly correlated with it, but never outperformed. The theory behind the quant strategy was that enough of the high-risk deals would close to pay for the ones that didn't. It could probably work in a market with a lot of high-risk deals. But in a market where spreads are tight and the deals are few, if the strategy lost money in even one deal, it would have a really hard time making it back."

Carlson continues, "There are a lot of portfolio management judgments you make along the way that can really add a lot of value in risk arb, such as varying the position size and weighting relative to risk." Especially, he adds, in complex deals with idiosyncratic pricing periods, puts or calls, or other features "where trading judgment can add a lot of value." For instance, Carlson says, in complex deals "where you're either creating a put or a call, depending on how the deal is structured, our philosophy has always been that if we can create a free put, we'll do it. But we don't want to create a free call. We'd already be stuck with a residual long exposure if there's a crash or untoward market volatility—and in that case, having set ourselves up with a put rather than a call would help the overall portfolio."

Although Carlson emphasizes his fundamental and inherently selective approach to risk arb, he hastens to clarify, "We look at every deal—of a certain size—because you never know when you're going to get the opportunity to go into it. An unattractive spread may widen out. Being prepared beforehand is a big deal. In other words, we go through the fundamentals first. Then, if we think the deal will happen, we determine, 'Do I like the spread, given the risk?' We don't start with spread. Our general rule of thumb is that if the spread is reflecting a 40 percent annual return, these days, then the deal isn't likely to get done."

Reminiscing a bit, Carlson pegs the first quarter of 1988 as the best ever, for risk arbitrageurs "because we had a lot of competitive deals." The October 1987 market crash had driven valuations across the market down to very low levels, he recalls. "So as we came into the first quarter, you started to see bids—a lot of them were LBOs, but not all—and when other potential buyers started to see those bids, they'd go, 'Whoa, that's really cheap!' because stock prices were so depressed. So the bidding commenced—and all that competition produced a great period in risk arbitrage. But it was a function of coming off the bottom with valuations that left a lot of room to raise bids. There is less room now, though we do still see competitive bid situations. Just not full-scale bidding wars, unless it's a company that's very misunderstood by the market."

Picking Up the Nuances

Fundamentally, Carlson reflects, "what the risk-arb business teaches you in a hurry is to be a very quick study. You have to learn a lot about the companies and the industries in a very short time—and do it yourself. You've got to know: How many things can go wrong? What are the issues? Who are the regulators? What are the financing conditions? And what can I glean from the merger agreement? Is there something in it that stands out as an unusual risk? All those questions must be answered very quickly." He adds, "Now, the longer you're in the business and the more things you've seen, the quicker it is to get through all of that stuff."

Carlson continues, "The most valuable advice I ever got came after a conversation I had with an investment banker. He warned, 'They're only going to tell you what they want you to hear.' It's actually good advice for all areas of investment. You have to realize that companies are pretty sophisticated; they're only going to tell you what they want you to hear. So you have to know what they're really saying. They're not going to give you inside information—you shouldn't be getting inside information—but it's important to pick up the nuances, the changes of tone, in what they say."

A downside of working in risk arbitrage, notes Carlson, is that there is no unique sourcing of ideas. "That's the one thing I don't like. You get your ideas from the front page of the *Wall Street Journal*. Your universe is the same as every other arb's—so the trades get crowded, no matter how you try to be creative in defining that universe or stretching your portfolio." While Carlson Capital has been known, on occasion, to take a low-key activist approach to a deal, it "doesn't go looking for that stuff," Carlson says. "It's highly time-consuming and I'd rather not be in the press. While we express our opinions—especially around votes and on our view of values—that's because it's our fiduciary duty to do so if we can create value. But it's not our fiduciary duty to get in the press." All too often, Carlson adds dismissively, the press is chasing purported takeover candidates—and "rumortrage," as he calls it, is strictly a bull market business. "Chasing the latest rumor is a tough way to make a living." Carlson adds, "I've seen guys who had 'rumortrage' as a large part of their strategy and they tend to do really well when the S&P is up 15 percent. But when the S&P corrects 10 percent, not only do the stocks go down, but they lose all the takeover premium at the same time, so it hurts."

The advice he gives to neophyte risk arbs looking to follow in his footsteps, says Carlson, really applies across the investment field: "One, have passion for the business. You've got to really love it—and to love what you do is the greatest blessing you can have. Two, you've got to be extremely intellectually curious to find out everything you can about all sorts of businesses, that really helps in risk arb—but you also need to be imaginative in identifying risks. You always have to be thinking, 'What could go wrong?' Finally, you need a high degree of skepticism—bordering on cynicism. You can't take anything at face value."

Carlson continues, "Those are the differentiating characteristics." The absolute prerequisites, of course, are "being smart and hardworking, with a high degree of ethics," he notes. "But without a passion for digging into things and finding out why," a Carlson wannabe won't go far. By contrast, the discipline of thinking in spread terms and constantly analyzing the upside of trades relative to the downside gets easier with experience, says Carlson with confidence. What isn't

as learnable, he admonishes, is skepticism. "Sure, start with the documents, read the merger agreement, go through the 10-K. There are
no shortcuts. But don't get lulled into thinking, as some people do,
that nothing else matters 'if the merger agreement is airtight.' What's
going on in the companies matters. If you think there's a problem
making someone want to get out of a deal, that makes it a highly risky
place to be. You just can't rely on an 'airtight' merger agreement."

As evidence, Carlson pointed, during a May 2016 interview, to "the
Energy Transfer/Williams deal as the poster child for what is supposed
to be a very tight merger agreement. It includes very few outs for
Energy Transfer." Nonetheless, Carlson added, "At this point, I don't
think either company *wants* to do the deal. Early on, before the spread
really blew out, everybody said, 'Yes, I know that the energy market
has deteriorated and this is now a bad deal for Energy Transfer, but
they can't get out.' Well, we'll see."

Not quite two months later, Carlson—who said he'd stopped following the deal by the time of our May interview because his firm
had long since jettisoned its small position—was proven prescient.
A Delaware judge ruled in late June 2016 that Energy Transfer could
indeed walk away from its "airtight" $33 billion merger deal without
paying a break-up fee.

Such is the value of informed skepticism, as some background color
on that ultimately busted deal illustrates. Energy Transfer Equity, then
trading around $37-$38, had initiated the fun and games with an
unsolicited bid in June 2015, saying it had been pursuing Williams
Cos., another pipeline operator, for six months. The news sent WMB's
shares soaring to over $57 from about $46. Not 30 days later, amid
turmoil in oil and gas prices, ETE reaffirmed its ardor for WMB,
describing an offer valued at $53 billion, or $64 a share. Arbs who
rushed in were to sorely disappointed, however. By the time the deal
was inked in late September 2015, the price had been negotiated
down to $37.7 billion, or $43.50 a share, in line with the continued
decline in energy prices.

But oil and gas prices kept sinking—and the arb spread widening.
In January 2016, with ENE's shares falling under $8 a share and its
own stock trading under $20, Williams' board deemed it appropri-
ate to put out a press release affirming its commitment to that pur-
portedly airtight merger deal to combat "market speculation" that it
wouldn't close. When that didn't work, Williams sued Energy Transfer

in Delaware and Texas courts in April 2016 over its alleged cold feet, and legal wrangling on both sides began in earnest. Clint Carlson made his prediction to me a month later, which came true for all intents and purposes when the Delaware Chancery court ruled in late June that tax issues entitled ENE to call off the deal, and half of Williams' board quit. Yet appeals of that decision dragged on until March 2017, when the Delaware court upheld Energy Transfer's exit from the agreement. Even then the lawyers weren't finished, as Energy Transfer took a demand for a $1.48 billion termination fee to the court, which didn't dismiss it until the end of 2017.

It's not that Carlson predicted the saga's every twist and turn. He didn't have to. By May 2016, he knew he'd seen that movie before, and spared his clients the rerun.

CHAPTER FOURTEEN

James Dinan

If you love investing and you love human psychology, risk arbitrage is an amazing business. All of a sudden, you're not just investing, you're playing a very intellectual game. You're thinking almost like in a chess game. The best arbs see the moves—like Bobby Fischer—three, four moves ahead. They see the ending long before the audience has figured out who done it. They can capitalize on the winners by loading up—and also can get out of the others, before they become real losers.

"THE BIGGEST CHANGE I've seen in merger arb is the availability and cost of information. A kid with Wi-Fi has 99.9 percent of the information I have. Thirty years ago, there were only twenty firms with all the information we had." The upshot, says James Dinan, the founder of Manhattan-based hedge fund York Capital Management, is that "there's no information advantage anymore in risk arbitrage, there's only a judgment advantage. . . . Arbitrageurs obviously need to have good quantitative skills, but you don't need *great* quant skills. You *do* need great judgment, though—and judgment is basically understanding human behavior, the human condition. Because in arbitrage, the decisions are made by humans; arbitrage is driven by individuals. Every individual has a unique personality, so you almost want to be a student of human psychology—but if you love investing and you love human psychology, risk arbitrage is an amazing business."

With a thick shock of silver hair and dark, expressive eyebrows, Dinan, fit and trim at fifty-seven, could have been placed at the glass conference table in his offices in the GM Building by a Hollywood casting director. But York Capital's founder, near universally known as Jamie, is the real thing. A self-made billionaire ($1.8 billion, according to *Forbes*' latest calculations), Dinan has long employed risk arbitrage to help power his event-driven multi-strategy hedge fund from its modest 1991 beginnings—roughly $4 million scraped together in 1991 from former colleagues at Donaldson, Lufkin & Jenrette—to around $17 billion in AUM at last count. With offices spread around the globe, primarily in New York, London, and Hong Kong, York Capital combines a renowned focus on deep, fundamental research and investment selection with disciplined risk management to try to generate consistent risk-adjusted returns across business and market cycles—and has accomplished that quite nicely, more often than not.

Which, make no mistake, is the point. Dinan traces his fascination with risk arbitrage back to his first job, in 1981. He had but one job offer coming out of the University of Pennsylvania's Wharton School that year, from DLJ's investment banking group. The Worcester, MA native moved to New York and found himself "the most junior guy in the department, so I was the one who got stuck with doing all the work." Luckily for Dinan, his arrival at DLJ more or less coincided with a considerably splashier one—Texas oil man T. Boone Pickens chose DLJ as his investment banking shop that year when he decided to use his Mesa Petroleum to make David vs. Goliath hostile bids for oil giants Cities Service and Gulf Oil. "What I quickly discovered, from an investment banker's perspective," recalls Dinan, "was that there is a business called merger arbitrage. People like Bob Rubin and Ivan Boesky were calling DLJ—and their calls were being referred to me. The good news is that I really didn't know what Boone was thinking because I wasn't high up enough, but I did tell them what was in the approved script."

Those Guys Are Going to Make a Lot

It didn't take the young banking trainee long to catch on to what the arbs were up to. "I soon figured out what these guys actually did—because you're there—and Boone has just bid like $50 a share for the company. But you know that in your models he's willing to go up to $65—and the stock is trading at $52." It dawned on Dinan: "These guys who are buying this stock at $52 are going to make *a lot* of money. They don't know it yet, but you know it, and you're thinking, that's a great business." Dinan quickly realized that, while he couldn't invest in deals that DLJ was involved in, there was nothing (in those days) keeping him from trading other arb situations in his own account. "I think I started with $10,000, but I did pretty well, just using my banker thought process—and the market was quite inefficient at the time."

Thoroughly intrigued, Dinan headed to Boston in the fall of 1983 to pick up his Harvard Business School credential. But not before arranging a summer job doing risk arbitrage under another DLJ alum, George Kellner, who just a couple of years before had started Kellner DiLeo & Co. Reminisces Dinan, "I was lucky that my boss at DLJ made the introduction to George, and he offered me the job. But it's funny how history changes over time, depending on who is doing the remembering. George remembers me as being this really smart guy he knew at DLJ and that's the reason he offered the summer job. The problem is that George left DLJ about a month before I joined the company. It's just a little inconvenient fact."

Nonetheless, that summer gig led to an offer of a full-time job with Kellner after the younger man finished his MBA, and Dinan leaves no doubt that he "was very fortunate that Kellner DiLeo embraced two things—research and risk." Coming from DLJ, famed at the time as the brokerage house that research built, Kellner had made sure, says Dinan, that "Kellner DiLeo was a research-driven merger-arbitrage shop—just like Goldman's risk-arb operation. There were other guys who had a different model—and I don't mean insider trading. There were guys who just would call their ten friends and buy what everybody else was buying. They didn't do their own work. I learned to do the work."

Dinan recalls one deal he worked on as an intern that indelibly impressed on him the importance of digging into primary research. "Harold Simmons was rumored to be trying to take over a timber company in Medford, Oregon in the summer of 1984. I picked up the phone, called the local newspaper out there, and talked to the business editor. He was really happy to talk to me, because he was also the sports editor, the prom editor—but he *was* on the ground out there. I remember him saying, 'I don't know what's going on, but there are lots of guys coming here in black Lincoln town cars. Does everybody from New York wear dark suits?' I answered, 'yeah, pretty much.' He replied, 'Well, they are all dark suits here. There are none of those—you know, where the pants are different from the jacket.' Now, that could have meant a million things," Dinan reflects. "But it *probably* meant there was action in Medford and it dovetailed with what we knew was going on in New York—and with what we thought the deal timeline was. I was the only one to call that editor because he was at just a little blip of a paper. But that's the kind of research we used to do."

In another instance, Dinan recalls, he was trying to value the old United Airlines, which at the time owned Westin Hotels. "I remember literally going to the Plaza Hotel, because Westin owned the Plaza, and picking up a brochure from the lobby that listed every Westin property. I went through it and valued every room based on the room rates. I actually came up with an independent valuation that was much, much closer to what Bob Bass ultimately paid for Westin than the number Wall Street was using, which was just a multiple of EBITDA." But these days, adds Dinan, with just a tinge of regret in his voice, "even here, people don't do that kind of work anymore. You can get so much online." It just goes to show, Dinan concludes, that the factors that define success in merger arb—as in any business—"are dynamic, not static." And, today's virtually universal access to data in the information age "has pulled judgment to the fore."

Feeling the Pain

Judgment, likewise, is crucial to risk taking—the other essential element in Dinan's schooling in the merger-arb arts at Kellner DiLeo. He was extraordinarily fortunate, says Dinan, in being exposed to both the up- and the downsides of risk appetite. "They were willing to take risk, put conviction behind your names—taking the view that you loaded up on high-conviction names. If you were going to have fifty positions they weren't all going to be 2 percent." This stood in sharp contrast, explains Dinan, to the tack taken at that time by many of the prop desks, like PaineWebber's and, particularly, Dillon Read's. On most prop desks, positions were sized uniformly. "At Kellner, if you really loved something, you sized it appropriately. Now, in some cases they had a very large a position—like in United Airlines—and when it didn't happen, it hurt a little bit—as in *a lot*. So I learned about risk management in the tails by experiencing the very real pain."

The experience left Dinan convinced that "the reality of merger arbitrage is that you can lose a lot of money if you are wrong. So if you really want the strategy to work, you have to take positions that can make *a lot* of money if you are right." This makes it imperative, in his view, "to not just do the super-safe stuff, but to embrace risk by doing the open-ended stuff." Indeed, Dinan opines, "the problem with Long-Term Capital Management was that *all* they were doing was picking up nickels and dimes in front of a steamroller. There were no dollar bills, there were no Benjamins, in that strategy. But they did have the tail risk that it could all end badly—and that's why it did. When you cut to the chase, that's when genius failed, to paraphrase the title of Roger Lowenstein's excellent book. And if there is one thing I have learned—and really learned by living it in this business—it is that the losers are what kill you in the merger-arbitrage space."

Avoiding them isn't easy, concedes Dinan. "One of my partners has a wonderful line I like to use: 'Seen the movie, know the ending.' Well, avoiding the losers is basically seeing hundreds and hundreds of movies and remembering those endings. You don't actually *know* what the ending is, but you know what it *could* be. Then you have to have the discipline to say, 'Yes, if this works, I'm going to make money here.' But that doesn't mean I know if it's a good risk/reward. For that—and this is not that sophisticated—you're looking at the spread as reflecting the relative probabilities that you'll capture the opportunity. If it's a big spread, the relative probabilities are maybe not so good."

Deals are seductive, Dinan continues. "There's this tendency—and everyone is guilty of it—when you see a nice spread, see a big return, it's like a moth to a light bulb. You're just drawn to it. But just because it looks like a big, juicy spread doesn't mean you're supposed to do it. You don't have to dance with every girl at the party, if I can be a bit chauvinistic for a moment. The deal may appear attractive, but if there's anything just a little off about it, there are plenty of others. Because the real key is avoiding losers. You are going to miss some of the winners as a result, but remember, you're making nickels and dimes when you are right and losing lots and lots of money when you're wrong. You can pass up a lot of good investments if the benefit is that you skip the disasters."

Avoiding Antitrust

Dinan points out, for instance, that York Capital has historically tried to avoid taking positions in deals involving antitrust issues, like those that felled the Halliburton/Baker Hughes and Office Depot/Staples deals during the waning years of the Obama administration—even though "most of them work out." Probabilities just really don't apply, he notes, whenever one person is the king maker—and that includes judges and presidents. He has also learned, he says, that there are two kinds of hostile deals—ones he calls institutionalized, in which a company under attack is suddenly being driven by the bankers and lawyers and therefore the outcome is predictable, to a degree. The others, Dinan adds, are hostile bids where a founder still owns 25 percent or more of the company, making it usually a small- or mid-sized deal. Of those, he says, "Guess what? The rules don't apply. It's not an institutionalized process."

Then too, warns Dinan, "Every once in a while, you get a larger deal you think is institutionalized, but then you realize the board members are *all* the CEO's buddies. There's a local law firm, not Skadden Arps, representing him, and McDonald & Co. out of Cleveland is the banker. It has been engaged for $100,000, as opposed to the typical $2 million, but it has been promised a $25 million success fee. Stay away from those. You don't have to play. The outcome is binary and all the analysis you have done, all the probabilities built into your best models—they don't apply when it's just one person, one decision." Besides, adds Dinan, who is an enthusiastic advocate of probabilistic thinking, "no matter how sure you are that something will happen, there's always a bit of uncertainty."

"I've always had the view that the most dangerous part of merger arb is when you get what you think is a really good piece of information—whether in a conversation, from a company presentation at an investor conference, or even from a legal document or press release. At the time, it's a fact to you, and you put it into the mental algorithm you're creating by synthesizing all of this fuzzy and hard information—and actually arrive at the right outcome. This is almost like a type-2 error in statistics. The analysis is correct; you just didn't realize that you had bad data. That's the scary thing about data—even if it's right, data has a lifespan of uncertain length. What is fact today could be totally wrong tomorrow. You just don't know. So some of the biggest mistakes we make are ones where the process isn't wrong, *the data changed—or was never right in the first place.* And by all means, if someone is telling you something they shouldn't be telling you, assume it's bad information. If someone's telling you 'Company A is going to bid,' or 'they're going to raise their bid,' or 'I've got three white knights lined up'—they're speaking from a position. If a guy claims he's got three white knights, he ain't got nothing."

Risk perceptions, of course, vary quite a bit, notes Dinan. "I find that people who own very plain vanilla-type transactions underestimate risk and people in very complicated situations overestimate the risk. So when in doubt—and you've heard this ad nauseam—embrace complexity. Complexity is your friend. For the simple reason that it is where you can add value."

Cockroach Theory

York Capital, as a firm, has never used leverage to make returns work, adds Dinan. It prefers to go up the complexity curve instead. "For several reasons. One, it's harder. Two, there are fewer people who want to play out there, while there are any number of firms that love sidling up to safety—doing boring 6 percent–8 percent type deals." Dinan's attitude is, "you only live life once, you might as well make it a little more exciting. Once you reach a point where you can pay the bills, you might as well do something that's challenging as opposed to clipping muni bond coupons." Nonetheless, Dinan cautions, "when you embrace complexity, you had better have rules to follow." One rule he follows is that when a hitch appears in a deal, "there's never just one. I call it the cockroach theory of investing. When you see one, get out, because there are more to come."

He also tends to avoid deals where the contract "is really just an option." It is conditioned on financing being raised, for instance. "Just avoid the spreads where the buyer has a get-out-of-jail-for-free card. And be much more careful about cash deals versus relative value deals. Stock for stock deals are relative value, so you don't have to worry so much about systemic issues. But in cash issues you do, as we saw in the financial crisis."

Dinan says that York actually went into the crisis in 2007 with very few deals on its books, "mainly because spreads had been so tight—it wasn't like we were rocket scientists and knew that Bear Stearns was going to blow and the subprime market would crash and all the bridge financings would get hung up when the banks got stuck. But I remember thinking, 'Now all the spreads are really wide,' and they were almost all private equity deals. So I had one simple rule: it was a question of 'deal or no deal.' We played it in the office. 'Imagine you're Henry Kravis, and you're Tom Lee.' So everybody put their dunce caps on and we went through the deals. 'Do we want to buy Harmon International?' KKR had a contract to buy it, but the answer was really simple, 'No, don't do that deal'" And KKR didn't, invoking a rarely used "materially adverse change" clause. "Or what about Chris Flowers," Dinan continues. "In Flowers's place would we want to buy Sallie Mae? *Hell, no.* That deal never happened either." But those failed deals were the exception, Dinan points out, even amid the financial crisis. "I forget how many we did, but we went down the list and there were eight or ten of them—strategic deals that made sense—that we took positions in. Every single one of them closed. It was common sense."

York Capital's founder further reflects, "I do believe that one of the things that makes a good arbitrageur today is a willingness to view the asset class as *part* of a model portfolio as opposed to *the* portfolio. There are times when, cyclically, spreads go out and you can take advantage. We're in one of those right now [May 2016]. But there are times when there's very little to do. The dedicated players, like the merger fund folks, still have to do it. But I think the good arbitrageurs know when it's time to leave the party—and they have a good party, somewhere counter-cyclical, to go to—because we're party animals." For some investors, Dinan points out, that business is even buying busted arb deals. "Eddie Lampert used to publicly—and privately—say that he loved buying deals the arbs were puking out. There's often real value to be found in playing the busted side of arb deals. That's one of the things I'm not good at, although others do it quite well. Which leads me to say it's important to know your libido—know what you're comfortable with."

Beware of Safe Spreads

What Dinan is comfortable with, it turns out, aren't safe-spread deals. "I always worry, 'It's 20 down and 50 cents up.' That's LTCM, not a lot of fun." Instead, he prefers situations where "there are a couple of bucks down, but there's *a lot* of money up. I have no idea what the probabilities are. But I've often found the best ones were where you didn't really know what the values are. In the high-tech world, in bio-tech, oftentimes you're surprised by the upside—but you had a floor." Dinan pointed during our early May interview, as an example, to the takeover speculation then-swirling around biotech firm Medivation, a specialist in immunology with a promising portfolio of cancer drugs. He began narrating the story: "Sanofi made a hostile bid at $52.50—probably a low bid. The stock is averaging $62 now. We had bought it because it was rumored in the papers to be in play. Then Sanofi approached—Medivation stock opened around $55—and we bought a bunch more. I read the corporate governance documents first. Is there a path to control? It's a Delaware corporation.

God bless Delaware—Joe Biden country—love Delaware. Stay away from Ohio. Never, ever, do a deal in Ohio. Bad things happen there. Ohio statutes are the worst. Maryland—dangerous. Stay out of Spiro Agnew country. You've got to learn. But back to Medivation. I don't know what it is going to go for. It could go for $80. But I do know that I have a $52.50 hard stop on the downside, and the French usually have a couple of extra bucks in their pockets to get something done. Sanofi has a good reputation as a buyer. It's the kind of situation I like. My kind of libido." As it turned out, Sanofi dropped out of the bidding for Medivation when Pfizer entered into the hunt, and the American drug giant ended up winning its prize in August 2016 with a bid even higher than Dinan's estimate—$81.50 a share, or $14 billion.

"There's a famous scene in *Harry Potter*," says Dinan. "There's an old sorcerer's hat, called the sorting hat. Harry is told that 'the hat chooses you.' Well, to some extent, I think the investors choose you." What he's getting at, Dinan explains, is that "the investors who come to us are oftentimes very different from those who might go to a plain vanilla merger-arbitrage fund. They are looking for higher returns, greater complexity. They not only want it and appreciate it—they're a lot more understanding if it doesn't always work. As a result, we get away with taking more risk. But we will also be penalized more if we de-risk and play it safe. So yes, when we have a tough six or nine months, we do hear, 'you suck' from some people. But we also have a lot of big, long-time investors whose message is, 'we want up-capture. We don't want you neutered. Forget belts and suspenders, we want a creative manager who will take risk.' I truly believe, in most markets, the more you move out the risk curve, the better the risk/reward is. Because the crowd is in the 'safe' stuff."

Control the Downside

Yet even if York's default position, as Dinan says, "is we want to play"—embrace risk to capture rewards—he's infinitely fonder of the upside, and therefore is normally meticulously careful in trying to control his downside by doing two things: investing incrementally, starting with a "non-full, 25 percent position," and dynamically "growing it in size as the risk goes down"—assuming it does. "The big discipline is that if the facts change and you wouldn't own it, you sell it. It's really simple. People hate to sell something that's down a buck. They've got no problem selling it if it's up a buck. But if it's down, they're hoping that at least they'll get their money back. Remember, hope is not a strategy. That's dumb."

To reinforce that verdict, Dinan conjures the memory of an arbitrage trade that ultimately worked for York "but was really nerve-racking," in large part because the firm didn't follow Dinan's incremental position-sizing rule. It was Hertz Corp.'s 2011 hostile bid for Dollar Thrifty Automotive Group. "Somehow we ended up with 16 percent–17 percent of Dollar Thrifty. So we had to file a 13-D with the SEC, and everyone knew what we owned. But we also owned Hertz, so we were long the combination. Hertz had bid $72, and at one point Dollar's stock spiked to over $80. But then risk went off. This was in 2011 and there was an antitrust issue, so Dollar Thrifty dropped into the $50s. Avis registered its interest as a white knight but then dropped out to buy Avis Europe, instead. Eventually, Hertz sweetened its bid to $85.50, all cash, and we got out in November, 2012. But one thing you need to learn is that the scariest positions are the ones you can't get out of. That was an outlier, even for York."

Dinan is well-known to readers of the sports pages as the third member of a triumvirate of New York financiers who bought what was the perennially cellar-dwelling Milwaukee Bucks NBA franchise in 2015. The trio has so far had some success lifting the Bucks' fortunes with fresh players and the promise of a heavily state-subsidized new arena — the team won more than half its games in the 2016–17 and 2017–18 seasons, only to lose in the first round of the playoffs each year. (Avenue Capital's Marc Lasry and Fortress Investment's Wes Edens have acted as point men in the venture and the Wall Streeters recently played to Milwaukee fans, announcing that they'd brought in local sports icon Aaron Rodgers, the Green Bay Packers quarterback, as a limited partner.)

But ask Dinan how he unwinds and it's spending countless hours watching his three children compete in their favorite sports that springs to his lips. Then he adds, "Little-known fact about me: I love do-it-yourself projects. It drives my wife up the wall sometimes, but I'm extraordinarily proficient with all types of power tools and I love building countertops, putting up wallpaper and moldings, and painting." All skills that likely come in handy, since Dinan has a lot of homes to keep up—in Katonah, NY; Nantucket; Miami and the Caribbean; as well as in Manhattan.

In like vein, billionaire-appropriate references to exotic and mildly dangerous adventure journeys—climbing Kilimanjaro, piloting dugout canoes through Dutch Guiana, camping with the polar bears on the Norwegian Arctic archipelago of Svalbard—sprinkle Dinan's conversation. (on Svalbard, the Chateau Lafitte he brought along froze. "It's rough, camping out in the freezing cold. The fancy wine I brought to drink freezes, I found out, if it gets cold enough. It essentially crystalized in our plastic cups. I should have brought Two Buck Chuck, or whatever they call it.") But the point of his exotic stories, one way or another, is often the depth of Dinan's obsession with Wall Street and its deals. Or, as he puts it, "I'm very anal, so I have a satellite phone and the whole bit. Usually call in the morning and at the end of the day—these days. At some point, you have to let go. When I was younger it was harder." And the satellite phones were much larger. When climbing Kilimanjaro during the difficult market in 1996, Dinan recounts, he took along a first-generation satellite phone that required a satellite dish "the size of a suitcase" and weighing eighty pounds. Dinan hired an extra porter just to carry the gear up the mountain with him. "For $15 for the week," says Dinan with a smile.

It all fits, when you think about it. A value orientation. Self-reliance. Extreme price sensitivity, compulsive attention to detail, calculated risk-taking. Tailor-made for merger arbitrage.

CHAPTER FIFTEEN

Drew Figdor

The way guys lose a lot in this business is by going down swinging on a deal they held before it broke. This job is not about rocket science. It's about hustle, hard work, diligence—and no ego. Because if you think you're smarter and right on deals, you're going to go down the tubes too often. My approach is always trying to control risk by not assuming I'm right versus the market.

DREW FIGDOR, GENERAL partner Tiedemann Investment Group and portfolio manager of TIG's event-driven global merger-arbitrage strategy, found his passion for finance at "a ridiculously young age," he reports—though he has no idea where it came from. "My dad was a research chemist but once I started reading about M&A deals in the newspaper, the story lines just fascinated me." In fact, confides Figdor, a favorite family story relates to a pit stop they made one summer in Minneapolis while traveling across the top of America in camper. "I asked my dad for a quarter and I bought the *Wall Street Journal*. Then I sat down on the corner and read the paper." He was eleven years old.

It was no great leap then, for Figdor—after graduating magna cum laude from the University of Connecticut in 1983—to enroll in NYU's Stern School evening program to study finance. Nor was it a stretch for Figdor to choose to analyze hostile versus friendly deal performance for his master's thesis—amid the era's booming M&A environment. "Essentially, the thesis was that the perception of risk doesn't match the reality. When you're in a hostile deal, there's a perception that it may not work, there's no commitment, they may walk. So there's a high perception of risk and a low perception of the opportunity set." Figdor studied the deals announced over a year, and allows that his results were probably biased simply by the timing of his observations in the mid-1980s. But he found that hostile deals outperformed the friendly ones by an astonishing 11 percentage points. "The conclusion was that the market misprices both risk and the opportunity set."

Figdor had toiled for a year right out of college as a PaineWebber financial analyst before snaring a job in the strategic planning department of Gulf & Western that permitted him to pursue his MBA. With that degree and his thesis in hand, he joined TIG as an arbitrage analyst in 1986, just six years after its founding by Wall Street legend Carl H. Tiedemann. By 1992 he was a general partner and in 1993 Figdor became sole portfolio manager of the TIG Arbitrage Fund.

Still youthful and lithely athletic despite the scattered flecks of gray in his sandy hair that testify to the thirty years he's worked in risk arbitrage, Figdor comes across as just as smitten with the M&A business today as he was as that eleven-year-old. While the business has changed dramatically over his career, Figdor remains captivated by its myriad challenges. "There's a very different information flow now," he wryly allows. Most obviously, he's no longer ripping news updates every twenty minutes from a noisy "ticker" machine tucked inside a closet or paying someone to fax just-filed 10-Ks up from Washington. "Parts of the business today are quite commoditized. Spread merger arbitrage, as of right now [April 2016] is somewhat attractive given the market moves that we've had and the dislocations. But it goes through cycles. I would argue that spreads on friendly deals last summer were—almost typically—priced too tight. Especially relative to the low interest rate environment."

With interest rates very low, Figdor goes on, "you're playing for a smaller spread. Your up/down is worse today than it would have been in a different period, simply by the fact that interest rates are so low. If interest rates were 5 percent, the spread today would be $2 instead of $1. The market, I think, doesn't price that well, because it looks at deals and says, 'Okay, we're earning 4 percent, interest rates are zero or 1 percent. Good enough.'" But the downside isn't the same today—it's worse," in relation to the shrunken upside.

In general, adds Figdor, the risk-arb portfolios on offer in times of market optimism are uninspiring—and ones on offer in times of market stress are attractive. "I feel really strongly that what we do well—at least historically—is going towards the light—risk—when it's ugly. That's when you're compensated. "The best examples are real ones, so think about 2008." In that monumentally ugly financial crisis year, Figdor continues, "my top-six positions traded at a gross discount to the spread terms—if the deal terms were 100, they were trading at 75 to 80. So, on average, they had 25 percent to 33 percent upside. All of them were going to be determined within a short time. Good or bad. And your downside was, let's assume, still 25 percent–33 percent. In other words, you were trading at one up, one down—given a tremendous discount *for the perception of risk*. All six of those deals closed on the original terms. So, in the fourth quarter of '08, our portfolio was not disadvantaged and ended positive."

You Can't Commoditize Fear

Indeed, says Figdor, "I have a strong belief there is no merger that I like or dislike: It's the spread that matters. It's the opportunity that is there or is not there. What you're really looking for are areas of the market that are less commoditized or more stressed, because the market does an inefficient job of pricing risk." For instance, he adds, "hostile deals trade the same to me today as they traded in 1985—there's been no commoditization because you can't commoditize fear. While the opportunity set varies over time, the overall win/lose ratio and the profits from each deal are fairly constant."

To illustrate, Figdor points to Westlake Chemical's pursuit of Axiall Corp. during the first half of 2016. "Westlake made a hostile bid for Axiall, at the end of January, at a 109 percent premium over prior-day price, and the stock pretty immediately ran up to around $17 on a hostile bid of just about $20 a share. So the deal was trading at a discount of $3—which was pretty much unheard of, historically. The market was pricing in fear because it looked at Westlake's history. The last time it had made a bid, which was a number of years earlier, it had eventually walked away from it. So Westlake was viewed with skepticism and the market was pricing in this tremendous up/down. But once we did the research, we could tell that Westlake was commit-ted—all that had to happen to close that gap was for them to launch a proxy contest, which is a fairly low-cost/low-risk alternative, as M&A tactics go. They did launch a proxy fight, the spread tightened by $3, and we were able to monetize the trade."

Risk, allows Figdor, fascinates him endlessly—and it's a fascination that has paid dividends to TIG's investors in spades. "One of the things we've done well, historically, is increase our exposure at times when markets turn fearful—as in 2008, 2011, 2015, and other times. When markets swooned in July/August of 2015, our portfolio went from 62 percent gross long invested to 105 percent gross long, because I was offered a different opportunity set. That's been fairly consistent through time. Some of that thought process goes back to liking hos-tile deals. The study I did in grad school has been really formative for me because it was about how people price risk and how they give you a portfolio of opportunities. There's a perception that *risk is bad*. I see it in how I see people invest—the focus these days is on friendly announced deals because they're perceived as low risk. Yet complex deals in today's market are priced one up, three down, one up four down—while a friendly deal is one up, 20 down, one up 30 down. So what's a better bet in a diversified portfolio?"

No Index Hugging

Figdor continues, "Theoretically, we're in the business of absolute return alpha generation. So focusing on a portfolio of non-correlated research ideas, which totally depend on my team's ability to research and differentiate the trade—that is where I want to be. By definition, whether I'm right or wrong, it's alpha: it's independent, it's non-correlated." Thus, to put it bluntly, Figdor's style is the polar opposite of index-hugging. It also tends to the very short-term. Figdor explains, "Our focus is really looking for short-dated events where we can focus our research, our time, and our trading because they have less risk. I'll give you current example. There was news last Friday [April 1, 2016] that Virgin America—which both Alaska Air and JetBlue were bidding for—would likely be bought by Alaska Air on Monday. Now, airline deals are scary. Oil prices impact them, labor impacts them, time, volatility—it can be extreme. But we looked at that and said, 'Okay, if the event is on Monday, how much risk do I have from Friday to Monday? I own all the event risk. But I don't have very much in the way of oil risk, labor risk, fundamental risk.' Those *could* hit you over the weekend but have a much lower probability of being significant and/or hitting at all. The market *knew* this on Friday—in fact, that afternoon, at 3:50, there was another report out saying the winner of the bidding contest would be announced Monday. You'd actually have an outcome, in days. What you're trying to do in a deal is put yourself in position to win the call option. In this particular case, it wasn't *rumortrage*. The auction process had been widely reported—first in the *Wall Street Journal*, as I recall. Now, it was going to succeed, or not, in short order. Yet despite all that information being out in the market, on Friday you could have bought Virgin America at $39 a share. When the deal was announced on Monday, the deal was priced at $57. So, does the market price risk and opportunity correctly? Clearly not."

Figdor continues, "One of my analysts walked in Monday morning and said, 'That's crazy. Who would have thought $57?' But I said, 'That's why we do it. People don't price in that opportunity set.'" Figdor goes on, "They're like, 'Well, the stock's at $39, so the deal will be done at $45.' But the reality is, through time, those stocks are bid higher. There were two bidders, significant potential synergies. The EBITDA of Virgin America is $300 million and, for synergy—we were tossing around anywhere from zero to $300 million. Well, Alaska Air has since come out with an estimate of their own of $225 million in synergy. That's a powerful number—$300 million of EBITDA and $225 million of synergy. I'm continuously fascinated with how the perception of risk affects market prices."

Risk, Within Limits

Figdor did not, however, back up the proverbial truck and load his portfolio with Virgin America that Friday. "I owned a position. I wish I had a bigger one. We looked at it, but one of the things we try to do well is consistently apply the rules we've learned to protect ourselves—while taking risk—in our thirty years of doing this. In this specific case, our rule is to own [no more than] 100 bips, because it's a deal that will be on the tape on Monday and you'll see how it goes. We have guidelines for hostile deals, too. If they meet a certain criteria, the position size should be X. Bigger, if they launch a tender with financing and no antitrust, etc.—for higher quality. What you're trying to do is protect yourself when taking risk, balance it out."

He continues, "Portfolio position sizes in up-for-sales should be similar. Years ago, I bet big on a rumored Savient Pharmaceuticals up-for-sale deal. It was a terrible loss, I was totally wrong—and it was a bigger position than anything else. I had thought, 'I *know* this one is good.' We learned from that. We make mistakes and we learn. We initiated rules that say, 'the percentage that we allow in each position is X.' In the Savient case, we underestimated the risk the deal wouldn't happen, and we underestimated the downside. So *process* is key. When you're looking at an up-for-sale, the longer-dated the process is, by definition, the crappier that prospect is for us." Thus, adds Figdor, "when Virgin Atlantic had formally put themselves up for sale three months earlier, it was a crappy process. You had to own it for probably three months. Didn't know what their motivation was. Didn't know a lot of things. But take that same event on a Friday, and say that on Monday they're either going to sign a merger agreement or fail—that's a better trade."

It's not that Figdor is risk-averse, far from it, but he's careful to put the odds on his side. Being conscious of how risk changes over time in deals is a big part of that. "Hiding under a rock [during a market crisis] is not a good strategy—it doesn't work because I truly believe the losses will find you. If you're not actually trying to make money, the losses will find you, and you won't be making money—so, net-net, you're probably going to lose money. I am always looking for the opportunity in risk, because it's always mispriced."

A contrarian to the core, Figdor is quite happy operating in the risk-arb universe *after* a big deal falls apart. "When a Shire/AbbVie breaks, all the deal spreads blow out. But it makes no sense for most of them to widen, because at least 90 percent are in different, uncorrelated, businesses." Figdor cites the successful 2015 Medtronic/Covidien deal as an example. "Even though it was also a tax inversion and broadly in the same economic sector as Shire/AbbVie, it wasn't the same deal. Medtronic was trading at a 3 percent–4 percent gross spread the day before Shire/AbbVie collapsed—and traded at a 12–15 percent gross spread the day after. Clearly, it was then a better risk."

Research to the Max

But Figdor doesn't rely solely on changing spread relationships to make portfolio decisions. He also "maxes out research." The TIG approach, he explains, is DIY: "We travel to directly meet with companies, competitors, regulators." So, the day after Shire/AbbVie fell apart, when Medtronic and Covidien had an analyst meeting in Minneapolis, Figdor flew out to attend. "I was with Medtronic's CFO for an hour-and-a-half—along with twenty of my competitors. That's a unique opportunity, because you're *there*. You're looking them in the eye when you're asking them questions. It's old-school, which is something we really believe in. Our approach is really looking for deep alpha, where research makes a difference—where you can ask the person a question and judge for yourself the answer. So we were there, and he was defending his deal just a day after the other one blew up. Which was what most of the questions were about. It wasn't about what the government would do next because it had just done something. At that point, the question was whether Medtronic still wanted to do the Covidien deal. Well, their commitment seemed strong and the spread was four times wider, so I stuck with my Covidien position, which was small. Now, it wasn't easy to do—in the face of the massive amount of pain I was taking—on our Shire position and throughout the portfolio. But that didn't matter. You still have to take risk, despite crazy pain because that's when opportunity is there—the spread was four times as wide."

Another time Figdor recalls his hands-on approach to research proving its worth involved the 2012 merger of Hertz and Dollar Thrifty. With the deal stuck in regulatory limbo, he travelled to a car rental franchise show in Vegas "to hang out with Hertz and Dollar Thrifty, but more importantly, with their competitors and the franchisees." His questions ran the gamut. "What do you think of the deal? What are the economics? Who's the buyer of the divested assets?" Figdor says he was literally just walking around the Vegas coliseum when he saw a guy whose badge said he ran one of the trade associations. "I asked, 'Who do you think is the buyer for the divested assets?' He answered, 'Not me, but my friend.'" With that, Figdor's concerns about the deal foundering on antitrust divestiture issues melted away.

Again, it's a tenet of faith for Figdor that "risk is not priced linearly." He posits, "Think about a deal that suddenly has an antitrust problem. A 'safe' deal goes from no perceived issues to a second DOJ request for information. Now, what's the likelihood of the deal blowing up from there? Maybe 20 percent more risk. But the spread doesn't go from $1 to $1.20. It goes from $1 to $2, or to $2.50. That's a nonlinear reaction. Still, it's tricky—it's an interesting debate about risk/reward because if the deal breaks, you're not losing a rate of return, you're going to lose money. It's a balancing act. But I find that a lot of the opportunity lies in these nonlinear relationships."

When events turn against one of his risk-arb positions—as inevitably happens from time to time, concedes Figdor, what he does "depends." The rule, he says, "basically is that if you spot risk rising, be the first to sell because it's always good to exit the position. We have catch-phrases, internally—things like, 'Your first sale is your best sale.' But that's *not* true as much if a deal just suddenly breaks because then *everybody knows*—that's just the outcome—so you have to go back to your research. For instance, when Shire broke and the news hit the tape, the deal was over. In that situation, it's actually better if you buy because everyone else is panicked and running for the door. On average in those cases, it's probably better to hold, at least for a bounce. But our strategy, in general, is just to take our hits and move on to fight another day."

Capital Preservation, First and Foremost

Figdor stresses, "Capital preservation is the key to the risk-arb business. It is by design supposed to be an absolute return business and if you have negative numbers, you're going to have very unhappy clients. I was working here at TIG as a young analyst in 1987 and it was a disastrous experience. The portfolio was losing a million bucks a day—mostly because of how it was constructed going into the crash—and it was only $20 million to begin with." But that searing 1987 experience taught Figdor lessons he's never forgotten. "I have to run a tight, absolute-return, strict, merger-arbitrage business, because restructurings—in a tough market—get crushed. I saw how much money we lost. I heard the clients complaining, 'I thought you were absolute return. You really aren't.' When you're losing 20 percent as the world goes ugly, that's what happens. So when I took over the portfolio in '93, I made sure that I was very strict about doing what we told clients we'd do. If you tell the client that you will only lose 1.5 percent, maximum, in any position, you have to stick to that, if the situation arises, and move on."

The ironic thing about that, Figdor continues, "is that clients mostly tend to appreciate it only in retrospect. In other words, 2008 was a really dark period for us—even though we made money—because everybody was taking money out of the fund. Partly, because they *could*. We didn't gate them. But they were also fearful. It wasn't until a year later that they were all like, 'Wow, that was an awesome job. I'm going to give you more money.' This just shows that patience and perseverance are key to a long-term, absolute return business."

It's no mean feat, Figdor adds, "But you've got to have the mindset that when bad things happen, it *isn't* a bad thing. It's an *opportunity*—to find a risk in a good way." Reminisces Figdor, "One of the better events that ever happened to me was when the European Union blocked the GE/Honeywell merger. I lost a small amount when the deal broke because I had been doing what I say I do—selling my position down as the deal started going bad—so that by the day the EU ruling came down, I had virtually no position in it. It wasn't that I was genius, it was just that I'd already taken my losses along the way. But when that deal collapsed, the spreads on every other proposed deal blew out, and the ones that had antitrust issues blew out *a lot*. In fact, I would argue, that one 'EU black box regulatory decision' is still blowing out European deal spreads today—making it one of the best events, ever, from my perspective as an arbitrageur."

Another point Figdor stresses to his young colleagues is that "often what's *not* said is just as important as what's said." He tells a story about some particularly telling nonverbal communication at the Milken/Drexel conference in 2007 to make his point. "LBOs were already widening out to big spreads, credit was disintegrating, and the market was wobbling. I was walking up to the buyers in every deal represented at the conference and testing a theory, saying, 'Your deal is economically cracked. Financing costs are going through the roof. What do you do?' It got funny when I walked up to someone from a private equity shop that had a deal to buy Penn National Gaming. I had barely started my spiel when he literally fell over backwards trying to get away from me. Now, if the deal were fine, you're not doing that. If the deal's not fine, that's what you're doing. You have to be sensitive to what's said and not said—and how."

Testing Theories

One reason he's effective in gleaning information from corporate executives, institutional shareholders, regulators, and the like, says Figdor, is that he tries "not to be a mooch." He explains, "you want to be a value-added. Instead of asking a 'dumb arbitrage' question, which insults your source because he knows he's being used, ask a theoretical question about value and provide a perspective. That changes the dynamic of the conversation and increases the quality of the answer. So we're always trying to test a theory—not asking open-ended questions."

When something significant goes awry in the portfolio, Figdor adds, "I go home, hug my wife and kids, and try to remember that there's always tomorrow in this business—that if you learn from your mistakes, you'll succeed." Then, Figdor and his team work through "a process we call an experience transformer. It starts with what we did right, what we did wrong, what we can do better next time—from a positive perspective. That's the key. One of the things I learned the hard way is that if you're yelling at someone about a mistake at nine o'clock in the morning, 'You idiot, you lost me money. What the— were you thinking?' everybody in the shop is working on eggshells. No one's thinking about making money and you're not thinking about it, either. Opportunities are lost."

The proposed inversion merger deal between Allergan and Pfizer blew up late on a Monday afternoon in April 2016, as Figdor sat being interviewed for this profile. A release from Treasury Secretary Jacob Lew's office moved across the news wires, outlining a packet of changes to tax and merger regulations. The hum of conversation on TIG's trading desk in the adjacent room instantly got louder, more intense, as analysts and traders put their heads together or worked their phones and computers furiously. Very soon, an analyst signaled to Figdor from the door of the conference room and the arb quickly excused himself to scan the release and confer with colleagues. What didn't happen was notable—no screaming, no yelling, no audible swearing—on Figdor's part or anyone else's. Just practiced teamwork.

Within ten minutes, Figdor was back in the conference room, relaying the news, apologizing for the interruption, and suggesting we pick up the interview after the dust settled. Two weeks later, when we did, Figdor jumped right into providing a blow-by-blow. "Lew's notice included a three-year look-back provision on inversion deals—and the second I saw 'three-year look-back,' I knew we were screwed. The whole structure of the law and M&A practice up to that point was two years. If you considered a merger that was done for corporate tax efficiency, the tax code stated that two years was the cool-off period to be considered part of a plan. But they did a per se rule—said those two-year tests no longer applied—that anything done within three years was assumed to be done with the intention of combining. That Treasury release strapped on those dramatic assumptions, and I pretty much knew right away that was the end of deal, no matter what Pfizer wanted."

Trading-wise, Figdor went on, "Pfizer didn't move. Our short in the name was up less than 1 percent from the close of trading—and it was pretty simple for me to cover 100 percent. At the end of the day, I no longer had the right to be short Pfizer because, in our opinion, there'd be no deal, or only a restructured one. The risk of being wrong was less than 1 percent. As I said, your first trade is often your best trade, as long as the outcome isn't in the market. It obviously wasn't, because the parties hadn't said anything. The government had just put out a notice. On the other side of the trade, we sold 20 percent of our position in Allergan at $225, which is about what we'd expected from a risk/reward perspective, and that's how I went home. The following day, Allergan traded as high as $245, and within the next two days, we sold the bulk of our position, realizing an average price of $235-ish. So the downside was $30–$40, a 12 percent to 15 percent loss, which was annoying and painful, but it is what it is. The market doesn't care what your cost basis is. It's irrelevant, get over it. The good news, just as I would expect, was that all the other deals blew out; the spreads widened significantly—and we took advantage of that."

Not Rocket Science

Figdor adds, "in the twenty-three years I've been doing this, I've had losses on only eight deals that met or exceeded 1.5 percent of the portfolio, which isn't great, but clearly shows that we manage losses. Our objective is a bit odd—to take losses *quicker*. Essentially, never assume that you're smarter than the market—that's a fool's game. And manage the portfolio through time. The way guys lose a lot in this business is by going down swinging on a deal they held before it broke. This job is not about rocket science. It's about hustle, hard work, diligence— and no ego. Because if you think you're smarter and right on deals, you're going to go down the tubes too often. My approach is always trying to control risk by not assuming I'm right versus the market. We work hard, as a team, to be open and honest with each other and ourselves about our research and constantly reassess our positions. One thing we've measured for years is how fast we can sell out of a position; change our viewpoint from positive to negative, because that's really how success is rated. As it turns out, we've only owned 60 percent of all deals that have broken, and of those, on average, by the day they've broken, we've owned less than 30 percent of our original position. That speaks to our consistent approach to our *process*."

In fact, Figdor opines, "If you have a full position in a merger, either you think there are no issues, antitrust or otherwise, or you're insane." As soon as there's a whiff of any issues, TIG is scaling back its position. For a risk-arb fund, it doesn't run an especially diversified book—maybe twenty-five names, with 5 percent–6 percent of assets, maximum, in any one. "But we try to have a concentrated book of ideas, when they become near-dated," Figdor concludes. "*We're not a buy and hold merger-arb spread shop.* Instead, we focus heavily on being a complex, trade the events, creative shop."

Risk arb, Figdor clearly knows, is in large part an art, and risk management isn't rocket science. His genius lies in the highly disciplined and thoughtful processes he applies to wield the art in the service of creating alpha for clients.

CHAPTER SIXTEEN

Jamie Zimmerman

Litespeed does lots and lots of fundamental research work on the acquirer and the target, as well as on the industry involved, trying to understand why they're doing the deal, what they see, who the people are, and what the incentives are. Distressed deals likewise require tons of research. It's always perversely fun to come across a bankrupt entity that got in over its head because it bought another company for too much money. You can go back to the original proxy and compare what they said they they'd accomplish with what wound up happening. Nobody goes into those things thinking they won't be successful. But sometimes it doesn't work, for any of a whole host of reasons.

ASK JAMIE ZIMMERMAN to describe what she does for a living and she instantly responds, "I'm like an investigative reporter looking for value with a financial event overlay. The numbers only tell you so much about the past and you have to figure out what they're going to be for the next year; nobody knows that for sure. But you *can* analyze and predict it," she adds emphatically.

Yet the direct and plain-spoken Zimmerman, who manages billions of dollars in event-driven assets for investors in Litespeed Partners, the hedge fund she founded in 2000, never intended to make her mark on Wall Street. Not that her schoolgirl aspirations were in any way blinkered as she grew up in prosperous Scarsdale, New York—Zimmerman set her sights on becoming the first woman on the Supreme Court. When Sandra Day O'Connor beat her to the punch, nominated by President Reagan just months after Zimmerman's 1981 magna cum laude graduation from Amherst College, she nonetheless continued, undaunted, on to the University of Michigan Law School. While there, Zimmerman—who now, at fifty-seven, is renowned in investment circles for her still-boundless energy—picked up both a JD and a master's in English Literature in the time it takes most grad students to earn just one degree. She also acquired an unshakable conviction that the *last* thing she wanted to do was spend her life practicing law. Casting about after graduation, Zimmerman fixed on her love of writing and "had all sorts of weird interviews—the DA's office, a bank, *Sports Illustrated*." But nothing truly struck a chord.

To buy herself time, in 1984 Zimmerman took a job clerking for a bankruptcy judge in New York's Southern District. "The code had just been rewritten in 1978, so it was pretty new and it took a while for the courts to knock it around, so I pretty much knew as much about it as anyone—having studied it from the beginning," Zimmerman explains. "But I really had no idea what I wanted to do. All I knew was that what I had thought I wanted to do was making me quite miserable."

Searching for inspiration, Zimmerman went to her five-year reunion at Amherst with a mission—poll her classmates to find ones who were enjoying both their work and their lives. The doctors, she discovered, "were sweating it." Those who had gotten Harvard MBAs and had become consultants "were spending most of their time stuck in a Howard Johnson's near some plant in the middle of nowhere; the investment bankers were working 24/7." Only her classmates who'd become bond traders, Zimmerman says, "were doing well financially, having a lot of fun and had lives that made me think, 'Okay, I'm going to do that.'" The more she analyzed it, Zimmerman continues, the more she realized that the idea of making calculated bets appealed deeply to her. "That's what had felt wrong about being in law, just being an advisor. I like to be the risk-taker, it turns out."

Looking for a Segue, Finding a Calling

Looking to act on that insight, Zimmerman recalls, she consulted friends already working on Wall Street. They pushed her towards corporate finance but she wound up "almost by accident" falling into a job in the risk-arbitrage department at L. F. Rothschild—as it happened, just two weeks before Ivan Boesky was arrested for insider trading. Zimmerman adds, "I was hired by Michael Gordon, who was then L. F. Rothschild's cohead of research—and I remember his future partner (in Angelo Gordon), John Angelo, who then was head of arbitrage at Rothschild, congratulating me for having the guts to join an arbitrage group at the time! But, really, when I started, I was just looking at it as a segue. I wanted to make some real money before trying journalism." The thing was, Zimmerman—whose words and thoughts tumble out in conversation at a breakneck pace, frequently making unexpected connections while probing and challenging assumptions, her own and others'—was almost immediately sucked in by the pace, excitement, and challenges she found on L. F. Rothschild's arb desk.

Its culture of rapid research and equally rapid decision-making, she found, was right up her alley. Zimmerman's intensity, passion, and anything-but-timid voice quickly turned colleagues' heads. Risk arbitrage, she pretty much immediately grasped, "is a how much and when strategy. There's a monetization or an exchange of one security for another, or for some cash," and the risk is simply that it doesn't happen. What's more, that Zimmerman entered the business just as the mid-1980s M&A boom was being thrown into reverse by the Boesky scandal—as well as by the subsequent prosecution and disintegration of Mike Milken's junk bond machine—actually worked in her favor, "as a result of my experience in bankruptcy law." She had been hired at Rothschild, Zimmerman explains, primarily to handle bond market opportunities and "when all the distressed situations and bankruptcies suddenly started falling into the laps of the people in the arb department—and they seized on them as opportunities—the workflow played to my strengths. We ended up being very busy. It was great for me." Indeed, in addition to all the rapidly unraveling LBOs serving up distressed opportunities, Texaco sought Chapter 11 protection late in 1987 in what, at the time, was the largest corporate bankruptcy ever. (The oil giant filed for bankruptcy in a desperate—and ultimately unsuccessful—maneuver to try to avoid a huge jury award in a Texas lawsuit brought by Pennzoil after it lost a bitter 1983 bidding war for Getty Oil to Texaco.)

From L. F. Rothschild, Zimmerman moved to Dillon Read in 1988 to focus on arbitrage and bankruptcies. She wound up primarily working under Alan Curtis, a legendary arbitrageur. "He was demanding," Zimmerman remembers, "and he was a great mentor. I learned a lot from him." She illustrates with two stories. In one, a financial company deal she'd invested in cratered when news hit the ticker that fraud was discovered in one of its auto loan portfolios. "I had lost a million dollars in a minute—which was a lot of money back then—and I was literally nauseous. Friends were asking if I was about to throw up. I walked into Alan's office, shaking. I was a wreck. But he simply said, 'You couldn't see fraud in an auto loan portfolio. How could you know that? You didn't do anything wrong.' Then he added, 'But yes, we lost this money, so let's get going onto the next thing.'"

Zimmerman's second Alan Curtis story is also about an arb deal involving the merger of two banks. One had foreclosed on a piece of real estate, arousing fears in the market that the deal would be delayed if an expensive environmental cleanup were mandated on the plot. Zimmerman says she did extensive research into the situation, calling local officials, realtors, and even journalists to try to substantiate the rumors—as well as calling the state department of natural resources with jurisdiction in the case. With the bureaucrats, she used her legal training to get chummy on the phone and elicited a regulator's insight that even if the company had exposure, it would be capped at $1 million. On that basis, Zimmerman pronounced the deal "plain vanilla"—and the firm stood pat on what she remembers as a 4.99 percent position. "But, of course, one day, the stock just dropped like a rock, let's say from $36 to $28, and I'm getting crucified because I'd said it was plain vanilla. It turned out that one of the reporters I had talked to decided to write a story saying the deal might be delayed." Zimmerman continues, "Well, I sat there calling everybody involved in the deal, telling them they had to put out a press release about the cap on any potential liability. But we took it on the chin all afternoon. It wasn't until the next morning that they put out a release, the selling pressure let up and the stock bounced back up to $36. All the time it had been cratering, Alan had been screaming at me, 'Why did you say it was plain vanilla?' But I stood my ground, and we bought more of it, too, on the dip. Then of course, *after* the stock rebounded, he wanted to know why we didn't buy more!" Zimmerman chuckles, "By the way, I think it's good to have people around you who are demanding of themselves and others—and Alan was great in that regard."

Do Your Own Work

Zimmerman reflects, "What I learned is just to do my own work, know what you're doing, and have faith in your own judgment. Whatever you can learn makes your predictive abilities better, and it is all about performance, not appearance." She muses, "It was so much different from being a lawyer. In that profession, there was so much concern about how you looked to the outside person. But the whole investment industry is just interested in what's the right answer. It doesn't matter if you sound like an idiot on the phone, as long as you wind up getting the right answer, you know what I'm saying?"

The late 1989 collapse of the proposed highly leveraged buyout of UAL by the airline's employees isn't an event whose details spring to Zimmerman's mind nearly thirty years after the fact. "I was a junior-junior, so it wasn't my deal. But what I do remember is that after that, all deal financing just disappeared. And my boss at Dillon Read retired." (The firm had been heavily and publicly involved as arbs in the UAL deal.) "At that point, I decided to move on and interviewed at both Oppenheimer's distressed unit and American Securities' risk-arb department. I remember Neil Goldstein at American Securities telling me that there was *never* going to be any arbitrage business ever again, so I should go to Oppenheimer and do distressed. He was right for at least four years."

Zimmerman notes happily, however, that the early and mid-1990s "turned out great for restructurings. I mean fabulous. That's why I've always thought that risk arbitrage and bonds and bankruptcies are just different sides of the credit cycle. It used to be—at least, until QE skewed things—that you could always count on one or the other to be serving up very interesting investment opportunities. If there was no financing, you had a lot of restructurings; if there was a lot of financing, there was lots of M&A—and risk arbitrage. There was always something interesting to do to make money in the event space." Long story short, Zimmerman stayed at Oppenheimer until 1997, when Toronto Dominion Bank recruited her to head up research for a new business push into risk arbitrage and special situation portfolios. The very next year, however, the bank's commitment to the business proved unexpectedly shallow. Long-Term Capital Management's swift demise and the attendant financial crisis spooked the bank into slashing its allocation to the event-driven space. Unsurprisingly, Zimmerman—whose second child had been born in late 1997—took that as a sign and started sounding out potential investors. It was time to start her own firm.

Birthing Pains

Which is precisely what she did, launching Litespeed Management and its Litespeed Partners hedge fund in October 2000. Much of her initial capital was supposed to have come from a friend with a high-tech business, a plan that imploded with the internet bubble. Litespeed ended up debuting with a modest $4 million in assets, much of it raised from her former bosses. Zimmerman's timing, clearly, was less than auspicious. But fate had already dealt her a crueler blow, the sudden death of her husband in early 1998. Says Zimmerman, "the truth is that at that point, I should already have been seeded by someone long ago—if my husband hadn't died and I didn't have two little kids. Everyone said, 'Uh-oh, wait, wait, are you sure?' Finally, I said, 'Well, to hell with this. I'm good at this. I'm just going to start'." Barely pausing for breath, she adds, "we got assets up to like $3.5 billion at one point, which was sort of amazing. We're not at $3.5 billion anymore now, but we'll get there again."

A life-long athlete who spent the summer after her Amherst graduation biking cross-country from Oregon to Virginia with friends, Zimmerman named Litespeed for her favorite brand of racing bikes—but Litespeed, the hedge fund, did not find its business accelerating rapidly. She admits to naively expecting assets to simply pour in as word of her better than 22 percent gain in her first full year in business spread. Instead, Litespeed's AUM were still only mid-double-digits after two full years in business, so she hired a marketer to help raise assets. But everything came together for Litespeed in 2003. Zimmerman turned in her best-ever performance, up 45 percent; her hedge fund ended the twelve months with north of $120 million in assets. That December *Barron's* featured an interview with Zimmerman headlined "Damsel in Distress." From there, Litespeed's asset base took off—until 2008, when like so many other hedge funds, she was wrong-footed by the collapse of Lehman Brothers and, despite hedges, closed the year down 21 percent. Zimmerman rebounded more than 30 percent the following year and has been rebuilding since.

Being able to invest in the full range of event-driven situations, from bankruptcies to M&A, Zimmerman stresses, gives Litespeed an advantage. "Because you understand where equities can go and you understand, on the other hand, what happens when people can't repay the debt in their capital structure—and that opens up a whole host of tricks to us, as investors." In fact, she continues, "a lot of the debt restructurings in which we've made the most money have been where we have bought a bond that got turned into a stock." She cites American Airlines as an example. "We were a very large bondholder in it during the bankruptcy. We bought a lot of the bonds at prices beginning at like 17 cents on the dollar, 20 cents, 23 cents. Those bonds ultimately were bid up to something like $1.20 on the dollar. Then we exchanged a lot of them for shares. We wound up making a huge return because we caught the airline cycle right. What started out as restructuring ended up with a consolidation in the industry."

The great advantage of risk arbitrage as a discipline, notes Zimmerman, is evident in looking at how many of today's multistrategy hedge funds all started out as arb funds. "Why was that?" she asks, pausing not quite a beat before answering her own question. "Because it's a risk management system. You assume contract law governance, you assume people don't actually enter into contracts—spend money on attorneys and financial advisors—to *not* complete a transaction. So risk arb is really mostly about how to evaluate risk, how to size positions, understand how much the upside will be, when you will get it, and what the potential downside is." And at the other end of the cycle, in bankruptcy workouts, that same contractual framework can be worked in reverse.

Zimmerman, who stacks up as "conservative" versus most other hedge fund managers for only rarely using even a tiny bit of leverage in Litespeed's portfolio, reiterates that the first thing she considers when looking at a risk-arb deal is its potential downside. "I mean, any of the deals is just a trade. So the questions are what are you risking and what can you expect to get? It's just a question of risk and reward. Plus, how sure are you of your estimates of your downside and upside?" Zimmerman continues, "then, before you can put yourself into a position to get lucky if a bidding war or whatnot breaks out, you first have to decide, 'How to size this?'" It's always tempting, she notes, to simply focus on potential rewards, "but it's much more disciplined to look at what could wrong; what do I lose if it goes wrong? And how big can I afford to be in this, if it does go wrong?" She concludes vehemently, "The *last* thing you want to do is kill yourself. You have to live to fight another day. If you size yourself appropriately and something goes wrong, you can go and make the money back somewhere else."

Playing Through the Cycle

She adds, "Litespeed does lots and lots of fundamental research work on the acquirer and the target, as well as on the industry involved, trying to understand why they're doing the deal, what they see, who the people are, and what the incentives are." Distressed deals likewise require tons of research, she acknowledges. "It's always perversely fun to come across a bankrupt entity that got in over its head because it bought another company for too much money. You can go back to the original proxy and compare what they *said* they'd accomplish with what actually wound up happening. Nobody goes into deals thinking they won't be successful. But sometimes it doesn't work, for any of a whole host of reasons." Zimmerman continues, "Look at Ralcorp. It spun off Post within four years of taking it over. Or look at Manitowoc, which bought Enodis in 2008. It worked, but now they're splitting it off under pressure from activists."

Timing is the other crucial—and uncertain—element in risk arbitrage and, really, all event-driven investing, notes Zimmerman. "We have a position in Globalstar right now [summer 2016], and it's taken three-and-a-half years from the notice of proposed rule-making to get a ruling circulated on the FCC's eighth floor. That is insane—a ridiculously long period of time. But the notion of how much and when is really what determines the rate of return. If you know something is a tender, it's thirty days, or if it's a merger, maybe it's ninety days, or if it involves a very long regulatory process, maybe it takes nine months or even a year. Whatever it is, we try to be conservative on timing and our rate of return requirement obviously has to take that into account. But that shouldn't only apply to risk arb, it should really be true for every investment. Otherwise, there tends to be an undisciplined assumption that the market will just take you where you need to go," Zimmerman opines. "For me, the higher the risk I see in a deal, the greater rate of return I demand."

Where Zimmerman parts company with many fellow arbs and event investors is on the question of hedging. "Often we play around and don't hedge everything or hedge things only partially—if we're very certain that one and one might equal three," she says. "But only after doing exhaustive fundamental research, and we always know our downside." Her reason: "Sometimes it is actually more risky to hedge. Look what happened in the Pfizer/Allergan deal." When the Treasury rewrote its tax policy in a surprise move to block the proposed tax-inversion merger in the spring of 2016, she explains, "as a risk arb, you would have lost *less money* if you had ignored conventional practice and had *not* shorted the acquirer. Because the shares of Pfizer, the acquirer, actually *rose* in price when the deal broke. Pfizer is around $34 today and it was trading down as low as $28," before the Treasury squashed the deal."

Value Investing with an Event Overlay

Shifting gears as smoothly as she does while driving her Mercedes AMG wagon—Zimmerman calls its staid "mommy-mobile" exterior "perfect camouflage" for getting up to 135 mph on the highway with impunity—she theorizes that a reason many risk arbs also do bankrupt-cies and restructurings is tied to the increasing complexity of corpo-rate balance sheets. Arbs, she notes, have to be comfortable analyzing complex securities and arcane conversion ratios to assess valuations. "We're value investors with an event overlay." But value investors with an advantage, she stresses. "The beautiful thing about risk arb and restructurings is that oftentimes you get monetized without having to wait for market liquidity. Maybe someone refinances you out of a bond you bought for 60 cents on the dollar at par. So the great thing about these strategies is that you can be market-neutral or uncorrelated to the market. Your position can be monetized without you having to sell it in the market—and since you don't actually have to sell, you can only make one mistake in a position—a bad purchase—not two."

When something does inevitably go awry, Zimmerman doesn't nec-essarily follow received wisdom in the risk-arb space. "We don't sell broken deals instantly. Take Australia's Treasury Wine Estates. There was talk of a bid for it in 2014 by KKR and of an additional bid by Rhone Capital and TPG. The KKR bid was for a takeout at A$5.30, and we thought it would happen. But they called off the auction on a Sunday night conference call from Australia. It was in September and I was coming home from the Hamptons. I was in someone's car listen-ing into this call—and the stock fell from, I want to say, like A$5.30 to A$4.20 immediately. We wound up keeping it. Not long enough—because it went higher after we finally sold. I think it's at A$9 today. But it turned out that the company was right to resist those bids. They had just hired a new CEO and he turned it around—with a big assist from a weakening Australian dollar. As it fell they were able to export wine to meet soaring demand in the Far East. They were absolutely right to call off the auction. It was a real missed opportunity for KKR and TPG. Who knows why they didn't increase their bids? Anyway, you shouldn't always sell a deal stock on a break."

Another example, says Zimmerman, was Shire Pharmaceuticals after the Shire/AbbVie deal broke. "I think Shire came all the way back. You have to have a sense of what you think the risk/reward is for hold-ing or covering." Likewise, Office Depot. After the 2016 ODP/Staples deal was scotched by the courts, Zimmerman says, "we covered the Staples but we still own the ODP. It is trading at less than four times EBIDTA and nobody's really been running the company. I'm not say-ing it's a growth stock, but I don't think it's disappearing tomorrow, either. We'll see." Interviewed in late May 2016, Zimmerman was also holding on to Litespeed's position in Allergan, despite the recent failure of its planned inversion merger with Pfizer. "Allergan, you can argue, once they get $40 billion from selling their generics business to Teva Pharmaceuticals in the next week or two, and start buying back stock, is going to move higher. So why would you sell it now? Then, there's Pfizer. Why would you necessarily rush to cover it? They clearly want to buy something. You've got all these companies bidding for things like Medivation, outfits with long pipelines and no cash flow. Who knows how the market will perceive what gets paid if Pfizer were to go for assets like that? So maybe it's best to leave that short out there." (Pfizer traded at just under $35 a share at the time of the interview and about the same on Aug. 22, 2016, when it announced the purchase of Medivation for $14 billion, or $81.50 a share. A little more than a month later, Pfizer traded under $30 a share, but it is back around $36 and change as this nears print.) "There's no one way to play arbitrage positions," Zimmerman firmly avers.

Nor is there just one way to analyze risk-arbitrage situations, in Zimmerman's book. During the early part of Office Depot and Staples's most recent attempt to merge, she says, Litespeed stayed away from the deal. "I actually expected the FTC to turn down the plan," Zimmerman says, because she had looked at the political backgrounds of the five FTC commissioners, the legal record of the head of its antitrust division, and position papers that staffers had published on the FTC website. Once the dispute got into the federal courts, however, Zimmerman put her legal background heavily into play and reevaluated. It was no contest in the courtroom, she decided, between the opposing litigators. "It seemed from the beginning that the lead attorney for Staples was just doing a dance" around the less-experienced counsel for the FTC. "We thought that meant the judge would rule against the FTC, but it turned out we were wrong."

It's precisely because outcomes can be unpredictable, despite best efforts at research, contends Zimmerman, that it's crucial to correctly size arb positions in a portfolio. Doing so is a kind of risk management system, she explains, that's inherent in the practice of risk arbitrage. "Basically, if you're going into a deal," she observes, "it's because you think it's going to happen. But in your portfolio, you have to size it so that if it breaks, you don't lose more than a month's profit—or whatever you think is a measure of an amount that you're going to be able to make back in short order." Zimmerman continues, "You have to remember these are essentially bets; you're not always going to get them right. What's more, when you're wrong about a position, you can't let it get in your brain so it defeats you. You have to pick yourself up and do the next deal." Which might involve hanging onto at least a piece of that broken position.

Active, but not Publicly Activist

Litespeed has so far eschewed joining other risk arbs in taking publicly activist positions to "hurry along" the consummation of potential deals. But that doesn't mean Zimmerman has shied away from acting as a "responsible shareholder" behind the scenes when she sees that Litespeed might influence a management. "It's just that nobody knows we're active. If you get too big or too noisy, and it's in the headlines that you own a ton of stock, you have an illiquid position. You don't want that, so we think you have to balance your activism with your ability to get out if you're wrong." She continues, "I think every investment fund is active to the point that we know a lot of managements and they usually know what we think—because that's our job." In one case, Zimmerman recalls, Litespeed had a position in a spinoff that didn't seem to be gaining traction and she urged the CEO to hire a branding firm. When she later found out nothing was happening because his calls to the branding outfit weren't being returned, Zimmerman says, "We introduced them and got very involved."

In another instance, Litespeed took a 6 percent or so position in Bradken, then a mildly distressed Australia-based international supplier of consumable mining equipment, beginning in May 2015. Best-known on trading desks by its ticker symbol, BKN AU, Bradken is the global leader in mill liners and crawler shoes, with world-class production facilities in Canada, India, the United States, and China. These products, responsible for 80 percent of Bradken's revenues, are the "razor blades" of mining—dependent on production levels, not capital expenditures. Their Quebec mill liner plant is automated and best-in-class. Their Kansas foundry for engineered products is unique in its ability to forge large, complicated parts, such as train frames and torpedo tubes. When Zimmerman first acquired its shares, Bradken was trading down around A$2.35 after rejecting as inadequate an A$2.50 a share buyout offer from Pacific Equity Partners and Koch Industries. Very soon thereafter—that June—Bradken issued A$70 million of redeemable convertible preference securities—convertible at a mere A$2 a share—to a consortium consisting of Chilean industrial group Sigdo Koppers SA and CHAMP Private Equity. Nick Greiner, Bradken's chairman, was also CHAMP's deputy chairman. Says Zimmerman, "The conflicts of interest were clear. With the board acting in other than shareholders' best interests, Bradken traded down to under A$1 share."

Headlines quickly followed, suggesting that Litespeed suffered an A$11 million "puncture" on the position. But Zimmerman did not give up, instead upping Litespeed's position to around 13 percent at rock-bottom prices. (In Australia, you are not an insider until you reach 15 percent.) Bradken's Greiner—who earlier had been pressured to step down as the premier of New South Wales for acts "contrary to known and recognized standards of honesty and integrity," and who had been fined in connection with bid-rigging in a takeover involving U.S. buyout firm Castle Harlan—did not take kindly to Zimmerman calling to suggest his actions were anything but friendly to shareholders. In response, Zimmerman became determined to wage a proxy contest in Australia and began calling other shareholders. Over just a few weeks, Litespeed reached out to each and every institutional shareholder of the company and succeeded in forcing changes to Bradken's board without actually filing anything official. Greiner, and two other directors aligned with him, agreed to step down, along with Bradken's long-time CEO Brian Hodges. With Litespeed's blessings, one continuing board member, Phil Arnall, stepped in as Bradken's new chairman and interim CEO. But amid the board turmoil—and obviously lacking a new leader with a plan—the company's shares slid to A$0.485 at year-end 2015.

Recounts Zimmerman, "We visited Arnall and the board in Australia that December and later met with Paul Zuckerman, the front-running candidate for CEO, in New York. We shared with Paul all the information we had gathered about who was dead wood and who was important to the company's future, as well as what buyers we thought were circling for what assets. I think we were most adamant that he should take his compensation in stock because we thought he would be incentivized to make a lot of money for himself and the shareholders. On February 15, 2016, the newly constituted Bradken board officially hired Zuckerman, most recently the CEO of a division of Fletcher

Building Ltd., as CEO as of March 1. Having met Zuckerman at our offices in January, we were very excited to see him take the helm. On April 26, Zuckerman hired Boston Consulting Group to advise on 'supply-chain savings and driving down back-end costs.' Bradken drifted up to $A1/share by the second quarter's end."

Zimmerman continues, "Then, on July 27, Zuckerman issued a press release announcing a restructuring of Bradken's business model and executive management team, whittling down five segments to three and forcing the retirement of several former executives. On August 23, 2016, investors heard forecasts from Zuckerman for the first time. He confirmed our EBITDA projections and outlined pro forma cost savings." Concludes Zimmerman, not even trying to conceal the hard-won satisfaction in her voice, "A few days after the third quarter's end, Bradken announced a deal to be acquired by Hitachi Construction Machinery for A$3.25/share. CHAMP and Sigdo converted their holdings to equity. Had their preference shares been redeemed at par rather than converted to equity, we would have been paid an additional A$0.25/share. But Bradken traded up to A$3.20/share on October 4, 2016."

Zimmerman attributes her uncommon sangfroid in the face of risk-taking uncertainty and the occasional, inevitable defeats and reversals in investing to her lifetime of active engagement in competitive sports. A three-sport athlete at Amherst—who has really never slowed down and looks it—she vividly remembers being "the oldest child of an athletic guy who coached all our teams" beginning in the youngest grades. She adds, "I've always encouraged my daughters to be out there, too, because I've always really believed it was important for them to learn that you will not experience the joy of victory without risking the agony of defeat. If you don't feel comfortable living through that—if you don't learn young that it's okay to lose, because what really matters in life is to pick yourself up and keep going—it's a real handicap. Everybody trips. It's what you do after you trip—do you pick yourself up and keep going, or do you give up?—that distinguishes long-time winners from losers." She reiterates, "You can only know the joy of victory if you're willing to risk defeat. It's just not realistic to expect never to trip, even if you're always going for the win."

Drawing further on her thirty years of experience in Wall Street, Zimmerman reflects on her career: "The *idea* of serving on the Supreme Court was quite nice. It was very much '*a contribute to society*' sort of idea. But *the day-to-day* of being a judge or an advocate—as opposed to a risk-taker—just wasn't me. If someone had actually sat me down while I was in school and said, 'Hey, Jamie, that's not really who you are,' I might have had a straighter shot." As the mother of two daughters, she adds, "I've always told them, 'You have to go to school and learn as much as possible because nobody really knows what the next thing is going to be. You have to be open-minded and full of skills, so you can see it and maneuver towards it—as the world keeps changing, cyclically.'"

Excellent coaching.

CHAPTER SEVENTEEN

Keith Moore

Most money that goes into mutual funds is parking money. People don't want to take big risks with it. It's hard to make significant money in any other strategy without taking a lot of risk. But risk arb, played conservatively, can compound pretty consistently.

KEITH MOORE SET up our meeting, not in a gilded midtown tower, but midafternoon in the quiet garden of a venerable neighborhood Irish pub not far from the suburban Huntington, NY, railroad station. Balding and bespectacled, he comes off more as a college professor than as a veteran Wall Street risk arb and the author of the most comprehensive text on the practice of risk arbitrage. But Keith M. Moore,

PhD, CFA, is both. What he makes no pretense of being is "a master of the universe."

The Long Island native, whose passions range from tuna fishing to teaching the finer details of merger arbitrage, over the last forty-plus years has built a remarkable career encompassing stints on the floor of the Big Board; at Gruss & Co.; Neuberger & Berman; Donaldson, Lufkin & Jenrette; Jupiter Capital (a small hedge fund); and Kellner Dileo—before switching sides of the Street to serve as managing director and event-driven strategist at brokerage firm MKM Partners and now, at FBN Securities. In between, he found time to earn a doctorate in finance at the University of Rhode Island and fulfill faculty assignments, not only there, but also at St. John's University and New York University. A second fully revised and updated edition of his authoritative textbook, *Risk Arbitrage: An Investor's Guide*, first published by John Wiley & Sons, Inc., in 1999, has just been released in hardcover, and perennially resides in MBA program bibliographies, worldwide.

"Listen, I've been the luckiest guy in the world as far as I'm concerned, in both business and my personal life. I've got an extraordinary

The New York Stock Exchange. Wikimedia Commons.

wife, great family, and friends. Risk arbitrage is a tremendous business. There were many years that I loved it so much—I couldn't believe they paid me to do what I did. It was so challenging, competing with the smartest people in Wall Street. I couldn't wait to get to Huntington train station to pick up the newspaper and figure out what we should be doing today. At the office, it was electric."

Moore says that within two weeks of taking a summer job for specialist James Gallagher on the floor of the NYSE, his sixteen-year-old self was so infatuated with the investment business that he not only gave up "the lawn business mega-conglomerate that was paying for my fishing trips," he ditched plans to study engineering, and started "making a pain-in-the-neck of myself" around trading desks during every school vacation. Gallagher, a neighbor of Moore's parents, took the neophyte under his wing and introduced him to Albert Cohen, a veteran risk arb who worked with Joe Gruss. Gallagher advised the young man, "If I heard it once during a week, I heard it five times, 'if you ever get a chance to work for Al Cohen, you've got to do it.' After a while, it gets in your mind."

Soon Gallagher's specialist firm was acquired by Gruss & Co. and the young college student started spending every spare vacation minute hanging around the Gruss arb desk "trying to figure out what the heck they were doing." When he landed back in New York with a new wife and a freshly minted BS from the University of Rhode Island, however, Moore discovered his timing was bad. It was the bear market summer of 1974. "Even though Jim Gallagher loved me and this guy loved me and that guy loved me, there were no jobs. Even if I had been the partner's son—in 1974, it wasn't happening." Moore put Wall Street dreams on hold and took a job as a credit analyst at Chemical Bank. It proved an invaluable education in the nitty-gritty realities of balance sheets and income statements, says Moore. "And it was pretty easy to transfer that skill over to the equity business when I finally got the chance."

The Good Wife

Moore continued hanging around the Gruss & Co. trading desk every chance he got, and within a year his luck turned. "Al Cohen had switched over to Neuberger Berman and his arbitrage analyst left to take a teaching job at Stanford Law," Moore reminisces. "I went up there and met formally with everybody. When I got home, I told my wife it went really well but that I had doubts. I'd spent so much time there, I knew they screamed and yelled and threw phones at the younger guys." His wife, normally a very demure woman, Moore says, responded, "Come on, you have been waiting for this chance for years." He took the leap and today reflects, "Sure, working at Neuberger was stressful at times, but it was a priceless education. A couple of the young guys who were regularly berated right alongside me are now running some of Wall Street's best-respected hedge funds. We were incredibly fortunate."

The arbitrage community was still quite small in the late 1970s, Moore recalls. There were only eight or ten firms, and Neuberger's arb desk connected to all of them via private phone lines. "One for Ace Greenberg at Bear Stearns; one for the future Treasury secretary, Robert Rubin, who was running Goldman Sachs's arbitrage desk; and so on. I was terrified whenever the Goldman light flashed. I'm not sure why. I never met Bob Rubin in person, and on the phone the man always treated me like a prince. Anyway, I got to learn the business by interacting with all these people for six or seven years. It was very hard to leave. Al taught me about business and life and how to treat people. I'll always be indebted."

But opportunity had knocked, before Moore turned thirty. "Donaldson, Lufkin & Jenrette, which George Kellner had just left with his arb team came to me and said, 'We'd like you to restart our arbitrage business.' So off I went to DLJ, and hired a team. It was a great firm, and it was a great period, in the 1980s, for risk arbitrage. We did quite well." Until, to be sure, the crash of 1987. "I now refer to it as 'the mini blip' when I teach," says Moore archly. "But we were on track for a record year going into it, and the whole thing—and then some—got wiped out."

Moore's luck returned the following year, however. His mentor, Al Cohen, left Neuberger Berman to start up his own firm and—casting about to replace him—Neuberger called Moore. He and his entire DLJ arbitrage team decamped for Neuberger Berman, where Moore didn't just run risk arbitrage but also added convertible arbitrage and closed-end fund trading on the floor of the NYSE to his portfolio. But Moore soon discovered that he was in a ticklish situation at Neuberger. "What you have to know is that Neuberger lost a ton of money in arbitrage in the 1987 crash. Within the first two months I was at

Neuberger in 1989, during the pendency of the bid by UAL's pilots and management to buy the airline, I got called into a very, very senior partner's office. He tells me, 'I know you're very sensitive to the fact that we lost a lot of money and some guys are really not happy about us being back in the arb business. But I want you to be aggressive.'" Moore recalls, "I knew I was dead then. I couldn't win. If I'm aggressive, these people hate me, and if I'm not aggressive, he hates me—and he is the power in the firm."

Saved by Puts

At that juncture, Moore adds, "We were already positioned in UAL— and I was frightened about the downside—as I usually am. But in UAL, I remember to this day, we had bought puts on our entire position. They were way-out-of-the-money puts—the strike had to be about $20 below the price. Every day, they decayed and they decayed and they decayed. At one point, as the negotiations dragged on, I turned to my trader—a fantastic woman—and said, 'Maybe we should get out of those things. We're wasting money.' She said, 'I'll look into it.' After a few more days, I saw we still had the position and asked why. She said, 'There's no market for them, and besides, they're down so much, why bother?' Well, I wish I could take credit for the decision to hold onto those puts because when the deal cracked they saved all of our jobs. I never saw a put trade like that before. It traded at around $100, eventually. It saved my rear. 'Be aggressive.' Risk arbitrage is a great business though."

Moore and his team stayed with Neuberger Berman another six years—during which, he says, he tried and failed to sell the firm's partners on adding a risk-arbitrage option to their line-up of mutual fund offerings as an alternative for investors looking for a "safe place to park money." If they had only gone with his plan, Moore ruminates—pointing to the success of several mutual funds specializing in risk arbitrage—"What they would have under management would dwarf what they have now." Moore adds, "Most money that goes into mutual funds is parking money. People don't want to take big risks with it. It's hard to make significant money in any other strategy without taking a lot of risk. But risk arb, played conservatively, can compound pretty consistently."

In early 1997, Moore was hired by a small hedge fund start-up. But after it dawned on the fund's top management that June that risk arb could result in losses—in part, when a federal judge allowed the FTC to block the first attempt by Office Depot and Staples to merge—Moore changed his career trajectory. "We made the money back elsewhere and it worked out," Moore shrugs. But he had quickly signed a contract to write his now classic textbook on risk arb and "started writing like a demon. I needed a break. I was worn down by that hedge fund experience."

Academic Turn

By the time *Risk Arbitrage: An Investor's Guide* was published, Moore was already deep into PhD research. He'd decided to turn his long-time sideline, teaching arbitrage to night students in NYU's Stern School of Business (where he'd picked up his own MBA) into an academic appointment and needed the credential. He'd found interacting with students enjoyable ever since he'd stepped in, on short notice, for an adjunct who'd been "unavoidably detained—Ivan Boesky," Moore explains. But he now believes that going back to the University of Rhode Island for his doctorate "in my mid-forties was probably the dumbest thing I've done." He taught for four years as an assistant professor of economics and finance at St. John's, "but found that some academics just didn't like someone from Wall Street invading their turf." Eventually, Moore gave in to the entreaties of an old friend, George Kellner of Kellner Capital Management to join his firm. Moore served as Kellner's co-CIO, portfolio manager of the KDC Merger Arbitrage Fund, and director of risk management, until deciding after a number of years to explore arb research from the sell side. He took a position running MKM Partners' event-driven group in late 2009 and switched to FBN Securities as a managing director and event-driven strategist in 2015.

One lesson, says Moore, that has been driven home to him time and again in risk arb is that "whenever things really get bad—and you have that feeling in the pit of your stomach that everything's going to go to hell—every time, so far in my life—that has been when you should just close your eyes and buy." The problem is, Moore allows, "You might be early. Certainly, in 2007, I was early. But when everybody's trying to go in the same direction—it's almost always time to go in another." Moore adds, "another thing I've noticed is that even though many practices in Wall Street have gotten a lot more sophisticated over my career, how people behave hasn't changed. While there are a lot of people doing risk-arbitrage trading, many haven't been around long enough to go through even a cycle or two. Which means their reactions tend to be very knee-jerk—and that creates opportunities. In part, that's because they lack the experience to react differently. But it is also because mechanical risk management systems force many risk arbs to make decisions they might not otherwise have made."

It used to be, Moore reflects, "the managing partner might say, 'we've had this guy for five years, he's good. If he's telling us not to sell now, maybe we should give him some rope.' Today, those people don't get rope. That's why Office Depot was trading at just $3.40 a share this week" (in the immediate aftermath of a federal judge blocking its second attempt to merge with Staples). Moore notes the total irony that he—along with a good chunk of the arb community— was wrong-footed not once but twice by the bust-up of deals to merge the office superstore operators. While the busted deals were separated by almost twenty years, they were classic examples, Moore avers, of both inexperience in the ranks of risk arbs and the immutability of human nature.

To this day, says Moore, he loves conducting arb research in the courtroom, usually alongside antitrust counsel he has hired. "Some of my biggest opportunities came out of going to court, listening to a case—having backgrounded myself beforehand—and using my experience and common sense to figure out what the judge was going to decide before he or she rendered the decision. I've done it, I don't know how many times—I've been lucky."

Courtroom Drama

Except when he wasn't. The 2016 proposal to try once again to combine Office Depot and Staples, which activist firm Starboard Value had been promoting for more than a year before it was unveiled, was a case in point. Moore recalls that he was initially leery. The FTC would have to reverse its opposition to the earlier 1997 merger plan. Completing the transaction would leave the office superstore market dominated by just one 800-pound gorilla, doubling the market's concentration and creating a company fifteen times larger than its nearest rival. Starboard, Staples, and Office Depot argued that the market landscape had dramatically changed since the earlier FTC decision and that the superstores needed a merger's cost savings to compete with the likes of Amazon and Walmart. Says Moore, "I had big arguments with clients and friends. They kept referring to a document from the 2013 Office Max/Office Depot merger in which the FTC said, in effect, 'there's no problem in the corporate market.' But when I looked at it, the document said that was because there was competition from Staples and Office Depot. I thought about that and decided, 'if they're the only two, then there *is* a problem.'"

He arrived at the court proceedings, Moore says, prepared for the FTC to win but also intent on keeping an open mind. "I sat there for ten days, reading four hundred pages of transcript a night—although that was tough for me. As a sell-side analyst now, when I'm not calling clients, they're not sending orders." What Moore saw in the courtroom was the FTC attorneys making a number of "unforced errors. It seemed, from the testimony and the way the judge was reacting that the Staples side had the stronger case." Though acutely aware, as Moore says, that "sizing up judges is tricky," by the time the FTC rested its case, he'd decided that it was Staples's case to lose. He eagerly awaited the presentation of the companies' case by their lead defense attorney, Weil, Gotshal & Manges partner Diane Sullivan, whom the *American Lawyer* had described as "a hired bazooka."

Instead, says a still-stunned Moore, "there was no Staples/Office Depot presentation. The defense rested. I thought I understood why. There were technical explanations. Besides, the FTC attorneys really did such a bad job." But the upshot, as Moore retells the story, is that courtroom observers didn't get to gauge the judge's reactions to the superstores' case until closing arguments. That was the day, he adds, all of the arbitrageurs who'd previously been content to merely send their lawyers to the hearings "showed up in droves. Which was a good thing. The judge's sharp questioning of the superstores' defense team during closing arguments spooked the arbs and they ended up saving some money." When the judge retired to decide the case, Moore says, "I told clients I saw the probabilities as 60 percent/40 percent, which is not good. When I go into these things, I want the odds 80 percent or 90 percent in my favor. Unfortunately, it turned out

I was 60/40 the wrong way." Adds Moore, given his track record in Staples/Office Depot deals, "I probably shouldn't pay attention if there's a third time around."

Teachable Moments

As a professor, though, Moore embraces busted deals as teachable moments. "When a deal is breaking, you really need to figure out what the clearing price is—if you haven't already. At what price is an institutional investor or a sell-side analyst going to finally, after they catch up on their work, say, 'Hey, you know what? This thing is trading here—but really it should be trading higher'." Moore observes, "When they're in the midst of losing a lot of money, somehow people don't go through that exercise fast enough. A lot of them try to do it on the fly, which is not good for human decision making, because then emotion and risk management take over." The relationship between that clearing price and a stock's current trading price, advises Moore, is what determines whether an arb should immediately dump a broken deal stock. "As much as I loved my mentor, Al Cohen, we had a running disagreement because he liked to keep the stocks in a broken deal when he made a mistake," reminisces Moore. "He was always convinced we'd make our money back. Over time, he was pretty much correct. But that depends on, (a) the possibility of recovering any money compared with where you think the stock should trade after people's emotions die down, and (b) you being very disciplined about looking at those positions as a percentage of your entire portfolio," mindful that a rising tide raises all ships.

In fact, Moore did some of his doctoral research on the topic. "If you hold onto shares in broken deals, you tend to get a good rate of return—over time," he wrote. But if you dissect that rate of return by doing what's called an event study—which separates the return attributable to the market from the return from the specific stock—you find that the rebound is almost all beta. The alpha is insignificant. So you don't want to kid yourself. If you want to play for the market return, hold on to a busted stock."

To be good at arbitrage, says the risk-arb professor, a practitioner needs certain technical skills: a combination of a financial background in analysis and modeling and a legal background in antitrust and corporate transactions. "But on top of those, one of the biggest things somebody needs to stick around in this business—I learned it from my boss, Al Cohen—is discipline. If you don't have discipline, it's very easy to make big mistakes. And if you make a big mistake, you lose people a lot of money—bad things happen." With just a touch of irony Moore also notes, "I've also learned that if you're too cautious, that doesn't work well, either. The funniest thing about the business, I've found, is that people who blow up funds because of what looks, from the outside, like a lack of discipline, sometimes get hired back or raise additional capital more easily than their perhaps too-disciplined rivals. In other words, I've learned that my innately conservative nature is not necessarily a good thing in the arbitrage world. I had to teach myself to be more aggressive to generate better returns, without abandoning my disciplines."

Wall Street, observes Moore, "has a tendency to swing between super highs and super lows—and it affects you, your daily behavior, and especially your decision making. I've learned that you've got to temper it on both sides. If everything is going great, maybe you ought to throttle it back a little bit—because you don't know what's around the corner. On the contrary, when things get really bad, it's not the end of the world—and there are opportunities out there—if anything, better opportunities."

The professor is not, however, a big fan of traditional position limits as a way to keep arbs out of trouble. "When I was running money for numerous firms, I'd always be given position limits. It seemed like it was written in the Bible somewhere, and I could never understand it. But I was constantly told I could put up to 10 percent of my available capital—but no more—into any one deal." Moore says he repeatedly protested, "That doesn't make a lot of sense. I could have 10 percent in a stock that could go down $20. Or I could have 10 percent in a stock that could go down $5. You'd be better off setting an overall loss limit. But I never got anybody in Wall Street to buy into that. Except me, so I made my own rule." As a PhD student, Moore made the evaluation of portfolio allocation rules a part of his dissertation research. "I tested the 10 percent maximum position versus a 2 percent maximum loss rule and then I tested a dual rule—you could risk up to a 2 percent maximum loss, but put no more than 10 percent of capital in any one position—and my simulations showed that the combination rule produced the best results—as I implicitly expected all along. The weird thing was that it also showed that as risk went down under that rule, returns went up. Bingo, though not by a lot."

In recent years, as a sell-side advisor, Moore hasn't had to wrestle much with portfolio allocation questions and he says he's still enjoying "interacting with really smart people. Some of them are frightening, they are so smart." But the work has its frustrations, like being asked for advice on deals in foreign markets where "(a) no one calls me back and (b) if they do, they don't understand me and I don't understand them. I wish I could help, but if I can't do the research—like Dirty Harry said—'A man's got to know his limitations.'"

PART TWO

The View from the Other Side— The CEOs

CHAPTER EIGHTEEN

William Stiritz

"The mantra driving everything right now is shareholder value—
enhancing shareholder value," observes eighty-three-year-old William
Stiritz, the cereal industrialist, competitive thoroughbred owner—"there
is no tougher game"– and prominent fan of St. Louis culture and
lifestyle. "There are outside advisors representing institutional money
telling corporations how they should act. They play into the hands
of the transactions-oriented mergers and acquisitions bar, investment
bankers, activists, and arbs—who always argue for the near-term

maximization of shareholder value. Maybe a quick deal is one thing for an institution—they're indifferent to the tax consequences. But individuals who have owned a company over the long-term—and certainly the people who work there—have very different interests. And we haven't had that debate in this society as much as we should have."

DON'T JUMP TO the conclusion that those are the nostalgic musings of "some old guy living in the past." Or make a far worse mistake and doubt for an instant Stiritz's deep and abiding appreciation for the capitalist economy that made possible his transformation from a kid doing odd jobs just to get through high school in the Ozarks in the late 1940s, to a "whale CEO" whose better-than 61,000 percent cumulative return to investors over thirty-five years (versus a relatively paltry 3,750 percent for the S&P 500 Total Return Index) ranks him second, behind only media magnate John Malone, in the alpha-generating pantheon of U.S. corporate leaders, according to calculations that Fundstrat, the independent market research boutique, ran in 2015 (somehow leaving Warren Buffett out of its tally).

"Retiring" simply isn't an adjective that can be used to describe Bill Stiritz. Still fully engaged in business and management, he serves as chairman of Post Holdings, Inc., the branded cereal, breakfast foods, and active nutrition company that he spun out of Ralcorp Holdings at the beginning of 2012—and whose market valuation, it should be noted, increased more than fourfold in the ensuing five years. Stiritz, who had been chairman of Ralcorp from the time of its own spinout in 1994 (from Ralston Purina), astutely jumped horses to Post not long after spending much of 2011 employing a stubborn "just say no" defense to fend off serial "bear hug" takeover bids for Ralcorp from ConAgra Foods Inc.

While some contemporary accounts record ConAgra as the "victor" in what ultimately turned out to be a twenty-month-long campaign to control Ralcorp, ConAgra's conquest proved pyrrhic at best. After Stiritz turned down first ConAgra's $4.9 billion and then its $5.2 billion offer for Ralcorp (even though the bids, when made, valued the target company at better than a 20 percent premium to market), ConAgra initially seemed to lose interest in pursuing Ralcorp. ConAgra began a spate of smaller, unrelated acquisitions in late 2011, even as Stiritz prepared to spin Post Holdings out of Ralcorp, leaving the latter a "pure play" in the private-label food business that ConAgra had been so adamant in pursuing earlier that year. But then in November 2012, ConAgra swooped back into the picture with an all-cash "bear hug" bid of $90 a share, or $5 billion, for what remained of Ralcorp's assets. Including assumed debt, the transaction, once completed, set ConAgra back a cool $6.8 billion—but it allowed the maker of Chef Boyardee pasta to proclaim itself also the top U.S. producer of private-label foods. Wall Street's arbitrageurs and activist investors, who had been less than enthralled by Ralcorp's stock performance since Stiritz refused to negotiate with ConAgra—and his subsequent spinoff of Post—rejoiced all the way to the bank.

Whatever celebrations took place in and around ConAgra's long-time Omaha, Nebraska headquarters, however, proved fleeting. The company's high-profile move into private label foods quickly proved a bust. Within three years, ConAgra had a new CEO—who boasted of a renewed focus on branded foods—and who dumped what was left of Ralcorp into the hands of TreeHouse Foods for roughly $4 billion *less* than ConAgra had paid for those assets. In the process, ConAgra also abandoned the city of its founding for hip new quarters in Chicago's Merchandise Mart—jettisoning more than 1,000 salaried Omaha headquarters employees along the way.

Revival Artist

Not merely a legendary corporate chieftain renowned for his deft shepherding of capital, Stiritz also dabbled in private equity between 2000 and 2006 via St. Louis's Westgate Group LLC. He allows, too, that he "invested a little in an arb fund years ago, to get a better understanding of the strategy." He underlines, "I understand very well how risk arbitrage serves a vital market function in keeping prices rational and efficient. But my role has been managing *all* of the shareholders' assets, and an unsolicited 'bear hug' to buy out existing shareholders is potentially an *existential* threat to corporations."

Stiritz got his start in applying his own brand of creative and innovative company-building and value creation to corporate assets in 1981 when, as a group vice president at Ralston Purina, he proposed a daring strategy for reviving the company's fortunes. Ralston's shares had flat-lined for at least a decade and—thanks to championing by board member Mary Wells Lawrence (a founder of ad agency Wells, Rich Greene), Stiritz appreciatively recalls—his plan won over the rest of the company's directors. Stiritz was then tapped, at only forty-six, as the CEO of an ungainly foods conglomerate with hundreds of disparate and largely disconnected businesses scattered around the United States and the globe.

It was his dream assignment—"figuring out how to make Ralston's assets earn more money; how to transform the organization from a very tired bureaucracy into a creative, adaptive, innovative one that did just wonderful things." The young CEO soon proved himself a shrewd analyst of value, adept at devising an almost endless string of timely divestitures, acquisitions and spinoffs that brought clarity, enhanced cash flow, and rising profits to Ralston's Checkerboard Square headquarters. He also began judiciously buying back the company's undervalued shares in the early 1980s, boosting shareholder returns long before the technique became a much-used and abused management fad. Along the way, Stiritz, a big proponent of decentralized management, crafted four new listed companies out of underperforming Ralston Purina assets that he decided would thrive better on their own—Ralcorp, Agribrands, Energizer, and Post. Stiritz served as chairman of each of the spun-out outfits while also keeping a steady hand on the helm of Ralston Purina until late 2001, when he got an offer he didn't think he could refuse for the pet food business. Faced with that "bear hug" bid from Nestle, the Swiss foods behemoth, at a 36 percent premium to Ralston's prebid trading level—and, importantly, assured that St. Louis would become the headquarters of Nestle's newly combined pet food operations—Stiritz agreed to a $10 billion cash takeover. Over his tenure, Ralston Purina's pretax margins had expanded from 9 percent to 15 percent, its return on equity more than doubled, and a dollar invested in the company morphed into $57.

No Silver Spoon

Raised by his grandparents in northwest Arkansas, Stiritz says the place where he grew up was so rural that the probability he'd ever make it out of the area was "no better than even money." Even when he did, adds Stiritz, "You would have put very low probabilities on me achieving much." Had he ended up as a country lawyer or maybe running the local hardware store, he muses, he would have been considered a smashing success. But luck—which Stiritz unabashedly calls, along with randomness, the biggest variable in life—intervened. After just two years at a state college, Stiritz quit to join the Naval Aviation Cadet Program and ended up as a navy flier. Assigned as the legal officer for his squadron, he found himself at the JAG Corps' Naval Justice School in Newport, Rhode Island, preparing for mock trials with classmates—including a couple of graduates of Harvard Law School. Recalls Stiritz, "I was the advocate for the other side in some mock trials versus those guys. With that experience and others at Northwestern University while picking up a bachelor's degree in business after I was discharged, I began to realize that I could compete at any level."

While describing himself as "a great reader of all kinds of literature from early childhood on," Stiritz says his literary taste changed in the navy, where he spent a lot of time in the library reading books on organizational structure. He recalls "studying how all kinds of systems work—starting with the Navy's BUPERS (bureau of naval personnel) manual and then fixing on business organizations." Stiritz's focus on systems design only sharpened upon his return to civilian life as he continued his education at Northwestern: "another great stepping stone in my preparation for life. When I look back, I think, 'my gosh, the incremental, broad experiences in dealing with all sorts of people in all sorts of situations—it was just almost an immaculate preparation for the myriad challenges in trying to create value as the head of a shareholder-owned company.'"

Reflects Stiritz, "I came from an unusual background, and I think the only reason that I'm sitting here in this very, very nice office looking out into a wonderful garden is that I always had—not the idea, it was more of an intuition—that any time you marched into a new place you had to ask: 'What's going on here? What are these people here for? What is really happening?' Just try to gauge, what is the environment here and how do I act?" He also came to realize, Stiritz continues, "there are laws and there are rules and there are guidelines—but those are all subject to analysis. 'Well, what's going on here? What *is* the environment?' If you live strictly by rules, you're badly served. There's not too much in life that is fixed, not even the laws. Reality is subjective and ethics are cultural rather than fixed in stone. So you have to be very critically analytical. But first, you must have gotten lucky and been gifted with a set of genes or some tribal background strong in critical analysis. Then, over time, you have to learn how to adapt, change, and get in sync—more than that, get ahead of wherever the environment is moving."

Stiritz also credits his success to a life-long appreciation of strategy and probability—inculcated through early exposure to competitive games. "In high school, although I always had outside jobs, I found time to play a lot of poker. I played some chess, too, and I also played a lot of bridge—including duplicate bridge," where the focus was on relative performance, not just the best score. Indeed, he calls winning the duplicate bridge championship at the University of Arkansas "one of the great achievements in my early life." Stiritz also has been known to draw comparisons between the skills he learned as a kid at the poker table—calculating odds, reading personalities, and the willingness to make large bets when the odds are in your favor—with those needed to be a stellar capital allocator. He ventures the opinion that the same skill set is likely critical to success in the world of risk arbitrage. "The best game for future arbs would probably be poker at a real meaning-ful level. I believe that game requires all the skills of an arbitrageur. You have to be analytical, you have to be able to calculate the prob-abilities of the cards, and you have to be able to read personalities. Try to second-guess what the CEO and the board will do. Plus, you have to have money management skills to be able to stay in the game."

Seizing Opportunities

When Stiritz joined Ralston's marketing unit in 1963 after short stints at Pillsbury and at a firm doing advertising work for Ralston, he was gobsmacked by the company's potential. "It was almost like some-one rolling up to the frontier in a covered wagon back in, say, 1850, and saying, 'Gee, look at all this land. It could all be mine. I could stake out land rights.' I realized that the company had, my gosh, such opportunities—if we could do certain things," Stiritz adds. "Back then, Ralston was still being run by members of the founding family." In one sense, he elaborates, it "was just a wonderful family enterprise. Very paternal. I wish all companies could be like that." For instance, says Stiritz, "Kurt von Schuschnigg, who had been the chancellor of Austria in 1938, was teaching here at St. Louis University, and I wanted to study history under him. I applied to their masters pro-gram and earned the degree—but Ralston paid for it, for chrissakes!

Although that degree was unrelated to business, there *were* invaluable lessons that came out of those studies that were very relevant to business. I have Donald Danforth to thank for that. He was the second generation of the founding family to be running the company back then—a gifted paternalistic leader in my view—not that he was ever given any credit. He later was ousted by a political faction of professional managers who called him incompetent."

On the other hand, Stiritz quickly acknowledges, Ralston Purina—during its third generation of family control—became a very "muddied up" and poorly organized outfit, its management riven by internecine warfare and dominated by "absolute masters at office politics," who unfortunately weren't very good managers. "In fact, if they would have merited a C-minus in management, I'd have been surprised," says Stiritz, who freely admits almost being done in, early in his career, by the challenges of navigating Ralston's bureaucratic shoals. "This Darwinian struggle for who gets the big job, who gets the next job, who gets to be the boss, and so on was the difficult part. In fact, at one time, I was put on probation. They called me in and said, 'We're not sure you belong here.' That worried me a bit, so I changed some of my prickly behavior. Some people call it cynicism; I call it realism—but it's offensive at times, so I learned to curb it."

Others at Ralston recognized, though, Stiritz continues, "that I had some ability to see things differently—I call it 'the immigrant's advantage.' I wasn't hindered by assumptions about the institution, could bring a fresh perspective—and that I had learned enough human relations skills to manage not to get fired." Not to mention to eventually work his way to the top of Ralston's management ranks. What he learned, first and foremost over those twenty-odd years, "before I got the big job in organizational life," as Stiritz puts it, "is that you have to be able to get along with people. The other big lesson was that you have to be constantly analyzing. You analyze, you analyze some more, and then you analyze yet again. You have to have an analytical skill set that has you always challenging the assumptions you are given, to try to create a decent business, to evaluate people, and to work to create win-wins in negotiating to affect change." He stresses, "I'm a win-win negotiator rather than a win-lose negotiator—and there's a big difference. I discovered by age ten or twelve that it was much better to give in when it didn't hurt too much, to let the other side win, than it was to drive for the hardest bargain."

The reason, says Stiritz firmly—now that he has more than fifty-five years of management experience and countless M&A deals under his belt—is that no matter whether you're a buyer or a seller, a principal, an arb, or an activist trying to size up the game from the outside, "nothing is fixed, *everything is situational* and no two deals are alike. So the person—or the institution—involved in this game must possess critical analytical skills—and be able to imagine all sorts of outcomes. He or she must also understand the personality and the institutional background of both the bidder and the target company."

Wielding Pruning Shears

On becoming Ralston's CEO, the tool Stiritz most frequently reached for was the pruning shears, and he was unsentimental about where he cut. The St. Louis-based company's ownership of the hometown St. Louis Blues hockey team and its "Checkerdome" arena were the first to go, in 1983. Jack in the Box restaurants, which Stiritz had personally overseen in his days as a group vice president, were sold off in 1985. Then came the 1986 sale of Ralston's U.S. farm animal feed business, Purina Mills, the very foundation on which William H. Danforth had started the company in 1894. But Stiritz also tried his hand at acquisitions, buying Continental Baking, the baker of Wonder Bread and Hostess snacks, in 1984 and the Eveready Battery Co. in 1986. The white bread business proved more difficult to turn around than Stiritz had expected. Sold in 1995 to Interstate Bakeries, Hostess ended up in bankruptcy in 2004. The battery unit, however, rebranded Energizer, became one of Stiritz's acclaimed spinoffs in 2000.

"The problem with large corporations, where they've developed a centralized command structure over multiple divisions—I think it's fair to say—is that they are less creative, less adaptive, less inventive than a company that is spun out and freestanding. Spinouts are simply better-incented and their managers will think about the task much more intentionally. Their managers are much more engaged, much more involved, than, say, a senior product manager at P&G on product X—to name a company that has been a laggard over the years." Stiritz elaborates, "At one time, P&G was a paragon. When I first got into the game, back in 1960 or 1961, it was considered a model for other managements. But over time, they were badly led and became

a dinosaur, lacking in adaptability. They've shown a few signs lately—
I sound critical and I shouldn't. Because until you put yourself into
their shoes—maybe the circumstances are different than they look.
But creating a new organization eliminates a lot of what was holding
a company back."

Stiritz's ability to rapidly size up what a business was worth—and
how that value might be enhanced—helped him immeasurably as he
set about rationalizing Ralston's operations. Characteristically, however, he disclaims extraordinary prowess. "You can size up any business very quickly simply by asking for the profit and loss statement on
a current-year basis. Give me two or three years' background and really
just the immediate year ahead—then maybe a longer-term plan for a
year after that—and in an hour's time I can make heads or tails out of
it." Once he grasped a business's underlying value, what's more, it was
Stiritz's wont to realize it, either under Ralston's corporate umbrella
or outside of it. When he found the market offering attractive prices
for the conglomerate's misfits, he would sell them off. But often when
he perceived that an under-performing business's long-term value was
far in excess of the immediate return a sale would produce, Stiritz
turned to spinouts. "I'm a big believer in spinouts," he explains, "first,
because they are very advantageous to shareholders from a tax viewpoint but also because they are simply the ultimate form of reorganization for better results."

The first spinout he did, in 1994, was of Ralcorp, a collection of
cereal, baby food, cookie and cracker, and sundry other businesses—
even ski resorts. Stiritz calls it "a perfect example" of why he favors the
technique. "Ralcorp is a case study of a group of assets that originally
were just *buried* within the corporate conglomerate called Ralston
Purina. It was three or four layers down in terms of management levels, an insignificant hobby business, with low shares of market, low
returns. What do you do with it? I tried a number of things, within
Ralston, and none of them worked. So finally I said, 'Well, we're going
to spin it out.'" Stiritz acknowledges that he was not the first CEO to
convince his board to spin out assets to shareholders to form a new
company. "The difference was that I saw it as a way to create a new
organizational model. I stayed with Ralcorp as its chairman, inserted
its management, and allocated the resources of the company to what
we should be doing. But the key to my success was picking very good
managers for Ralcorp and its spinoffs." He continues, "there were

several, but three especially come to mind: Pat Mulcahy at Energizer, Bill Armstrong at Agribrands and, most importantly, Rob Vitale at Post Holdings. I met Rob in the private equity venture I got involved in. Working with him, I came to see him as the most talented manager I'd come across in all my experience running companies and serving on multiple corporate boards. What I'm trying to say is that when you're running a complex enterprise, the art of selecting good managers is critical to success."

Spinning Gold

When Stiritz started working on the Ralcorp spinoff in 1994, he recalls, "the business was worth just a few hundred million dollars and it ended up being sold for $5 or $6 billion." Likewise, he notes, his 2012 spinout of Post Holdings from Ralcorp has so far created "another $4 billion to $5 billion—and the game goes on." The magic in a spinoff, Stiritz explains, arises from the liberation of the new company from the old. "Throwing out the old organizational chart, redrawing the boxes, and then creating a new organizational chart for a new company with a different group of shareholders and a different mindset." Says Stiritz, "It is almost as if some kid with a small lamp rubs the damn thing and out pops this amazing transformation." He goes on, "I took very ordinary people who had been involved with an organization in Ralston Purina and their personalities were *transformed*. It was amazing to see. That included people whose abilities—before the spinoff—I had personally disdained when I observed them in meetings. But when we put them in this different situation, I'll be damned if they weren't transformed— became just incredible managers. So I became a big fan of spinoffs."

Those transformations, Stiritz insists, were largely unrelated to changes in the ways the new company paid managers. "It wasn't the incentives. I think we overplay in this society the idea that somebody can make a million dollars now instead of making $55,000." Hesitating briefly to consider his words, Stiritz adds, "No, it has something to do with the new situation capturing a person's mind. So he thinks about it around the clock. He wakes up in the middle of the night. He's now under a lot of stress, has anxiety about getting it right. But people just *like* to be responsible and to run things themselves. They also like being able to quit playing bureaucratic corporate games. I've seen it time and time again. At Beech-Nut Baby Food; at Keystone, the ski resort in Colorado. Even at the St. Louis Blues, before we got rid of them."

In 1998, Stiritz arranged for Ralston Purina to do a second spinout. This one, dubbed Agribrands, was an international collection of animal feed businesses that the conglomerate had retained when it sold William Danforth's domestic Purina Mills operation two years earlier. It included, says Stiritz, "a great business in the Philippines and one in Korea and probably another thirty nice companies overseas—all derivative of the old domestic animal feeds business—and I figured its market value was about $500 million, plus or minus, at the time. We tried to sell it; nobody wanted it. So I thought, 'I'll take this and I'll run it as the CEO.' It was a fit with my personal plans at the time—so I spun it out. The goal, really, was an eventual merger of equals between Ralcorp and Agribrands, but I wasn't able to effectuate it. After a few years, we did announce a merger of equals, and that's where we made our mistake: putting a fair exchange value of $39 a share on Agribrands. One of the bankers went up to Minnesota and sold Cargill [the mammoth privately-held agricultural products conglomerate that even then had annual revenues topping $50 billion] on making a competing bid. I received a call from its CEO one morning. He said, 'We are going to make an offer for Agribrands.' After some back-and-forth attempts to elude the bear hug, I was unable to evade it. He first offered $50 and we ended up at $55, which then was reduced by the cost of a silver parachute I had gotten the board to quickly institute. All employees were to get a year's salary even if they'd only been at Agribrands for a day. So by the end of 2000, Agribrands had been acquired. Yes, I was very poorly served by that particular banker. But you have to blame yourself for something like that. If I knew then what I know now, I'd have just said no."

Playing the Larger Game

"To make a long story short," continues Stiritz, "that was a hand I played that came out—from my perspective—badly. It was just very badly played. But it was an experience that later served me well when I got into the Ralcorp/ConAgra situation. If you play a hand two or three times, it's a great advantage—to be able to go back and recognize some analogies and metaphors—so it was later of great value for me to have been through that Agribrands experience." What losing control of Agribrands drove home to Stiritz, he elaborates, is that "the problem with a bear hug situation is it captures market value only at a static moment in time. It ignores the potential value of the management's imagination and creativity and the adaptiveness of the asset over time. Particularly, if you then also calculate the tax consequences of an immediate sale, to my mind, in the great majority of cases you'd be better off saying, 'No, get out of here,' to the activist investor, to the arbs, and to the bidder attempting a bear hug."

The technique assumes, he goes on, "that life is not dynamic, doesn't change. Take the dough because it's $10 a share more than whatever the bankers are coming in with. But the banker is conflicted. He wants to do the deal. There will always be some arb players pushing for the deal. But their only responsibility is to make the extra dollar for their investors—nothing broader. The various players in these dramas don't have much respect for me or any CEO. They don't see the big picture; it's a curious role that they play."

It follows that Stiritz doesn't have much time for arbitrageurs. "They serve their own purposes," he allows. "I can understand that, it's their game. But in the larger game, they play only a small role. So I don't have a lot of personal sympathy or identification with arbs, as a class." Reflecting on all the forces arrayed against him when Cargill targeted Agribrands, Stiritz saves his harshest words for lawyers. He recognizes, though, "they have only a limited role to play as counselors and admittedly it's an important one." He recalls, "There was a lawyer, a dominant figure in M&A at the time, who scared the bejesus out of the board, saying 'you have a duty to the shareholders. You've been offered $50 a share and your merger of equals agreement stated a value of $39. You *should* take it.' There also was an activist stirring things up. But I take the blame in that the board decided to take the Cargill offer—much to my regret every time I think about it. I wake up now and again, restacking some old experience. Often, it's that one. I say to myself, 'Gee, you played that very badly; you should be ashamed of yourself.'"

Then Stiritz cuts himself a bit of slack. "The reality is that any CEO who hasn't played the M&A game before is at a great disadvantage when his company is targeted in a transaction. He does not understand the game he's suddenly involved in. It's like a new guy at the poker table. You have to have two or three marks at the table if you're going to make money. The old guys who play the game repeatedly—the bankers and the lawyers—*know* how it's played." But, he asks, "If I can't even spell 'arbitrageur,' how can I know that game? The shares move quickly into concentrated hands, where the calculations are simply about time and returns, probabilities and information. Often, that doesn't serve society at large—all stakeholders."

Stiritz catches himself quickly, adding, "That sounds like a moralistic statement and I'm the last guy who should ever be preaching." He reiterates, "In the abstract, M&A and arbitrage assist in the long-term efficient allocation of resources." Stiritz allows that the threat of a hostile bid can also serve as a needed wake-up call to a somnolent corporate management. "Wait a minute, we may be doing something wrong, maybe we better get rid of this thing. It's a drag on us."

Nonetheless it's clear that Stiritz firmly believes that *good* managements and boards are far better positioned to look after the interests—not only of long-term shareholders but of all the others inevitably entwined in a company's fate. "You also have the interests of the employees and their communities to consider," even though those interests rarely enter into the negotiations. The way it typically works, notes Stiritz, is "the banker will come to you saying, 'Well, they've offered $85, but you can get them up to $90.' The banker's job—primary function—is earning commissions. This may or may not serve the interests of all of a firm's shareholders. To be sure, investment bankers play a vital role—good ones are invaluable—and are to be cultivated. My point is that the CEO must have the ability to use bankers wisely. You can get yourself into a box—the lawyers are happy from the outset, the bankers are getting their commissions, and the top level of management has a golden parachute. I made a ton of dough out of that deal but I would have been a lot better off, over time, keeping control of Agribrands. We could have doubled it or tripled it in terms of value."

No Fan of Instant Gratification

At heart, Stiritz concedes, "I'm just not a big fan of selling out for the immediate benefit of the activist. I don't think that this is particularly an admirable character in the big play of U.S. corporate capitalism—*shareholder-owned* capitalism. We have so many players feasting on this wonderful pie. There's the long-term shareholder, and his interests are one thing; then there are the institutional money managers for the local fire departments, the unions, and the teachers—these are tax-shielded investors and they're completely indifferent to when they take a profit. They simply roll the money over into something else, so they have their own interests. Then there are all the others whose interests are primarily transactional: the investment bankers, the lawyers, the arbs."

Stiritz emphasizes, "everything is situational and you just have to be able to read the circumstances. Maybe there are times when you should go ahead and sell to somebody. Every deal is different; sometimes a little bit and sometimes dramatically different. The most important— and often underrated—ingredient, always, is management's imaginative power. When you are generating options, seeking solutions to a problem, imaginative power is a real strength—being able to handicap an off-the-wall option. What can we do? What are the probabilities that we can bring it off?" Then he adds, just a tad sardonically, "Also, *try* to keep your personal stuff out of it."

Which brings to Stiritz's mind ConAgra's almost two-year-long campaign, beginning in 2011, to acquire Ralcorp. He regards the episode as "the pièce de résistance" of his career. "That cake you baked that you've been studying how to put together for your entire life. I couldn't have modeled it any better." Stiritz continues, "The very interesting thing was the situation was changing every day as ConAgra made one bid and then sweetened it. I think most of the arbitrageurs made the wrong bet. They probably thought that the company would be sold—probably for mid-value—three or four dollars more than the initial bid. They might have been guessing what I'd do based on how I mishandled the Agribrands situation. They probably didn't calculate either offer's consequences for long-term shareholders. So maybe some Wall Street people lost a bit of money when I just said no near the end of my tenure at Ralcorp. But that story didn't end there. ConAgra came back and bought Ralcorp eventually—made that huge mistake."

It's Never Over

Stiritz muses, "The whole thing makes a great case study, but the moral at the end of it is that it's never over. The game goes on. Everything evolves. Eventually, ConAgra made a stunning recovery (after jettisoning Ralcorp) under a new CEO. The old CEO, who had pushed the deal . . . retired. Institutional memory these days is so short: when one game is over, that door is closed and no one recognizes you or remembers or cares, really, what role you played in the history of a company. That's the brutal reality. You can never declare victory. The evolution goes on."

Focusing again on the episode's particulars, Stiritz notes, "A big thing I had learned from my Agribrands situation—which came in very handy when I got involved with ConAgra—came out of asking our legal people to give me a little white paper on the background of takeover attempts when companies had employed the 'just say no' defense. There was a famous court case—Paramount back in the 1980s—demonstrating that you *could* 'just say no.' All the other tactics, the staggered boards, entering into conflicting contracts, and so on, are only temporary defenses. 'Just say no' is really the only defense that is viable in the long-term. If you want to stay independent, you can—*if* you have the board's confidence that you're the one to lead them to even better numbers. But there's a bias against that defensive tactic in Wall Street. In the end, lots of times it comes down to the chemistry between individuals—'I'm bigger than you.' It's almost a throwback to animalistic behavior, and you'll see that in board meetings where it's expressed in terms of dominance—and it does play a role in the so-called bear hugs."

After fielding the first phone call from ConAgra CEO Gary Rodkin, Stiritz quickly put the Ralcorp legal team's research into takeover defenses to use. "I distributed legal's paper to the board, showing that you can 'just say no' when you can make the case that the company's long-term value exceeds its current value. Now that case of course rests upon some assumptions—and you can game the assumptions— we hope with some credibility. I had not done that in the Agribrands situation. But in the case of Ralcorp—and, my guess is, with any company under a similar attack—you could probably have bankers come in with a projection of future earnings that says the company is worth X instead of this miserable price being offered. That way, when the outside lawyers come into the boardroom and try to scare the directors into thinking, 'Gee, I don't have anything at stake in this and it's my duty to shareholders and so on,' a strong-minded CEO can tell the lawyers to pack it in and talk with the other directors on a more informed basis. Convince them to hold out for a better long-term return even if the proffered immediate payout is greater than, say, the immediate value, if you did it on an objective basis."

Playing the Long Game

In standing adamantly against ConAgra's bear hug, there's no doubt Stiritz assumed the role of that "strong-minded" CEO leading his board. He concedes, "There's no question that Ralcorp was a case where that happened." Not that it was a slam dunk, Stiritz adds. "I put off meeting with Rodkin; kept coming up with excuses to buy time to extricate Ralcorp from his grasp. I got the bankers involved. Then the bank—Credit Suisse at the time—recommended an entirely different transaction to the board. I was Ralcorp's chairman, but even the company's co-CEOs were against my spinout plan. They proposed selling out to a private equity group that was going to load the company with junk finance. And while the negotiations were going on, there was, of course, a big shift in ownership, with long-term shareholders selling out to arbs. But again, for the CEO, it gets back to this: You just have to have an independent mindset and be willing to stake yourself, your reputation, your leadership of the group—the tribe, the company, the people who work there—on 'just saying no.' You have to be willing to say to them, 'I've got it figured out and I'm going to do it this way, and if it works to the short-term disadvantage of the stock, clipping off 10 or 15 or 20 bucks, so be it. Over the long-term, we'll create more value.'"

He continues, "I'm reluctant to use the Churchill phrase 'my finest hour,' but of all the things that I've done through the years, it was. Because Post's subsequent success and its organizational model were the result of over forty years of studying how a business should be organized. It's a variation on the private equity corporate model. In Post, you have the benefits of a KKR-like model—managed with the intent and the insight to get the assets to yield the most, and to do that with alacrity—but with the flexibility of a shareholder-owned piece of paper. So the investor isn't paying 2 and 20 and isn't stuck in the paper for a duration of ten years or so. The private equity guys rent an asset for a duration whereas a Post can thrive for generations. There's a difference and someday it will be appreciated."

As an aside, mentions Stiritz, "John Paulson is the one arb I know of who had a big position in Ralcorp and didn't sell it when we got

ConAgra to go away in 2011, though he had hoped, I'm sure, that I would quickly sell Ralston for $98 a share when ConAgra first came around. Then again, he's more than an arbitrageur. He stayed with it. It's a question of research, I guess. A lot of arbs, on a formulaic basis, simply got out when that deal didn't happen. Paulson did a lot of information gathering, valuation work, stayed, and became a big shareholder of Post when we spun it out. John actually made a trip out here, came to my house for dinner and gave me a bit of advice on peddling cereal. I said, 'John, that's not your bag.' Later, I met him for breakfast once in New York City. I suspect he's out of Post by now, but he rode it up for a while. So there are arbs—and then there are arbs."

Many of the arbitrageurs who quickly buy into proposed deals have tax situations that are more favorable to short-term gains than most investors do, Stiritz concedes, "but for the long-term share-holder, honestly, a bear hug works to their disadvantage. And it damn sure works to the disadvantage of many of the managers and of the people who work in the company. They will be 'synergized'— that's such a sterile term; the dark side of capitalism. In calculating value, we always put in 'synergy.' We can buy something for a six multiple of EBITDA and now it's worth ten or twelve or fourteen times EBITDA. But that 'synergy' is an abstraction. When you bring it back to flesh and blood, it is not so much fun. As the leader of the corporate body you have a responsibility to the people who work there and not just to immediate 'shareholder value.' So I don't like the outsiders who come in, who have nothing in the game other than some damn precedent coming out of some case in Delaware, but who insist, 'You have this responsibility.' My mental response is 'Get out of here.' They just don't think it through. It's because of their narrow interest. They try to define what's good for the corporation strictly from the viewpoint of a shareholder—an institutional share-holder—who pays no taxes and can roll the money over quickly. But, to be fair, in the role they play, they can only offer a viewpoint. It's the board's decision—hopefully led by a talented CEO—how best to respond in these situations. Outsiders have limited knowledge of the company's potential."

Indeed, observes Stiritz, "many of the actors in corporate deal-making dramas have limited roles, period. Meanwhile, the guy who works as a foreman on the line in Jonesboro, Arkansas gets a [pink] slip, and he's got a kid in Arkansas State Teacher's College or somewhere—so his whole life is changed. I know, in theory, maybe I carry that too far. Maybe 'creative destruction' is a source of economic strength; results in getting the most productivity out of finite resources. But on a human basis, it's the pathos in the economic play."

Stiritz opines, "On a micro basis, I've enjoyed the good fortune, luck, to successfully engage in these corporate chess moves allocating capital. The question is always, do you take the money and run when somebody comes in and makes you an offer? Finding the answer is much more complicated than simply listening to the lawyers trying to dictate, 'You have an ultimate duty to the shareholders.' That is nonsense. Doing that is just an abdication of your responsibilities or it's a recognition of your own pathetic qualities as a manager."

The long-time CEO is not completely unsympathetic, however, to the plight of corporate chieftains facing bear hugs or other hostile bids. "Most average managers came out of sales or finance or operations and they have had *no* experience with M&A. Listen, I have been on that side and I've lost a lot of sleep over the consequences. When a typical CEO is faced with this offer: 'Gee, I'll give you $100 and your company is only worth $90,' he is, in so many cases, thinking of his own life situation, probably nearing retirement: 'I'll get a big payday, I've got a golden parachute, I'll get the house in Florida, and my wife is ready.' In other words, they look at the personal side of it and say, 'Okay, you've forced me into it.' They throw the company into the brier patch and laugh all the way to the bank."

A CEO, Stiritz makes clear, in the final analysis must rely on his or her own counsel—not on outsiders. They have to be very discerning, Stiritz adds, in identifying their advisors' motivations. He recalls, for instance, getting a call "out of the blue" one morning not long after ConAgra first made known its designs on Ralcorp. "It was from a banker I'd worked with in the past. He said, 'Gee, I'm going to be in town.' So I said, 'Come by and we'll have coffee.' He came up to my house in his chauffeured car 'just dropping by to say hello.' We had the coffee, but when I thought about it later—about the questions he had asked—he was really trying to gauge, 'How will this guy react when we offer him that?' Sure enough, his firm actually turned out to be working for ConAgra. It was a part of the game. But it takes time to understand that." He adds, "I can't tell you—looking back on many experiences—boards I've served on and companies I have run—how many times I've wished I could play it over again. 'What might have been'—those words sadly resonate."

Self-Reliance

Stiritz's conclusion: A CEO has to rely on himself and on his own knowledge, which makes it tough. "Most managers haven't been through M&A transactions before and quite often, you see them make mistakes. Not only about the present value of the company. If you look out over the longer term, they make really big mistakes—particularly failing to calculate the long- or short-term capital gains taxes on an all-cash offer. So it often turns out the shareholder wealth question was badly answered. Very often, when you calculate it from an individual shareholder's viewpoint, he would have been much better off holding the stock, assuming a good adaptive management group that would have been creating capital gains over time." He adds, "I can't tell you how many times I have made that mistake—cashing out, taking the capital gain, and then watching the company go on to greater value. That's based on my experience of serving on many, many boards and seeing many buy and sell decisions."

The risk is especially high, Stiritz feels, in hostile deals. "I dare say, if you took the bear hug companies—did an index of twenty-five or thirty or fifty of them over the last thirty years—and did an in-depth study of how they likely would have done had they stayed independent you would say, 'Well, they probably would have done a lot better.' They would have adapted or maybe the board simply should have gotten rid of the CEO and brought in a transformative figure. Unfortunately, however, most boards today don't have that ability. We've seen a transformation over the last thirty years—from boards that were much more reliant on the CEO, deferred to him and allowed him to lead—to boards that claim independence. Whoever invented the term 'lead director' didn't do the capitalist system any great favor. We were better off with the older system where we relied upon the CEO and his managers to lead the company rather than an independent board with independent directors. There is a new set of rules today that—when you delve into them—tie the hands of management a great deal. They prevent a CEO from considering the larger interests and ongoing nature of the company rather than an immediate deal."

Ignoring the Immediate Dollar

Stiritz attributes his own astonishing long-term record of creating shareholder value to luck, yes, but also to "ignoring the immediate dollar"; something that even as chairman and CEO required him to act powerfully enough and persuasively enough to bring his boards along.

"It's a question," explains Stiritz, "of what's the long-term value? You could almost say—whatever the algorithm employed in the present value of the long-term calculation—that it's a by-guess and a by-gosh—it's absolutely subjective. So it takes a willingness to assume these risks, to bet that we can make these assets work in a different fashion, and that over time it will work out. It's having the self-confidence to say, 'We *can* do it. We won't take an immediate payout and head for Florida to retire.' It's just doing it in the longer-term. Which works to the advantage *of people*. I get a *little* satisfaction every now and then when I bump into somebody and they say, 'I really appreciated you being involved in such-and-such. My wife and I are living the good life now because that experience was great.' But, again, most of my career has been luck. I don't want to take too much credit, I've just been at the right place at the right time and been willing to take the calculated risk that we would be adaptive and inventive as time goes on." Still, those happy encounters are infinitely easier to take, Stiritz confesses, than occasionally "being confronted—not directly, but just by reading the body language—by folks whose careers were sunk by something I have done. That's heart-rending. To repeat, I've made mistakes, played hands badly that I wish I could replay."

As a proof of his assertions that bear hugs tend to short-change the potential of well-managed assets, Stiritz points to the dramatic increase in the valuation of Post Holdings since its spinout. "The static bear hug," he reiterates, "says, 'Here's what you're worth, based on today's value.' But that is not reality. The game changes constantly." When ConAgra first made its interest in Ralcorp's private label food operations known, it also made its *dis*interest in the cereal business evident. Sizing up the situation after "just saying no" to ConAgra's bid, Stiritz quickly arranged to spinout the undervalued cereal operation to Ralcorp's shareholders and to take charge of the newly independent Post Holdings, as chairman.

To Stiritz's mind, "The value that has been created in Post since then is all based on this idea of the management's expertise, creativity, inventiveness, and adaptiveness—which were triggered by 'just saying no.' In the end, it's like a father figure or mother figure saying, 'It's okay, kids, we'll be okay.' It's a leap of faith for the board to say that the management can bring about the necessary changes, because the environment is changing constantly. The managerial quality that's really the most important is creativity—to generate ideas and alternatives and be able to handicap them and select the ones that have the best shot—and then get people in place to bring them about. I mean, good management is an art and I don't think we revere that as much as we should. At Post, my greatest managerial accomplishment was selecting Rob Vitale as the leader, as I said, he is the one most responsible for the company's great accomplishments."

Nonetheless, Stiritz stresses, "Again, the biggest variables are randomness and luck. I want to emphasize, everything is situational. There really aren't rules you can fall back on, so critical analysis is key. In the end, we gladly take credit for the good outcomes but the odds were probably high that things could have worked out differently.

"All of us who have managed to end up in that one-tenth of one-tenth, of one-tenth of 1 percent—doing so well in life—we're in the right country at the right time in the country's evolution and development. And we happen to have been fortunate enough to end up with excess wealth. It doesn't have too much to do with us specifically. It was just that the circumstances were right and we happened to hit long shots. Against all odds, we ended up here, and we should all always remember that. You try to be as humble as you can but you just cannot be humble enough."

Continuing in a reflective vein, Stiritz again emphasizes, "The management mantra driving everything now is 'enhancing shareholder value.' Few question it. But my recollection, when I was back at Northwestern and asking, 'What is the ultimate responsibility of somebody managing a company?' is that the answer I heard—which I admit may be warped by my experiences since—was that there's a duality and then some. 'You owe a responsibility to the shareholders, yes, but you also owe a responsibility to your managers, to your leaders in the various operations, probably to people working with you as partners, and to your employees. Then, if to a lesser degree, you owe an obligation to the community—to the environment and to the people who draw their sustenance and livelihood from the companies in the area.' I've always believed that—though sometimes, I'm sorry to say, I haven't practiced it. But I've regretted it when I've played purely the immediate shareholder value variable."

The bigger question, posits Stiritz, "is really, what the hell is the whole thing about? We have 300 million or so people in this country and we try to provide jobs for them. If people are not occupied, they get into all kinds of trouble. So we try to create a system that will create jobs for them. To do that, over the long term, I suspect that driving toward maximum productivity—which business does so well—is not the answer in and of itself. There's got to be a better equation for society as a whole—one that allows for sometimes not being quite as productive as we could be—if, at the same time, we're providing good lives for people."

As for Stiritz, he focused on enhancing shareholder value with the long-term interests of *all* "shareholders" in mind. Still does. And that's all too rare today.

CHAPTER NINETEEN

Paul Montrone

I always like to say, when something goes wrong, that there are two types of people. There are people who point fingers and then there are people who look in the mirror. I'm a mirror person. If something goes wrong, I'm not blaming anybody. I look in the mirror and ask, 'What did I do wrong?' or 'What did I learn from this?' or 'What would I do differently if I were going to do it again?' I take personal responsibility. Then I learn.

SILVER-MANED AT SEVENTY-SIX, but as imposingly tall and erect today as he must have appeared a half century ago as a young ROTC cadet, Paul Montrone delivers those lines in tones tinged with the authority that comes only from experience. Yet over a long and eventful business career that encompassed countless strategic mergers, acquisitions, divestitures, spinoffs, and corporate restructurings—even a few bankruptcies along the way—as well as dramatic internal corporate growth and industry-leading expansion into electronic commerce, the wins Montrone chalked up far exceeded the setbacks. As the CEO of Fisher Scientific International Inc. from the time the venerable purveyor of laboratory tools was spun out of Henley Group at the end of 1991—until its merger with Thermo Electron in 2006, a deal which created Thermo Fisher Scientific Inc.—Montrone oversaw an almost endless stream of transactions that transformed a company once derisively referred to on Wall Street as one of "Dingman's Dogs," into *the* global powerhouse serving the scientific community.

An underperforming domestic manufacturer and distributor of test tubes, centrifuges, and such when Montrone took its helm in 1991, by the time of its 2006 merger with Thermo, Fisher's reach spanned the globe. It was the predominant supplier to research, testing, and clinical laboratories in 150 countries—with over 600,000 products and services—and the company's annual sales had risen from $760 million to about $6 billion. Over those fifteen years under Montrone, moreover, Fisher's equity value soared from roughly $200 million to $12 billion and its compound annual return to shareholders registered a blistering 26 percent.

Fisher Scientific's roots go back to a young Pittsburgh engineer's organization of that region's first commercial supplier of laboratory gear in 1902. Founder Chester Fisher and his sons proudly ran the company for most of the next approximately eighty years (and took it public in 1965). But in 1981, Allied Corp.—which was soon to turn its attention to acquiring much bigger fish—swallowed up Fisher Scientific. The purveyor of laboratory products then endured a decade of management upheaval and benign neglect as Allied, led by Edward L. Hennessy, Jr.—who was determined to prove his mettle by diversifying away from Allied's roots as a quotidian chemicals and oil producer—rose to prominence as a major player in the heyday of Wall Street's merger mania. Prominent among his subsequent deals were Allied's high-profile 1983 "white knight" takeover of Bendix

Corp. for $1.8 billion. It was an arb-pleasing last-minute maneuver, which saved Bendix from a "Pac-Man defense" Martin Marietta had launched in a desperate move to save itself from what had been an apparently successful but headline-grabbing and scandal-tinged hostile bid initiated by Bendix chairman William Agee.

Then, almost before the dust settled, in 1985, came Allied's block-buster $5 billion merger with the Signal Cos. That deal made aerospace the largest business segment in the conglomerate newly renamed Allied-Signal (Subsequently AlliedSignal and then Honeywell). But it also made Allied-Signal's C-suite the focus of intense speculation by media, investors, and employees because it gathered under one patched-together roof three corporate deal titans—not one of whom was known as a shrinking violet. Or even as deferential.

C-Suite Intrigue

Ensconced in that C suite with Hennessy, whose new title was chairman and CEO of Allied-Signal, was Signal Cos. chairman and legendary conglomerateur Forrest N. Shumway as the combined companies' vice chairman. Also included was Michael D. Dingman, an erstwhile investment banker—most recently Signal's president—who enjoyed an outsized reputation as a management whisperer. Hennessy brought Dingman in as president of Allied-Signal with the promise that Hennessy would step aside—five years down the road—to make him Allied-Signal's CEO. It was Dingman, widely followed in Wall Street for his marketing savvy and deal-making chops, who was widely credited with taking the lead in sparking the clandestine conversations-turned-negotiations that led to the Allied-Signal merger.

Just two years earlier, Dingman had pulled off combining Wheelabrator-Frye, the New Hampshire-based manufacturing company he had spent twelve years building, with Signal in a $1.5 billion *premium-less* stock swap. Engineered by the two CEOs, who were old friends, that deal folded Wheelabrator into Signal as a way for Shumway's overly diversified holding company to acquire Dingman's reputedly "mythical management team" in one fell swoop. The premium-less transaction, a rarity in the merger-mad 1980s, left Wall Street speculators and arbs, who'd driven both companies' shares up sharply on rumors of a pending deal, grumbling and licking their wounds.

Thus, the widespread anticipation of pending fireworks in Allied-Signal's C-suite might have been explained by the three executives' Brobdingnagian reputations alone. But there was also this: In the midst of his negotiations to rescue Bendix, Hennessy had agreed to make Bendix's Bill Agee the president of Allied only to push him out within days. What's more, though he had thus far succeeded in ignoring such niceties with impunity, Hennessy *was* usurping his board's prerogatives in promising to make Dingman CEO.

What wasn't widely appreciated at the time was that there was actually a fourth formidable executive in that volatile mix—Paul Montrone. Essentially, at that point, he was Dingman's secret weapon; his finance and operations wingman. A PhD in finance—who had fulfilled his ROTC active duty requirement by working as one of Robert McNamara's whiz kids in the Pentagon in the late 1960s—Montrone had served as Dingman's CFO and unofficial second in command since 1970. When Wheelabrator had merged with Signal, the two executives led the entire management team's exodus from New Hampshire to Signal's La Jolla headquarters. Montrone was named Signal's co-executive VP—right alongside the fellow who had been Signal's president until unseated by Dingman. Subsequently, when Hennessey and Dingman started negotiating the Allied-Signal merger, Montrone had what turned out to be a crucial seat at the table.

"Unknown to anyone outside," Montrone recalls, "the deal fell apart early in the negotiations. Then Hennessey reached out and tried to recruit *me* to become president of Allied to ease the fallout from the Agee fiasco. I agreed to meet with him, but when I did the main thing I was trying to do was to breathe life back into the AlliedSignal deal, which I accomplished." As Montrone remembers it, "I said, 'Ed, if you want to hire me, the best way to get that done is to get the merger done.' He asked, 'Can we get it done? There's lots of resistance.' I said, 'I think we can pull it off. We just have to tweak a few things.' So I quietly reignited the discussions between Hennessey, Dingman, and Shumway that ultimately got the Allied-Signal deal done. Helped put it back on track."

Yet when the new Allied-Signal's organizational chart came out, Montrone's new post looked like only a lateral move—exactly as he wanted it. Explains Montrone, "These were three very powerful CEOs and I was the middleman—stoking all those deals, to a certain extent.

I had very good relationships with each of them. The funny thing is that when Allied and Signal merged—and all three of those guys were still there—they wanted *me* to be the chief operating officer." He was adamant, says Montrone, "No, I'm not going to take that job. I'm not going to work in that position for those three huge deal guys. I had already worked for them, in one way or another—at least two of them. I knew my chance of success was zero." First Boston's star M&A banker Bruce Wasserstein, who had worked the deal, was incredulous, Montrone reports. He remembers Wasserstein telling him, "I don't believe this, you turned that job down? You could be the chief operating officer of *this big thing*." Montrone remembers his reply as, "Bruce, forget about it. I don't want to be on the front-lines, with all those generals behind me, watching and prodding me." He elaborates, "I figured they were going to be battling with one another and I'd be in the middle, so I stepped aside and let somebody else do it."

It proved a deft move, though the explosive C-suite soap opera Montrone and many spectators expected was short-circuited by—what else, with all those deal makers in the same room?—yet another blockbuster deal. Barely a month after formally assuming his new role as Allied-Signal's president, Dingman was said to have volunteered at a secret board meeting in the fall of 1985 to give up that post. Instead, he would head up a motley collection of $3.5 billion in assets—spread across thirty-five companies employing some 25,000 people in areas ranging from soda ash to real estate—which AlliedSignal was preparing to jettison. It turned out that after spending years building up to the $5 billion merger of his chemicals giant with Signal's massive aerospace and engineering core, Hennessy decided, in a dramatic about-face, to concentrate Allied-Signal in just three industries: aerospace, electronics, and chemicals. Whether Hennessy was actually surprised that Dingman raised his hand or felt he had cleverly maneuvered him into volunteering, Dingman—who frequently boasted of his prowess in turnarounds—never publicly professed anything but delight in the change of circumstances. He threw himself into planning the spinout, which he named "Henley Group," an homage to an English town famed for rowing regattas, but Wall St. wags cynically dubbed "Dingman's Dogs." There was just one glitch: Paul Montrone.

A Close Escape

While no doubt delighted to be getting Dingman—and a raft of middling to troubled operations—off of his plate, Hennessy had been plenty impressed with Montrone during the Allied-Signal negotiations and wanted to keep him with "mother"—even after Montrone had turned down the COO job. "Hennessey knew he had a bit of a problem with his board," says Montrone, "after jettisoning both Agee and Dingman as successors. So while he was happy to let Dingman do the spinoff, he wanted me to stay at Allied-Signal as the eventual president. I considered myself at that point a corporate hostage. But I agreed to go along with Ed to get the deal done." So when Hennessy soon permitted Dingman to transfer a sizeable team of loyal managers over to Henley, Montrone was conspicuously not among them. Indeed, it was not clear until the following March, when details of the proposed Henley spinoff were filed with the SEC, that Dingman and Montrone's persistent back-channel lobbying had finally convinced Hennessy to relent. Montrone moved to Henley as its president, and acquired a 49 percent stake in New Hampshire Oak, the control vehicle Dingman set up to increase his stake in Henley.

To say that Montrone was relieved was an understatement. He had been quoted in a contemporaneous *New York Times* article calling being left behind in Allied-Signal "an emotional trauma"—albeit one he was determined to surmount. But Hennessy clearly was not alone in appreciating Montrone's skills as an executive. A *Fortune* article, published before Montrone's emancipation from Allied-Signal, reported that executive recruiters had named him one of the nation's top ten managers in their forties with the right stuff to be CEOs. When he ended up as president of Henley Group instead, Montrone told the *New York Times* that the opportunity for continued association with Dingman and the challenges of leading the new organization would more than suffice. "Everybody dreams of being their own boss, but I think that is a little idealistic. Mike and I have enough of a relationship so that this is about as close as I am going to get, without the dream world" (Kenneth N. Gilpin and Lee A. Daniels, "Business People; Allied-Signal Executive Shifting to Henley Post," *New York Times*, March 3, 1986).

Looking back now, Montrone reflects, "I knew Dingman—knew he could handle me and I could handle him." Besides, Montrone continues, "Mike was an excellent strategy guy in addition to having a real talent for marketing to Wall Street—and Mike also appreciated operations and the importance of financial controls—he really knew how important the controls are. Essentially, we were a good team. We complemented each other."

The Early Years

Reaching back to some of his earliest experiences with Dingman in the 1970s, Montrone elaborates, "We took Wheelabrator, which was a basically a little industrial cleaning company—the Wheelabrator was a machine used to abrade industrial equipment to clean it—and turned it, over the years, into an environmental company—right when that was trendy. But first we had to form Wheelabrator-Frye out of Equity Corp." Dingman had forked over $500,000 in 1968 to purchase, along with a partner, the troubled old-line closed-end investment company. Under prior management, explains Montrone, Equity Corp. had run afoul of securities regulators by taking control positions instead of merely investing in public companies. So it took Dingman until the end of 1970 to get the SEC to approve Equity's reregistration as an operating company. Then, however, he lost little time. Dingman merged Equity Corp. with three other companies in which it held substantial stakes, two of which were Wheelabrator and Frye. Says Montrone, "I don't think there's been another four-way merger since that one in 1971. But then, it was obvious to Mike that he had brought only one guy, Steve Shulman, with him from Wall Street and he needed to assemble a management team."

Montrone was hired as senior vice president and CFO of what was still called Equity Corp. in June of 1971, as Dingman started that process and later assumed comparable positions at Wheelabrator-Frye. He continues, "It was Mike who had the strategic vision. The Clean Air Act was passed in 1970 and Mike realized that the 'fabric filter system' that was attached to Wheelabrator machines (which otherwise created a lot of dirt in factories) was, essentially, an air pollution control device. It wasn't called that back then but that's what it was. So Mike said, 'Hey, we're going to be an environmental company because we have a foothold right here in air pollution.' Then we got into water pollution; then we got into garbage-to-energy." Indeed, "it was all

Mike's vision," Montrone reiterates, that created the company that the pair sold to Signal Cos. in 1983 for $1.5 billion. "I learned from a great strategist when nobody else was seeing the possibilities."

"Dingman's Dogs"

Scarcely three years after the Signal-Wheelabrator merger, investors were certainly betting on strategic vision in August of 1986 when they poured an eye-popping $1.2 billion into "Dingman's Dogs," the Allied-Signal castoffs, including Wheelabrator, in Henley's IPO. The Henley Group's initial public offering was the largest industrial underwriting ever in the United States up to that time even though its constituent companies were producing copious red ink and even though the funds raised, according to the offering documents, were to be devoted to unspecified future acquisitions. Indeed, the next month Henley acquired IMED Corp., a maker of intravenous solution pumping systems for hospitals for $163 million in a move to bulk up its scientific businesses.

But most of Dingman and Montrone's early focus at Henley was on organizing it into three main units: the Fisher Scientific Group, the Wheelabrator Technologies Group, and a catch-all manufacturing unit. Numerous strategic acquisitions and partial divestitures in all three areas followed—prominently including, the very next year, the initial public offering of not quite 7 million shares of Wheelabrator Technologies, which raised $119 million. It was the first of a long series of deals to emerge from Henley, which Dingman essentially ran as an incubator—engineering creative transactions to maximize shareholder value and, not incidentally, increase the equity stakes held by Dingman and his loyal executive team. Businesses were regularly taken public through the sale of noncontrolling interests to the public—gaining independent stock valuations—while at the same time raising cash for yet other investments. From all indications, investors and their brokers loved it, routinely paying premiums for the opportunity to directly share the risk of operating the monoline spinoffs with Henley.

Montrone multitasked in the late 1980s, as Wheelabrator Technology's chairman and CEO as well as Henley's president. With its spinoff from Henley, Wheelabrator increased its focus on growing its waste-to-energy business, and in the process it became a bigger factor in the waste industry. Always strategizing and mindful of building relationships, Montrone quickly decided that industry leader Waste Management could be a great synergistic partner for his company. "So we targeted them," says Montrone. "We got big enough and powerful enough that they had to notice us." He also had Wheelabrator collaborate with Waste Management on some projects and invited its key executives to corporate outings—building the relationship until the waste disposal giant ultimately decided to take Wheelabrator over, making it a majority-owned subsidiary in a 1990 transaction. Wheelabrator's annual shareholder returns under Montrone's leadership between 1987 and 1990 were 22 percent compounded. "Almost all of our deals," Montrone reflects, were things we targeted; we were always strategizing."

On His Own

The next year, Montrone assumed the CEO role at Fisher Scientific when it was spun out from Henley. Finally at the helm of a company in which Henley—and his long-time boss, Dingman—held only a tiny, derivative stake (an option to buy 15 percent of the company under certain conditions)—Montrone started to methodically build out his own strategic vision of a global scientific supply powerhouse. His strategizing, Montrone says, was evident in the changes he quickly made to the Fisher's marketing motto. "When we started, Fisher described itself as 'the oldest and largest distributor of scientific products in North America.' That was it." He then deconstructs that pitch. "Okay, oldest: that's great; largest: that's pretty good; distributor: not that great; North America: not that great. We decided we had to change the tag line. So we called ourselves, 'The world leader in serving science.' That was the first thing we threw out, and I figured I'd hear from Hewlett Packard or IBM or a bunch of big companies saying, 'How are you claiming to be *the* world leader? *We're* serving science.' But no company said a word. The only recoil we got was from the SEC—we put that line in some filing and they came back and said, 'If you're going to make this statement you've got to prove to us that you're the world leader.' So we took it out of our filings. But that was it. 'The world leader in serving science' became our marketing mantra."

The new tag line was seminal in developing his strategic vision for Fisher Scientific, Montrone explains, because it focused the company globally and "explicitly said we weren't just a distributor, we were going to do whatever we could to service our customers. That became the thesis on which we built our company. Every step was in the direction of doing whatever it took." "I have a little salesman in me," explains Montrone, who grew up in Scranton, Pennsylvania, and worked his way through the local Jesuit college, the University of Scranton (graduating magna cum laude, valedictorian of his class, and with a ROTC commission), in a variety of jobs. But his favorite college gig was selling books door-to-door—a job in which he quickly learned the value of building a strategy—along with the value of direct customer contact.

"In those days there was a collection called the *Great Books of the Western World*. I wanted to get a set for myself—and the way I could was by selling enough of them, door-to-door. So I became one of their best salesmen. I loved it. Those were the days when you could actually knock on doors. Now if you knock on the door, somebody might shoot you. Our society has changed. But back then, they'd come to the door and be polite. I learned a lot about sales. We had a memorized pitch and six or eight 'closings'—you'd try each of them in turn until one worked. If you got down to the last one, it was really a polite way of saying, 'I understand you don't want to buy these books—meaning you want to be a dunce all your life'—a little bit of an insult. A final attempt to shame them into buying. If that failed, you were out the door. It taught me so much about the psychology of sales and a close—leading them along, mentally."

The *Great Books*, Montrone reminisces, were a division of Encyclopedia Britannica, and he quickly learned to take advantage of the company's sales tools. "You could pay, I think it was a buck a lead, to get a list of people who had already bought the encyclopedias and then you could pay probably two bucks a lead for the names of people who had actually responded to an ad offering a descriptive pamphlet about the *Great Books* series. Right away, I experimented with the lists." From that data emerged Montrone's sales strategy, "Okay, I'm buying the $2 names first because they are my highest odds that somebody's interested. The Encyclopedia Britannica owners list was pretty good, too. I stopped knocking on random doors. It was worth a buck or two a lead because our commissions were good." To Montrone, the lesson was unmistakable. "Advertising pays. People could be completely captured by a sales pitch. I was shocked—what did I know, I was just a college kid. But it works. I was quite successful."

An Early Reality Check

Then "a stupid thing came along," says Montrone, that provided another invaluable lesson. "I was a part-time salesman, still in college, when they hired a new sales manager. He didn't want any part-timers. Now, as a commission-only sales rep, I didn't cost him anything unless I produced—and was one of the best producers in the region. But when they put him in charge, he just killed off one of his best sales people—me! It was an unbelievably stupid business move. But I told myself, 'Boy, if this is the way business works, I'll do okay.'"

Not eager to go into either business or the military straight from college and unable to afford MBA tuition, Montrone fell back on his contacts and relationships. "These days it would be called networking," says Montrone, "back then it was just working relationships I'd built." A former professor knew someone at Columbia University and heard grants were available for enrollment in Columbia's doctoral program in finance. The professor urged Montrone to apply. "I never thought I'd be an academic, though I was always fascinated by research and analysis—and became very fascinated by operations research, which was just emerging as a field while I was in grad school."

Three years later, doctorate in hand and facing imminent active duty status, Montrone again got lucky. "I somehow found out that a Columbia professor knew Alain Enthoven, who had left Rand and was doing operations research at the Pentagon, and he reached out for me. To this day, when I see that professor, he always says, 'Montrone, I saved you from getting killed in Vietnam.' I was coming out of Columbia with all my work in operations research—just when that was a sweet spot in the McNamara Pentagon." Assigned to the Office of the Secretary of Defense for Systems Analysis, Montrone did wartime simulation models, cost-effectiveness studies and logistics. "I was doing really advanced computer work—the Pentagon had a basement filled with the biggest computers anyone had seen, all linked together." Today, Montrone shakes his head, noting wryly that he didn't grasp back then the technological revolution those connected computers presaged. "How stupid of me. I never conceived of them as anything but big adding machines, probably just getting bigger. It was the late 1960s. Apple wasn't even founded until 1976." Besides, his primary mission was accomplished. "I came out of the service as a captain, having served my country, albeit oddly, by saving taxpayers billions—and never had to wear the uniform, except in ROTC."

Lessons Applied

Nonetheless, Montrone allows, early lessons in sales and in the military served him well. "I always liked to be in touch with the customers; to understand their mentality, even as the CEO." In fact, he adds, "one reason I was ready to sell Fisher Scientific in 2006 was that Fisher had gotten so big, it was hard for me to maintain that personal touch. Hard to get in front of the customer and find out what was really going on." Notes Montrone, "I'm very sympathetic to these very big companies. The CEO becomes an administrator, a human resources person, a board process machine—and very dependent on people down the line to understand what's going on. But in a huge company, everybody is not going to be a home-run hitter. You're going to have some subpar performers with the good ones, and I don't like that." Trying to maintain a bit of direct customer contact at Fisher when its sales force numbered over 1,500 Montrone recalls, "I realized it was like an army, so I dug out one of my old military manuals. I sensed we needed communications all up and down the organization. The military is impressive in a lot of respects—and unimpressive in certain others—but I realized I had to rediscover how a general knows what the hell's going on out on the front lines because I was losing contact with the customer experience." Generals, Montrone rediscovered, have radio operators reporting from the frontlines up to headquarters. "So in each sales district, we added an administrator to collect information from the sales people and feed it up to Fisher's executives. That way, we had some visibility at the top about what the heck's going on with the customer, and particularly, what's going on with competitors. But the bigger you are, the harder it is."

Still, a CEO's primary concern, opines Montrone, has to be value creation. "If you're going to overpay for something, you're not going to create value. And even if you don't overpay, you've still got to execute." Every now and then, he acknowledges, Fisher ran into an execution problem on his watch. "We'd do a deal and say, 'these are the cost savings and we'll execute it over six or twelve months,' but then we'd miss. The Street would get PO'd and the stock would drop. So our stock didn't go straight up, it zigzagged." Wall Street, observes Montrone, likes to focus on the short term. "But I never worried too much about short-term results. I stayed in touch with the big investors so they knew what was going on—and the fundamental analysts, when they were still around. Your stock can always drop over the short term. But if you do reasonably well over a period of time, you'll be at the high end of your industry range again and investors forgive you."

Montrone declares that although they have their place, he's "never been big on business consultants, management books, and that kind of stuff." Yet he did cut out a *Wall Street Journal* op-ed piece [originally published on October 21, 1993] that management guru Peter Drucker penned, called "The Five Deadly Business Sins." Every time Fisher bought a company or brought in a new management, he says, "I always handed it out at the meeting and said, 'Read this.' One of the deadly sins Drucker listed was 'worshipping at the altar of high margins.' Another was investing in today and starving the future." Montrone exclaims, "Talk about two ways to kill a business. General Motors and Kodak are two great examples."

Montrone continues, "Public companies are especially vulnerable to worshipping at the altar of high margins. Today, that's why I always love having a private company that's competing with a publicly held one. The public company has to worry about earnings per share; it's got to worry about short-term investors—and all that stuff at least partially drives what the CEO is doing. Whereas a private company can say, 'Holy jeepers, there's an opportunity! I'm going to kill my earnings this year to do that.' Then, it outruns the public company."

Listed Company Blues

What's more, Montrone suggests, "process" has become more important to many big publicly-held companies than returns. "To me, the only reason to be a public company today is if you can get an extraordinary multiple, and therefore, a very low cost of capital. If you're just an ordinary company plugging away, my philosophy is it's actually a disadvantage to be public." He adds that today's companies have more opportunities to utilize leverage—with structured finance often allowing them to raise money without giving up equity—than were available even when he was running Fisher Scientific. "It's a very big change; one that tax laws have not kept up with." Early in his career, reflects Montrone, he'd strive to win investment-grade credit ratings and the lower borrowing costs they'd entail. But "the funny thing is, as the junk bond market developed, I didn't even *want* to be investment grade. I always kept my ratios in later companies, like Fisher, just *below* investment grade. I didn't want to risk being downgraded because of an acquisition. Then, all of a sudden, everyone would ask what's wrong with the company?"

It's an insight Montrone uses in investing for his New Hampshire–based trust company and multi-family office, Perspecta Trust. "One of the things we do is junk bonds. It's not what I would call a broad portfolio. It's very selective, based on deep research and analysis. But once in a while, we will see an issue and say, 'this really should be investment grade, but it's junk.' So we find out why. Usually, I'll call the CFO and he'll say, 'I don't *want* to be investment grade.' I understand that. But that means it's an investment opportunity, an underrated bond."

Generating good long-term returns in business, first of all, requires luck, says Montrone. "Beyond that, my criteria for the businesses I want to be in today are threefold: I want to be part of a big industry, I want to have the wind at my back, and I don't want to compete with the Chinese." Practically in the same breath, he qualifies. "It's not as if you can't make a lot of money in companies where the wind is in your face, but you have to have a strategy for coming out on top and it's not as much fun." Fisher Scientific, he remembers fondly, ticked off all three of his ideal-company boxes. "We were in a huge industry, we had the wind at our back—health care, science. And not so much competition. We started as a distributor, and as such, weren't really competing with any of the foreign guys. Distribution is a local business. Gradually we did get into manufacturing—and there was foreign competition there. But it was in Europe. It wasn't in Asia. As a matter of fact, we led the march into Asia. We watched our industry very carefully all the time since our goal was to become a bigger and bigger part of it. We were always strategizing. At each step we took, we had to add value. And that takes a lot of discipline." Montrone continues,

"Any time you overpay for something or do anything crazy, it sets you back, and it takes a while to catch up again."

To illustrate how his early experience in systems operations research influenced his analytical approach throughout his career, Montrone points to Fisher's diversification into organic chemicals. "Although it was essentially a distributor when we acquired it, Fisher already happened to be also manufacturing *inorganic* chemicals for some customers," he says. After taking Fisher's reins, Montrone immediately set out analyzing how it could grow its businesses. "We started out looking at our very strong customer base; wanted to increase our market penetration with them. How? Well, one obvious way was by also distributing *organic* chemicals. The leader in that business was Sigma-Aldrich. They sold direct. No sales force, a strong market position, a strong brand. We met with them and said, 'Hey, we'd love to distribute your products.' The answer was, basically, 'We don't need you; we're doing just fine.' Tried a few more times, to no avail." But Montrone didn't give up, instead searching the globe for rival maker of organic chemicals. "We found a small subsidiary of Johnson & Johnson in Europe that made organic chemicals. The operation didn't really fit their strategy. We worked at it and eventually bought it, putting Fisher into organic chemical manufacturing and distribution."

It was a milestone, avers Montrone, because the acquisition enhanced "the biggest asset we had: channel power. As a distributor, we were a meaningful factor in our customers' businesses. In our industry, the Fisher brand was strong and we kept making it stronger by providing more products and services. Also, by not being afraid to get into manufacturing, if we had to, to get product to distribute. Companies selling direct were up against a strong competitor in Fisher—even if we couldn't distribute *their* products. Our going into organic chemicals dramatically affected Sigma-Aldrich. They had to put a sales force together, change the way they were doing business. We were in front of their customers anyway, and those customers had been looking for an alternative. Sigma-Aldrich had been so strong in organic chemicals that its customers didn't feel it was competing for their business. When we suddenly showed up with competitive organics—with our name on them and our reputation—boom! Sigma-Aldrich had underestimated our channel power and was stuck worshiping at the altar of high margins." And Sigma-Aldrich ultimately caved, adding distributors to its sales operations.

A Focus on Returns

Montrone also attributes his success at Fisher to "not being a cutter of overhead," despite his early experiences as a CFO. "I actually like overhead." He attributes the insight to a postmortem he read on Coca-Cola's infamous *New Coke* fiasco. Coke had learned the hard way that marketing should be treated as an investment, not as an expense. "So I look at *all* overhead as an investment, whether in marketing, or research, or people, or anything else. You had better just make sure you make a return on it." He reiterates, "It's not enough to just minimize overhead. You have to pump money into the things that are going to generate a return. The investments that yield the biggest payoffs are in people. The tech companies know that full well. That's all they're investing in—people." Then he quickly qualifies, "Of course, I'm not trying to waste money. I've always insisted you need to have strong financial controls to make sure it is a good investment."

A good CEO, reiterates Montrone, is always strategizing. "You have to be thinking ahead about what's going on in your company, in your industry. What's going on elsewhere. Always watching competitive moves." In fact, he created a staff at Fisher descriptively but inelegantly called, "I want to see everything that moves—Any rival, any customer, doing anything new, any deals—however small—any innovations." He put his right-hand man and partner Paul Meister in charge. "I told them, if something moves and we don't know about it, you guys are going to be killed. The idea was to have some visibility to what was happening around us, not just internally. It became part of the dynamics." The group proved its worth many times over, Montrone says, particularly "during the internet boom, when people were throwing money at anything tech. We noticed a particular technology company being funded by Wall Street and realized, 'Okay, we can't ignore this.' It could have done the equivalent in our industry to what Amazon did when it switched into supplying books and then began building warehouses that just knocked Barnes & Noble and Borders out of the way."

Montrone clarifies, "it was an online procurement system for scientific instruments, for health care products—and Wall Street was pouring money into its development." As a public company, Montrone recalls, Fisher Scientific couldn't afford to match that level of funding.

"So we pulled together seven other companies in various distribution and supply businesses in science and health care and got them to agree to finance the creation of a new entity, essentially to try to do the same thing." Had the companies individually tried to finance the project, says Montrone, they would have cratered their earnings. "So we all funded it a little bit. We hired a bunch of techies to develop a competing technology at least as good as the one the Street was funding. When we got it, we essentially blew them away. They couldn't raise their next round of funding because we all had established market positions and business relationships as well as our equivalent technology." The new venture's mission accomplished, Montrone concludes, the distributors' group unwound it. "We shared the new technology and some used it and some didn't. But we had to attack that rival procurement system strategically to protect our businesses."

Strategic Endgame

Always strategizing for ways to set his companies apart from the crowd, and an indefatigable networker, Montrone since Wheelabrator days had been inviting business contacts, not to golf, but to an annual bocce tournament at his New Hampshire lake house. The exclusive gatherings, which over the years drew real estate magnates and a Supreme Court justice as well as Wall Street and corporate participation, took on added strategic significance when he and his executive team first started eying Thermo Electron as a potential acquisition. "We invited its CEO, Marijn Dekkers, to the bocce tournament." Montrone explains that Fisher was already a distributor of some Thermo products, so the invitation didn't raise eyebrows. "That went on for a couple of years," Montrone notes, "so when it came time to start making a deal, it wasn't a cold call. We already had a relationship, a little trust." While Thermo, the smaller company, actually ended up—atypically—as the acquirer in their 2006 transaction, Fisher was the instigator, Montrone insists. "We had two or three other synergistic opportunities at that point and the main reason we went with Thermo versus the others was to get an increase in our valuation."

By then it had become evident to him, says Montrone, that the character of the stock market had changed dramatically. Back in the day, he reminisces, "analysts would come and talk with us. But in the last few years that we were running Fisher, we'd hardly ever see an analyst. It was a new era, the era of modeling." To Montrone's practiced eye, this has had a subtle but harmful impact on managements' abilities to distinguish themselves in terms of market multiples. "One of the distinguishing characteristics of a Henley or a Wheelabrator was Mike Dingman. Our shares, because of Mike, always commanded a premium multiple. He was going to do things differently." But, continues Montrone, "in Fisher's latter years, a different kind of pattern emerged as the Street switched to modeling from following companies. It meant that almost nothing we did as a company made much difference in our multiple. We were lumped into an industry *and got the industry's multiple*. In fact, if there were rewards, they went to companies with *bad* performance. If you had lousy performance, your stock might drop off temporarily. Then, as long as you reasonably came back, your multiple would go right back up into the industry range."

Frustrated by that dynamic, Montrone was determined to break Fisher out of Wall Street's valuation straitjacket in his last deal. His idea was to turn the tables on the modelers by capitalizing on the way the Street was anchoring valuations by industry. "Thermo was only half our size but had a much stronger multiple because they were considered a technology company. So rather than us buying them, they bought us." Adds Montrone, "It was a high-risk deal from the point of view of us selling out to them—their management doing the takeover. While a lot of our shareholders by then were short-term investors—arbs and the like—we still had many long-term investors—and the tax-free, stock-for-stock exchange that we negotiated meant that we were giving them shares in the merged company. We had to have pretty high confidence that the merger actually was going to happen, that the multiple on the combined companies would work up somehow, and that the cost savings and synergies would materialize. So we stayed on the board, with Paul Meister as chair, as we got to know Thermo even better." Adds Montrone, "I was getting out, so we didn't want our loyal shareholders to think we were abandoning them."

The strategy worked even better than Montrone had dared to hope. "The question had been, could we take the Fisher earnings—which were double the Thermo earnings—and get the market to accord all those Fisher earnings an elevated Thermo multiple just by merging the companies? I told the board, 'They'll probably give us half.' But I was wrong. They gave us the whole multiple. It was the most stunning thing I'd ever seen. The modelers went in, added Fisher's earnings to Thermo's, and then applied the elevated Thermo multiple to the combined earnings. So the multiple on Fisher's earnings contribution went up, up, up! It was the multiple of the industry that mattered. All these ETFs and such just add fuel to that."

Reflecting, Montrone shrugs. "I mean, it's right and it's wrong. It's capitalism at work in its current version. So what you want to do is try to capitalize on it."

CHAPTER TWENTY

Peter McCausland

Some of the arbs were blatant about their pursuit of short-term profits.
Some of them had fancy offices and came out of Goldman Sachs—like
the guy at Eton Park [Eric Mindich]. Then there was John Paulson.
I liked talking to Mr. Paulson. He seemed to listen to me. But then the
next day, they said they weren't voting for us. There were a few other
arbs that I thought were pretty coherent. There were several who tried
to engage in discussions about the packaged gas industry worldwide, or
Delaware corporate law, like the Eton Park guys. But it was all a ruse.

The conversations were just a way to try to find a point of vulnerability to put pressure on us. During that process, we said some arbs were really bad, none were great, but some were okay. But by the time the votes came in, we knew none of them were okay. The arbs and activists were all invested in a potential transaction—and we were fighting that transaction. . . . In our case, the arbs ran into a company that was really run for the long term.

CLEARLY, WALL STREET'S risk arbitrageurs and activists don't rank highly on Peter McCausland's hit parade. It's odd, perhaps, to think that McCausland, himself a lawyer by training, once ran a legal firm specializing in M&A. Indeed, it might strike you as even more than passingly odd if you knew that McCausland built his company not only organically but also by making nearly 500 acquisitions over his thirty-three years at its helm. Very possibly, you might even brush off his contempt for the Street as certifiable—if you were told McCausland walked away from that enterprise—his personal wealth enhanced by a cool $1 billion—after he negotiated a surprise, $10.3 billion takeover of his company in late 2015.

That singular transaction, including assumption of $2.8 billion of debt, put a total enterprise value of $13.4 billion on the company McCausland founded in 1982. It was not only a higher multiple of EBITDA than paid in any combination in the consolidating packaged gas-distribution industry, before or since, the price was more than double a notorious offer McCausland and his company's board were roundly criticized for rejecting only four years earlier. And, just for good measure, the deal represented a better than 50 percent premium to the company's one-month average share price prior to the announcement as well as a 20 percent-plus premium to the stock's fifty-two-week high. To the lucky few shareholders who had purchased the company's shares on its 1986 IPO—and held for the long term—the company McCausland founded delivered a breathtaking 13,000 percent return, versus 700 percent on the S&P 500 over that span. And McCausland himself was very notably among those long-termers.

The sixty-seven-year-old executive is now an occasional gentleman farmer who favors bow ties and khakis when visiting the 450-acre estate near Philadelphia he and his family are preserving. He lives most of the year in Florida and also enjoys a place on Nantucket. Despite his tone in the opening quote, McCausland is not a crank or impossible to please. Far from it. But the company McCausland spent more than three decades nurturing as it grew from a single Connecticut industrial gas distributor with $3 million in annual sales—for which he paid $5 million—into a dominant force in the packaged gas industry with $5.5 billion in annual revenues was Airgas. *That Airgas.* And he never wanted to sell it. After fighting an epic Wall Street battle to fend off that earlier "grossly undervalued" merger bid, McCausland explains, "I had hoped that I could just step back to nonexecutive chairman and Airgas would remain independent. But the chances of that were pretty small."

Drawing the Battle Lines

Based in Radnor, Pennsylvania, Airgas was the leading supplier of canisters of industrial, medical, and specialty gases, plus sundry related products and services, in the United States. Between 2009 and 2011, Airgas was the target of one of the longest, nastiest, knock-down, drag-out hostile takeover campaigns in recent memory. The management of Air Products, a bulk producer and distributor of industrial gases and specialty materials, also based in Pennsylvania, had opportunistically commenced the hostilities while Airgas's shares, which had changed hands comfortably above $60 before the financial crisis, were still lagging, down around $48. An occasional supplier to—and sometimes rival of—Airgas, Allentown-headquartered Air Products coveted Airgas's unparalleled distribution platform, with more than 1,400 locations, and deep relationships with over a million customers coast-to-coast.

But the companies were frenemies of long standing. "There was nothing they could do to convince me that they were a good company," McCausland avers. "I had known them for too long. Their culture was antithetical to ours. All's well that ends well—but it was a traumatic thing to go through for a long time. On the phone until four o'clock in the morning in meetings; staying up all night reading briefs. But we just weren't going to go down without a fight. I threw my heart and soul into it."

After the Airgas board decided to go to the mat over Air Products' unwanted advances, the ensuing nearly eighteen-month-long take-over saga encompassed almost everything the genre has to offer. It was JPMorgan and Cravath, Swaine & Moore for the suitor versus Goldman Sachs, Bank of America, and Wachtell, Lipton, Rosen & Katz for the prey. There were initial secret flirtations utterly spurned followed by a public bid *at a lower price* also rejected out of hand. There was a fully financed tender offer in which the bid was teasingly ratcheted higher in three steps from $60 to $70 a share; numerous bitter accusations of skullduggery and scurrilous behavior; a proxy contest that succeeded in replacing three members of Airgas's stag-gered board, momentarily even unseating McCausland; followed by the ironic spectacle of Air Products' handpicked-directors siding with Airgas. The hostile takeover attempt also included several independent analyses that pegged Airgas's value at up to $78 a share as well as numerous Delaware Chancery Court proceedings in multiple suits and countersuits, one of which was appealed to that state's Supreme Court and, more than a year after the hostile bid was publicly announced, a 158-page decision reluctantly supporting the Airgas board's use of a poison pill to fend off the bid and confirming the Airgas board's fidu-ciary duty to reject an offer it deemed inadequate. Finally, Air Products slunk away, empty-handed, and two years later replaced its CEO after activist Bill Ackman's Pershing Square Capital Management took a stake in its sagging shares.

McCausland and Airgas, meanwhile, got back to business. In the company's 2011 annual report, the founder wrote to shareholders:

> There's a feeling you get when you finally break free of a traffic jam and see only open road ahead. It's more than relief. It's a sense of optimism and freedom as you retake charge of your own destiny.
>
> That's where we are today at Airgas. The global recession and Air Products' unsuccessful hostile bid for our company are both in our rear view mirror, and we are back where we belong—delivering on the promise of an operating model, a platform for growth and a workplace culture that are unmatched in the industry.

By early 2015, however, storm clouds were unmistakably gathering again over Airgas. McCausland watched apprehensively as a promi-nent activist investor, Elliott Management's Paul Singer took a large position in the Airgas shares—even as McCausland was fending off renewed private inquiries from Air Products. McCausland read the handwriting on the wall and with the support of the Airgas board quietly sprang into action, looking "for a good company that would value Airgas appropriately and, as importantly, believe in our culture and growth potential." McCausland found that suitor in France's Air Liquide. It wasn't just the deal's $13-plus billion valuation that he liked. Says McCausland, "Very quickly Air Liquide announced that only four or five Airgas jobs were going to be lost. All the synergies came from their Air Liquide Houston operation; 800 people were laid off there. They took their merchant business and packaged business and moved them into Airgas's Radnor headquarters, adding a little over $2 billion in sales to our $5.5 billion. They are still going to run their big pipeline system out of Houston, but our people will be running a much bigger bulk and packaged gas business here. We're very proud that Air Liquide is taking our business model, our platform, our people—and that Air Liquide is so pleased with this whole thing. That offsets some of the disappointment in Airgas not being an independent company anymore."

A Question of Trust

McCausland reflects, "I'm not going to say that activism hasn't helped turn around some bad companies—where boards didn't replace managements when they should have, or approved lousy acquisitions. It's hard to condemn *all* activism. But I always argue that one-size-fits-all doesn't work in either corporate governance or in activism. Maybe Air Products deserved to have a Bill Ackman go in there and shake things up; they did a terrible job for their shareholders for so long. But companies like Airgas—which at that point, even with a depressed stock price, had returned 18 percent a year, compounded, to shareholders—*we should have been given the benefit of the doubt*. Shareholders *ought* to trust management if it has met certain performance levels over the years."

He elaborates, "I won't say there weren't times when our stock price dropped more than the market or the very large caps. We were a small-cap and then a medium-cap in a cyclical business. But our stock *always* rebounded more than the market and our returns were remarkably stable. I mean, we never had a down year in same-store sales of gas or cylinder rent, which were two-thirds of our sales and the real driver of our business. Until the Great Recession, that is, when gas sales and cylinder rent actually went down 14 percent. Yet for the fiscal year ended March 31, 2010, which pretty much coincided with the worst of that downturn, our cash flow from operations set a record." Airgas, McCausland explains, "had reduced expenses pretty dramatically, which we had rarely done before because we were just very expense-disciplined all the time; we had never had reductions in force or things like that. But in the financial crisis, we reduced our workforce by 10 percent. Our working capital and capital expenditures shrank. We paid off debt. And our cylinder rent just kept flowing in. It's one of the very good things about the business."

McCausland hastens to make clear that Airgas's strong cash flow in the recession, and sharp earnings rebound the following fiscal year—despite the distractions and expenses involved in fighting off Air Products—were neither automatic nor a fluke. "It goes to show you how amazing our associates—led by Mike Molinini, our COO—were. We said to them, 'Look, we'll focus on fighting off Air Products. You guys run the company, deliver the earnings. Control what you can control. We'll do the very best we can.' They took it on themselves to just outperform. It was amazing. When we won, I made sure that they knew that they were the ones who were responsible for us winning. During the hostile takeover attempt, many of our fundamental shareholders left us, and it was the Airgas associates who saved the company for the ones who didn't sell their shares. That was important for them to hear because they had tried so hard."

The company's smart rebound was the payoff, McCausland avers, "from the very long time we took to develop our business model and philosophy." Also, from years spent developing and nurturing "a decentralized, entrepreneurial management structure in a flat organization that took pains to keep decision making as close to its customers as possible." McCausland proudly adds that Airgas's performance under duress offered proof that "we did a very good job aligning our goals, objectives, and compensation over the years, through a lot of trial and error. We had a very leveraged compensation system—with much more at risk than the average company. That meant that the top 400, if they made full bonus for a year, would get a bonus of 50 percent of their cash compensation. Plus, we had a stock options plan that wasn't top-heavy, unlike most big companies' plans. It went deep into the organization instead because getting stock options makes employees feel like owners." Moreover, the operating rebound could only happen, says McCausland, because of all the time and attention Airgas had, for the previous thirty years, poured into "trying to get better at meeting our customers' requirements, developing the best interfaces with them." This involved developing multiple channels— outside sales, inside sales support, telesales, e-commerce, catalogues, outbound telemarketing, a big strategic accounts program. "We had process specialists helping food freezer manufacturers or steel makers or welders. We had a huge welding process group. We had supply chain experts. We spent a very long time developing how we interfaced with customers. We took a long time making our 480 acquisitions and then standardizing and improving businesses processes." At the same time, Airgas internally developed things like its small bulk gas program, nationwide distribution centers, sophisticated logistics for its hard goods, a national specialty gas platform. It essentially became a first-class operating company, the founder avers.

Extraordinary Due Diligence

Even in a consolidating industry, Airgas's 480 acquisitions over little more than thirty years was a prodigious pace. And they weren't all tiny. Besides numerous independent bottled gas distributors, they included, over time, the packaged gas businesses of rivals Puritan Bennett, BOC, Linde and Air Products; the safety products telesales company IPCO; the equipment rental company Red-D-Arc; and the U.S. bulk gas business of Linde. McCausland explains that as a young acquisition lawyer, "My mantra had been that the businessman made the decision whether to buy a company but it was my job to make sure that the price was the price. The agreed price might be $50 million," he goes on, "but if you're assuming all sorts of contingent liabilities, the real price could end up being a lot higher. Or, if the company had bad business practices, there could be looming litigation. So when I started the Airgas acquisition program, one of our central tenets was to be very, very good at our due diligence. Another was to be very careful in our contract drafting, so if something did come up, the liability would go back to the former owner. We brought that rigor to all our deals."

If the proof is in the pudding, Airgas was very rigorous indeed. While most companies doing multiple acquisitions end up reporting year after year of serially recurring "non-recurring" events and charge offs, Airgas's financials were remarkably free of write-offs. Says McCausland, "We took one big write-off when we sold a company called Rutland Tool. We had bought it thinking it went well with our business and it really didn't. It was the only big mistake we made. But we had a lot of gains over the years, so over the entire history of the company, the difference between our GAAP earnings and our adjusted earnings was less than 2 percent." For comparison's sake, he throws out the tidbit that, at bête noir Air Products, the difference between GAAP and adjusted earnings "is 40 percent–50 percent." Many investors, McCausland notes, "think that special charges don't count, but they are very important over time."

The Airgas founder readily acknowledges, "A company is owned by the shareholders and ultimately you have to run it so that the value of their investment goes up." But, he cautions, "If you don't cultivate your customers and take good care of them—and do the same with your employees—well, you might do okay for a few years. But in the long run, you're not going to create value. That's where you run into the long-term versus short-term thing—and the investment community is much more focused on the short-term. There's constant pressure on them. They are paid for short-term results. You've got a lot of fast-buck artists on Wall Street who want to make millions."

Conservative Values

There can be little doubt in the mind of a visitor to the McCausland family's Philadelphia-area farm that his predilections fall solidly on the side of long-term value. The main house is a thoughtfully restored country manse designed by Gilded Age architect Horace Trumbauer (known for the Philadelphia Art Museum, New York Evening Post Building, Harvard's Widener Memorial Library, among other buildings.). While there was an original structure on the property dating back to 1764, and an addition built in the 1830s, says McCausland, "Trumbauer was brought in to redo the whole place when George Widener bought it in 1912 and he made it really special." The famed architect also built indoor tennis courts and horse and sheep barns on the property, but Widener—the scion of an exceedingly wealthy Philadelphia streetcar and railroad magnate—didn't live to enjoy them. He went down on the *Titanic*.

For all the mansion's storied history, it is its location that is truly extraordinary. Situated only about fifteen miles from the congestion and high-rises of center city—and just minutes from the bustle of the Main Line—it is surrounded by nearly 450 bucolic acres of woods, pastures, and meadows, long known as "Erdenheim Farm." The land has been devoted to agriculture since the colonial era. Explains McCausland, "It was going to be sold to developers and broken up, so my wife and I, in 2009, decided to take a flyer and buy it." To complete the transaction, which also involved a local conservation foundation, the McCauslands agreed to preserve the farm as mostly open space in perpetuity. They gave it, in trust, to their adult children in 2015, when the senior McCauslands moved to Florida. The younger generation runs the property as a working farm, with community outreach "to reconnect people with where food comes from." The agricultural operation grows seasonal fruits, vegetables, and herbs that are sold at its farm stand and is home to prize-winning livestock, Morgan horses, and free-range chickens, as well as an apiary.

It is a real-life display, in a sense, of the kind of old-fashioned, truly conservative values that attracted McCausland to the bottled gas business in the early 1980s. "I had worked as a lawyer for an industrial gas company and there were a lot of things I liked about the business. Your principal assets were high-pressure chromoloy steel cylinders that last practically forever. We had some very old ones from the early twentieth century still in service. Your other principal assets were cryogenic vessels that last thirty to fifty years. They have no moving parts and are rarely moved. All you had to add was some working capital and it was a nice business. I also liked that it was a business where progress was very incremental—you didn't have to go out and swing for the fences." The analogy reminds McCausland of the attitude he worked to inculcate in his Airgas associates: "The business was about getting on base. It doesn't matter how you get on base—a hit, a walk, get hit by a pitch. Sometimes you have to lean out over the plate, sometimes you get a broken-bat single—as long as you get there." He adds, "That sort of incrementalism was very appealing to me—where you can build a little bit here, a little bit there, until you get the flywheel going—and I thought all the chemistry was interesting, too."

"Not Interested"

McCausland continues, "Another attraction was Airgas's incredibly diverse customer base"—among them, hospitals; medical and dental practices; welders; industrial users of refrigerants, ammonia, process chemicals, and specialty chemicals. "To deal with that diversity, we developed a very decentralized business model; gave a lot of autonomy and responsibility to the front-line people who had to deal with customers. In many ways, it was a local business and it was how well you did at the local level that ultimately determined your success. A customer, for instance, will be more willing to take a price increase if you've done a great job for him, solved his problems, done things to make him more successful. To do that, you've got to develop people who like autonomy and responsibility but are still willing to be held accountable; still willing to communicate the information you need as a public company to deal with shareholders. So it took a very long time to develop our business model and philosophy."

McCausland makes it abundantly clear that he wasn't in the least tempted to bail out when Air Products came calling. "First of all, we had such growth potential. We were becoming an operating company at that time and were about to launch SAP, our first enterprise software system, all across our acquisitions. We had a lot of work to do and we were confident we could create a lot of value for our shareholders. Secondly, our stock price had fallen down to the low $40s in the financial crisis, so the timing of Air Products' bid was very opportunistic. We certainly didn't want to sell it at just a 30 percent 40 percent premium to a very depressed number—well below where we had traded before. Finally, we knew Air Products really well and didn't care for them. They had long been big in bulk gas sales and tonnage, the big pipeline business. In early 2002, when they sold their packaged gas business to us, they had acted like they did us a favor. But, in fact, they had run it into the ground. We did the deal anyway, realizing that it could be very valuable in the right hands, because it did a lot of volume in high-end specialty gases. Air Products had been one of our suppliers for a long time at that point and it became our largest supplier after we bought their packaged gas business. That was part of the deal, for us to give them more business."

A more congenial supplier/customer relationship did not, however, evolve from more transactions. McCausland elaborates. "They had treated us pretty badly in the mid- to late-1990s, so we had built a couple of air-separation plants in Oklahoma and Arkansas to replace some bulk supplies that we had been sourcing from Air Products." Once those bulk gas plants were up and running, recalls McCausland, it turned out that "another huge customer of theirs" decided to switch to Airgas as a supplier. "That could have been like a shot across the bow for them," he ruminates. But Airgas didn't really have designs on Air Products' bulk gas market. "We were more interested in acquiring additional packaged gas businesses—that was our strength—and we still had a lot of work to do to build out our national platform."

McCausland continues, "After we bought Air Products' packaged gas business in 2002, we followed up by buying BOC Group's packaged gas unit in 2004 and Linde's packaged *and* bulk gas businesses in 2007." That last transaction overnight took Airgas's share of the bulk-gas market to 10 percent, transforming it into a sizeable direct competitor to Air Products—almost unintentionally—as well as making Airgas one of only two vertically integrated gas suppliers in the United States. As McCausland explains, "Linde hadn't really wanted to sell its packaged gas business but the FTC was requiring them to divest their bulk division to gain approval to acquire BOC—and they knew the FTC would okay us as a buyer for their bulk unit. So we told them we would buy the bulk unit *only* if we also got the packaged business. They had a lot of debt from the acquisition, so they agreed." As a result, as 2010 began, Airgas was operating sixteen bulk gas air-separation plants around the nation, producing roughly 30 percent of the gas it was selling—and was squarely in Air Products' crosshairs.

Air Products, McCausland relates, had made its first behind-the-scenes takeover overture in mid-October 2009, when its CEO, John E. McGlade, verbally offered him $60 a share, all-stock, for Airgas—an "insulting" offer that the Airgas board rebuffed out of hand. Slightly more than a month later, McGlade followed up with an unsolicited letter to McCausland repeating the same bid. When the Airgas board also spurned that advance, McGlade came back in mid-December with a letter proffering $62 a share, in a mix of cash and paper. Again, McCausland and the Airgas board turned thumbs down. Those come-ons had all been made in private, and Air Products said nothing more over the holidays. On January 4, 2010, McCausland sent a letter reiterating to McGlade that his bids "grossly undervalued" Airgas. But Air Products was not taking "just say no" for an answer. On February 4, Air Products' CEO replied with a letter making a formal unsolicited—*and reduced*—$60 a share all-cash offer for Airgas. McGlade released the letter to the public the next morning, while telling the press he was prepared to launch a hostile proxy fight if this offer was spurned as his multiple private advances had been.

The Sparring Begins

McGlade's "lowball" public bid, McCausland scornfully notes, was below what Airgas traded at shortly before the Great Recession, although it represented a 38 percent premium to Airgas's closing share price of $43.53 on the day the letter was sent. Including debt, the Air Products bid was valued at about $7 billion. The Airgas founder adds, "I knew that our chances weren't great. I just wasn't going to go down without a fight—and the Airgas Board of Directors was fully supportive." Within twenty-four hours, both sides filed suits. Air Products went to Delaware Chancery Court on the night of February 4, accusing McCausland of trying to "entrench himself" by improperly blocking his board from considering its bids. The next afternoon, Airgas fired back, suing Air Products' law firm, Cravath, in Pennsylvania state court, alleging conflict of interest and breach of confidentiality. "Cravath had been Air Products' long-time attorney," McCausland concedes. "But they also had been our attorney on financings for ten years, doing twenty Airgas deals. In fact, we concluded that Air Products was planning their hostile takeover bid with Cravath while Cravath was representing *us* in a bond issue. After they got paid for that bond issue, Cravath said, 'Well, we can't work for you anymore.' So we sued them—I'm not allowed to tell you anything about the settlement terms," he adds, "except that the Airgas board approved them."

Airgas formally rejected the $60 bid, on February 9 and Air Products responded two days later commencing a fully financed tender offer at $60. The nasty battle was just beginning. A week later, Air Products amended its Delaware suit, alleging the Airgas board wasn't acting in good faith in resisting its takeover proposals. It also put in the record an attempt to rebut Airgas's "disingenuous" charges about Cravath's conflicts by intimating that Airgas's primary investment banker, Goldman Sachs, was similarly conflicted by recent assignments from Air Products.

Low Blow

McCausland, still visibly angry even six years later, recounts a "low blow" that followed. He awoke the next morning, he says, to read a *New York Times* headline asking, "What Was the Airgas Chief Thinking?" The February 12, 2010 *Times* story by Steven Davidoff Solomon and Peter J. Henning—clearly lifted virtually straight from Air Products' amended legal filing in Delaware—reported that McCausland's adversaries claimed he'd committed a breach of fiduciary duty by exercising options to acquire 300,000 Airgas shares on January 5. It went on to note that McCausland took that action, "the day after Airgas rejected for a second time a friendly overture from Air Products." Then the writers thoughtfully calculated what the story described as McCausland's "immediate unrealized gain," and opined, "Exercising the options certainly benefits him tax-wise and could look like possible insider trading. When Mr. McCausland exercised these options, he possessed material nonpublic information about Airgas. . . ." The item added, "Under the so-called 'classic' theory of insider trading set forth in the Supreme Court's decision in *Chiarella v. United States*, a corporate officer or director who trades his company's shares while in possession of confidential information about its future plans or prospects breaches a fiduciary duty to shareholders. The question that comes to mind is the same asked of Brett Favre after a particularly untimely interception: *'What was he thinking?'* "

"*Insider trading!*" McCausland exclaims. "The news agencies all picked it up: 'McCausland accused of insider trading.' My kids read it! The truth is that I cleared the options exercise with the Airgas general counsel and with Wachtell—and that I was entitled to those options—those shares were reserved for me. All I had to do was pay the fixed exercise price and tell the company to issue them. I did it because I'd have more votes. *And I didn't sell the shares!*" His lawyerly demeanor reasserting itself, McCausland explains, "There is federal case law saying that merely exercising an option is *not* insider trading. Air Products was very careful. They didn't *say* in their court filing that I had violated insider trading regulations. What they said was that

I was an insider and exercised options. They framed it in a way to generate interest in the press and worked closely with the *New York Times*' 'Deal Professor' columnist during the entire saga. But that's the kind of fight they put on. They claimed that I was entrenched, that I would never sell my baby, that I controlled the board. All kinds of stuff. I had worked pretty hard for our shareholders over the years but Air Products thought we would just cave."

Instead, Airgas dug in its heels, formally rejecting the "grossly undervalued and highly opportunistic" Air Products tender offer on February 22 while also decrying its suitor's "personal attacks and deceptive statements." Air Products responded in kind and the stage was set for a full-frontal war fought on multiple levels—and it dragged out for another year, to the dismay of many a short-term oriented Wall Street risk arbitrageur. Concedes McCausland, "Even our own advisors gave us only a small chance of staying independent. They said, 'Air Products might not get you, but your chances of staying independent through this are very small.' The *Times*' 'Deal Professor' column agreed, saying it would 'take a miracle' for Airgas to survive as an independent company."

Into the Hands of Arbs

The Airgas founder, however, was undeterred. Naively, perhaps, he believed Airgas's twenty-plus year track record of "tremendous share-holder value creation" and transparent communications would stand it in good stead with its investors in the battle. Instead, he watched in mounting disgust as Air Products quickly disadvantaged Airgas—through what the *New York Times* columnist later called the suit-or's "masterful strategy—manipulating its offer price to place almost half of Airgas's shares into the hands of the arbitrageurs—a power-ful shareholder base willing to accept its offer" (Stephen Davidoff Solomon, "Winners and Losers in the Airgas Poison Pill Case," *New York Times*, February 16, 2011) McCausland doesn't mince words. "Air Products' CFO—Paul Huck—would tell the arbs he was going to raise the bid, but he wouldn't tell them how much. It was obvi-ous he wanted them to buy more and more shares and that he was manipulating the arbs. The federal securities laws are supposed to prevent a bidder from making selective private disclosures. But every time he raised the bid, more of the old shareholders would sell, and the arbs would get more of the shareholder base. So very quickly, 60 percent was short-term money. A lot of the fundamental funds just hit the bid, because they're so smart—they think—that they can always just redeploy the money profitably. And hitting the bid gooses up their quarterly results."

Airgas and McCausland lost most of the early skirmishes in the legal battle. In March, the Delaware chancellor assigned to the case, William B. Chandler III, set a potential trial date in the litigation, as requested by Air Products, that severely limited Airgas's options on the timing of its annual meeting. Airgas then set its annual meeting for Sept. 15. By mid-May, Air Products had filed proxies naming its nominees to the Airgas board and detailing three bylaw changes it wanted. The most significant would have compelled Airgas, whose nine-member board served staggered terms—with three seats up for election at each annual meeting—to push forward the date of its 2011 annual meeting to January, or only about four months after its 2010 annual meeting. In effect, that change would give Air Products a chance to quickly capture two-thirds of the seats on the Airgas board. The stage was set for a long, hot summer of charges and counter charges as both companies worked to curry favor among the arbs who by then held a majority of Airgas shares.

With so much hot money in Airgas shares, acknowledges McCausland, "there was no question that the majority of shareholders wanted the company sold—didn't want us to keep fighting. But the board represented *all* the shareholders—and its structure included staggered terms." McCausland took considerable heat during the takeover battle for defending Airgas's staggered board structure but he remains unrepentant. "To say that a staggered board is antidemocratic and not shareholder-friendly and all that is nuts. The U.S. Senate is like a staggered board, with one-third of its seats up for election every two years. Both the Senate and the staggered board provision permitted under Delaware corporation law are examples of governance structures that moderate the impact of the popular will in favor of continuity."

Arbs as Shareholders

McCausland doesn't deny that the Air Products battle took a toll. "It was not a great time in my life. I felt we were being treated pretty unfairly because our shareholders weren't loyal—despite the very good returns we had generated for them over the years. I felt our shareholders should have stayed loyal to us instead of selling to the arbs. That was the most disappointing thing. I mean, arbs are arbs. Although we tried to persuade them and had a great investment thesis, we had no real expectation of loyalty there. In fact, it was frustrating having to meet with them whenever they wanted. But our advisors told us we had to because the arbs had become our shareholders. So we spent all kinds of time with them on the phone. Some of those characters were *really awful*. Such blowhards—they'd threaten and cajole. We tried to treat everybody as special; hoped we could reason with them. But the arbs and activists were so invested in the transaction happening, they wouldn't listen to our plans for long-term growth. I must say, however, that there was one really special thing during that very stressful time— how the legacy Airgas board acted. They were incredible despite the huge amount of pressure placed on them—especially John van Roden, who became chairman, and Lee Thomas, who met with arbs with the management team. The entire legacy board contributed to the defense and all of them did a great job for the Airgas shareholders."

Over that summer, McCausland recalls, "I went up to New York City on probably ten different days. We tried to convince the biggest activists, like Eton Park and Paulson & Co., to back us. Then we would meet with groups of the smaller arbs at our proxy solicitor's office, maybe ten at a time. We took a couple of our board members to one or two of these sessions. They consumed *a lot* of my time. I'd say, 'Hey, look. I know you are an arb fund, but you just made an investment in a great company.' Yet not one of them voted for us. They would engage us in discussions about our business model and poison pills and staggered boards; they'd tell us our rivals were getting stronger, and would want to talk about our results. But all they really wanted to do was put more pressure on us; find a weak spot."

He goes on, "They wanted to sow seeds of doubt, fear—I got letters accusing me of the worst crimes against shareholders you can imagine." One incident still rankles: "We went up to meet one guy. We were told he's a class act, the dean of arbitrageurs. He was perfectly cordial in the meeting. Then he wrote this terrible letter about the way he said I treated shareholders. It really, really angered me. I never responded to it." McCausland shrugs, "Then again, the letter shouldn't have surprised me given the tenor of the battle from the outset. But I had never been involved in a hostile deal before. I thought that you could reason with some arbs. Get them to see it was crazy, what was going on. Here was a company that had returned 18 percent per year compounded. The largest independent packaged gas company in the best market in the world. If it were ever to be sold, why would it not be sold under circumstances where you could maximize the purchase price as opposed to letting it go to a hostile bidder while the stock was depressed? That's how I approached it. Some *seemed* reasonable. None of them voted for us."

Institutional Hypocrisy

What did surprise McCausland was that the index funds in his shareholders' base more or less automatically voted with the arbs. "Now, I'd put the index funds in the arb category—maybe at the other end of the spectrum from the worst of the arbs—but they're in there." The Airgas founder goes on, "Here's just one example: We went to see a major, highly regarded institutional investor to try to get them to vote their index funds with us. I had previously met that firm's chairman and CEO. Airgas had a 401(k) plan run through them with some $1 billion in it. So their top executive called in his corporate governance guy and about thirty others and we made our pitch. But they didn't vote for us. They voted to throw me out as chairman. They pretty much told me they were going to do that at the meeting. So I asked, 'Why? We've generated 18 percent a year, compounded, for shareholders. We've been totally transparent, never had a scandal, never restated earnings. We're the perfect fiduciaries.' Then I added, 'Besides, it's a bad deal.' "

McCausland continues, "The institutional investor's head of corporate governance replied, 'Well, we're an index fund, which means we hold more Air Products than Airgas—and a bad deal for you is a good deal for them—so it's a good deal for our shareholders.' I said, 'That could help you today, it might even help you tomorrow, but if you don't reward good governance, how can you expect good governance? In the long run, how can you expect managers to work their asses off for shareholders like you, when you're saying, 'It's okay if someone rips you off, as long as we own part of them, because we'll benefit more?' "

Scarcely pausing for breath, McCausland argues, "There's a hypocrisy there that's unspeakable. They've got a huge corporate governance group today. It's pure short-termism. The whole system is broken; it promotes transactions, trades. That institutional position means any time a big company comes after a little company, if the deal looks good for the big company, they're going to vote for it regardless. That makes no sense; it just promotes transactions. That's the arbs' whole thing, too. They are invested in a transaction being completed, not in a company over the long term. It is really sad because it's completely at odds with what customers and associates—the two most important things for running a business—are looking for. Namely, long-term commitment."

With its Sept. 15 shareholder meeting fast approaching—and with straw counts of proxy votes showing it on the verge of losing to Air Products—Airgas threw a Hail Mary. It announced that, if shareholders voted down its suitor's proposals, it would hold its own annual meeting the following June and hold votes to both destagger the board and elect the majority of its members. Airgas also filed documents with the Delaware court claiming that Air Products' proposed bylaw amendments didn't pass legal muster. Airgas was playing for time, as it had been all along, McCausland explains. "As long as we had the staggered board, we had at least several more quarters to outrun Air Products' lowball bid with our earnings." But Air Products fired a salvo of its own, barely a week later. It sweetened its bid for Airgas to $65.50 a share, or $5.48 billion in cash.

Losing the Vote

The vote came. When the proxies were counted, the fast money had won. Air Products' slate of directors was elected, temporarily relieving McCausland of his seat, and its bylaw amendments, including the one advancing the date of Airgas's next annual meeting, also passed. Recalls McCausland, "That was a low point. We were looking at losing control of the board and the whole thing." Though plenty affronted, he didn't surrender. The bylaws amendments won by Air Products contained a loophole permitting the Airgas board to add a new seat to bring McCausland back aboard—albeit not as chairman—as long as they got a "nationally recognized expert in corporate governance" to verify McCausland's suitability. "So we had to pay $100,000 to some lawyer to say that I was qualified when I had founded the company and had run the company and had been chair of the board and had been on several other public company boards! Our shareholders, including some of our very large institutional shareholders, voted for that! What kind of nonsense was it to put me through something like that? They just wanted the company sold."

The future looked bleak indeed for the Airgas team three weeks after the proxy vote, when the Delaware Chancery Court upheld the new bylaws. Says McCausland, "That was the lowest point—when he ruled that four months is a year. In effect, he said we had to hold our next annual meeting barely more than four months after our 2010 meeting—before our fiscal year even ended." The court based its ruling on purported "ambiguity" in Airgas's charter. "But that was so stupid," McCausland protests. "Air Products had the exact same language in its own bylaws and said, in other public filings, that it meant three-year board terms. But their lawyers came up with this theory, which had been talked about in Delaware legal circles as a way to weaken the takeover protection afforded by staggered boards."

Wall Street's sell-side analysts had incurred McCausland's wrath early that year when some of them dropped research coverage of the take-over target, "on the excuse that they only follow companies that trade on fundamentals. I kept urging them, 'Look at our earnings,' but to no avail. It's a lot of work to dig in and understand what a takeover bid is about, what the target's potential is, and how long it's likely to take before its value outruns the bid." Although a couple of analysts did express some initial qualms about the price, what remains seared in McCausland's memory is that "not even one stuck with us, saying, 'This company is worth more than the bid.' Then again, most of them covered Air Products, too."

Turning the Tide

Still, McCausland—and Jay Worley, Airgas's director of investor relations—persisted. After the proxy defeat, the two started double-teaming analysts on phone calls, "trying to shame them into covering us again because our earnings had continued to grow." Incessant phone calls over about three weeks, says McCausland, finally convinced three analysts to issue research reports, "two of which included price targets *above* Air Products' bid. Once those came out, others jumped in. But that wasn't until probably ninety days before the final ruling." Still, the timing was fortuitous. Airgas's legal team managed to submit the analysts' estimates to the Delaware court "as evidence that there were people out there with higher twelve-month targets for the stock than the bid. We even had one at $90 or so," remembers McCausland.

In the meantime, Airgas had immediately appealed the Chancery Court decision upholding Air Products' bylaw changes to Delaware's Supreme Court. And, critically, McCausland, his legal team, and Airgas's remaining longtime directors went to work on the board's newbies. Recalls McCausland, "We painted them into a corner. They didn't want to side with us but by the last week of October they didn't really have a choice."

Air Products had paid each of its nominees $100,000 to agree to stand for the Airgas board in the proxy battle but the newly elected board members ended up voting—along with Airgas's remaining legacy board members—that Air Products' sweetened $65.50 a share bid was "grossly inadequate." That Airgas board vote most likely caused "heart attacks," as one news story put it, among some of the hedge funds speculating on a deal. But McCausland cheerfully credits it to "excellent advice" from Wachtell, Lipton. He elaborates, "The three new directors insisted on having their own lawyer, so we gave them their own lawyer. Then they insisted on adding a new investment banker. The new banker, Credit Suisse, came in with a *higher* valuation—$78 a share—than the two we already had. Faced with that, one of the new directors said, 'We have to protect the pill.'"

Then Airgas's board dashed off an ultimatum of sorts to Air Products' CEO, saying in part, "We read with great interest your, and your chief financial officer's, trial testimony . . . that Air Products is attempting to acquire Airgas for the *lowest* possible price. In contrast, our obligation is to seek the *greatest* possible price. . . . Each member of our board believes that the value of Airgas in any sale is meaningfully in excess of $70 per share. We are writing to let you know that our board is unanimous in its willingness to authorize negotiations with Air Products, *if* Air Products provides us with sufficient reason to believe that those negotiations will lead to a transaction at a price that is consistent with that valuation." The Airgas legal team then had the board follow up with a public announcement, the following week, claiming that Airgas was worth at least $78 a share—not so much to get that specific number out, explains McCausland, "but to make it clear to the court that we weren't just saying no; we were *not* saying we were *never* for sale."

The real surprise for much of the Street and for the financial commentators who had been hanging crepe for Airgas since it lost the proxy vote came a few weeks later. On November 23, the Delaware Supreme Court reversed the lower court's bylaw ruling, five to zero. They decided, a still-greatly-relieved McCausland enthuses, "Look, a staggered board is a creature of the Delaware statute and it's clear that the original Airgas bylaws established terms of three years for the directors. The lower court decision was firmly rejected."

Yet the legal wrangling still dragged on, with the litigation's focus turning to the validity of Airgas's poison pill and whether its board had the right to refuse to redeem the pill in the face of what it believed to be an inadequate offer. The Chancery Court on December 3 prodded both Airgas and Air Products to file additional arguments, broadly hinting the issue now boiled down to price. Six days later, Air Products unveiled a $70 a share "best and final" offer for Airgas. The bid was a ploy by his adversaries, explains McCausland, to pressure the court to rein in poison pills if a suitor was threatening to walk away from a deal that offered a premium price to the target's shareholders. The Airgas board remained steadfast. On December 22, it (including the three new directors nominated by Air Products) unanimously rejected the $70 bid as "inadequate," reiterating that Airgas was worth at least $78 a share.

The Wheels of Justice . . .

The ball was back in the hands of the court. A "mini-trial" in the matter was called for January 25. But Chancellor Chandler didn't issue his lengthy decision until February 15, 2011—nearly eighteen months after the first skirmishes between Airgas and Air Products. "He was reluctant to rule that our pill was valid," McCausland observes, "but he had to, because he had to follow precedent. So he wrote a 150-page opinion, with 514 footnotes—to follow precedent! Not only did he rule in our favor, but he wrote that the members of the Airgas board were 'quintessential fiduciaries,' which was pretty great." Air Products' McGlade, for his part, issued a sour statement about Airgas's "entrenched" board, concluding, "We have decided to withdraw our offer and move on." Airgas's legal advisors at Wachtell, meanwhile, celebrated by having "great hats made for the entire winning team, with angels' wings and 'Team Miracle' on them," recounts McCausland.

The Airgas founder thanked his lawyers, his "amazing board and Airgas associates," as well as his lucky stars. "I'll tell you, when we lost the proxy contest and I got thrown off the board with two other directors—if Air Products had come in then and raised the bid to $75—our board might have taken it." Even later on, he reflects, "We had bankers' opinions and, if they had raised the price higher, we would have had to take a look at it. They *should* have bought us. They needed us so badly. After all, Airgas eventually went for $143 a share—more than twice Air Products' 'best and final.'"

How McCausland and the Airgas board pulled off that capstone deal adds still more layers of guile and cunning to the saga. Ironically, the opportunity arose in part from the woes that befell Air Products after Airgas slipped from its grasp. McCausland summarizes: "They continued to post bad results and special charges; the stock fell way down. Wall Street hated them. Then Bill Ackman bought 10 percent—and they just gave him three board seats—without a proxy fight. The reconstituted board fired the CEO and brought in Seifollah Ghasemi—whom I had known for thirty years because he used to be at British Oxygen Co.—to run the search committee. We had dinner at Erdenheim farm after he went on the board. Then Seifi picked himself as Air Products' new CEO. The day Seifi got the job, he called me. A few weeks later, he flew up to Nantucket to visit me at my place there. We had lunch."

Meals with Friends

It became something of a routine, McCausland recounts. "For a year, every couple of months, Seifi would ask me to have dinner, saying he had something new to discuss. Then, in the spring of '15, he called me to an 'emergency' lunch in downtown Philadelphia, at the Rittenhouse Hotel. We sat down and he said, 'Peter, you're going to lose the company.'" The Airgas founder continues, "He told me this activist—Paul Singer, of Elliott Management—came to see him. Seifi said Singer told him that 'McCausland is washed up; his growth days are over' and that 'he wants me to buy Airgas.' Seifi added that Singer also told him that he had institutional shareholders in tow." McCausland says he responded, "Well, I hope you told him to go away." But Seifi replied, "No, I met with him for an hour." McCausland queried, "Well, did you tell him you don't want to buy the company?"

Ghasemi then admitted he'd said, "We'd be interested if it were for sale." McCausland remembers retorting, "Oh, thanks, Seifi!" Shaking his head, he adds, "Seifi was supposed to be my friend."

But McCausland already knew that Singer had taken a position in Airgas. "Another industry CEO had called me earlier and told me that Elliott had been in to see him and made the same case. 'McCausland's entrenched, a shitty manager.'" But the other industry leader had also told McCausland, "I disabused Singer of that. I told him that I thought you were one of the best managers in the industry." Thus forewarned, McCausland told Ghasemi at the Rittenhouse, "Look, I'm not afraid of Singer." The next week, Singer's Elliott Management filed a form 13F with the SEC for the first quarter of 2015 showing a large stake in Airgas. "But then, very quickly, they went away," in the second quarter marvels McCausland. "Sold. I don't know why, but they went away at a small loss, and they had bought a lot of shares."

His old friend at Air Products, however, wasn't as easily discouraged. "Seifi called me to a couple other meetings and made a proposal, stock for stock, no premium. I said, 'We don't want your stock, Seifi, and we would never sell for no premium.'" More meetings followed, McCausland recounts, and "eventually his bid worked up to a small premium, 15 percent or 20 percent, but still stock for stock, and he was talking about spinning off or selling the two divisions that weren't gasses, so I knew I had some time."

McCausland quietly went to work. "I talked to about ten different parties. Air Liquide got really interested. We shared some public information but compiled in a way that the public doesn't usually see and that really got them excited." But Air Products got busy, too. McCausland continues, "Seifi called me to another dinner. He brought along an investment banker's book and ripped out a page showing that the overlap between our two companies' shareholder bases was 86 percent. He said, 'Peter, your shareholders want this,' meaning, 'I'll go right to them.' I said, 'Well, Seifi, you said you'd *never* do a hostile.' He replied, 'Look, I don't *want* to do a hostile.'"

After that dinner, McCausland says, he went home and "consulted with the board and our lawyers again. But meanwhile, Air Liquide's interest in doing a deal with us was heating up." So he called Ghasemi and once again stalled, telling him that the Airgas board was going on retreat in Arizona in early November and would discuss his bid then. When the Air Products CEO doubted that promise, McCausland says he told him, "Seifi, everything you've told me in the last year-and-a-half, I've taken to the board." Ghasemi agreed to wait.

Meetings, in Secret

McCausland went into high gear, arranging for a team of five from Air Liquide "to spend a day-and-a-half here at the farm with me and my team. They were very interested. But I had to make sure that Air Products didn't launch something before Air Liquide and Airgas could get together—that might have made Air Liquide back away. Foreign companies generally don't like contentious deals. So I called Seifi and said, 'I need some more information for my board about this $300 million synergy number you gave me.' Seifi proposed another lunch, again at the Rittenhouse Hotel, and we agreed to have it on the Friday before the Airgas board was gathering in Arizona. Seifi told me he wanted to bring along his lawyer and the guy who runs Air Products' gasses business. Well, we got there at ten in the morning and listened to their presentation with the expectation that the meeting would extend through lunch. The $300 million in cost synergies, it very quickly turned out, were only $200 million. The other $100 million was to come from sales synergies. We asked a few questions and it was over in forty-five minutes." When his team stood up to leave, McCausland adds, "Seifi asked, 'What about all this lunch?' and looked shaken. The week before, Valeant had blown up in Bill Ackman's face and Seifi may have needed Ackman to come after us with him. He looked really uncertain, so I just said, 'We're off to the meeting in Arizona.'"

What Ghasemi didn't know, McCausland explains, was that he had been doing a lot of traveling in preparation for that Airgas board meeting in Arizona. "I had been in Rome for the IOMA (International Oxygen Manufacturers Association) meeting the week before and while I was in Europe, I met with other industry CEOs, including taking a trip to Paris to secretly meet with Benoît Potier, the CEO of Air Liquide. I already knew him but we wanted to talk about our deal. Then, I went up to New York the next Thursday—the day before the Air Products lunch—and actually cut the deal with Pierre Dufour, the number 2 guy at Air Liquide. So when we met with Air Products that Friday, we actually had an agreement in principle with Air Liquide.

The only question was whether the lawyers could pull it together in time for our Arizona board meeting. But, of course, they did, and we signed the Air Liquide deal in Arizona."

McCausland reflects, "It was huge. The end of a year-and-a-half search to find a good deal because we didn't think we could dodge a bullet twice. And it all culminated in a series of meetings and events that took place over a very short time. The principal terms were negotiated without any bankers or lawyers. We did the whole thing with Air Liquide's executives to keep it very quiet." McCausland admits to melancholy on his part and on that of long-time colleagues as they watched Airgas disappear into Air Liquide, but concedes, "a lot of them got wealthy—a just reward for their incredible hard work and dedication over the years. The price—a very pleasant surprise and reward for our loyal shareholders—was more than twice Air Products' 'best and final'!"

Their coup owed in part to guile and in part to luck, muses McCausland. Airgas was the only sizeable industrial gas company with operations almost entirely in the United States. The industry's four global players had all been investing heavily in emerging markets, particularly in Asia, "which weren't doing well at all," he observes. "China was a total mess. South America was going south. Brazil, once such a great economy, was a mess. By contrast, we were such a pure company. Two-thirds gas sales and rent, a wonderful platform, a wonderful business. So our huge U.S. position, our market presence with 1,400 locations, over a million customers, was suddenly extremely attractive—after years of hearing nothing but 'the U.S. is post-industrial; businesses are leaving the country.' Anyway, all of a sudden, the world changed, and people said, 'We need more exposure in the U.S.' That's a reason we got such a good price."

Another, McCausland notes, "is that good companies in our industry always go for high multiples. I wanted to get 14 times EBITDA because the record had been 12.5 or 13 times—and Airgas was better than that company." Indeed, McCausland boasts, "When Air Liquide did their due diligence, they couldn't believe how clean the company was. Their head of finance in Paris told me, 'In most acquisitions, you can find a place to build a reserve here or there. But there's nothing here.' In fact, she enthused, 'We've bought a lot of companies that had all kinds of reserves, but your people are so good and your balance sheet is so clean and your finance practices are state of the art.'"

"It made me feel great, but I think it made them feel great, too."

Risk Arbitrage Decision Tree

Five Initial Questions

1) What is the spread? What is the annualized return?
2) What are the regulatory issues/hurdles?
3) What are the conditions of the merger agreement?
4) What is the strategic rationale for the deal?
5) What is the downside if the deal breaks?

Company Analysis

1) Who is the buyer?

- What is financial condition of buyer? Balance sheet, coverage ratios?
- Reputation? History on past acquisitions?
- Size of buyer? Will this acquisition significantly alter buyer strategy/structure?
- Why does buyer want to merge . . . strategic, financial, etc.?
- Does acquirer own stock in the target? How much?

2) Who is the seller?

- Financial condition of seller?
- Nature of business of seller? Same as that of buyer?
- What are seller's reasons for merger?
- Are there pending litigation or environmental liabilities for the seller?

3) Combined company going forward

- Will transaction be accretive/dilutive? At what point will it become accretive?
- Are there synergies and cost savings? How much?
- What do the pro-forma financials look like? Does it make strategic sense?

Financing

1) How will merger be funded? Stock, cash, LBO?
2) Is funding in place? Is it a condition? Do they have commitments from banks?
3) Are they confident that funding will not be an issue?
4) (If a stock deal) How many shares will be issued? Very dilutive?

Background

1) Is the deal friendly or hostile?
2) How did the merger come about? Who approached whom?
3) Did the seller put itself up for sale? If so, why?
4) Were other bidders involved? What is likelihood of a higher bid?
5) Was an auction conducted? What kind? Sealed or closed bids?
6) Who were the investment banks and legal advisors for each company?

Conditions

1) What are the conditions to complete the merger?
2) Is due diligence complete or still a requirement?
3) Is the merger contingent on financing?
4) Which regulatory approvals are conditions of the merger?
5) What vote/tender required by target company? Acquirer vote required?
6) Under what conditions can either company terminate the merger?

Regulatory Issues

1) Hart-Scott-Rodino

   - Any overlap in businesses?
   - 15 calendar days for a tender; 30 calendar days for a merger

2) FTC/Justice Department approval

   - Will merger be anticompetitive? Horizontal and/or vertical issues?
   - What percent of its market's share will the combined company have?

3) SEC must approve merger proxy

   - How long will this take?
   - Proxy reads: Q&A, Background, Projections, Conditions.

4) Individual state approvals

   - Insurance
   - Public utility

5) Specific industry approvals

- Banks: Federal Reserve
- Utilities: Federal Energy Regulatory Commission
- Communications: Federal Communications Commission

6) Foreign regulatory approvals

- European Union (EU) approval
- China State Administration for Market Regulation (SAMR) approval
- Other foreign countries approval

Risk vs. Return Issues

1) What is the spread on the deal? Annualized return?
2) Where will stocks go if deal breaks? What is the downside?
3) What are the odds of nonconsummation of the deal? What could go wrong?
4) What are the odds that another buyer comes in and bids higher?
5) Is transaction definitive, letter of intent, or just preliminary talks?

Deals

Example #1 (January 2007)

Molecular Devices Corp. (MDCC-$35.18-OTC) agreed to be acquired by Canadian analytical device company MDS Inc. (MDZ-$17.30-NYSE). Molecular Devices provides high-performance measurement tools for high content screening, cellular analysis, and biochemical testing. Under terms of the transaction MDCC shareholders will receive $35.50 cash per share, valuing the transaction at approximately $615 million. The transaction is subject to regulatory approval as well as the tender of a majority of MDCC shares, and is expected to close in the first quarter of 2007.

• MDCC	$35.500
• Net Dividends & Short Interest	0.000
	35.500
• Purchase (January 29, 2007)	34.950
• Plus Transaction Costs	.005
	34.955
• Gross Profit	$0.545
• Gross Profit %	1.56%
• Holding Period (close March 13, 2007)	43 days
• Annualized Rate of Return	13.05%

Example #2 (February 2007)

New River Pharmaceuticals (NRPH-$63.25-OTC) agreed to be acquired by British pharmaceutical company Shire plc (SHP-GBP1,080 pence-London). New River and Shire developed VYANASE, a drug used for the treatment of Attention Deficit and Hyperactivity Disorder, and through the acquisition Shire will capture the full economic value of VYANASE. Under terms of the agreement New River shareholders will receive $64.00 cash per share, valuing the transaction at approximately $2.6 billion. The acquisition is subject to the approval of Shire's shareholders, the tender of a majority of the outstanding New River shares as well as antitrust approval and is expected to close in the second quarter of 2007.

• NRPH	$64.000
• Net Dividends & Short Interest	0.000
	64.000
• Purchase (February 22, 2007)	63.050
• Plus Transaction Costs	.005
	63.055
• Gross Profit	$0.945
• Gross Profit %	1.49%
• Holding Period (close April 13, 2007)	50 days
• Annualized Rate of Return	10.72%

Example #3 (March 2007)

Dollar General (DG-$21.15-NYSE) agreed to be acquired by private equity firm Kohlberg Kravis Roberts & Co. Dollar General is a discount retailer with 8,260 neighborhood stores selling consumable basic items that are frequently used and replenished, such as food, snacks, health and beauty aids, and cleaning supplies. Under terms of the agreement Dollar General shareholders will receive $22.00 cash per share, valuing the transaction at approximately $7.3 billion. The transaction is subject to Dollar General shareholder as well as regulatory approvals and is expected to close in the third quarter of 2007.

• DG	$22.000
• Net Dividends & Short Interest	0.050
	22.050
• Purchase (March 14, 2007)	20.920
• Plus Transaction Costs	.005
	20.925
• Gross Profit	$1.125
• Gross Profit %	5.37%
• Holding Period (close July 14, 2007)	122 days
• Annualized Rate of Return	15.84%

Example #4 (April 2007)

Global Imaging Systems (GISX-$28.89-OTC) agreed to be acquired by Xerox Corp. (XRX-$18.50-NYSE). Global Imaging provides office technology solutions to middle-market business, providing contract services for automated office equipment including copiers, facsimile machines, printers, and network integration solutions. Under terms of the transaction Global Imaging shareholders will receive $29.00 cash per share, valuing the transaction at approximately $1.5 billion. The transaction is subject to a majority of Global Imaging shares being tendered as well as regulatory approval and is expected to close in the second quarter of 2007.

• GISX	$29.000
• Net Dividends & Short Interest	0.000
	29.000
• Purchase (April 3, 2007)	28.610
• Plus Transaction Costs	.005
	28.615
• Gross Profit	$0.385
• Gross Profit %	1.34%
• Holding Period (close May 8, 2007)	35 days
• Annualized Rate of Return	13.84%

Example #5 (May 2007)

aQuantive, Inc. (AQNT-$63.79-OTC) agreed to be acquired by software giant Microsoft Corp. (MSFT-$30.69-OTC). aQuantive is a digital marketing company that provides integrated digital marketing technologies. Under terms of the agreement aQuantive shareholders will receive $66.50 cash per share, valuing the transaction at approximately $6 billion. The transaction is subject to aQuantive as well as regulatory approval and is expected to close in the second half of 2007.

• AQNT	$66.500
• Net Dividends & Short Interest	0.000
	66.500
• Purchase (May 25, 2007)	63.810
• Plus Transaction Costs	.005
	63.815
• Gross Profit	$2.685
• Gross Profit %	4.207%
• Holding Period (close September 20, 2007)	118 days
• Annualized Rate of Return	12.84%

Example #6 (June 2007)

Komag, Inc. (KOMG-$31.89-OTC) agreed to be acquired by digital storage company Western Digital Corp. (WDC-$19.20-NYSE). Komag is a supplier of thin-film disks that are the primary high-capacity storage medium for digital data. Under terms of the agreement Komag shareholders will receive $32.25 cash per share, valuing the transaction at approximately $1 billion. The transaction is subject to a majority of shares being tendered as well as regulatory approval and is expected to close in the third quarter of 2007.

• KOMG	$32.250
• Net Dividends & Short Interest	0.000
	32.250
• Purchase (June 29, 2007)	31.720
• Plus Transaction Costs	.005
	31.725
• Gross Profit	$0.525
• Gross Profit %	1.650%
• Holding Period (close August 7, 2007)	39 days
• Annualized Rate of Return	15.76%

Example #7 (July 2007)

Chaparral Steel Company (CHAP-$84.04-OTC) agreed to be acquired by Gerdau Ameristeel Corporation. Texas-based Chaparral Steel produces structural steel beams, steel bar products, and has a recycling business. Under terms of the transaction Chaparral shareholders will receive $86.00 cash per share, valuing the transaction at approximately $4.4 billion. The transaction is subject to Chaparral shareholder as well as regulatory approval and is expected to close in the fourth quarter of 2007.

• CHAP	$86.000
• Net Dividends & Short Interest	0.100
	86.100
• Purchase (July 27, 2007)	82.630
• Plus Transaction Costs	.005
	82.635
• Gross Profit	$3.465
• Gross Profit %	4.190%
• Holding Period (close September 30, 2007)	65 days
• Annualized Rate of Return	23.25%

Example #8 (August 2007)

CheckFree Corp. (CKFR-$46.23-OTC) agreed to be acquired by information management company Fiserv, Inc. (FISV-$46.52-OTC). CheckFree provides online banking, electronic payments and billing, and infrastructure and services. Under terms of the agreement CheckFree shareholders will receive $48.00 cash per share, valuing the transaction at approximately $4.4 billion. The transaction is subject to CheckFree shareholder as well as regulatory approval and is expected to close in the fourth quarter of 2007.

• CKFR	$48.000
• Net Dividends & Short Interest	0.000
	48.000
• Purchase (August 20, 2007)	45.500
• Plus Transaction Costs	.005
	45.505
• Gross Profit	$2.495
• Gross Profit %	5.483%
• Holding Period (close December 1, 2007)	103 days
• Annualized Rate of Return	19.16%

Example #9 (September 2007)

Applix, Inc. (APLX-$17.78-OTC) agreed to be acquired by Canadian business software company Cognos (COGN-$41.53-OTC). Applix develops business analytics software used for performance management and business intelligence to assist with strategic planning, forecasting, consolidations, reporting, and analytics across financial, operational, sales, marketing, and human resources departments. Under terms of the agreement Applix shareholders will receive $17.87 cash per share, valuing the transaction at approximately $339 million. The transaction is subject to regulatory approval as well as a majority of Applix shares being tendered into the offer and is expected to close in the fourth quarter of 2007.

• APLX	$17.870
• Net Dividends & Short Interest	0.000
	17.870
• Purchase (September 5, 2007)	17.570
• Plus Transaction Costs	.005
	17.575
• Gross Profit	$0.295
• Gross Profit %	1.670%
• Holding Period (close October 16, 2007)	41 days
• Annualized Rate of Return	14.94%

Example #10 (October 2007)

NAVTEQ (NVT-$77.20-NYSE) agreed to be acquired by Finnish cell phone maker Nokia (NOK-$39.72-NYSE). NAVTEQ is a leading provider of comprehensive digital map information for automotive systems, mobile navigation devices, Internet-based mapping applications, and government and business solutions. Under terms of the agreement NAVTEQ shareholders will receive $78.00 cash per share, valuing the transaction at approximately $7.7 billion, net of cash. The transaction is subject to NAVTEQ shareholder as well as regulatory approval and is expected to close in the first quarter 2008.

• NVT	$78.000
• Net Dividends & Short Interest	0.000
	78.000
• Purchase (October 22, 2007)	75.550
• Plus Transaction Costs	.010
	75.560
• Gross Profit	$2.440
• Gross Profit %	3.230%
• Holding Period (close January 31, 2007)	101 days
• Annualized Rate of Return	11.56%

Example #11 (November 2007)

The Genlyte Group (GLYT-$94.25-OTC) agreed to be acquired by Royal Philips Electronics (PHG-$41.61-NYSE). Genlyte is a manufacturer of lighting fixtures, controls, and related products for the commercial, industrial, and residential markets. Under terms of the agreement Genlyte shareholders will receive $95.50 cash per share, valuing the transaction at approximately $2.7 billion. The transaction is subject to a tender of a majority of shares as well as regulatory approval and is expected to close in the first quarter of 2008.

• GLYT	$95.500
• Net Dividends & Short Interest	0.000
	95.500
• Purchase (November 27, 2007)	94.000
• Plus Transaction Costs	.005
	94.005
• Gross Profit	$1.495
• Gross Profit %	1.590%
• Holding Period (close January 10, 2007)	44 days
• Annualized Rate of Return	13.01%

Example #12 (December 2007)

Adams Respiratory Therapeutics (ARXT-$59.74-OTC) agreed to be acquired by U.K.-based Reckitt Benckiser (RB-GBP2,914 pence–London). Adams is exclusively focused on the development, commercialization, and marketing of pharmaceuticals for the treatment of respiratory disorders under the brands Mucinex and Delsym. Under terms of the agreement Adams shareholders will receive $60 cash per share, valuing the transaction at approximately $2.3 billlion. The transaction is subject to the tender of a majority of Adams shares as well as regulatory approval and is expected to close in the first quarter of 2008.

• ARXT	$60.000
• Net Dividends & Short Interest	0.000
	60.000
• Purchase (January 4, 2008)	59.500
• Plus Transaction Costs	.005
	59.505
• Gross Profit	$0.495
• Gross Profit %	0.840%
• Holding Period (close January 23, 2008)	19 days
• Annualized Rate of Return	15.92%

Example #13 (January 2008)

Ventana Medical Systems (VMSI-$89.05-OTC) agreed to be acquired by pharmaceutical and diagnostic company Roche Holdings (ROG-CHF195.8-London). Ventana develops, manufactures, and markets instrument/reagent systems that automate tissue preparation and slide staining for diagnosing and treating cancer and infectious diseases. Ventana fended off Roche's hostile $75.00 bid, announced in June 2007, and following due diligence, Roche agreed to acquire Ventana for $89.50 cash per share, valuing the transaction at approximately $3.4 billion. The transaction is subject to the tender of a majority of Ventana shares, as regulatory approval has already been obtained. The transaction is expected to close in the first quarter of 2008.

• VMSI	$89.500
• Net Dividends & Short Interest	0.000
	89.500
• Purchase (January 23, 2008)	88.860
• Plus Transaction Costs	.005
	88.865
• Gross Profit	$0.635
• Gross Profit %	0.715%
• Holding Period (close February 7, 2008)	15 days
• Annualized Rate of Return	17.16%

Example #14 (February 2008)

ChoicePoint (CPS-$48.40-OTC) agreed to be acquired by British Publisher Reed Elsevier (REL-GBP 637 pence–London). ChoicePoint provides businesses, government agencies, and non-profit organizations with DNA identification services, background screenings, drug testing administration services, data visualization, data analytics, teleservices, database and campaign management services. Under terms of the agreement ChoicePoint shareholders will receive $50 cash per share, valuing the transaction at approximately $4 billion. The acquisition is subject to ChoicePoint shareholder as well as regulatory approvals and is expected to close in the summer of 2008.

• CPS	$50.000
• Net Dividends & Short Interest	0.000
	50.000
• Purchase (February 27, 2008)	48.050
• Plus Transaction Costs	.005
	48.055
• Gross Profit	$1.945
• Gross Profit %	4.040%
• Holding Period (close July 15, 2008)	139 days
• Annualized Rate of Return	10.5%

Example #15 (March 2008)

BladeLogic (BLOG-$28.05-OTC) agreed to be acquired by enterprise software company BMC Software (BMC-$32.52-NYSE). BladeLogic provides data center automation software to enterprises, service providers, and government organizations to browse, provision, configure, patch, audit, and remediate physical and virtual servers designed to lower operating costs. Under terms of the transaction BladeLogic sharehoders will receive $28 cash per share, valuing the transaction at approximately $800 million. The transaction is subject to the tender of a majority of shares as well as regulatory approval and is expected to close in the second quarter of 2008.

• BLOG	$27.500
• Net Dividends & Short Interest	0.000
	27.500
• Purchase (March 17, 2008)	27.500
• Plus Transaction Costs	.005
	27.505
• Gross Profit	$0.495
• Gross Profit %	1.800%
• Holding Period (close April17, 2008)	31 days
• Annualized Rate of Return	20.9%

Example #16 (April 2008)

LifeCell Corp. (LIFC-$50.78-OTC) agreed to be acquired by Kinetic Concepts (KCI-$39.66-NYSE). LifeCell supplies biological products for soft tissue repair for orthopedic and urogynecologic surgical procedures and burn and periodontal procedures. Under terms of the agreement LifeCell shareholders will receive $51.00 cash per share, valuing the transaction at approximately $1.7 billion. The transaction is subject to the tender of a majority of shares outstanding as well as regulatory approval and is expected to close in the second quarter of 2008.

• LIFC	$51.000
• Net Dividends & Short Interest	0.000
	51.000
• Purchase (April 24, 2008)	50.500
• Plus Transaction Costs	.005
	50.505
• Gross Profit	$0.495
• Gross Profit %	0.980%
• Holding Period (close May 19, 2008)	25 days
• Annualized Rate of Return	14.1%

Example #17 (May 2008)

Electronic Data Systems (EDS-$24.49-NYSE) agreed to be acquired by Hewlett-Packard (HPQ-$47.06-NYSE). Electronic Data Systems offers systems and technology services, business process management, management consulting, and electronic business including the management of computers, networks, information systems, information processing facilities, business operations, and related personnel. Under terms of the agreement EDS shareholders will receive $25 cash per share, valuing the transaction at approximately $13.9 billion. The transaction is subject to regulatory as well as EDS shareholder approval and is expected to close in the second half of 2008.

• EDS	$25.000
• Net Dividends & Short Interest	0.050
	25.050
• Purchase (May 21, 2008)	24.290
• Plus Transaction Costs	.005
	24.295
• Gross Profit	$0.755
• Gross Profit %	3.100%
• Holding Period (close August 31, 2008)	102 days
• Annualized Rate of Return	11.0%

Example #18 (June 2008)

Superior Essex Inc. (SPSX-$44.63-OTC) agreed to be acquired by South Korean cable company LS Corp. Superior Essex manufactures and supplies a broad portfolio of wire and cable products for the communications, energy, automotive, industrial, and commercial & residential end-markets whose products include magnet wire, fabricated insulation products, and copper and fiber optic communications wire and cable. Under terms of the agreement Superior Essex shareholders will receive $45 cash per share, valuing the transaction at approximately $900 million. The transaction is subject to the tender of a majority of Superior Essex shares as well as regulatory approvals and is expected to close in the third quarter of 2008.

• SPSX	$45.000
• Net Dividends & Short Interest	0.000
	45.000
• Purchase (June 30, 2008)	44.630
• Plus Transaction Costs	.005
	44.635
• Gross Profit	$0.365
• Gross Profit %	0.818%
• Holding Period (close July 31, 2008)	31 days
• Annualized Rate of Return	9.50%

Example #19 (July 2008)

Philadelphia Consolidated Holding Corp. (PHLY-$58.45-OTC) agreed to be acquired by Tokio Marine Holdings (8766-JPY 4,080 yen–Tokyo). Philadelphia Consolidated designs, markets, and underwrites specialty commercial property and casualty insurance products. Under terms of the agreement PHLY shareholders will receive $61.50 cash per share, valuing the transaction at approximately $4.7 billion. The transaction is subject to PHLY shareholder as well as regulatory approval and is expected to close by the end of 2008.

• PHLY	$61.500
• Net Dividends & Short Interest	0.000
	61.500
• Purchase (July 24, 2008)	58.250
• Plus Transaction Costs	.005
	58.255
• Gross Profit	$3.245
• Gross Profit %	5.570%
• Holding Period (close December 1, 2008)	130 days
• Annualized Rate of Return	15.43%

Example #20 (August 2008)

UnionBanCal Corp. (UB-$73.68-NYSE) agreed to be acquired by Mitsubishi UFJ Financial Group, Inc. (8306-JPY 839-Tokyo). San Francisco-based UnionBanCal Corporation is a bank holding company with $61 billion of assets and 337 banking offices in California, Oregon, and Washington. Under terms of the agreement UnionBanCal shareholders will receive $73.50 cash per share, valuing UnionBanCal at approximately $10.1 billion. The transaction is subject to a minimum tender condition but is not subject to any Japanese or U.S. bank regulatory or antitrust approval. There is no financing condition to the transaction.

• UB	$73.500
• Net Dividends & Short Interest	0.520
	74.020
• Purchase (August 18, 2008)	73.180
• Plus Transaction Costs	.005
	73.185
• Gross Profit	$0.835
• Gross Profit %	1.14%
• Holding Period (close September 26, 2008)	39 days
• Annualized Rate of Return	10.53%

Example #21 (September 2008)

CryoCath Technologies Inc. (CYT-C$8.23-Toronto) agreed to be acquired by medical device company Medtronic Inc. (MDT-$50.10-NYSE). CryoCath is a medical device company that develops catheter cryotherapy products used for the treatment of atrial fibrillation. Under terms of the agreement CryoCath shareholders will receive C$8.75 cash per share, valuing the transaction at approximately C$400 million. The transaction is subject to CryoCath shareholder as well as regulatory approval and is expected to close in the fourth quarter of 2008.

• CYT	$ 8.750
• Net Dividends & Short Interest	0.000
	8.750
• Purchase (September 29, 2008)	8.300
• Plus Transaction Costs	.005
	8.305
• Gross Profit	$0.445
• Gross Profit %	5.36%
• Holding Period (close November 12, 2008)	44 days
• Annualized Rate of Return	43.84%

Example #22 (October 2008)

Imclone Systems (IMCL-$68.76-OTC) agreed to be acquired by Eli Lilly & Co. (LLY-$33.82-NYSE). Imclone is a biopharmaceutical company that develops and commercializes drugs designed to treat patients with cancer, including growth factor blockers and aniogenesis inhibitors. Under terms of the agreement Imclone shareholders will receive $70 cash per share, valuing the transaction at approximately $6 billion. The transaction is subject to regulatory approval as well as the tender of a majority of shares outstanding and is expected to close by the end of November 2008.

• IMCL	$70.000
• Net Dividends & Short Interest	0.000
	70.000
• Purchase (October 16, 2008)	67.360
• Plus Transaction Costs	.005
	67.365
• Gross Profit	$2.635
• Gross Profit %	3.912%
• Holding Period (close November 21, 2008)	36 days
• Annualized Rate of Return	39.12%

Example #23 (November 2008)

Omrix Biopharmaceuticals (OMRI-$24.88-OTC) agreed to be acquired by Johnson & Johnson (JNJ-$58.58-NYSE). Omrix is a biopharmaceutical company that develops, manufactures, and markets protein-based biosurgery and passive immunotherapy products. Under terms of the agreement Omrix shareholders will receive $25 cash per share, valuing the transaction at approximately $500 million. The transaction is subject to the tender of a majority of shares outstanding as well as regulatory approval and is expected to close in late 2008 or early 2009.

• OMRI	$25.000
• Net Dividends & Short Interest	0.000
	25.000
• Purchase (November 25, 2008)	24.600
• Plus Transaction Costs	.005
	24.605
• Gross Profit	$0.395
• Gross Profit %	1.600%
• Holding Period (close December 29, 2008)	34 days
• Annualized Rate of Return	16.94%

Example #24 (December 2008)

Mentor Corp. (MNT-$30.93-NYSE) agreed to be acquired by healthcare giant Johnson & Johnson (JNJ-$59.83-NYSE). Mentor develops, manufactures, and markets a broad range of products for the medical specialties of plastic, reconstructive, and general surgery and urology. Under terms of the agreement Mentor shareholders will receive $31.00 cash per share, valuing the transaction at $1.1 billion. The transaction is subject to the tender of a majority of Mentor shares outstanding as well as antitrust approval and is expected to close in early 2009.

• MNT	$31.000
• Net Dividends & Short Interest	0.000
	31.000
• Purchase (December 5, 2008)	30.500
• Plus Transaction Costs	.005
	30.505
• Gross Profit	$0.495
• Gross Profit %	1.622%
• Holding Period (close January 23, 2009)	49 days
• Annualized Rate of Return	11.92%

Example #25 (January 2009)

Advanced Medical Optics (EYE-$21.97-NYSE) agreed to be acquired by Abbott (ABT-$55.44-NYSE). Advanced Medical Optics develops products for ophthalmic care including cataract surgery, laser vision correction (LASIK), and other eye care products. Under terms of the transaction AMO shareholders will receive $22 cash per share, valuing the transaction at approximately $3 billion. The transaction is subject to the tender of a majority of AMO shares outstanding as well as regulatory approval and is expected to close in the first quarter of 2009.

• EYE	$22.000
• Net Dividends & Short Interest	0.000
	22.000
• Purchase (January 13, 2008)	21.470
• Plus Transaction Costs	.005
	21.475
• Gross Profit	$0.525
• Gross Profit %	2.45%
• Holding Period (close February 24, 2009)	42 days
• Annualized Rate of Return	20.96%

Example #26 (February 2009)

PharmaNet Development Group, Inc. (PDGI-$4.94-OTC) agreed to be acquired by private equity firm JLL Partners. PharmaNet provides early- and late-stage consulting; Phase I clinical studies and bioanalytical analyses; and Phase II, III, and IV clinical development programs. Under terms of the transaction PharmaNet shareholders will receive $5.00 cash per share, valuing the transaction at approximately $250 million. The transaction is subject to the tender of a majority of PharmaNet common stock as well as regulatory approvals and is expected to close in the first quarter of 2009.

• PDGI	$5.000
• Net Dividends & Short Interest	0.000
	5.000
• Purchase (February 5, 2009)	4.790
• Plus Transaction Costs	.005
	4.795
• Gross Profit	$0.205
• Gross Profit %	4.28%
• Holding Period (close March 20, 2009)	43 days
• Annualized Rate of Return	35.79%

Example #27 (March 2009)

CV Therapeutics, Inc. (CVTX-$19.88-OTC) agreed to be acquired by Gilead Sciences, Inc. (GILD-$46.32-OTC). CV Therapeutics is a biopharmaceutical company primarily focused on applying molecular cardiology to the discovery, development, and commercialization of small molecule drugs for the treatment of cardiovascular diseases. Under terms of the transaction CVTX shareholders will receive $20 cash per share, valuing the transaction at approximately $1.4 billion. The transaction is subject to the tender by at least a majority of shares outstanding as well as regulatory approvals and is expected to close in the second quarter of 2009. There is no financing condition to the transaction.

• CVTX	$20.000
• Net Dividends & Short Interest	0.000
	20.000
• Purchase (March 16, 2009)	19.650
• Plus Transaction Costs	.005
	19.655
• Gross Profit	$0.345
• Gross Profit %	1.76%
• Holding Period (close April 16, 2009)	31 days
• Annualized Rate of Return	20.38%

Example #28 (April 2009)

Sun Microsystems, Inc. (JAVA-$9.16-OTC) agreed to be acquired by Oracle Corp. (ORCL-$19.34-OTC). Sun Microsystems develops and sells software and networking hardware. Under terms of the agreement Sun shareholders will receive $9.50 cash per share, valuing the transaction at approximately $7.5 billion. The transaction is subject to Sun shareholder as well as regulatory approvals and is expected to close in the third quarter of 2009.

• JAVA	$9.500
• Net Dividends & Short Interest	0.000
	9.500
• Purchase (April 28, 2009)	9.120
• Plus Transaction Costs	.005
	9.125
• Gross Profit	$0.375
• Gross Profit %	4.11%
• Holding Period (close August 10, 2009)	104 days
• Annualized Rate of Return	14.30%

Example #29 (May 2009)

VNUS Medical Technologies Inc. (VNUS-$28.96-NYSE) agreed to be acquired by Covidien plc (COV-$35.72-NYSE). VNUS Medical Technologies Inc. is a leader in medical devices for the minimally invasive treatment of venous reflux disease, a progressive condition that is the underlying cause of varicose veins. Under the terms of the transaction VNUS shareholders will receive $29.00 in cash, valuing the deal at roughly $440 million. The transaction is subject to shareholder and regulatory approval and is expected to close in the second quarter of 2009.

• VNUS	$29.000
• Net Dividends & Short Interest	0.000
	29.000
• Purchase (May 8, 2009)	28.680
• Plus Transaction Costs	.005
	28.685
• Gross Profit	$0.315
• Gross Profit %	1.10%
• Holding Period (close June 17, 2009)	40 days
• Annualized Rate of Return	9.88%

Example #30 (June 2009)

Addax Petroleum Corporation (AXC CN–C$49.33-TSE) agreed to be acquired by China Petroleum and Chemical Corp (Sinopec) (SNP-$75.86-NYSE). Addax Petroleum is involved in the exploration and production of oil and gas in the Middle East and Africa. Under the terms of the agreement, shareholders of Addax will receive C$52.80 in cash per share valuing the transaction at C$8.3 Billion. The deal requires acceptances of at least 66.66 percent of Addax shares outstanding as well as regulatory approvals from both Canada and China. The offer is expected to close by mid-August 2009.

• AXC CN	C$52.800
• Net Dividends & Short Interest	0.100
	52.900
• Purchase (June 24, 2009)	49.000
• Plus Transaction Costs	.010
	49.010
• Gross Profit	C$3.890
• Gross Profit %	7.94%
• Holding Period (close August 24, 2009)	61 days
• Annualized Rate of Return	46.84%

Example #31 (July 2009)

Noven Pharmaceuticals, Inc. (NOVN-$16.48-OTC) agreed to be acquired by Hisamitsu Pharmaceutical Co., Inc. (4530-JPY 3,270–Tokyo). Noven Pharmaceuticals researches and develops prescription pharmaceuticals focused in transdermal drug delivery. Under terms of the agreement Noven shareholders will receive $16.50 cash per share, valuing the transaction at approximately $430 million. The transaction is subject to the tender of a majority of shares outstanding as well as regulatory approvals and is expected to close in the third quarter of 2009.

• NOVN	$16.500
• Net Dividends & Short Interest	0.000
	16.500
• Purchase (July 21, 2009)	16.340
• Plus Transaction Costs	.005
	16.345
• Gross Profit	$0.155
• Gross Profit %	0.95%
• Holding Period (close August 19, 2009)	29 days
• Annualized Rate of Return	11.77%

Example #32 (August 2009)

Charlotte Russe Holding (CHIC-$17.39-OTC) agreed to be acquired by Advent International Corp. Charlotte Russe is a mall-based specialty retailer of fashionable value-priced apparel and accessories targeting young women, with more than 500 stores in the United States and Puerto Rico. Under terms of the agreement Charlotte Russe shareholders will receive $17.50 cash per share, valuing the transaction at approximately $400 million. The transaction is subject to regulatory approval as well as the tender of the majority of shares outstanding and is expected to close in the fourth quarter of 2009.

• CHIC	$17.500
• Net Dividends & Short Interest	0.000
	17.500
• Purchase (August 28, 2009)	17.350
• Plus Transaction Costs	.005
	17.355
• Gross Profit	$0.145
• Gross Profit %	0.84%
• Holding Period (close September 28, 2009)	31 days
• Annualized Rate of Return	9.70%

Example #33 (September 2009)

Sepracor Inc. (SEPR-$22.90-OTC) agreed to be acquired by Dainippon Sumitomo Pharma (4506-JPY 979–Tokyo). Sepracor is a specialty pharmaceutical company with a focus on central nervous system and respiratory disorders. Under terms of the agreement Sepracor shareholders will receive $23 cash per share, valuing the transaction at approximately $3 billion. The transaction is subject to regulatory approvals as well as a tender of the majority of shares outstanding and is expected to close in the fourth quarter of 2009.

• SEPR	$23.000
• Net Dividends & Short Interest	0.000
	23.000
• Purchase (September 14, 2009)	22.790
• Plus Transaction Costs	.005
	22.795
• Gross Profit	$0.205
• Gross Profit %	0.90%
• Holding Period (close October 13, 2009)	29 days
• Annualized Rate of Return	11.16%

Example #34 (October 2009)

Starent Networks (STAR-$33.74-OTC) agreed to be acquired by networking equipment maker Cisco (CSCO-$22.81-OTC). Starent provides infrastructure equipment used by mobile operators to deliver multimedia services to their subscribers. Under terms of the transaction Starent shareholders will receive $35 cash per share, valuing the transaction at approximately $3 billion. The transaction is subject to regulatory as well as Starent shareholder approval and is expected to close in the first half of 2010.

• STAR	$35.000
• Net Dividends & Short Interest	0.000
	35.000
• Purchase (October 22, 2009)	33.650
• Plus Transaction Costs	.005
	33.655
• Gross Profit	$1.345
• Gross Profit %	4.00%
• Holding Period (close September 28, 2009)	101 days
• Annualized Rate of Return	14.25%

Example #35 (November 2009)

Burlington Northern Santa Fe Corp. (BNI-$98.30-NYSE) agreed to be acquired by Berkshire Hathaway (BRK/A-$100,600-NYSE). Burlington Northern operates a railroad system throughout the United States and Canada. Under terms of the agreement Burlington shareholders will receive $100 in cash and Berkshire common stock per share, valuing the transaction at approximately $44 billion. The transaction is subject to the approval of 66 2/3 percent of Burlington Northern shares not already held by Berkshire as well as regulatory approval and is expected to close in the first quarter of 2010.

• BNI	$100.000
• Net Dividends & Short Interest	0.660
	100.660
• Purchase (November 5, 2009)	96.980
• Plus Transaction Costs	.005
	96.985
• Gross Profit	$3.675
• Gross Profit %	3.79%
• Holding Period (close February 11, 2009)	98 days
• Annualized Rate of Return	13.92%

Example #36 (December 2009)

Livingston International Income Fund (LIV-U-C$9.47-Toronto) agreed to be acquired by Canada Pension Plan Investment Board on improved terms. Livingston provides customs, transportation, and integrated logistics services at 100 key border points, seaports, airports, and other locations in the United States and Canada. Under terms of the new agreement Livingston shareholders will receive C$9.50 cash per share, valuing the transaction at approximately C$500 million. Livingston had previously agreed to be acquired by CPPIB for C$8 cash per share. The transaction is subject to Livingston unitholder approval and is expected to close in the first quarter of 2010.

• LIV-U	$9.500
• Net Dividends & Short Interest	0.000
	9.500
• Purchase (December 21, 2009)	9.430
• Plus Transaction Costs	.005
	9.435
• Gross Profit	$0.065
• Gross Profit %	0.70%
• Holding Period (close January 19, 2010)	29 days
• Annualized Rate of Return	8.69%

Example #37 (January 2010)

Brink's Home Security Holdings (CFL-$41.00-NYSE) agreed to be acquired by Tyco International (TYC-$35.43-NYSE). Brink's is a full-service provider of residential and business security systems under its brand name Broadview Security. Under terms of the agreement Brink's shareholders will receive $42.50 value in cash and Tyco common shares, valuing the transaction at approximately $2 billion. The transaction is subject to Brink's shareholder as well as regulatory approvals and is expected to close in mid-2010.

• CFL	$42.500
• Net Dividends & Short Interest	0.000
	42.500
• Purchase (January 29, 2010)	40.930
• Plus Transaction Costs	.005
	40.935
• Gross Profit	$1.565
• Gross Profit %	3.82%
• Holding Period (close April 30, 2010)	91 days
• Annualized Rate of Return	15.12%

Example #38 (February 2010)

Bowne & Co., Inc. (BNE-$11.13-NYSE) agreed to be acquired by R.R. Donnelley & Sons Company (RRD-$19.89-NYSE). Bowne provides shareholder, marketing, and compliance communications services around the world. Under terms of the agreement Bowne shareholders will receive $11.50 cash per share, valuing the transaction at approximately $450 million. The transaction is subject to Bowne shareholder as well as regulatory approvals and is expected to close in mid-2010.

• BNE	$11.500
• Net Dividends & Short Interest	0.055
	11.555
• Purchase (February 24, 2010)	11.100
• Plus Transaction Costs	.005
	11.105
• Gross Profit	$0.450
• Gross Profit %	4.05%
• Holding Period (close June 15, 2010)	111 days
• Annualized Rate of Return	13.14%

Example #39 (March 2010)

SouthWest Water Company (SWWC-$10.44-NASDAQ) agreed to be acquired by J. P. Morgan Asset Management. SouthWest Water operates and manages water-supply and wastewater-treatment systems, some of which are owned by the company and are regulated public utilities and others are managed under contract. Under terms of the agreement SouthWest shareholders will receive $11.00 cash per share, valuing the transaction at approximately $450 million. The transaction is subject to SouthWest shareholder as well as regulatory approval and is expected to close in late 2010, or early 2011.

• SWWC	$11.000
• Net Dividends & Short Interest	0.050
	11.050
• Purchase (March 8, 2010)	10.300
• Plus Transaction Costs	.005
	10.305
• Gross Profit	$0.735
• Gross Profit %	7.13%
• Holding Period (close November 15, 2010)	252 days
• Annualized Rate of Return	10.18%

Example #40 (April 2010)

ATS Medical, Inc. (ATSI-$3.98-NASDAQ) agreed to be acquired by Medtronic, Inc. (MDT-$43.69-NYSE). ATS Medical develops, manufactures, and markets products and services focused on cardiac surgery, including heart valves and cryoablation technology. Under terms of the agreement ATS shareholders will receive $4 cash per share, valuing the transaction at approximately $370 million. The transaction is subject to ATS shareholder as well as regulatory approvals and is expected to close in the third quarter of 2010.

• ATSI	$4.000
• Net Dividends & Short Interest	0.000
	4.000
• Purchase (May 10, 2010)	3.930
• Plus Transaction Costs	0.005
	3.935
• Gross Profit	$0.065
• Gross Profit %	1.652%
• Holding Period (Close July 15, 2010)	66 days
• Annualized Rate of Return	9.010%

Example #41 (May 2010)

Sybase, Inc. (SY-$64.33-NYSE) agreed to be acquired by SAP (SAP-$42.43-NYSE). Under terms of the transaction, Sybase develops and sells enterprise software for data warehousing, web computing environments, and embedded computing. Sybase shareholders will receive $65 cash per share, valuing the transaction at approximately $5.8 million. The transaction is subject to the tender of a majority of shares outstanding as well as regulatory approvals and is expected to close in mid-2010.

• SY	$65.000
• Net Dividends & Short Interest	0.000
	65.000
• Purchase (May 25, 2010)	64.000
• Plus Transaction Costs	0.005
	64.005
• Gross Profit	$0.995
• Gross Profit %	1.560%
• Holding Period (Close July 22, 2010)	58 days
• Annualized Rate of Return	9.650%

Example #42 (June 2010)

American Italian Pasta Co. (AIPC-$52.87-NASDAQ) agreed to be acquired by Ralcorp Holdings, Inc. (RAH-$54.80-NYSE). American Italian Pasta Company produces and markets dry pasta in North America using durum wheat milling and pasta production technology. Under terms of the agreement AIPC shareholders will receive $53 cash per share, valuing the transaction at approximately $1.2 billion. The transaction is subject to the tender of a majority of AIPC shares outstanding as well as regulatory approval and is expected to close in the fourth quarter of 2010.

• AIPC	$53.000
• Net Dividends & Short Interest	0.000
	53.000
• Purchase (June 21, 2010)	52.600
• Plus Transaction Costs	0.005
	52.605
• Gross Profit	$0.395
• Gross Profit %	0.751%
• Holding Period (Close July 22, 2010)	31 days
• Annualized Rate of Return	8.720%

Example #43 (July 2010)

AmeriCredit Corp. (ACF-$24.11-NYSE) agreed to be acquired by General Motors. AmeriCredit is a national consumer finance company specializing in purchasing, securitizing, and servicing automobile loans. Under terms of the agreement AmeriCredit shareholders will receive $24.50 cash per share, valuing the transaction at approximately $3.3 billion. The transaction is subject to AmeriCredit shareholder as well as regulatory approvals and is expected to close by the end of 2010.

• ACF	$24.500
• Net Dividends & Short Interest	0.000
	24.500
• Purchase (July 22, 2010)	23.850
• Plus Transaction Costs	0.005
	23.855
• Gross Profit	$0.645
• Gross Profit %	2.704%
• Holding Period (Close November 15, 2010)	116 days
• Annualized Rate of Return	8.391%

Example #44 (August 2010)

McAfee, Inc. (MFE-$47.05-NYSE) agreed to be acquired by Intel Corp. (INTC-$17.67-NASDAQ). McAfee develops, sells, and markets computer security solutions with a focus on network security. Under terms of the agreement McAfee shareholders will receive $48 cash per share, valuing the transaction at approximately $7.7 billion. The transaction is subject to McAfee shareholder as well as regulatory approvals and is expected to close in the fourth quarter of 2010.

• MFE	$48.000
• Net Dividends & Short Interest	0.000
	48.000
• Purchase (August 20, 2010)	46.950
• Plus Transaction Costs	0.005
	46.955
• Gross Profit	$1.045
• Gross Profit %	2.226%
• Holding Period (Close November 30, 2010)	102 days
• Annualized Rate of Return	7.855%

Example #45 (September 2010)

The Student Loan Corporation (STU-$29.70-NYSE) agreed to be acquired by Discover Financial Services (DFS-$16.68-NYSE). The Student Loan Corp. is an originator and holder of student loans and provides other education financing products. Under terms of the agreement Student Loan shareholders will receive $30 cash per share, valuing the transaction at approximately $600 million. The transaction is subject to Student Loan shareholder as well as regulatory approvals and is expected to close in the fourth quarter of 2010.

• STU	$30.000
• Net Dividends & Short Interest	0.000
	30.000
• Purchase (September 28, 2010)	29.500
• Plus Transaction Costs	0.005
	29.550
• Gross Profit	$0.495
• Gross Profit %	1.678%
• Holding Period (Close December 15, 2010)	78 days
• Annualized Rate of Return	7.743%

Example #46 (October 2010)

The Gymboree Corp. (GYMB-$65.06-NASDAQ) agreed to be acquired by private equity firm Bain Capital Partners. Gymboree designs, manufactures, and retails apparel and accessories for children from birth to seven years of age, operating stores in the United States, Canada, and Europe. Under terms of the agreement Gymboree shareholders will receive $65.40 cash per share, valuing the transaction at approximately $1.8 billion. Gymboree may solicit acquisition proposals from third parties for a period of forty calendar days continuing through November 20, 2010. The transaction is subject to the tender of at least 66 percent of common shares outstanding as well as regulatory approvals and is expected to close in the fourth quarter of 2010.

• GYMB	$65.400
• Net Dividends & Short Interest	0.000
	65.400
• Purchase (October 21, 2010)	64.900
• Plus Transaction Costs	0.005
	64.905
• Gross Profit	$0.495
• Gross Profit %	0.763%
• Holding Period (Close November 23, 2010)	33 days
• Annualized Rate of Return	8.320%

Example #47 (November 2010)

Bucyrus International, Inc. (BUCY-$89.16-NASDAQ) agreed to be acquired by Caterpillar, Inc. (CAT-$84.60-NYSE). Bucyrus designs and manufactures high productivity mining equipment for the surface and underground mining industries. Under terms of the transaction Bucyrus shareholders will receive $92 cash per share, valuing the transaction at approximately $8.6 billion. The transaction is subject to Bucyrus shareholder as well as regulatory approvals and is expected to close in mid-2011.

• BUCY	$92.000
• Dividends	0.025
	92.025
• Purchase (November 23, 2010)	89.000
• Plus Transaction Costs	0.005
	89.005
• Gross Profit	$3.020
• Gross Profit %	3.393%
• Holding Period (Close April 15, 2011)	143 days
• Annualized Rate of Return	8.542%

Example #48 (December 2010)

Applied Signal Technology (APSG-$37.89-NASDAQ) agreed to be acquired by Raytheon Company (RTN-$46.34-NYSE). Applied Signal is a provider of advanced intelligence, surveillance, and reconnaissance (ISR) products, systems, and services that enhance global security. Under the terms of the agreement Applied Signal shareholders will receive $38.00 cash per share, valuing the transaction at approximately $500 million. The transaction is subject to the tender of a majority of Applied Signal's common shares outstanding as well as regulatory approvals and is expected to close in the first quarter of 2011.

• APSG	$38.000
• Dividends	0.000
	38.000
• Purchase (December 20, 2010)	37.770
• Plus Transaction Costs	0.005
	37.775
• Gross Profit	$0.225
• Gross Profit %	0.596%
• Holding Period (Close January 28, 2011)	38 days
• Annualized Rate of Return	5.643%

Example #49 (January 2011)

Massey Energy Co. (MEE-$62.86-NYSE) agreed to be acquired by Alpha Natural Resources Inc. (ANR-$53.73-NYSE). Massey Energy produces, processes, and sells coal of steam and metallurgical grades, primarily in the United States and sells to utility, industrial, and metallurgical customers. Under the terms of the agreement Massey shareholders will receive $10.00 in cash and 1.025 shares of ANR per share, valuing the total transaction at approximately $8.5 billion. The transaction is subject to regulatory approvals as well as the approval of shareholders of both companies and is expected to close in the second quarter of 2011.

• MEE	Sell Short ANR (1.025 × $53.73)	$55.070
	Cash	10.000
• Net Dividends		0.060
		65.130
• Purchase (January 31, 2011)		62.860
• Plus Transaction Costs		0.010
		62.870
• Gross Profit		$2.260
• Gross Profit %		3.595%
• Holding Period (Close May 31, 2011)		120 days
• Annualized Rate of Return		10.934%

Example #50 (February 2011)

Beckman Coulter (BEC-$83.13-NYSE) agreed to be acquired by Danaher Corp. (DHR-$50.60-NYSE). Beckman Coulter is a manufacturer of biomedical testing instrument systems. Under the terms of the agreement Beckman shareholders will receive $83.50 in cash per share, valuing the total transaction at approximately $5.8 billion. The transaction is subject to the tender of a majority of Beckman's common shares outstanding as well as regulatory approvals and is anticipated to close in the second quarter of 2011.

• BEC	$83.500
• Net Dividends	0.190
	83.690
• Purchase (February 24, 2011)	82.820
• Plus Transaction Costs	0.005
	82.825
• Gross Profit	$0.865
• Gross Profit %	1.044%
• Holding Period (Close April 30, 2011)	65 days
• Annualized Rate of Return	5.865%

Example #51 (March 2011)

Lubrizol Corp. (LZ-$133.96-NYSE) agreed to be acquired by Berkshire Hathaway (BRK/A-$125,300-NYSE). Lubrizol develops, sells, and produces specialty additives used in transportation and industrial finished lubricants. Under terms of the agreement Lubrizol shareholders will receive $135 cash per share, valuing the transaction at approximately $9 billion. The transaction is subject to Lubrizol shareholder as well as regulatory approvals and is expected to close mid-year 2011.

• LZ	$135.000
• Net Dividends	0.360
	135.360
• Purchase (March 24, 2011)	133.700
• Plus Transaction Costs	0.005
	133.705
• Gross Profit	$1.655
• Gross Profit %	1.238%
• Holding Period (Close June 15, 2011)	83 days
• Annualized Rate of Return	5.443%

Example #52 (April 2011)

National Semiconductor (NSM-$24.12-NYSE) agreed to be acquired by Texas Instruments (TXN-$35.53-NYSE). National Semiconductor designs, develops, manufactures, and markets a wide variety of analog and mixed-signal integrated circuits for the information appliance, personal computing, consumer, and communication markets. Under terms of the agreement National Semiconductor shareholders will receive $25 cash per share, valuing the transaction at approximately $6.5 billion. The transaction is subject to National Semiconductor shareholder as well as regulatory approvals and is expected to close in the second half of 2011.

• NSM	$25.000
• Net Dividends	0.000
	25.000
• Purchase (April 20, 2011)	24.080
• Plus Transaction Costs	0.005
	24.085
• Gross Profit	$0.915
• Gross Profit %	3.799%
• Holding Period (Close September 30, 2011)	163 days
• Annualized Rate of Return	8.507%

Example #53 (May 2011)

International Coal Group (ICO-$14.53-NYSE) agreed to be acquired by Arch Coal (ACI-$29.89-NYSE). International Coal mines coal in northern and central Appalachia and the Illinois basin. Under terms of the agreement International Coal shareholders will receive $14.60 cash per share, valuing the transaction at approximately $3.4 billion. The transaction is subject to the tender of a majority of shares outstanding as well as regulatory approvals and is expected to close in the second quarter of 2011.

• ICO	$14.600
• Net Dividends	0.000
	14.600
• Purchase (May 2, 2011)	14.430
• Plus Transaction Costs	0.005
	14.435
• Gross Profit	$0.165
• Gross Profit %	1.143%
• Holding Period (Close June 14, 2011)	43 days
• Annualized Rate of Return	9.703%

Example #54 (June 2011)

BJ's Wholesale Club (BJ-$50.35-NYSE) agreed to be acquired by a consortium consisting of CVC Capital Partners and Leonard Green & Partners. BJ's Wholesale operates a wholesale club chain in the eastern United States offering grocery items, general merchandise, and automotive services. Under terms of the agreement BJ's shareholders will receive $51.25 cash per share, valuing the transaction at approximately $2.8 billion. The transaction is subject to BJ's shareholder as well as regulatory approvals and is expected to close in the fourth quarter of 2011.

• BJ	$51.250
• Net Dividends	0.000
	51.250
• Purchase (June 29, 2011)	50.250
• Plus Transaction Costs	0.005
	50.255
• Gross Profit	$0.995
• Gross Profit %	1.980%
• Holding Period (Close October 10, 2011)	103 days
• Annualized Rate of Return	7.016%

Example #55 (July 2011)

Petrohawk Energy Corp. (HK-$38.19-NYSE) agreed to be acquired by BHP Billiton (BHP-$91.55-NYSE). Petrohawk Energy is an oil and gas company that explores for and produces natural gas and crude oil in the United States. Under terms of the agreement Petrohawk shareholders will receive $38.75 cash per share, valuing the transaction at approximately $15 billion. The transaction is subject to regulatory approvals as well as the tender of at least a majority of shares outstanding and is expected to close in the third quarter of 2011.

• HK	$38.750
• Net Dividends	0.000
	38.750
• Purchase (July 29, 2011)	38.190
• Plus Transaction Costs	0.005
	38.195
• Gross Profit	$0.555
• Gross Profit %	1.453%
• Holding Period (Close August 19, 2011)	21 days
• Annualized Rate of Return	25.256%

Example #56 (August 2011)

Autonomy plc (AU/ LN-£25.20-London) agreed to be acquired by Hewlett Packard Co. (HPQ-$26.03-NYSE), as part of a larger restructuring. Autonomy is an enterprise information management company that makes software that automatically processes information in emails, web pages, and other sources of unstructured information. Under terms of the agreement Autonomy shareholders will receive £25.50 cash per share, valuing the transaction at approximately £7 billion. In addition, HP has confirmed its intent to spin off its personal computing business. The transaction is subject to regulatory approval from four separate jurisdictions and we expect the offer to close in October 2011.

• AU/LN	£25.500
• Net Dividends	0.000
	25.500
• Purchase (August 23, 2011)	24.850
• Plus Transaction Costs	0.025
	24.875
• Gross Profit	£0.625
• Gross Profit %	2.513%
• Holding Period (Pay October 17, 2011)	55 days
• Annualized Rate of Return	16.678%

Example #57 (September 2011)

Goodrich Corp. (GR-$120.68-NYSE) agreed to be acquired by United Technologies (UTX-$70.53-NYSE). Goodrich supplies aerospace components, systems, and services to commercial, military, general aviation, and space industries. Under terms of the agreement, Goodrich shareholders will receive $127.50 cash per share, valuing the transaction at approximately $18.4 billion. The transaction is subject to Goodrich shareholder as well as regulatory approvals and is expected to close in the first half of 2011.

• GR	$127.500
• Net Dividends	0.580
	128.080
• Purchase (September 30, 2011)	120.900
• Plus Transaction Costs	0.005
	120.905
• Gross Profit	$7.175
• Gross Profit %	5.934%
• Holding Period (Close March 31, 2012)	183 days
• Annualized Rate of Return	11.836%

Example #58 (October 2011)

Daylight Energy (DAY CN-C$9.85-Toronto) agreed to be acquired by China Petrochemical Corp. (600500 CH-CNY 7.92-Shanghai). Daylight Energy explores for and produces oil and natural gas in Alberta and British Columbia, Canada. Under terms of the agreement Daylight Energy shareholders will receive C$10.08 cash per share, valuing the transaction at approximately C$2.2 billion. The transaction is subject to approval by Daylight shareholders as well as Canadian regulators and is expected to close in late 2011 or early 2012.

• DAY CN	C$10.080
• Net Dividends	0.000
	10.080
• Purchase (October 20, 2011)	9.850
• Plus Transaction Costs	0.005
	9.855
• Gross Profit	$0.225
• Gross Profit %	2.283%
• Holding Period (Close January 15, 2012)	87 days
• Annualized Rate of Return	9.579%

Example #59 (November 2011)

Advanced Analogic Technologies (AATI-$5.74-NASDAQ) agreed to be acquired by Skyworks Solutions (SWKS-$16.31-NASDAQ) under revised terms. Advanced Analogic supplies power management semiconductors for mobile consumer electronic devices, such as wireless handsets, notebook and tablet computers, smartphones, digital cameras, and digital audio players. Under terms of the revised agreement AATI shareholders will receive $5.80 cash per share, valuing the transaction at approximately $200 million. The transaction is subject to the tender of at least a majority of shares outstanding and is expected to close in January 2012.

• AATI	$5.800
• Net Dividends	0.000
	5.800
• Purchase (November 30, 2011)	5.740
• Plus Transaction Costs	0.005
	5.745
• Gross Profit	$0.055
• Gross Profit %	0.957%
• Holding Period (Close January 10, 2012)	41 days
• Annualized Rate of Return	8.523%

Example #60 (December 2011)

Synovis Life Technologies (SYNO-$27.83-NASDAQ) agreed to be acquired by Baxter International (BAX-$49.48-NYSE). Synovis provides biological and mechanical products for soft tissue repair used in a variety of surgical procedures. Under terms of the agreement Synovis shareholders will receive $28 cash per share, valuing the transaction at approximately $325 million. The transaction is subject to Synovis shareholder as well as regulatory approvals and is expected to close in the first quarter of 2012.

• SYNO	$28.000
• Net Dividends	0.000
	28.000
• Purchase (December 27, 2012)	27.780
• Plus Transaction Costs	0.005
	27.785
• Gross Profit	$0.215
• Gross Profit %	0.774%
• Holding Period (Close February 14, 2012)	49 days
• Annualized Rate of Return	5.764%

Example #61 (January 2012)

Inhibitex, Inc. (INHX-$25.52-NASDAQ) agreed to be acquired by Bristol-Myers Squibb (BMY-$32.24-NYSE). Inhibitex is a biopharmaceutical company that discovers, develops, and commercializes novel antibody-based products, including treatments for hepatitis C. Under terms of the agreement Inhibitex shareholders will receive $26.00 cash per share, valuing the transaction at approximately $2.5 billion. The transaction is subject to the tender of at least a majority of shares outstanding as well as regulatory approvals and is expected to close in the first quarter of 2012.

• INHX	$26.000
• Net Dividends	0.000
	26.000
• Purchase (January 11, 2012)	24.350
• Plus Transaction Costs	0.005
	24.355
• Gross Profit	$1.645
• Gross Profit %	6.754%
• Holding Period (Close February 10, 2012)	30 days
• Annualized Rate of Return	82.177%

Example #62 (February 2012)

Taleo Corp. (TLEO-$45.82-NASDAQ) agreed to be acquired by Oracle Corp. (ORCL-$29.25-NASDAQ). Taleo provides cloud-based staffing management software for temporary, hourly, and professional employees. Under terms of the agreement Taleo shareholders will receive $46 cash per share, valuing the transaction at approximately $1.9 billion. The transaction is subject to Taleo shareholder as well as regulatory approvals and is expected to close in mid-2012.

• TLEO	$46.000
• Net Dividends	0.000
	46.000
• Purchase (February 9, 2012)	45.550
• Plus Transaction Costs	0.005
	45.555
• Gross Profit	$0.445
• Gross Profit %	0.977%
• Holding Period (Close April 5, 2012)	56 days
• Annualized Rate of Return	6.367%

Example #63 (March 2012)

Viterra Inc. (VT CN-C$15.91-Toronto) agreed to be acquired by Glencore International plc (GLEN LN-£3.894-London). Viterra operates grain handling and marking terminals and retail outlets, and processes grains. Under terms of the agreement Viterra shareholders will receive C$16.25 cash per share, valuing the transaction at approximately C$7.5 billion. The transaction is subject to Viterra shareholder as well as regulatory approvals and is expected to close in mid-2012.

• VT CN	C$16.250
• Net Dividends	0.075
	16.325
• Purchase (March 20, 2012)	15.800
• Plus Transaction Costs	0.005
	15.805
• Gross Profit	$0.520
• Gross Profit %	3.290%
• Holding Period (Close August 31, 2012)	164 days
• Annualized Rate of Return	7.320%

Example #64 (April 2012)

Ardea Biosciences (RDEA-$31.87-NASDAQ) agreed to be acquired by AstraZeneca (AZN-$43.90-NYSE). Ardea is a biotechnology company focused on the development of small-molecule therapeutics for the treatment of serious diseases, including lesinurad for the treatment of gout. Under terms of the agreement Ardea shareholders will receive $32 cash per share, valuing the transaction at approximately $1.3 billion. The transaction is subject to Ardea shareholder as well as regulatory approval and is expected to close in the second or third quarter of 2012.

• RDEA	$32.000
• Net Dividends	0.000
	32.000
• Purchase (May 7, 2012)	31.700
• Plus Transaction Costs	0.005
	31.705
• Gross Profit	$0.295
• Gross Profit %	0.930%
• Holding Period (Close June 20, 2012)	44 days
• Annualized Rate of Return	7.720%

Example #65 (May 2012)

Ariba Inc. (ARBA-$44.93-NASDAQ) agreed to be acquired by SAP AG (SAP-$57.32-NYSE). Ariba offers software, service, and network solutions that allow companies to source, contract, procure, pay, manage, and analyze their spend and supplier relationships. Under terms of the agreement Ariba shareholders will receive $45 cash per share, valuing the transaction at approximately $4.3 billion. The transaction is subject to Ariba shareholder as well as regulatory approvals and is expected to close in the third quarter of 2012.

• ARBA	$45.000
• Net Dividends	0.000
	45.000
• Purchase (June 5, 2012)	44.630
• Plus Transaction Costs	0.005
	44.635
• Gross Profit	$0.465
• Gross Profit %	1.044%
• Holding Period (Close August 1, 2012)	57 days
• Annualized Rate of Return	6.690%

Example #66 (June 2012)

Hughes Telematics (HUTC-$11.95-OTC BB) agreed to be acquired by Verizon Communications (VZ-$44.44-NYSE). Hughes Telematics designs and manufactures devices that provide real-time voice and data communications services and applications for use in vehicles, with applications outside automotive in development. Under terms of the agreement Hughes Telematics shareholders will receive $12 cash per share, valuing the transaction at approximately $1.4 billion. Apollo Management, who owns 62 percent of Hughes common shares, has agreed to vote in favor of the transaction, guaranteeing shareholder approval. The transaction is subject U.S. antitrust approval under Hart-Scott-Rodino as well as the publication to minority shareholders of an information statement. The transaction is expected to close in the third quarter of 2012.

• HUTC	$12.000
• Net Dividends	0.000
	12.000
• Purchase (June 1, 2012)	11.800
• Plus Transaction Costs	0.005
	11.805
• Gross Profit	$0.195
• Gross Profit %	1.652%
• Holding Period (Close July 26, 2012)	55 days
• Annualized Rate of Return	10.962%

Example #67 (July 2012)

Amerigroup Corp. (AGP-$89.88-NYSE) agreed to be acquired by WellPoint (WLP-$53.29-NYSE). Amerigroup is a multi-state managed healthcare company that serves primarily Medicare and Medicaid enrollees. Under terms of the agreement Amerigroup shareholders will receive $92 cash per share, valuing the transaction at approximately $4.4 billion. The transaction is subject to Amerigroup shareholder as well as state and federal regulatory approvals and is expected to close in early 2013.

• AGP	$92.000
• Net Dividends	0.000
	92.000
• Purchase (July 10, 2012)	89.450
• Plus Transaction Costs	0.005
	89.455
• Gross Profit	$2.545
• Gross Profit %	2.845%
• Holding Period (Close December 31, 2012)	174 days
• Annualized Rate of Return	5.968%

Example #68 (August 2012)

Talison Lithium (TLH CN-C$6.49-Toronto) agreed to be acquired by Rockwood Holdings (ROC-$47.34-NYSE). Talison produces lithium from its high-grade Greenbushes mine in southwestern Australia. Under terms of the agreement Talison shareholders will receive C$6.50 cash per share, valuing the transaction at approximately C$650 million. The transaction is subject to Talison shareholder as well as regulatory approvals and is expected to close in the fourth quarter of 2012.

• TLH CN	$6.500
• Net Dividends	0.000
	6.500
• Purchase (August 23, 2012)	6.420
• Plus Transaction Costs	0.005
	6.425
• Gross Profit	$0.075
• Gross Profit %	1.167%
• Holding Period (Close October 31, 2012)	69 days
• Annualized Rate of Return	6.175%

Example #69 (September 2012)

Medicis Pharmaceutical (MRX-$43.27-NYSE) agreed to be acquired by Valeant Pharmaceuticals (VRX-$55.27-NYSE). Medicis is a pharmaceutical company focused on treatments of dermatological, pediatric, and podiatric conditions. Under terms of the agreement Medicis shareholders will receive $44 cash per share, valuing the transaction at approximately $2.5 billion. The transaction is subject to Medicis shareholder as well as regulatory approvals and is expected to close in late 2012 or early 2013.

• MRX	$44.000
• Net Dividends	0.200
	44.200
• Purchase (September 21, 2012)	43.420
• Plus Transaction Costs	0.005
	43.425
• Gross Profit	$0.775
• Gross Profit %	1.785%
• Holding Period (Close January 15, 2013)	116 days
• Annualized Rate of Return	5.616%

Example #70 (October 2012)

PSS World Medical (PSSI-$28.62-NASDAQ) agreed to be acquired by McKesson Corp. (MCK-$93.31-NYSE). PSS World markets and distributes medical products and services to front-line caregivers in the United States. Under terms of the agreement PSS World shareholders will receive $29 cash per share, valuing the transaction at approximately $2.1 billion. The transaction is subject to PSS shareholder as well as regulatory approvals and is expected to close in late 2012 or early 2013.

• PSSI	$29.000
• Net Dividends	0.000
	29.000
• Purchase (November 14, 2012)	28.460
• Plus Transaction Costs	0.005
	28.465
• Gross Profit	$0.535
• Gross Profit %	1.880%
• Holding Period (Close January 31, 2013)	78 days
• Annualized Rate of Return	8.795%

Example #71 (November 2012)

Metropolitan Health Networks (MDF-$11.24-NYSE) agreed to be acquired by Humana (HUM-$65.41-NYSE). Metropolitan Health is a health care company that provides and coordinates health care services for Medicare Advantage, Medicaid, and other customers in Florida. Under terms of the agreement Metropolitan shareholders will receive $11.25 cash per share, valuing the transaction at approximately $750 million. The transaction is subject to Metropolitan shareholder as well as regulatory approval and is expected to close in the fourth quarter of 2012.

• MDF	$11.250
• Net Dividends	0.000
	11.250
• Purchase (November 8, 2012)	11.130
• Plus Transaction Costs	0.005
	11.135
• Gross Profit	$0.115
• Gross Profit %	1.033%
• Holding Period (Close December 22, 2012)	44 days
• Annualized Rate of Return	8.567%

Example #72 (December 2012)

YM Biosciences Inc. (YMI-$2.87-NYSE) agreed to be acquired by Gilead Sciences Inc. (GILD-$73.45-NASDAQ). YM Biosciences is a drug development company whose lead drug candidate, CYT387, will be used to treat myelofibrosis. Under terms of the agreement YMI shareholders will receive $2.95 cash per share, valuing the transaction at approximately $500 million. The transaction is subject to YMI shareholder as well as regulatory approval and is expected to close in the first quarter of 2013.

• YMI	$2.950
• Net Dividends	0.000
	2.950
• Purchase (December 12, 2012)	2.890
• Plus Transaction Costs	0.005
	2.895
• Gross Profit	$0.055
• Gross Profit %	1.900%
• Holding Period (Close February 5, 2013)	55 days
• Annualized Rate of Return	12.608%

Example #73 (January 2013)

MAP Pharmaceuticals (MAPP-$24.77-NASDAQ) agreed to be acquired by Allergan Inc. (AGN-$105.01-NYSE). MAP Pharmaceuticals is a biopharmaceutical company that develops treatments for respiratory and CNS diseases, and its current lead drug candidate is LEVADEX for the treatment of migraines. Under terms of the agreement MAP shareholders will receive $25.00 cash per share, valuing the transaction at approximately $800 million. The transaction is subject to the tender of at least a majority of shares outstanding as well as regulatory approvals and is expected to close in the first quarter of 2013.

• MAPP	$25.000
• Net Dividends	0.000
	25.000
• Purchase (January 23, 2012)	24.710
• Plus Transaction Costs	0.005
	24.715
• Gross Profit	$0.285
• Gross Profit %	1.153%
• Holding Period (Close February 28, 2013)	36 days
• Annualized Rate of Return	11.692%

Example #74 (February 2013)

Heinz (HNZ-$72.43-NYSE) agreed to be acquired by Berkshire Hathaway (BRK/A-$152,600-NYSE) and the Brazilian family office *3G Capital.* H. J. Heinz manufactures and markets processed food products including ketchup, condiments, sauces, frozen food, and soups. Under terms of the agreement Heinz shareholders will receive $72.50 cash per share and two $0.515 cash dividends, valuing the transaction at approximately $28 billion. The transaction is subject to Heinz shareholder as well as regulatory approvals and is expected to close mid-2013.

• HNZ	$72.500
• Net Dividends	1.030
	73.530
• Purchase (February 21, 2012)	72.200
• Plus Transaction Costs	0.005
	72.205
• Gross Profit	$1.325
• Gross Profit %	1.835%
• Holding Period (Close July 15, 2013)	144 days
• Annualized Rate of Return	4.651%

Example #75 (March 2013)

Gardner Denver, Inc. (GDI-$75.11-NYSE) agreed to be acquired by private equity firm KKR (KKR-$19.32-NYSE). Gardner Denver is a global producer of vacuum products and engineered compressors for industrial machinery uses. Under the terms of the agreement Gardner Denver shareholders will receive $76.00 cash per share, valuing the transaction at approximately $3.9 billion. The transaction is subject to Gardner Denver shareholder as well as regulatory approvals and is expected to close in the third quarter of 2013.

• GDI	$76.000
• Net Dividends	0.050
	76.050
• Purchase (March 14, 2013)	74.750
• Plus Transaction Costs	0.005
	74.755
• Gross Profit	$1.295
• Gross Profit %	1.732%
• Holding Period (Close August 15, 2013)	154 days
• Annualized Rate of Return	4.106%

Example #76 (April 2013)

D.E. Master Blenders 1753 NV (DE NA-€12.04-Amsterdam) agreed to be acquired by Joh. A. Benckiser (JAB). D.E. Master is a Netherlands-based coffee and tea producer spun off from Sara Lee in 2012. JAB has made a number of coffee acquisitions having recently acquired Peet's Coffee & Tea Inc. as well as Caribou Coffee Company. JAB made its initial proposal for D.E. Master Blenders in March, following the purchase of a 15 percent stake in 2012. Under the terms of the agreement D.E. Master shareholders will receive €12.50 in cash per share, valuing the transaction at approximately €8 billion. The transaction is subject to the tender of a minimum of shares outstanding as well as regulatory approvals and is expected to close midyear 2013.

• DE NA	€12.500
• Net Dividends	0.000
	12.500
• Purchase (April 25, 2013)	12.100
• Plus Transaction Costs	0.012
	12.112
• Gross Profit	€0.388
• Gross Profit %	3.203%
• Holding Period (Close August 30, 2013)	127 days
• Annualized Rate of Return	9.207%

Example #77 (May 2013)

NV Energy, Inc. (NVE-$23.44-NYSE) agreed to be acquired by MidAmerican Energy Holdings, a subsidiary of Berkshire Hathaway (BRK/B-$114.07-NYSE). NV Energy owns public utilities that generate and distribute electricity and transport and deliver natural gas in Nevada. Under terms of the agreement NV Energy shareholders will receive $23.75 cash per share, valuing the transaction at approximately $10 billion. The transaction is subject to shareholder as well as regulatory approvals and is expected to close in the first quarter of 2014.

• NVE	$23.750
• Net Dividends	0.380
	24.130
• Purchase (May 30, 2013)	23.420
• Plus Transaction Costs	0.005
	23.425
• Gross Profit	$0.705
• Gross Profit %	3.010%
• Holding Period (Close January 31, 2014)	246 days
• Annualized Rate of Return	4.465%

Example #78 (June 2013)

ExactTarget (ET-$33.72-NYSE) agreed to be acquired by Salesforce.com (CRM-$38.18-NYSE). ExactTarget is a cloud-based digital marketing platform based in Indianapolis, Indiana. Under terms of the agreement ExactTarget shareholders will receive $33.75 cash per share, valuing the transaction at approximately $2.5 billion. The transaction is subject to the tender of at least a majority of shares outstanding as well as regulatory approvals and is expected to close by the end of July 2013.

• ET	$33.750
• Net Dividends	0.000
	33.750
• Purchase (June 10, 2013)	33.590
• Plus Transaction Costs	0.005
	33.595
• Gross Profit	$0.155
• Gross Profit %	0.461%
• Holding Period (Close July 12, 2013)	32 days
• Annualized Rate of Return	5.263%

Example #79 (July 2013)

Sourcefire (FIRE-$75.43-NASDAQ) agreed to be acquired by Cisco (CSCO-$25.59-NASDAQ). Sourcefire provides cybersecurity solutions for businesses and government agencies. Under terms of the agreement Sourcefire shareholders will receive $76.00 cash per share, valuing the transaction at approximately $2.7 billion. The transaction is subject to shareholder as well as regulatory approvals and is expected to close during the second half of 2013.

• FIRE	$76.000
• Net Dividends	0.000
	76.000
• Purchase (July 23, 2013)	75.300
• Plus Transaction Costs	0.005
	75.305
• Gross Profit	$0.695
• Gross Profit %	0.923%
• Holding Period (Close October 15, 2013)	84 days
• Annualized Rate of Return	4.010%

Example #80 (August 2013)

Onyx Pharmaceuticals (ONXX-$123.58-NASDAQ) agreed to be acquired by Amgen Inc. (AMGN-$108.94-NASDAQ). Onyx Pharmaceuticals is a biopharmaceutical focused on developing therapies to treat cancer. Under terms of the agreement Onyx shareholders will receive $125 cash per share, valuing the transaction at approximately $10 billion. In June, Amgen proposed acquiring Onyx for $120 cash per share, prompting Onyx to explore strategic alternatives resulting in the acquisition by Amgen. The transaction is subject to the tender of at least a majority of shares outstanding as well as regulatory approval and is expected to close early in the fourth quarter.

• ONXX	$125.000
• Net Dividends	0.000
	125.000
• Purchase (August 29, 2013)	123.600
• Plus Transaction Costs	0.005
	123.605
• Gross Profit	$1.395
• Gross Profit %	1.129%
• Holding Period (Close October 1, 2013)	33 days
• Annualized Rate of Return	12.483%

Example #81 (September 2013)

Molex Incorporated (MOLX/A-$38.28-NASDAQ) agreed to be acquired by Koch Industries, Inc. Molex manufactures electrical connectors and components for commercial and consumer markets. Under terms of the agreement Molex shareholders will receive $38.50 cash per share, valuing the transaction at approximately $7.2 billion. The transaction is subject to shareholder as well as regulatory approvals and is expected to close by year-end.

• MOLXA	$38.500
• Net Dividends	0.480
	38.980
• Purchase (September 10, 2013)	38.300
• Plus Transaction Costs	0.005
	38.305
• Gross Profit	$0.675
• Gross Profit %	1.762%
• Holding Period (Close December 31, 2013)	112 days
• Annualized Rate of Return	5.743%

Example #82 (October 2013)

Edgen Group Inc. (EDG-$11.97-NYSE) agreed to be acquired by the Sumitomo Corporation (8053 JP-¥1,275-Tokyo). Edgen is a global distributor of energy and infrastructure specialty products such as pipes, valves, and related components. Under terms of the agreement Edgen shareholders will receive $12.00 cash per share, valuing the transaction at approximately $900 million. The transaction is subject to regulatory approvals and is expected to close before the end of 2013.

• EDG	$12.000
• Net Dividends	0.000
	12.000
• Purchase (October 2, 2013)	11.900
• Plus Transaction Costs	0.005
	11.905
• Gross Profit	$0.095
• Gross Profit %	0.798%
• Holding Period (Close November 21, 2013)	50 days
• Annualized Rate of Return	5.825%

Example #83 (November 2013)

ViroPharma Incorporated (VPHM-$49.51-NASDAQ) agreed to be acquired by Shire plc (SHPG-$135.81-NASDAQ). ViroPharma is a biopharmaceutical company with a specialty in rare diseases, including hereditary angioedema. Under terms of the agreement ViroPharma shareholders will receive $50.00 cash per share, valuing the transaction at approximately $4.2 billion. The transaction is subject to shareholder as well as regulatory approvals and is expected to close in early 2014.

• VPHM	$50.000
• Net Dividends	0.000
	50.000
• Purchase (November 11, 2013)	49.420
• Plus Transaction Costs	0.005
	49.425
• Gross Profit	$0.575
• Gross Profit %	1.163%
• Holding Period (Close February 10, 2014)	91 days
• Annualized Rate of Return	4.666%

Example #84 (December 2013)

UNS Energy Corporation (UNS-$59.85-NYSE) agreed to be acquired by Fortis Inc. (FTS CN-C$30.45-Toronto). UNS owns regulated electricity and gas distribution and production assets in Arizona. Under terms of the agreement UNS shareholders will receive $60.25 cash per share, valuing the transaction at approximately $4.3 billion. The transaction is subject to shareholder as well as regulatory approvals and is expected to close by the end of 2014.

• UNS	$60.250
• Net Dividends	1.740
	61.990
• Purchase (December 12, 2013)	58.850
• Plus Transaction Costs	0.005
	58.855
• Gross Profit	$3.135
• Gross Profit %	5.327%
• Holding Period (Close December 31, 2014)	379 days
• Annualized Rate of Return	5.130%

Example #85 (January 2014)

Beam Inc. (BEAM-$83.30-NYSE) agreed to be acquired by Suntory Holdings Limited. Beam is a premium spirits company with brands including Maker's Mark Bourbon, Pinnacle Vodka, Sauza Tequila, and Jim Beam Bourbon. Under terms of the agreement Beam shareholders will receive $83.50 cash per share, valuing the transaction at approximately $16 billion. The transaction is subject to shareholder as well as regulatory approvals and is expected to close in the second quarter of 2014.

• BEAM	$83.500
• Net Dividends	0.225
	83.725
• Purchase (January 13, 2014)	83.050
• Plus Transaction Costs	0.005
	83.055
• Gross Profit	$0.670
• Gross Profit %	0.810%
• Holding Period (Close April 15, 2014)	92 days
• Annualized Rate of Return	3.200%

Example #86 (February 2014)

Jos. A. Bank Clothiers, Inc. (JOSB-$62.08-NASDAQ) received an improved offer to be acquired by Men's Wearhouse (MW-$53.79-NYSE), and agreed to let Men's conduct due diligence. In March, Jos. A. Bank agreed to be acquired by Men's Wearhouse, completing a successful use of the "Pac-Man defense." Jos. A. Bank designs, manufactures, and retails tailored and casual clothing through over 600 retail stores nationwide. Under terms of the improved agreement Jos. A. Bank shareholders will receive $65.00 cash per share, valuing the transaction at approximately $1.8 billion. The transaction is subject to the tender of at least a majority of shares outstanding as well as regulatory approvals and is expected to close by the third quarter of 2014.

• JOSB	$65.000
• Net Dividends	0.000
	65.000
• Purchase (March 13, 2014)	64.200
• Plus Transaction Costs	0.005
	64.205
• Gross Profit	$0.795
• Gross Profit %	1.238%
• Holding Period (Close June 10, 2014)	89 days
• Annualized Rate of Return	5.078%

Example #87 (March 2014)

Nordion Inc. (NDZ-$11.52-NYSE) agreed to be acquired by Sterigenics, a portfolio company of private equity firm GTCR. Nordion is a global health science company and provides medical isotopes and sterilization technologies. Under terms of the agreement Nordion shareholders will receive $11.75 cash per share, valuing the transaction at approximately $750 million. The transaction is subject to shareholder as well as regulatory approvals and is expected to close in the second half of 2014.

• NDZ	$11.750
• Net Dividends	0.000
	11.750
• Purchase (April 23, 2014)	11.470
• Plus Transaction Costs	0.005
	11.475
• Gross Profit	$0.275
• Gross Profit %	2.397%
• Holding Period (Close August 15, 2014)	120 days
• Annualized Rate of Return	7.289%

Example #88 (April 2014)

Caracal Energy, Inc. (CRCL LN-£5.43-London) agreed to be acquired by Glencore Xstrata plc (GLEN LN-£3.185-London). Caracal is an oil and gas exploration company with operations in the African Republic of Chad. Under terms of the agreement Caracal shareholders will receive £5.50 cash per share, valuing the transaction at approximately £800 million. The transaction is subject to shareholder as well as regulatory approvals and is expected to close in the second quarter of 2014.

• CRCL LN	£5.500
• Net Dividends	0.000
	5.500
• Purchase (April 25, 2014)	5.410
• Plus Transaction Costs	0.005
	5.415
• Gross Profit	£0.085
• Gross Profit %	1.562%
• Holding Period (Close June 30, 2014)	66 days
• Annualized Rate of Return	8.638%

Example #89 (May 2014)

Aurora Oil & Gas Limited (AUT AU-A$4.18-Sydney) agreed to be acquired under improved terms by Baytex Energy Corp. (BTE CN-C$45.29-Toronto) after Aurora shareholders successfully pushed for a higher price. Aurora is an oil and gas company with operations in the Eagle Ford Shale in Texas as well as developments in other parts of Texas. Under terms of the revised agreement Aurora shareholders will receive A$4.20 cash per share, valuing the transaction at approximately A$2.5 billion. The transaction is subject to shareholder as well as regulatory approvals and is expected to close in the second quarter of 2014.

• AUT AU	A$4.200
• Net Dividends	0.000
	4.200
• Purchase (February 7, 2014)	4.080
• Plus Transaction Costs	0.005
	4.085
• Gross Profit	0.115
• Gross Profit %	2.815%
• Holding Period (Close June 13, 2014)	126 days
• Annualized Rate of Return	8.155%

Example #90 (June 2014)

Hillshire Brands (HSH-$62.30-NYSE) agreed to be acquired by Tyson Foods, Inc. (TSN-$37.54-NYSE). Hillshire Brands is a branded food products company whose brands include Jimmy Dean, Ball Park, and Hillshire Farm. Under terms of the agreement Hillshire Brands shareholders will receive $63.00 cash per share, valuing the transaction at approximately $8.4 billion. Hillshire Brands became the subject of a bidding war after the company agreed to acquire Pinnacle Foods in May, with Pilgrim's Pride first proposing to acquire Hillshire for $45 cash per share on May 27. The transaction is subject to the tender of at least a majority of Hillshire shares outstanding as well as regulatory approvals and is expected to close in the third quarter of 2014.

• HSH	$63.000
• Net Dividends	0.000
	63.000
• Purchase (June 30, 2014)	62.300
• Plus Transaction Costs	0.005
	62.305
• Gross Profit	0.695
• Gross Profit %	1.115%
• Holding Period (Close August 30, 2014)	61 days
• Annualized Rate of Return	6.675%

Example #91 (July 2014)

Trulia, Inc. (TRLA-$60.53-NYSE) agreed to be acquired by Zillow, Inc. (Z-$143.53-NASDAQ). Trulia operates a real estate search engine that helps users find homes for sale and provides other real estate information and services. Under terms of the agreement Trulia shareholders will receive 0.444 shares of Zillow common stock per share of Trulia, valuing the transaction at approximately $3.5 billion. The transaction is subject to approval by shareholders of both Trulia and Zillow as well as regulatory approvals and is expected to close in 2015.

• TRLA (1 TRLA = 0.444 Z ($149.87))	$66.540
• Net Dividends	0.000
	66.540
• Purchase (July 29, 2014)	62.200
• Plus Transaction Costs	0.040
	62.240
• Gross Profit	4.300
• Gross Profit %	6.909%
• Holding Period (Close February 15, 2015)	201 days
• Annualized Rate of Return	12.546%

Example #92 (August 2014)

InterMune, Inc. (ITMN-$73.45-NASDAQ) agreed to be acquired by Roche Holding AG (RHHBY-$36.51-OTC). InterMune is a biotechnology company focused on developing therapies for pulmonology and fibrotic diseases, with its main drug Esbriet approved for idiopathic pulmonary fibrosis in several countries and currently under review in the United States. Under terms of the agreement InterMune shareholders will receive $74.00 cash per share, valuing the transaction at approximately $8.5 billion. The transaction is subject to the tender of at least a majority of shares outstanding as well as regulatory approvals and is expected to close in 2014.

• ITMN	$74.000
• Net Dividends	0.000
	74.000
• Purchase (August 27, 2014)	73.150
• Plus Transaction Costs	0.005
	73.155
• Gross Profit	0.850
• Gross Profit %	1.162%
• Holding Period (Close September 26, 2014)	30 days
• Annualized Rate of Return	14.138%

Example #93 (September 2014)

TRW Automotive Holdings (TRW-$101.25-NYSE) agreed to be acquired by ZF Friedrichshafen AG. TRW manufactures and supplies automotive systems, modules, and components to global automotive original equipment manufacturers that include active and passive safety systems and electronics. Under terms of the agreement TRW shareholders will receive $105.60 cash per share, valuing the transaction at approximately $13 billion. The transaction is subject to TRW shareholder as well as regulatory approval and is expected to close in the first quarter of 2015.

• TRW	$105.600
• Net Dividends	0.000
	105.600
• Purchase (October 16, 2014)	100.140
• Plus Transaction Costs	0.005
	100.145
• Gross Profit	5.455
• Gross Profit %	5.447%
• Holding Period (Close March 31, 2015)	166 days
• Annualized Rate of Return	11.977%

Example #94 (October 2014)

Athlon Energy, Inc. (ATHL-$58.30-NYSE) announced it agreed to be acquired by Encana Corporation (ECA-$18.63-NYSE) on September 29, 2014. Athlon is an oil and natural gas exploration and production company with assets focused in the Permian basin. Under terms of the agreement Athlon shareholders received $58.50 cash per share, valuing the transaction at approximately $7 billion. The transaction was subject to the tender of at least a majority of shares outstanding as well as regulatory approvals and was completed on November 12, 2014.

• ATHL	$58.500
• Net Dividends	0.000
	58.500
• Purchase (October 15, 2014)	57.400
• Plus Transaction Costs	0.005
	57.405
• Gross Profit	1.095
• Gross Profit %	1.907%
• Holding Period (Close November 12, 2014)	28 days
• Annualized Rate of Return	24.866%

Example #95 (November 2014)

Allergan Inc. (AGN-$213.89-NYSE) agreed to be acquired by Actavis plc (ACT-$270.61-NYSE). Allergan is a health care company that develops and commercializes pharmaceuticals, biologics, medical devices, and over-the-counter products for ophthalmic and aesthetic applications. Under terms of the agreement Allergan shareholders will receive $129.22 cash and 0.3683 shares of Actavis common stock per share of Allergan, valuing the transaction at approximately $65 billion. Allergan was put "in play" in April 2014 when Valeant Pharmaceuticals made an unsolicited proposal to acquire Allergan for $48.30 cash and 0.83 shares of Valeant common stock per share of Allergan, or about $45 billion. Valeant increased the cash component of its proposal and was pursuing litigation to bring Allergan to the negotiating table but indicated they would not compete with the Actavis transaction.

• AGN (1 AGN = $129.22 + 0.3683 ACT ($259.75))	$224.890
• Net Dividends	0.050
	224.940
• Purchase (November 21, 2014)	209.090
• Plus Transaction Costs	0.005
	209.095
• Gross Profit	15.845
• Gross Profit %	7.578%
• Holding Period (Close April 30, 2015)	160 days
• Annualized Rate of Return	17.287%

Example #96 (December 2014)

Cubist Pharmaceuticals, Inc. (CBST-$100.65-NASDAQ) agreed to be acquired by Merck & Company, Inc. (MRK-$56.79-NYSE). Cubist is a biopharmaceutical company focused on the development and commercialization of antibiotics. Under terms of the agreement Cubist shareholders will receive $102.00 cash per share, valuing the transaction at approximately $8.3 billion. The transaction is subject to the tender of at least a majority of shares outstanding as well as regulatory approvals and is expected to close in January 2015.

• CBST	$102.000
• Net Dividends	0.000
	102.000
• Purchase (December 16, 2014)	96.730
• Plus Transaction Costs	0.005
	96.735
• Gross Profit	5.265
• Gross Profit %	5.443%
• Holding Period (Close January 21, 2015)	36 days
• Annualized Rate of Return	55.183%

Example #97 (January 2015)

NPS Pharmaceuticals, Inc. (NPSP-$45.86-NASDAQ) agreed to be acquired by Shire plc (SHPG-$219.26-NASDAQ). NPS is a biopharmaceutical company focused on developing therapies for patients with rare diseases. Under terms of the agreement NPS shareholders will receive $46.00 cash per share, valuing the transaction at approximately $5 billion. The transaction is subject to the tender of at least a majority of shares outstanding as well as regulatory approvals and is expected to close in the first quarter of 2015.

• NPSP	$46.000
• Net Dividends	0.000
	46.000
• Purchase (January 15, 2015)	45.570
• Plus Transaction Costs	0.005
	45.575
• Gross Profit	0.425
• Gross Profit %	0.933%
• Holding Period (Close February 20, 2015)	36 days
• Annualized Rate of Return	9.455%

Example #98 (February 2015)

Hospira, Inc. (HSP-$87.54-NYSE) agreed to be acquired by Pfizer, Inc. (PFE-$34.32-NYSE). Hospira provides infusion technologies as well as injectable drugs. Under terms of the agreement Hospira shareholders will receive $90.00 cash per share, valuing the transaction at approximately $17 billion. The transaction is subject to shareholder as well as regulatory approvals and is expected to close in the third quarter of 2015.

• HSP	$90.000
• Net Dividends	0.000
	90.000
• Purchase (February 19, 2015)	87.440
• Plus Transaction Costs	0.005
	87.445
• Gross Profit	2.555
• Gross Profit %	2.922%
• Holding Period (Close July 15, 2015)	146 days
• Annualized Rate of Return	7.305%

Example #99 (March 2015)

Catamaran Corporation (CTRX-$59.54-NASDAQ) agreed to be acquired by UnitedHealth Group, Inc. (UNH-$118.29-NYSE). Catamaran provides pharmacy benefit management solutions including point-of-sale claims management and prescription rebate management systems. Under terms of the agreement Catamaran shareholders will receive $61.50 cash per share, valuing the transaction at approximately $13 billion. The transaction is subject to shareholder as well as regulatory approvals and is expected to close in the fourth quarter of 2015.

• CTRX	$61.500
• Net Dividends	0.000
	61.500
• Purchase (April 7, 2015)	59.200
• Plus Transaction Costs	0.005
	59.205
• Gross Profit	2.295
• Gross Profit %	3.876%
• Holding Period (Close October 31, 2015)	207 days
• Annualized Rate of Return	6.835%

Example #100 (April 2015)

TNT Express NV (TNTE NA-€7.62-Amsterdam) agreed to be acquired by FedEx Corporation (FDX-$169.57-NYSE). TNT is a global delivery company serving small, medium, and global businesses. Under terms of the agreement TNT shareholders will receive €8.00 cash per share, valuing the transaction at approximately $5 billion. The transaction is subject to the tender of at least 80 percent of shares outstanding as well as regulatory approvals and is expected to close in the first quarter of 2016.

• TNTE NA	€8.000
• Net Dividends	0.000
	8.000
• Purchase (April 17, 2015)	7.590
• Plus Transaction Costs	0.005
	7.595
• Gross Profit	0.405
• Gross Profit %	5.3332%
• Holding Period (Close February 16, 2015)	304 days
• Annualized Rate of Return	6.402%

Example #101 (May 2015)

Omnicare, Inc. (OCR-$95.29-NYSE) agreed to be acquired by CVS Health Corporation (CVS-$102.38-NYSE). Omnicare provides geriatric pharmaceutical care services and related pharmacy consulting and other ancillary services. Under terms of the agreement Omnicare shareholders will receive $98.00 cash per share, valuing the transaction at approximately $13 billion. The transaction is subject to shareholder as well as regulatory approvals and is expected to close near the end of 2015.

• OCR	$98.000
• Net Dividends	0.220
	98.220
• Purchase (June 22, 2015)	94.300
• Plus Transaction Costs	0.005
	94.305
• Gross Profit	3.915
• Gross Profit %	4.151%
• Holding Period (Close December 31, 2015)	192 days
• Annualized Rate of Return	7.892%

Example #102 (June 2015)

Altera Corporation (ALTR-$51.20-NASDAQ) agreed to be acquired by Intel Corporation (INTC-$30.42-NASDAQ). Altera designs and manufactures programmable semiconductor circuits, chips, devices, and technology. Under terms of the agreement Altera shareholders will receive $54.00 cash per share, valuing the transaction at approximately $17 billion. The transaction is subject to shareholder as well as regulatory approvals and is expected to close in early 2016.

• ALTR	$54.000
• Net Dividends	0.540
	54.540
• Purchase (July 13, 2015)	50.150
• Plus Transaction Costs	0.005
	50.155
• Gross Profit	4.385
• Gross Profit %	8.743%
• Holding Period (Close March 31, 2016)	262 days
• Annualized Rate of Return	12.180%

Example #103 (July 2015)

Receptos, Inc. (RCPT-$227.86-NASDAQ) agreed to be acquired by Celgene Corporation (CELG-$131.25-NASDAQ). Receptos is a biopharmaceutical company focused on developing treatments for immune disorders including multiple sclerosis and ulcerative colitis. Under terms of the agreement Receptos shareholders will receive $232.00 cash per share, valuing the transaction at approximately $7 billion. The transaction is subject to the tender of at least a majority of shares outstanding as well as regulatory approvals and is expected to close in 2015.

• RCPT	$232.000
• Net Dividends	0.000
	232.000
• Purchase (July 22, 2015)	228.450
• Plus Transaction Costs	0.005
	228.455
• Gross Profit	3.545
• Gross Profit %	1.552%
• Holding Period (Close August 24, 2015)	33 days
• Annualized Rate of Return	17.163%

Example #104 (August 2015)

Precision Castparts Corporation (PCP-$230.25-NYSE) agreed to be acquired by Berkshire Hathaway, Inc. (BRK/A-$202,531.00-NYSE). Precision Castparts manufactures complex metal components and products for aerospace and industrial gas turbine applications. Under terms of the agreement Precision Castparts shareholders will receive $235.00 cash per share, valuing the transaction at approximately $37 billion. The transaction is subject to shareholder as well as regulatory approvals and is expected to close in the first quarter of 2016.

• PCP	$235.000
• Net Dividends	0.060
	235.060
• Purchase (August 26, 2015)	228.750
• Plus Transaction Costs	0.005
	228.755
• Gross Profit	6.245
• Gross Profit %	2.730%
• Holding Period (Close January 31, 2016)	158 days
• Annualized Rate of Return	6.307%

Example #105 (September 2015)

TECO Energy, Inc. (TE-$26.26-NYSE) agreed to be acquired by Emera Inc. (EMA CN-C$44.27-Toronto). TECO operates under its principal subsidiary Tampa Electric, providing retail electric service in Florida as well as natural gas distribution in New Mexico. Under terms of the agreement TECO shareholders will receive $27.55 cash per share, valuing the transaction at approximately $10 billion. The transaction is subject to shareholder as well as regulatory approvals and is expected to close by mid-2016.

• TE	$27.550
• Net Dividends	0.770
	28.320
• Purchase (September 9, 2015)	26.490
• Plus Transaction Costs	0.005
	26.495
• Gross Profit	1.825
• Gross Profit %	6.888%
• Holding Period (Close June 30, 2016)	295 days
• Annualized Rate of Return	8.523%

Example #106 (October 2015)

Rite Aid Corporation (RAD-$7.88-NYSE) agreed to be acquired by Walgreens Boots Alliance, Inc. (WBA-$84.68-NASDAQ). Rite Aid operates a retail drugstore chain across the United States and the District of Columbia. Under terms of the agreement Rite Aid shareholders will receive $9.00 cash per share, valuing the transaction at approximately $17 billion. The transaction is subject to shareholder as well as regulatory approvals and is expected to close in the second half of 2016.

• RAD	$9.000
• Net Dividends	0.000
	9.000
• Purchase (October 30, 2015)	7.900
• Plus Transaction Costs	0.005
	7.905
• Gross Profit	1.095
• Gross Profit %	13.852%
• Holding Period (Close September 30, 2016)	336 days
• Annualized Rate of Return	15.048%

Example #107 (November 2015)

Airgas, Inc. (ARG-$138.20-NYSE) agreed to be acquired by Air Liquide, SA (AI FP-€115.50-Paris). Airgas supplies gases and hard goods for industrial, medical, and specialty uses. Under terms of the agreement Airgas shareholders will receive $143.00 cash per share, valuing the transaction at approximately $13 billion. The transaction is subject to shareholder as well as regulatory approvals and is expected to close midyear 2016.

• ARG	$143.000
• Net Dividends	1.800
	144.800
• Purchase (November 24, 2015)	138.400
• Plus Transaction Costs	0.005
	138.405
• Gross Profit	6.395
• Gross Profit %	4.620%
• Holding Period (Close June 30, 2016)	219 days
• Annualized Rate of Return	7.701%

Example #108 (December 2015)

Keurig Green Mountain, Inc. (GMCR-$89.98-NASDAQ) agreed to be acquired by Jacobs Douwe Egberts BV. Keurig designs and manufactures personal and commercial coffee beverage brewing machines as well as the single-serve "K-Cups." Under terms of the agreement Keurig shareholders will receive $92.00 cash per share, valuing the transaction at approximately $14 billion. The transaction is subject to shareholder as well as regulatory approvals and is expected to close in the first quarter of 2016.

• GMCR	$92.000
• Net Dividends	0.325
	92.325
• Purchase (December 11, 2015)	89.150
• Plus Transaction Costs	0.005
	89.155
• Gross Profit	3.170
• Gross Profit %	3.556%
• Holding Period (Close February 29, 2016)	95 days
• Annualized Rate of Return	13.661%

Example #109 (January 2016)

Baxalta, Inc. (BXLT-$40.01-NYSE) agreed to be acquired by Shire plc (SHPG-$168.30-NASDAQ). Baxalta is a biopharmaceutical company focused on developing and marketing treatments for areas including hematology, immunology, and oncology. Under terms of the agreement Baxalta shareholders will receive $18.00 cash and 0.1482 shares of Shire ADRs, valuing the transaction at approximately $36 billion. The transaction is subject to approval by shareholders of both Baxalta and Shire as well as regulatory approvals and is expected to close in mid-2016.

• BXLT (1 BXLT = $18 + 0.1482 SHPG ($177.02))	$44.230
• Net Dividends	0.040
	44.270
• Purchase (January 21, 2016)	40.400
• Plus Transaction Costs	0.005
	40.405
• Gross Profit	3.865
• Gross Profit %	9.566%
• Holding Period (Close June 30, 2016)	161 days
• Annualized Rate of Return	21.686%

Example #110 (February 2016)

The ADT Corporation (ADT-$40.37-NYSE) agreed to be acquired by Apollo Global Management, LLC (APO-$15.55-NYSE). ADT provides security, monitoring, and automation services for homes and businesses. Under terms of the agreement ADT shareholders will receive $42.00 cash per share, valuing the transaction at approximately $12 billion. The transaction is subject to shareholder as well as regulatory approvals and is expected to close by June 2016. ADT is also permitted to solicit superior bids from parties during a forty-day "go-shop" period.

• ADT	$42.000
• Net Dividends	0.000
	42.000
• Purchase (February 25, 2016)	40.200
• Plus Transaction Costs	0.005
	40.205
• Gross Profit	1.795
• Gross Profit %	4.465%
• Holding Period (Close June 30, 2016)	126 days
• Annualized Rate of Return	12.933%

Example #111 (March 2016)

The Valspar Corporation (VAL-$107.02-NYSE) agreed to be acquired by The Sherwin-Williams Company (SHW-$284.67-NYSE). Valspar develops, manufactures, and distributes coatings and paints. Under terms of the agreement Valspar shareholders will receive $113.00 cash per share, valuing the transaction at approximately $12 billion. Alternatively, under certain defined regulatory outcomes, shareholders will receive $105.00 cash per share. The transaction is subject to shareholder as well as regulatory approvals and is expected to close by the end of the first quarter in 2017.

• VAL	$113.000
• Net Dividends	0.990
	113.990
• Purchase (February 25, 2016)	106.700
• Plus Transaction Costs	0.005
	106.705
• Gross Profit	7.285
• Gross Profit %	6.827%
• Holding Period (Close December 31, 2016)	276 days
• Annualized Rate of Return	9.029%

Example #112 (April 2016)

St. Jude Medical, Inc. (STJ-$76.20-NYSE) agreed to be acquired by Abbott Laboratories (ABT-$38.90-NYSE). St. Jude produces cardiovascular medical devices for a range of therapies and pain management applications. Under terms of the agreement St. Jude shareholders will receive $46.75 cash and 0.8708 shares of Abbott common stock per share, valuing the transaction at approximately $30 billion. The transaction is subject to St. Jude shareholder as well as regulatory approvals and is expected to close in the fourth quarter of 2016.

• STJ (1 STJ = $46.75 + 0.8708 ABT ($41.27))	$82.680
• Net Dividends	0.160
	82.840
• Purchase (April 28, 2016)	78.860
• Plus Transaction Costs	0.005
	78.865
• Gross Profit	3.975
• Gross Profit %	5.040%
• Holding Period (Close November 15, 2016)	201 days
• Annualized Rate of Return	9.153%

Example #113 (May 2016)

Celator Pharmaceuticals, Inc. (CPXX-$30.08-NASDAQ) agreed to be acquired by JAZZ Pharmaceuticals (JAZZ-$151.56-NASDAQ). Celator is a biopharmaceutical company focused on oncology with a drug candidate for the treatment of acute myeloid leukemia (AML). Under terms of the agreement Celator shareholders will receive $30.25 cash per share, valuing the transaction at approximately $1.5 billion. The transaction is subject to the tender of at least a majority of shares outstanding as well as regulatory approvals and is expected to close in the third quarter of 2016.

• CPXX	$30.250
• Net Dividends	0.000
	30.250
• Purchase (May 31, 2016)	29.980
• Plus Transaction Costs	0.005
	29.985
• Gross Profit	0.265
• Gross Profit %	0.884%
• Holding Period (Close July 12, 2016)	42 days
• Annualized Rate of Return	7.680%

Example #114 (June 2016)

LinkedIn Corporation (LNKD-$189.59-NYSE) agreed to be acquired by Microsoft Corporation (MSFT-$50.54-NASDAQ). LinkedIn is an online social platform for professional networks and talent solutions. Under terms of the agreement LinkedIn shareholders will receive $196.00 cash per share, valuing the transaction at approximately $25 billion. The transaction is subject to shareholder as well as regulatory approvals and is expected to close by the end of 2016.

• LNKD	$196.000
• Net Dividends	0.000
	196.000
• Purchase (June 29, 2016)	189.600
• Plus Transaction Costs	0.005
	189.605
• Gross Profit	6.395
• Gross Profit %	3.373%
• Holding Period (Close November 15, 2016)	139 days
• Annualized Rate of Return	8.857%

Example #115 (July 2016)

ARM Holdings plc (ARM LN-£16.72-London) agreed to be acquired by Softbank Group Corp. (9984 JP-¥5,703-Tokyo). ARM Holdings licenses their intellectual property and microprocessor designs to electronics companies. Under terms of the agreement ARM shareholders will receive £17.00 cash per share, valuing the transaction at approximately £24 billion. The transaction is subject to shareholder as well as regulatory approvals and is expected to close by year-end 2016.

• ARM LN	£17.000
• Net Dividends	0.038
	17.038
• Purchase (July 29, 2016)	16.710
• Plus Transaction Costs (0.1%)	0.017
	16.727
• Gross Profit	0.311
• Gross Profit %	1.859%
• Holding Period (Close September 30, 2016)	63 days
• Annualized Rate of Return	10.772%

Example #116 (August 2016)

Medivation, Inc. (MDVN-$80.56-NASDAQ) agreed to be acquired by Pfizer Inc. (PFE-$34.80-NYSE). Medivation is a biopharmaceutical company that develops treatments for cancer. Under terms of the agreement Medivation shareholders will receive $81.50 cash per share, valuing the transaction at approximately $14 billion. The transaction is subject to shareholder as well as regulatory approvals and is expected to close in the second half of 2016.

• MDVN	$81.500
• Net Dividends	0.000
	81.500
• Purchase (August 22, 2016)	80.400
• Plus Transaction Costs	0.005
	80.405
• Gross Profit	1.095
• Gross Profit %	1.362%
• Holding Period (Close October 15, 2016)	54 days
• Annualized Rate of Return	9.205%

Example #117 (September 2016)

Vitae Pharmaceuticals, Inc. (VTAE-$20.92-NASDAQ) agreed to be acquired by Allergan plc (AGN-$230.31-NYSE). Vitae Pharmaceuticals is a clinical stage biotechnology company developing drugs for psoriasis, other autoimmune disorders, and atopic dermatitis. Under terms of the agreement Vitae shareholders will receive $21.00 cash per share, valuing the transaction at approximately $500 million. The transaction is subject to the tender of at least a majority of shares outstanding as well as regulatory approvals and is expected to close in the fourth quarter of 2016.

• VTAE	$21.000
• Net Dividends	0.000
	21.000
• Purchase (September 19, 2016)	20.850
• Plus Transaction Costs	0.005
	20.855
• Gross Profit	0.145
• Gross Profit %	0.695%
• Holding Period (Close October 24, 2016)	35 days
• Annualized Rate of Return	7.251%

Example #118 (October 2016)

NXP Semiconductors NV (NXPI-$100.00-NASDAQ) agreed to be acquired by Qualcomm Inc. (QCOM-$68.72-NASDAQ). NXP designs semiconductors and software for mobile communications, consumer electronics, security applications, in-car entertainment, and networking. Under terms of the agreement NXP shareholders will receive $110.00 cash per share, valuing the transaction at approximately $46 billion. The transaction is subject to shareholder as well as regulatory approvals and is expected to close by the end of 2017.

• NXPI	$110.000
• Net Dividends	0.000
	110.000
• Purchase (October 31, 2016)	100.000
• Plus Transaction Costs	0.005
	100.005
• Gross Profit	9.995
• Gross Profit %	9.995
• Holding Period (Close September 30, 2017)	334 days
• Annualized Rate of Return	10.922%

Example #119 (November 2016)

Mentor Graphics Co. (MENT-$36.55-NASDAQ) agreed to be acquired by Siemens AG (SIE GR-€106.60-Frankfurt). Mentor Graphics provides software and hardware for design automation and system testing. Under terms of the agreement Mentor Graphics shareholders will receive $37.25 cash per share, valuing the transaction at approximately $4 billion. The transaction is subject to shareholder as well as regulatory approvals and is expected to close in the second quarter of 2017.

• MENT	$37.250
• Net Dividends	0.110
	37.360
• Purchase (November 18, 2016)	36.500
• Plus Transaction Costs	0.005
	36.505
• Gross Profit	0.855
• Gross Profit %	2.342
• Holding Period (Close April 30, 2017)	163 days
• Annualized Rate of Return	5.245%

Example #120 (December 2016)

CLARCOR Inc. (CLC-$82.47-NYSE) agreed to be acquired by Parker-Hannifin Corporation (PH-$140.00-NYSE). CLARCOR manufactures mobile, industrial, and environmental filtration products. Under terms of the agreement CLARCOR shareholders will receive $83.00 cash per share, valuing the transaction at approximately $4 billion. The transaction is subject to shareholder as well as regulatory approvals and is expected to close in the first quarter of 2017.

• CLC	$83.000
• Net Dividends	0.250
	83.250
• Purchase (December 20, 2016)	82.300
• Plus Transaction Costs	0.005
	82.305
• Gross Profit	0.945
• Gross Profit %	1.148%
• Holding Period (Close February 23, 2017)	65 days
• Annualized Rate of Return	6.447%

Example #121 (January 2017)

Ariad Pharmaceuticals Inc. (ARIA-$23.82-NASDAQ) agreed to be acquired by Takeda Pharmaceutical Co. Ltd. (4502 JP-¥4,724.00-Tokyo). Ariad is a biopharmaceutical company focused on developing and commercializing therapies for patients with rare cancers. Under terms of the agreement Ariad shareholders will receive $24.00 cash per share, valuing the transaction at approximately $5 billion. The transaction is subject to the tender of at least a majority of shares outstanding as well as regulatory approvals and is expected to close in the first quarter of 2017.

• ARIA	$24.000
• Net Dividends	0.000
	24.000
• Purchase (January 20, 2017)	23.750
• Plus Transaction Costs	0.005
	23.755
• Gross Profit	0.245
• Gross Profit %	1.031%
• Holding Period (Close February 17, 2017)	28 days
• Annualized Rate of Return	13.445%

Example #122 (February 2017)

Mead Johnson Nutrition Company (MJN-$87.79-NYSE) agreed to be acquired by Reckitt Benckiser (RB LN-£73.11-London). Mead Johnson manufactures and distributes pediatric nutrition products globally, including infant formula under the Enfamil brand. Under terms of the agreement Mead Johnson shareholders will receive $90.00 cash per share, valuing the transaction at approximately $19 billion. The transaction is subject to approval by shareholders of both companies as well as regulatory approvals and is expected to close in the third quarter of 2017.

• MJN	$90.000
• Net Dividends	0.825
	90.825
• Purchase (February 21, 2017)	87.500
• Plus Transaction Costs	0.005
	87.505
• Gross Profit	3.320
• Gross Profit %	3.794%
• Holding Period (Close August 15, 2017)	175 days
• Annualized Rate of Return	7.913%

Example #123 (March 2017)

Mobileye N.V. (MBLY-$61.40-NYSE) agreed to be acquired by Intel Corporation (INTC-$36.07-NASDAQ). Mobileye develops computer vision and machine learnings tools utilized primarily for autonomous driving systems. Under terms of the agreement Mobileye shareholders will receive $63.54 cash per share, valuing the transaction at approximately $15 billion. The transaction is subject to the tender of 95 percent of shares outstanding as well as regulatory approvals and is expected to close in the second half of 2017.

• MBLY	$63.540
• Net Dividends	0.000
	63.540
• Purchase (March 24, 2017)	60.800
• Plus Transaction Costs	0.005
	60.805
• Gross Profit	2.735
• Gross Profit %	4.498%
• Holding Period (Close August 15, 2017)	144 days
• Annualized Rate of Return	11.401%

Example #124 (April 2017)

Akorn Inc. (AKRX-$33.45-NASDAQ) agreed to be acquired by Fresenius SE & Co (FRE GY-€74.41-Munich). Akorn develops and manufactures specialty generic pharmaceuticals. Under terms of the agreement Akorn shareholders will receive $34.00 cash per share, valuing the transaction at approximately $5 billion. The transaction is subject to shareholder as well as regulatory approvals and is expected to close in late 2017.

• AKRX	$34.000
• Net Dividends	0.000
	34.000
• Purchase (April 24, 2017)	32.900
• Plus Transaction Costs	0.005
	32.905
• Gross Profit	1.095
• Gross Profit %	3.328%
• Holding Period (Close October 30, 2017)	189 days
• Annualized Rate of Return	6.427%

Example #125 (May 2017)

C.R. Bard, Inc. (BCR-$307.43-NYSE) agreed to be acquired by Becton Dickinson and Co. (BDX-$189.23-NYSE) in April 2017. C.R. Bard develops and manufactures medical technologies specifically in the vascular, urology, oncology, and surgical fields. Under terms of the agreement C.R Bard shareholders will receive $222.93 cash and 0.5077 shares of Becton Dickinson common stock per share, valuing the transaction at approximately $24 billion. The transaction is subject to shareholder as well as regulatory approvals and is expected to close in the second half of 2017.

• BCR (1 BCR = $222.93 + 0.5077 BDX ($184.77))	$316.740
• Net Dividends	–0.480
	316.260
• Purchase (May 22, 2017)	307.260
• Plus Transaction Costs	0.005
	307.265
• Gross Profit	8.995
• Gross Profit %	2.928%
• Holding Period (Close October 15, 2017)	146 days
• Annualized Rate of Return	7.319%

Example #126 (June 2017)

Whole Foods Market, Inc. (WFM-$42.11-NASDAQ) agreed to be acquired by Amazon.com Inc. (AMZN-$968.00-NASDAQ). Whole Foods is the leading natural and organic foods supermarket, operating approximately 460 stores across the United States, Canada, and United Kingdom. Under terms of the agreement Whole Foods shareholders will receive $42.00 cash per share, valuing the transaction at approximately $14 billion. The transaction is subject to shareholder as well as regulatory approvals and is expected to close in the second half of 2017.

• WFM	$42.000
• Net Dividends	0.000
	42.000
• Purchase (July 19, 2017)	41.730
• Plus Transaction Costs	0.005
	41.735
• Gross Profit	0.265
• Gross Profit %	0.635%
• Holding Period (Close August 31, 2017)	43 days
• Annualized Rate of Return	5.390%

Example #127 (July 2017)

Dominion Diamond Corporation (DDC-$14.08-NYSE) agreed to be acquired by The Washington Companies under an improved offer. Dominion Diamond owns interest in two major producing diamond mines in the Northwest Territories of Canada. Under the terms of the transaction Dominion Diamond shareholders will receive $14.25 cash per share, valuing the transaction at approximately $1.2 billion. In February, Washington made an unsolicited bid to acquire Dominion for $13.50 cash per share, which prompted DDC to pursue a sale process. The transaction is subject to shareholder as well as regulatory approvals and is expected to close in the fourth quarter of 2017.

• DDC	$14.250
• Net Dividends	0.000
	14.250
• Purchase (August 10, 2017)	14.080
• Plus Transaction Costs	0.005
	14.085
• Gross Profit	0.165
• Gross Profit %	1.172%
• Holding Period (Close October 15, 2017)	66 days
• Annualized Rate of Return	6.479%

Example #128 (August 2017)

Kite Pharma, Inc. (KITE-$177.90-NASDAQ) agreed to be acquired by Gilead Sciences, Inc. (GILD-$83.71-NASDAQ). Kite Pharma develops innovative immunotherapies designed to treat cancer patients. Under terms of the agreement Calpine shareholders will receive $180.00 cash per share, valuing the transaction at approximately $12 billion. The transaction is subject to the tender of at least a majority of shares outstanding as well as regulatory approvals and is expected to close in fourth quarter of 2017.

• KITE	$180.000
• Net Dividends	0.000
	180.000
• Purchase (August 29, 2017)	178.200
• Plus Transaction Costs	0.005
	178.205
• Gross Profit	1.795
• Gross Profit %	1.007%
• Holding Period (Close October 2, 2017)	34 days
• Annualized Rate of Return	10.813%

Example #129 (September 2017)

Rockwell Collins, Inc. (COL-$130.71-NYSE) agreed to be acquired by United Technologies Corporation (UTX-$116.08-NYSE). Rockwell Collins provides avionics and information technology systems to government agencies and aircraft manufacturers. Under terms of the agreement Rockwell Collins shareholders will receive $140.00 cash and shares of United Technologies common stock per share, subject to a collar, valuing the transaction at approximately $30 billion. The transaction is subject to shareholder as well as regulatory approvals and is expected to close by the third quarter of 2018.

• COL	$140.000
• Net Dividends	0.990
	140.990
• Purchase (October 3, 2017)	132.000
• Plus Transaction Costs	0.005
	132.005
• Gross Profit	8.985
• Gross Profit %	6.807%
• Holding Period (Close June 30, 2018)	270 days
• Annualized Rate of Return	9.201%

Example #130 (October 2018)

Advanced Accelerator Applications SA (AAAP-$81.00-NASDAQ) agreed to be acquired by Novartis AG (NVS-$82.58-NYSE). Advanced Accelerator develops diagnostic and therapeutic products for a variety of medical applications. Under terms of the agreement Advanced Accelerator Applications shareholders will receive $82.00 cash per share, valuing the transaction at approximately $4 billion. The transaction is subject to the tender of at least 80 percent of shares outstanding as well as regulatory approvals and is expected to close in first quarter of 2018.

• AAAP	$82.000
• Net Dividends	0.000
	82.000
• Purchase (October 30, 2017)	80.500
• Plus Transaction Costs	0.005
	80.505
• Gross Profit	1.495
• Gross Profit %	1.857%
• Holding Period (Close February 15, 2018)	108 days
• Annualized Rate of Return	6.276%

Example #131 (November 2017)

Cavium, Inc. (CAVM-$85.48-NASDAQ) agreed to be acquired by Marvell Technology Group Ltd. (MRVL-$22.34-NASDAQ). Cavium designs and develops semiconductors used in networking applications. Under terms of the agreement Cavium shareholders will receive $40.00 cash and 2.1757 shares of Marvell common stock per share, valuing the transaction at approximately $6 billion. The transaction is subject to approval by shareholders of both companies as well as regulatory approvals and is expected to close in mid-2018.

• CAVM (1 CAVM = $40 + 2.1757 MRVL ($22.40))	$88.740
• Net Dividends	−0.260
	88.480
• Purchase (December 4, 2017)	85.750
• Plus Transaction Costs	0.005
	85.755
• Gross Profit	2.725
• Gross Profit %	3.178%
• Holding Period (Close May 15, 2018)	162 days
• Annualized Rate of Return	7.160%

Example #132 (December 2017)

Regal Entertainment Group (RGC-$23.01-NYSE) agreed to be acquired by Cineworld Group plc (CINE LN-£6.01-London). Regal Entertainment Group operates over 500 movie theaters across the United States. Under terms of the agreement Regal shareholders will receive $23.00 cash per share, valuing the transaction at approximately $4 billion. The transaction is subject to approval by shareholders of both companies as well as regulatory approvals and is expected to close in the first half of 2018.

• RGC	$23.000
• Net Dividends	0.220
	23.220
• Purchase (December 8, 2017)	22.700
• Plus Transaction Costs	0.005
	22.705
• Gross Profit	0.515
• Gross Profit %	2.268%
• Holding Period (Close March 5, 2018)	87 days
• Annualized Rate of Return	9.516%

A Note On Methods

ONCE MARIO GABELLI convinced me, around year-end 2015, to translate his vision and zeal about the underappreciated criticality of risk arbitrage—not just to the functioning of the M&A process—but to the proper understanding of values and valuations on which the entire edifice of finance rests, this volume began taking shape. Mario already had a short list of monumentally successful arbs he wanted profiled and the idea to counterpoint those pieces by talking to a few highly successful corporate executives he suspected would have pungent perspectives on the practice of merger arbitrage "from the other side of the fence." We collaborated to fill out the list of *Merger Masters* interviewees and Mario then applied his considerable powers of persuasion to win the participants' assent to participating in the project.

The profiles that comprise this book are based on upfront and personal interviews that I conducted with each of those "merger masters"—usually in their offices—between February 2016 and June 2017. All of these initial conversations lasted for more than an hour. In most cases, they ran two hours or longer and they all were digitally recorded.

Mario and I had jointly developed a list of the questions about the interviewees' careers and approaches to merger arbitrage that we wanted all of the participants to address and I provided that list to each merger master in advance of our first meeting to help them gather their thoughts. That list also served to loosely organize all of the separate interviews around the same issues and themes in risk arbitrage. But it wasn't followed slavishly. Most of the interviews were one-on-one. A few participants asked finance, legal, or media associates to sit in on our sessions to backstop their memories, but they were rarely called on. My role during an interview was to get the conversation flowing with open-ended questions and then *to listen.* I probed with follow-up questions or redirected as needed but essentially let each of the merger masters unspool his or her own narrative.

In advance of each of the interviews, the Gabelli merger arb team provided me with invaluable background on many of the persons to be interviewed, often including insights into some of their recent investment activities and suggestions about which deals they might be willing to discuss. My own preparation for the interviews generally included refreshing myself on the key points of each of the merger masters' public biographies, most often by rifling through online back issues of the *Wall Street Journal, Barron's, Forbes, Fortune,* and— especially—the *New York Times,* to review contemporaneous accounts of deals in which their names were splashed in the headlines. In the cases of Guy Wyser-Pratte, Keith Moore and Karen Finerman, who already had penned notable books on risk arbitrage and their careers, I read their books. I also reread Regina Pitaro's invaluable *Deals, Deals and More Deals,* previously published by GAMCO.

As my initial interviews with each merger master were completed, the audio recordings were transcribed by a professional service and my real work began. First, listening to the audio myself to verify and correct the transcripts. Then reorganizing those recordings of stream-of–consciousness conversations into coherent profiles that accurately reflect the lives and career stories of the men and women we chose to interview. My writing style, inevitably, given my degree from Northwestern's Medill School, my quarter-century as a *Barron's* writer and managing editor, and subsequent tenure, now approaching twenty years, as editor and publisher of my independent investment journal, originally dubbed *Welling@Weeden* and now called *Welling on Wall St.,* is plainly reportorial.

The extensive quotations used in this volume are provided in the best journalistic tradition. They are the interviewees' words—accurately presented snippets of the conversations recorded in my initial interviews and also in the sometimes multiple short follow-up interviews that subsequently transpired (which were also recorded, transcribed, and verified). That is not to say that the language has not, at times, been cleaned up, digressions excised for clarity, or that misstatements of factoids (names, dates, and such) haven't been corrected—with the interviewees' approvals—when memory proved fallible against subsequent research and fact-checking.

Yes, each interview spawned considerable follow-up research, online and in libraries, to verify the narratives recounted and to more fully background or refresh this author in the specific deals and Wall Street milieus in which they took place. In instances where specific details were fleshed out by delving into contemporaneous press accounts or published Wall Street histories by other authors, those works are credited in the bodies of the profiles.

Finally, an invaluable resource and immense time-saver, as it turned out, was a private collection of around thirty overstuffed chronological scrapbooks focused on the business of risk arbitrage. Guy Wyser-Pratte has been compiling and maintaining the collection ever since he joined his father's Wyser-Pratte & Co. in the late 1960s. Guy very kindly allowed me to spend countless hours in his Connecticut office's store room-cum-library, pouring over those volumes and reading their accounts of predigital age Wall Street history in the making. Where material from Guy's treasure trove is mentioned in this volume, its original source is cited. Thank you, Guy.

— Kate Welling, May 2018

Index

hubris, 126
Huck, Paul, 285
Hudson General, 11
Huebsch, Ron, 169
human nature, 223
humiliation, 126
humor, 47–48
Hunter, Sam, 41
Hurwitz, Charles, 169

IBM, 261
Ichan, Carl, 12
IFB Managing Partnership, 154–55
imagination, risk and, 164, 175
IMED Corp., 260
Immelt, Jeff, 79
Inco, 52
incremental position-sizing rule,
    187–88
index fund, 140
index hugging, 193–94
industry multiple, 270–71
information, 99, 179, 181, 184
innovation, 88
inside information, 113, 133
insider trading, 6, 24, 27–28,
    47–48, 111–12, 181, 284–85
instant gratification, 243–44
institutional hypocrisy, 288–89
insurance, 160, 172
intellectual curiosity, 175
intellectual flexibility, 125–26
interest rates, 81, 84, 134, 273;
    compounding, 6, 153, 217, 221;
    Figdor on, 192; low, 192; short-
    term, 13, 167; zero, 81, 88, 120,
    148, 192
internationalization, of capital
    markets, 127
International Mining Corp., 79
International Nickel, 52
Internet bubble, 10, 13

InterNorth, 31
Interstate Bakeries, 238
intrinsic value, 172
investing: common sense, 113–14;
    distressed, 94–96, 153; event
    overlay and value, 210–11;
    global, 72; international, 133;
    principles of Singer, 62–63;
    psychology and, 9; Schoenfeld
    on M&A in distressed, 94–96;
    situational, 71
investors, 5, 6, 12–14, 79–82, 96
IPO market, 16
Irvine Ranch, 111
ISS, 97
ITT, 12
I've Got a Secret, 40
IWKA, 34–35

Jacobs, Harry, 25
Jacobson, Hans, 78
JetBlue, 194
Johnson, Lyndon B., 25
Johnson & Johnson, 267
John Wiley & Sons, Inc., 218
JPMorgan, 138
J. Ray McDermott & Co., 26
judgment, 86, 182
junk bonds, 205
Justice Department, 137, 139

KDC Merger Arbitrage Fund, 222
Kellner, George, *116*, 220;
    background of, 117; on being
    different, 124–26; Dinan and,
    180–81; on disciplined risk
    analysis, 121–23; discovering risk
    arbitrage, 118–19; early days of,
    119–20; education of, 117–18;
    family of, 119; father of, 117–18;
    harrowing experiences of, 121;
    on leverage, 121; Moore and,

of, 262; strategy of, 269–71; valuation and, 269–70; on Wall Street, 265; Waste Management and, 261
Moon Jae-in, 60
Moore, Keith, *217*; on Boesky, 222; career of, 218; courtroom drama of, 223–24; on deals, 225; on discipline, 226; education of, 218, 219, 222, 225; family of, 218–20; Gallagher and, 219; Kellner and, 222; on mutual funds, 221; at NYSE, 220; portfolio of, 220, 225, 226–27; on risk arbitrage, 221, 222–23, 225–26; teachable moments of, 225–27
morality, 89, 90
Morgan Stanley, 52, 96, 107, 154
Morrill, Vaughn, 39
motivation, Finerman on, 150–51
Mulcahy, Pat, 240
Mulheren, John, 156
Munger, Charlie, 80
Murray, Roger, 3
Musial, Stan, 121, *122*
Musk, Elon, 88
mutual funds, 217, 221
Mutual Shares, 75, 78, 86, 87

Nabisco, 155
Nash, Jack, 42, 101
National Bank of Hungary, 117
nationalism, 61
Nazis, 20, 51
NCR, 146
Nestle, 234
Neuberger Berman, 42, 219, 220, 221
New Hampshire Oak, 258
New York Post, 28
New York Stock Exchange, 7, 23–24, 120, *218*, 219

New York Times, 55, 258, 284
non-directional strategies, 169–70
Northrop Grumman, 139

Obama administration, 60, 68, 82, 98, 103, 124, 183
O'Connor, Sandra Day, 203
Odyssey Partners, 101
Office Depot, 82, 103–4, 183, 211, 212, 222, 223–25
oil, 51, 127, 128, 176
Omnicom Group, 134
Oncor Electric Delivery Co., 59, 71
Operation Match, 38, 39–40
Oppenheimer, 42, 43, 207
opportunistic thinking, 86–87
opportunities, Stiritz on, 236–38
options, 115
organizational charts, 240
outsiders, 247

Pacific Equity Partners, 214
PaineWebber, 191
Park Geun-hye, 60
partnerships, 32
passion, 175
patience, 34, 47–48, 198
Paulson, John, 53, *99*, 246; activism of, 105–6; background of, 100; at Boston Consulting Group, 101; Dow Chemical and, 106–7, 108; education of, 100; on FTC, 103–4; Gruss, M., and, 50–51, 158; on leverage, 102–3; McCausland and, 272; obstacles overcome by, 100–101; portfolio of, 102–3; on risk arbitrage, 102
Paulson & Co., 100, 103, 107, 287
peer-group analysis, 34
Penn Central, 42
Penn National Gaming, 199
Pennzoil, 205

Smith, Bonnie L., 129, 132, 136
Smith Barney, 41
Smith & Nephew, 97–98
Smurfit-Stone, 94, 95
Solomon, Steven Davidoff, 284, 285
Sortino ratio, 132
sourcing of ideas, 175
South Korea, 60–61
S&P 500 index, 50, 148, 175, 273
special charges, 279
special situations, 93–94
spinoffs, 14, 15, 76, 115, 213, 240, 260
spinouts, 238, 239, 257
spreads, *162*, 173; box, 43;
    Carlson on, 165; Dinan on safe,
    186–87; Figdor on, 192–93,
    201; Finerman on, 148; merger
    arbitrage and, 192; safe, 186–87;
    unattractive, 174
Sprint, 144
stability, 125
standard deviation, 135
Staples, 82, 103–4, 183, 212, 222, 223–25
Starboard Value, 223
Steinberg, Bob, 54
Steinberg, Saul, 13
Steinhardt, Fine, Berkowitz & Company, 12
Steinhardt, Michael, 12
Stephenson, Randall, 11, 15
Stewart, James B., 24
Stiritz, William, *231*; background
    of, 232, 234–35; on CEOs, 242;
    chess playing of, 236; on deals,
    244, 247–48, 249; education
    of, 235; on evolution, 244–45;
    family of, 234–35; on ignoring
    immediate dollar, 250–52; on
    immigrant's advantage, 237; on
    instant gratification, 243–44;

larger game of, 241–43; on
    lawyers, 242–43, 248; lessons
    of, 237; on long game, 246–49;
    on management, 237, 242,
    251; Naval career of, 235; on
    opportunities, 236–38; profit and
    loss statements, 239; on pruning
    companies, 238–40; Ralston
    Purina and, 233–34; as revival
    artist, 233–34; on self-reliance,
    249; on shareholders, 248; on
    shareholder value, 232, 252; on
    spinoffs, 240; strategy, 236; on
    tax, 242
stock-for-stock deals, 132–33
stock market: crashes, 85; emotional
    excesses in, 3; landslides, 85; over
    next decade, 9; sensitivity, 81;
    severe decline, 53–54; violent
    mood swings in, 3
strategic rationale, 134–35, 149
style drift, 152
subprime market, 185
Sullivan, Diane, 224
surprises, avoiding, 133–35
systems operations, 267

Tantalum Corp., 80
Tarnopol, Michael, 54
Tarr, Jeffrey, *37*; achievements of,
    38; analytical edge of, 42–43;
    background of, 39, 41; box
    spreads of, 43; computers and,
    42–43, 47–48; on crash, 48;
    discovering risk arbitrage, 41–42;
    education of, 38, 39; on insider
    trading, 47, 48; mathematics
    and, 46–48; as MIT professor,
    48; patience and humor, 47–48;
    scholarship of, 39; skill and
    aptitude of, 39; tax and, 43,
    44–45